Emerging Issues in MANAGEMENT RESEARCH

Edited by
P. DAVID JAWAHAR

BHARATHIDASAN INSTITUTE OF MANAGEMENT, TRICHY

EXCEL BOOKS

ISBN: 978-81-7446-603-7

First Edition: New Delhi, 2008

EXCEL BOOKS
A-45, Naraina, Phase-I
New Delhi-110 028

Published by Anurag Jain for Excel Books, A-45, Naraina, Phase I, New Delhi - 110 028
and printed by him at Excel Printers, C-206, Naraina, Phase I, New Delhi - 110 028

CONTENTS

Preface

The stress on research in Management Sciences these days should be on challenging traditional social sciences by moving beyond reflective knowledge to an active moment-to-moment theorizing, data collecting, and inquiring occurring in the midst of emerging structures.Research in Management Science has as its primary objective the advancement of knowledge and the theoretical understanding of the relations among variables. Research being a subset of Invention is exploratory and often driven by the researcher's curiosity, interest, or intuition.

Traditionally, basic Management Research has been considered as an activity that preceded Applied Management Research, which in turn preceded development into practical social or economic models. Recently, these distinctions have become much less clear-cut, and it seems that all stages will intermix with the fundamental discoveries being made alongside work intended to develop new models, and in areas where public and private sector partners collaborate in order to develop greater insight into key areas of interest. For this reason, some researchers now prefer the term frontier research.

Inquiry in Management Research creates a research cycle among four different types of knowledge: propositional knowledge (as in contemporary science), practical knowledge (the knowledge that comes with actually doing what you propose), experiential knowledge (the feedback we get in real time about our interaction with the larger world) and presentational knowledge (the artistic rehearsal process through which we craft new practices). The research process iterates these four stages at each cycle with deepening experience and knowledge of the initial proposition, or of new propositions, at every cycle. The process of research in Management Sciences should balance problem solving actions implemented in a collaborative context with data-driven collaborative analysis or research to understand underlying causes enabling future predictions about personal and organizational change.

Keeping these ideals in mind, Bharathidasan Institute of Management has conceptualized Athenaeum – a symposium for the teacher and the taught to interact on various facets of management research. In its second year now, Athenaeum 2008 called for papers on a broad spectrum of functional sub-themes. This year's themes range from studies on Entrepreneurship practices in Family Businesses to Enterprise wide Unified Processes in IT.

It is our pleasure to present this book comprising selected papers presented at Athenaeum 2008. The intent of this forum is to provide a unique opportunity for academicians and researchers to get to know about each other's research endeavors and provide a stage for meaningful deliberations. We believe that this presentation would be a useful source of reference to Scholars, Students and Management Practitioners.

P. DAVID JAWAHAR

Acknowledgements

This is a collection of research articles presented at the Second International Conference on Management Research – Athenaeum 08. To bring out a book of this genre requires the active support of so many people.

I express my whole hearted appreciation to all the research scholars who have contributed their brilliantly researched articles here. Their contributions will most certainly add to the understanding of management dynamics and would also help other researchers and practitioners.

I take this opportunity to thank Bharathidasan Institute of Management, Trichy for this honour. My thanks are due to Prof. M. Sankaran, Director, Bharathidasan Institute of Management for his tremendous support. I also thank all my colleagues for their assistance and support.

I am indebted to Dr. T. V. Subramanian, Management Consultant, Dr. Senthilkumar Muthusamy, Asst. Professor, Bowling Green State University, Dr. Partha Krishanamurthy, Bauer Faculty Fellow, University of Houston, Dr. B. Mahadevan, Professor, Indian Institute of Management, Bangalore, Dr. Srinivasan Raghavan, Director General Posts and Secretary to Government of India (Retd.), Dr. Prasanna Chandra, Director, Centre for Financial Management for their invaluable inputs and great support.

I would like to thank my student team for their untiring efforts and infectious enthusiasm that kept the whole project going. My thanks are also due to my secretarial assistants and office staff for their help. I am also thankful to Prof K Nigama for her immense support.

I would also like to thank Excel Books for once again doing the near impossible – bring out this book not only on time but also with great class.

About the Editor

P. David Jawahar has more than 20 years of experience in research, academics and industry. He heads the OB/ HR section of Bharathidasan Institute of Management, Trichy. He is also the Chairman of the Centre for Contemporary Management Research (CECMAR) – the research wing of Bharathidasan Institute of Management.

He was awarded his PhD in management by the University of Madras. His doctoral research examined the role of empowerment as a moderator of the effects of stress on individually and organizationally valued states. He is an avid researcher and has many research publications to his credit. His research interests include emotions in the work place, emotional branding and the role of emotions in cross cultural management. He has traveled widely and has visited many countries. He is also an accomplished soft skills trainer and has conducted many training programmes for leading corporate houses.

He has also published a book (edited) along with Ramesh Venkatraman titled "Perspectives on HR and IT Management"

1

Information Systems Requirement: From the Analytical Approach to the Construction of a Representation

BERNARD FALLERY*
FLORENCE RODHAIN*

Information Requirement elucidation has been intensively studied in MIS field. But yet, it had not gone far away. Why? Because people looked at it in an inappropriate way. Information Requirement had been considered from a positivism point a view, as a "positive data", that is to say something that has a "real" "existence" in an user mind. We believe that the constructivism perspective better explains the nature of information requirement. Information Requirement is a construction, being constantly constructed and re-constructed by several actors being influenced by all the systems (organizations, society, etc...) in which it lived.

INTRODUCTION

"Nothing is obvious. Nothing is given. Everything is a construction".
Gaston Bachelard,
La formation de l'esprit scientifique, 1938, 1982, p.14.

"In spite of all the rhetoric to the contrary, requirements definition remains a most important problem" (Telem 1988, p.549).

"REQUIREMENTS ANALYSIS CONTINUES TO BE THE MOST CRITICAL and most difficult activity normally undertaken in information system development" (Zmud et al.1993, p.176, typography respected).

Although the Information Requirement (IR) analysis is an old process, it is considered an important problem (Boar 1986, Telem 1988, Zmud et al, 1993) because it is one of the most difficult steps (Munro 1978); indeed the most difficult step in the life cycle of system development (Zmud et al, 1993). Why is this step acknowledged as the most difficult one?

* CREGO, Professor, University of Montpellier 2, Place E. Bataillon, FRANCE.

Because, according to many authors (McKeen et al, 1979, Davis et al, 1986, Leifer et al, 1994), a satisfactory IR analysis should *record* a *comprehensive whole* of the users' *real* requirements. However, the authors mention that it is difficult to achieve this exhaustivity and this exactness for many reasons:

- the users may be unwilling to express their requirements (Land 1982, Davis et al 1986, Reix 1995), because they don't want the changes that the new system will unavoidably provoke;
- the users are not always 'aware' of their needs (McKeen et al, 1979, Leifer et al, 1994);
- even if the users know their needs, they will not always be able to express them (McKeen et al, 1979).

Reading these authors' articles, one understands that the underlying general idea is that users do indeed have a need. Often, they either cannot express or even realize what those needs are. Therefore, the analyst's task is to reveal them. This idea according to which the requirement is «real» is always found in literature, even in the articles dealing with the prototyping process. Indeed, according to the authors, this technique (like the others) allows requirements that were pre-existing to the application to be revealed.

It is clearly evident that the authors consider the IR as positive and real data which is important to analyze. It is a typical positivism approach. Believing that it is possible *to take a census of all the real requirements* is to consider IR as positive data. Now, IR can also be considered as a construction. So the constructivism approach could also be used. The IR, far from being real, imposed and determined data, is, hence, on the contrary, data that is built by the subject, according to the way he or she interprets his or her background; in other words, according to his or her own interpretations. Consequently, one must study a subject's representations before studying his or her IR. If one considers the IR as a construction, the objective of the requirement analysis phase (the one of taking a census of the comprehensive whole of real requirements) becomes null and void. Indeed, the notions of completion and reality do not correspond to the notion of construction. Thus, the inability to take a census of a 'comprehensive' whole of 'real' IR is no longer a problem[1]. Furthermore, an exhaustive census of real requirements is not an objective any more as well. However, everything must still be done in order to satisfy the users. The objective of an analysis of the users' IR is to produce a list of requirements to be satisfied, which consequently result in the elaboration of an IS satisfying the users' needs.

Since the requirement is considered as a construction, *the analyst* becomes a fundamental actor in the process of requirement determination. His objective can no longer be to take a

---

[1] Criticizing the CSF method proposed by Rockart, Davis says: "The possibilities of failure with the method center on the ability of executives to respond with critical success factors that are correct, complete, and sufficient." (Davis 1979, p.57). This means that *a comprehensive whole of CSF does exist somewhere*. The analyst's task is to find that whole. To my mind, *a comprehensive whole of CSF* does not exist. What does exist are managers who have a vision of their organization. The analyst's task is not to lead the managers to 'The Way', the one and only list of the real CSF, but to determine a list of CSF which results in the elaboration of an IS which suits the user.

census of all the user's real requirements, but rather to propose a list of requirements that result in the elaboration of an IS that should satisfy the users. It is favourable to the process that the analyst be aware that, by taking part in the process of requirements determination, he has an effect on the expected results. Actually, if the individual is conscious of the ineluctability of his influence, he is more able to reduce it than if he were not conscious of it. As Watzlawick emphasizes:

> *"One cannot influence. It is, therefore, absurd to ask how influence and manipulation can be avoided, and we are left with the inescapable responsibility of deciding for ourselves how this basic law of human communication may be obeyed in the most humane, ethical, and effective manner." (Watzlawick 1978, p.11).*

Therefore, the analyst's influence can no longer be considered as a problem that must be removed. It is an inevitable notion. The objective is no longer to remove the problem of influence because there is no sense in it when a constructivism point of view is applied[2]. Then the objective is to reduce the influence to a minimum.

This approach, based on the consideration of the IR as a construction (constructivism approach) is not fully opposed to the approach based on the consideration of the IR as positive data (positivist approach). The aim of the former is neither to 'revolutionize' the analysis process of the IR, nor to change in any way the practices, but only to propose a different way to cope with a classical problem. Nobody in the literature surveyed seems to have explicitly considered the IR as a construction. On the contrary, the words the authors use show that the IR is always considered as a positive data (for example, when they use the word 'real' and all its derivatives). But sometimes the authors seem not to consider it wholly as positive data. For example, when they talk about the problem of the analysts' influence or about the intervention of their mental models. Thus, it is time to connect a constructivist epistemology to the IR because it fits in with the current beliefs. In order to

---

[2] Let's state that what I call constructivism is a point of view that shows how the radical distinction between subject and object can cancel out. My own conception of constructivism comes particularly from the reading of the Palo Alto Schoolmen's literature where the three most important key words are: **tolerance**, **responsibility** and **freedom**. In the book coordinated by Paul Watzlawick (1984): *The Invented Reality*, the authors (and particularly Watzlawick and Varela) suggest that the individual who agrees with the fact that the reality he perceives is an invention, his own invention, will be likely to follow the tracks that lead to tolerance, responsibility and freedom. If the individual acknowledges that he does not have access to the absolute reality, but that all the realities are made up (his own like the others' reality), he is not likely to reject his counterparts' conception without any further ceremony. The realities that the others invent or build themselves are as respectable as his, from which comes the idea of tolerance. Then, as the individual knows that his actions and decisions depend partly on the realities he invents can have an effect on the environment, he can't reject this environment but must recognize his contribution to its construction, from which comes the idea of responsibility. This individual doesn't fall into the trap of self-fulfilling prophecies. Now the individual knows that he is able to build his own representations (realities): he has access to the meta-knowledge, that is to say to the understanding of how he acts to know. So now, he can build adequate representations in relation to his project, and he does it better than other people who don't have access to this knowledge. As Watzlawick emphasizes (in the epilogue of *The Invented reality*), now the individual can *choose*:

> "This total responsibility would mean total *freedom*. Whoever is conscious of being the architect of his or her own reality would be equally aware of the ever-present possibility of constructing it differently. In the truest sense of the word, this person would be a heretic, that it, one who knows that choice is possible." (p.327).

demonstrate it, we propose the following plan:

- first, the problematic of the IR should be set out,
- secondly, an explanation as to why it is possible to consider the IR as a construct must be given,
- and then thirdly, a substitution of the word *construction* for the word *analysis* must be made in order to describe the process of determining the IR.

THE INFORMATION REQUIREMENT ANALYSIS

Even if the existence of the first step of IR analysis for the elaboration of an IS is uncontested, this fact was not always obvious. The marketing approach was born from the limits of an approach based on the production and then on the stock flow. In the same way, the 'by the requirements' approach in IS was born from the limits of the 'by the production' approach (1.1.). The latter, used today as the first step for the elaboration of an IS is considered as 'critical' by the authors who recognize that the quality of the IS depends on the first step (1.2.).

The 'By the Requirements' Approach Versus the 'By the Production' Approach

During the first decade of the computer era, the construction of information systems was not always based on users' requirements (Peaucelle 1977):

> *" The underlying idea of this period is that automation is progress, that the computer system is better than a manual system; the machine improves. This perspective remains deeply anchored in the implied postulates of today's computer scientists. Nonetheless it is formulated with less audacity. One mentions it cautiously even if it is modernized with the disguise of the database"* (*Peaucelle 1977, p.9*).

So the first computer period corresponds to the 'production approach':

> *"[...] before, one used to enter data into the computer then take it out. One would follow their flow. Once the data were available, one would distribute them. Once it was "made", one would try to sell them. Then the data were always used because of the state of computer scarcity in which (theoretically) the target consumers found themselves." (Peaucelle 1977, p.9).*

Then the marketing approach, based on the concept of requirement (Peaucelle 1977), replaced this production approach. Since then, for the IS topic, the result is an admission that the input matter depends on the output matter (Figure 1.) .

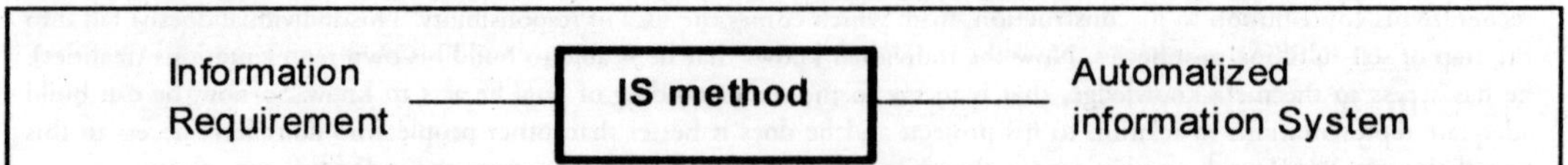

Figure 1: The second decade according to Peaucelle (1977): the automatized information system depends on the customer's IR (copy of Peaucelle's figure 1977, p.11)

During the second computer decade, the idea that it is necessary to understand the users' requirements before building an IS appeared. Then, the conception methods of IR elaborated since this period begin with a step of IR analysis.

A "CRITICAL" ACTIVITY!

Different methods have been elaborated to develop an application of an IS project. Most of them are based on the notion of project life cycle (Davis et al, 1986, Necco et al, 1987) which involves a cutting out of the development in successive steps. The process is linear. The research literature does not reveal the existence of a standard life cycle (Davis et al, 1986, Necco et al, 1987, Reix 1995). In 1970, Murdick already took a census of 17 different life cycles from IS authors' published work. Reix (1995) proposes a classic example of a life cycle, which is composed of 5 steps:

1. Prior analysis (research of the requirements);
2. Conception (research of the main principles of the solution);
3. Development (accomplishment of the solution);
4. Implementation (the setting up of the solution);
5. Maintenance.

According to Mendes (1980), it is around the mid 70's that the first empirical studies show the importance of the step of requirement analysis for the elaboration of effective IS. The step of IR analysis is recognized as the most important or the most critical element of the project life cycle (Taggart and Tharp 1977, McKeen et al, 1979, Zmud et al, 1993, Leifer et al, 1994, Mouakket et al, 1994). For Telem (1988), this is "the Achilles heel" or the 'cornerstone' of the management project life cycle. The latter metaphor implies that the phase of requirements analysis is the foundation on which the IS is based. A house is likely to fall if there are no foundations or if the foundations are unsuitable… in the same way, an IS is less likely to be performatory if the step of requirement analysis has been done perfunctorily. If the phase of requirements analysis is wrong, the whole IS resulting from it will be wrong as well (Leifer et al, 1994), since all errors in the first phase will effect other phases (McKeen et al, 1979, Mendes 1980, Mouakket et al, 1994), which explains how many failures in the IS field are due to a defect in the activity of requirement research (Cooper and Swanson 1979, Davis 1982, Telem 1988, Byrd et al, 1992). According to Telem (1988), the failures of the requirement analysis are also the main cause of failures in the IS field. Mendes seems to agree when he says that the failures observed in the developed IS result more from failures in the first step of analysis than from all the other steps. Moreover, according to him, the failures resulting from the first step have more effects on the quality of the IS than the ones resulting from the other steps. Gilhooley (1986) sums up the damages that happen in an organization when the phase of IR analysis is neglected:

- the conceived systems do not correspond to the users' requirements;
- the managers do not approve of them;

- they are difficult to maintain;
- the maintenance is very expensive (the costs of corrections of the failures inserted in the phase of requirement analysis are even higher than the ones inherent in the failures inserted in the other phases (Mendes 1980));
- they are not adequate to the plans of IS;
- the development budget and the time allowed to their elaboration have been exceeded.

So, the authors agree to recognize that the quality of the IS depends on the quality of the IR analysis phase. This is the most critical phase in a project life cycle of an IS development. A theoretical reflection about this phase does not seem superfluous because of the importance of this step. This reflection begins with the identification of the constructive factors of the IR.

THE "CONSTRUCTIVE" FACTORS OF THE IR: A CONSTRUCTIVISM APPROACH

The schema that allows the users' needs to lead to the adapted IS would ideally be such that the IS follows from the IR of the organization or of an entity of the organization. This is the analysis method which allows the passage from the needs to the deliverable (Figure 2):

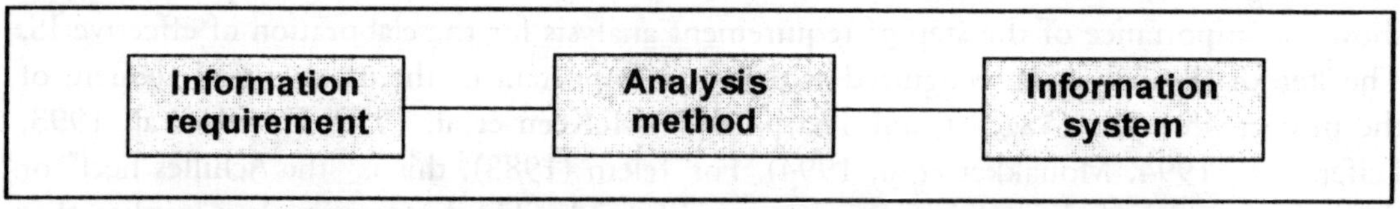

Figure 2: The ideal schema of the passage from the IR up to the adapted IS

Nevertheless, this schema can be completed. The elements that complete it can be called: 'the constructive factors of the IR' because they have an effect on these requirements. The factors include: the kind of IS, the technology, the economic context, the analysis method and the analyst. The first two factors show that the relationship between a requirement and a deliverable is not as linear as Figure 2 might suggest.

The Relationship between Requirement and Satisfaction: A Complex Relationship

According to some authors, the fulfillment of a requirement should lead to research toward the fulfillment of other requirements ("each fulfillment creates new need for other fulfillment" Rojot and Bergmann (1989, p.258) emphasize). Since then, one can catch a glimpse of a circular relationship between the requirement and fulfillment, because fulfillment can lead to the research of fulfillment of other requirements. In this circular relationship, is it always the requirement that engages the research of fulfillment? On the contrary, might one envisage that a fulfillment could cause the research of a requirement it could answer? Is the requirement always first? Couldn't the awareness of the possible fulfillment of a requirement lead to the state of the corresponding requirement? If it is generally admitted that the state of requirement is first and that the fulfillment follows, the inverse sequence is not to divert; actually, the possible fulfillment of a requirement may result in the state of requirement, because both these sequences are tightly linked.

The relationship between the requirement and its fulfillment or between the state of need and the regulation allowing to find again the equilibrium, is not linear. One cannot say that the need is always first and that, because of a single causal principle, the need leads to the research of strategies in order to fulfill it. In the same way, a unique simple causal relationship does exist between need and fulfillment in the process of determining the IR. Actually, the need is not always first and the satisfaction second, as one can understand from looking at Figure 2, which proposes only one simple linear causal relationship between a need and a deliverable (the IS). The complexity of the relationship between the need and the fulfillment can be illustrated in two different ways: considering the effects that the proposed fulfillment has on the requirements it should satisfy, and taking into consideration the potential of the IT.

The influence of the IS or when fulfillment can result in the need (Figure 3)

According to Mahmood (1987), there are two kinds of approaches to determine the IR for the development of an IS:

- the approach by the project life cycle (the 'traditional approach'),
- the approach by the prototyping technique.

The first approach identifies a succession of steps for the working out of the IS. The first step is the determination of the needs. It is a linear progression. The second approach consists in proposing very quickly to the users (Janson and Smith 1985, Davis et al, 1986, Seen 1984), an imperfect and incomplete solution (Reix 1995) which should answer the 'elementary' (Seen 1984) needs the users have stated. Once done, the prototype is presented to the users who can implement it and then propose some modifications. Then the analysts improve the prototype until it reaches the users' satisfaction (Seen 1984). This approach by the prototyping technique is particularly adapted to situations in which analysts do not understand the users' needs. In this case, the users are unable to articulate their needs (Alavi 1984, Janson and Smith 1985, Davis et al, 1986, Mahmood 1987, Seen 1984, Reix 1995). The method based on the project life cycle relies upon a linear approach of the development process. On the contrary, the prototype method is heuristic. The latter shows that the relationship between need and fulfillment is not linear and unidirectional but complex. From the statement of confused needs, the analysts build a prototype. This is the deliverable, thus the fulfillment. What happens when it is used? According to the authors, the users are likely to 'discover' their needs when they use the prototype. Did these needs exist before the proposed solution? Davis et al are likely to think so. Actually they declare: "The prototyping process is an heuristic process of a progressive discovery of the requirements" (Davis et al 1986, p.220) and "this way one grasps [with the prototyping process the requirements] by successive approximations" (Davis et al, 1986, p.218). Seen seems to agree with them and says that the recourse to prototyping allows a "clarification of the needs" (Seen 1984). Declaring that prototyping allows "the discovery" of the needs implies that the needs are pre-existent to the presentation and utilization of the prototype. One has "to grasp" these needs. In the same way, to state that prototyping allows "the clarification" of the needs, presupposes that the needs do exist and are confused. So the prototyping process is used in order to find these hidden needs. Since the users are not able to clearly state their needs, they remain unexposed. So, the aim is to bring the existing needs to light.

But how is it possible to think that the proposed solution does not have any effect on the users' needs? One can easily suppose that when the users discover the solution invented by someone else, they can consider it as a need that they have never thought of before. In addition, one can easily suppose that after discovering the solution, the users imagine other needs that could be satisfied by this solution. These needs were not pre-existent to the presentation of the prototype. Not to believe in the pre-existence of all the needs satisfied by the final IS conceived by the prototyping method is consequently to believe that the relationship between need and fulfillment is complex.

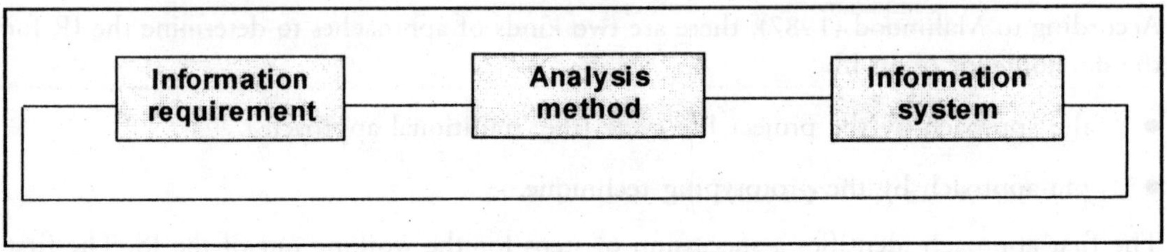

Figure 3: The IS has an effect on IR

The influence of the available technology, or when the lack of fulfillment results in the lack of need

"The definition of requirements is also called "analysis" in order to express the details of everything the IS must do", say Davis et al (1986, p.225). But when one defines what an IS must do, one should know that things can be done or cannot be done in accordance with the possibilities of the IT. According to Peaucelle, "IR are a non-technological description of the IS" (1977, p.12). But, when one describes the IR, even if trying not to think about the IT, one may describe it keeping in mind that it can be defined in technological terms. Therefore one is likely to think about the existing technology that allows the description of the needs.

So the technology has an effect on IR, as Peaucelle emphasizes:

> *"IR are the main raw material of the conception method. In reality, this is not totally true. Some people explicitly admit this. The available technology is a very powerful guide that one follows (even if it is implied) in order to say what is possible to do, hence what must be done." (Peaucelle 1977, p.11, typography respected).*

In a way, the lack of fulfillment must result in the lack of need. "Who worried about recording sounds a hundred years ago?" Alain wonders. According to him, the need of recording sounds did not exist before the fulfillment (the sound recorder) created the need of recording sounds (so the lack of fulfillment leads to the lack of need). But now that this fulfillment does exist, many people can express their needs, which recording techniques can answer. Would these requirements have been expressed before the fulfillment had existed?

In the same way that the technology has an effect on IR, reciprocally the IR have an effect on the technology (b, figure 4). Actually, this is because technological progress is (at least in part) conditioned by potential needs which it can answer.

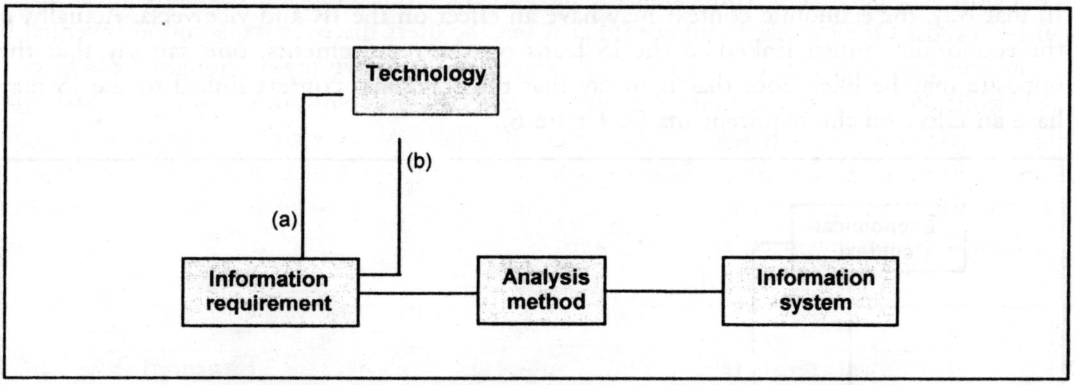

Figure 4: The technology has an effect on IR and reciprocally

The Demand Linked to the Economic Context

As society is supposed to answer people's needs, the IS services are likely to answer users' IR the same way. So if the IS services need something, it is because users need something. Therefore, the existence of the IS services is built on their customers' requirements. So it is in the interest of the IS services that the customers have needs.

In another way, some IS services develop particular products and abilities. When these IS services analyze their customers' requirements, is it not in their interest to act so that the users' requirements coincide with their products and abilities which are able to answer fulfill their requirements?

Therefore, there is an interaction between the IS services' requirements and the customers' requirements as the following figure shows:

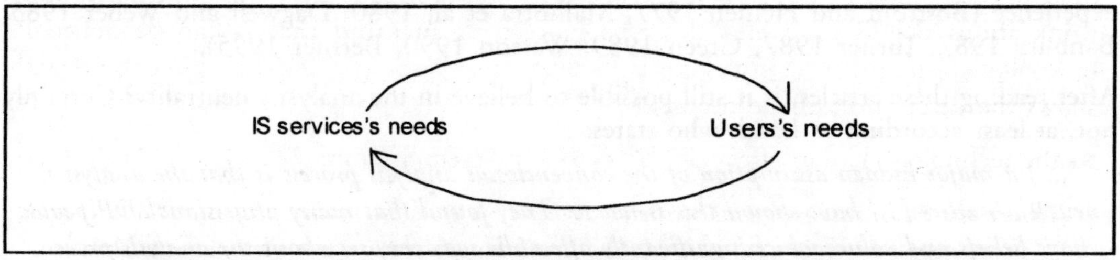

Figure 5: There is an interaction between IS services's requirements and users' requirements

Moreover, one can conceive that the analysts who have to "detect" the users' IR, may turn these requirements more or less into the category of problems that they are able to work out. Generally speaking, it is in the analysts' interest to lead the users' IR so that the available technical solution allows them to satisfy their own purposes. So, the analysts may turn the users' needs into deliverables which they are the most qualified to answer. In the same way, they may turn these requirements into solutions that require abilities that they do not have, because they need these abilities to remain competitive in their employment market. Thus, the users' requirements turned a bit into their own concerns may offer them the opportunity to gain new abilities, hence to answer their own interests.

In that way, the economic context may have an effect on the IR and vice versa. Actually, if the economic context linked to the IS leans on the requirements, one can say that the opposite may be likely too, that is to say that the economic context linked to the IS may have an effect on the requirements (a, Figure 6).

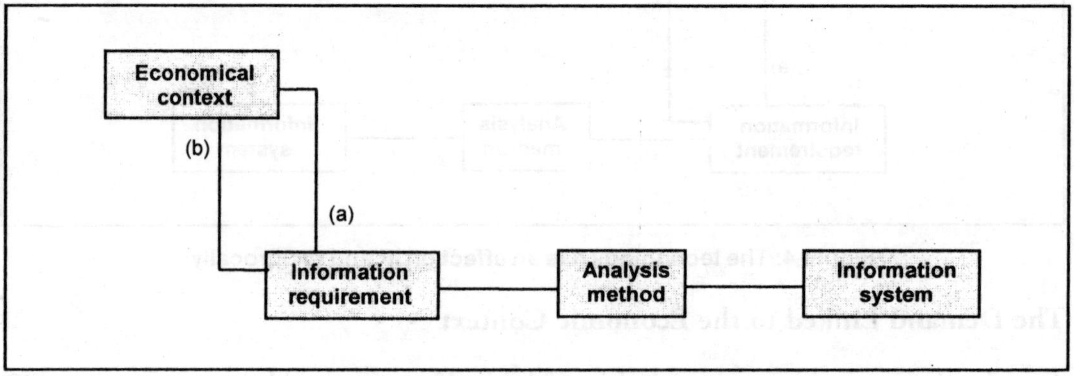

Figure 6: The economic context has an effect on the IR, and vice versa

The Unavoidable Analyst's Subjectivity

The previous paragraph asserts that users' IR may be influenced by the analysts (b, Figure 7). These can also influence the choice of the analysis method according to their abilities and preferences (a, Figure 7). Bernier (1995) observes that some authors followed the tracks proposed by Mason and Mittroff in 1973. These reveal that the research in IS may benefit from a reflection on the way the analyst's psychological type effects on the way he conceives the systems. Since then, some authors state that analysts may act according to their beliefs and models (the user's model, the organization's model...) they made up from experience (Bostrom and Heinen 1977, Malhotra et al, 1980, Dagwell and Weber 1983, Banbury 1987, Turner 1987, Green 1989, Watson 1990, Bernier 1995).

After reading these articles, is it still possible to believe in the analyst's neutrality? Certainly not, at least according to Land, who states:

> *"[...] a major hidden assumption of the conventional analysis process is that the analyst is neutral. Studies [...] have shown this is not so. They found that many professional DP people have beliefs and values which significantly affect the way they set about the analysis process, which distort their model of what the real world is like, and which influences the designs they prefer." (Land 1982, p.63).*

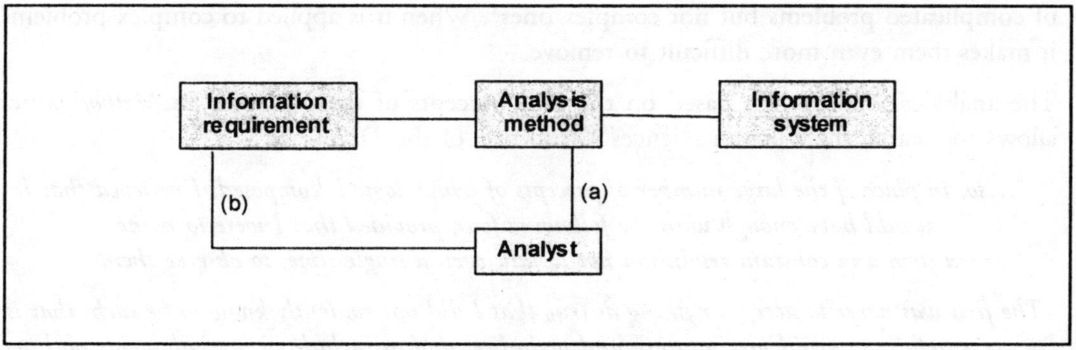

Figure 7: The analyst's influence

The Lack of Neutrality of the Analysis Methods

Are the analysis methods used to elaborate the IR neutral with regard to the requirements? Observing the working of the prototyping process shown in paragraph 1.1.1., the answer is in the negative, because the prototyping method can have an effect on the users' requirements. More generally, Leifer et al emphasize that the analysis methods do have an effect on the collected information: "it should be no surprise that techniques of gathering information determine the kinds of information gathered" (Leifer et al, 1994, p.276). And I think that this information should reciprocally have an effect on the users' requirements at different moments during the analysis process. For example, when the users discover the list elaborated by the analyst that is supposed to fit with their requirements, their vision of their IR is likely to evolve in accordance with this list elaborated by an IS specialist (Figure 8).

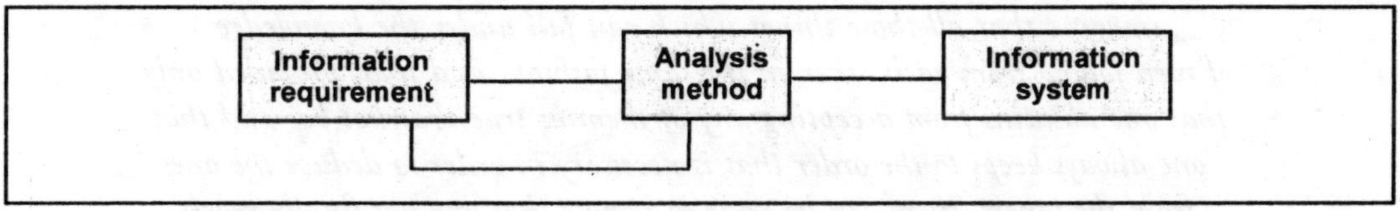

Figure 8: The analysis method has an effect on the IR and vice versa

After presenting the "constructive factors of the IR", now it is advisable to wonder about the word *analysis*. Considering that the requirement is a construction, it is awkward to keep the word *analysis*, connoted in a decisive manner by the four precepts of the *Discourse on Method* by Descartes, as Le Moigne remarks. So we prefer to use the word *construction* rather than the word *analysis*.

FROM THE ANALYSIS OF DATA TO THE CONSTRUCTION OF A REPRESENTATION CONSIDERED AS SATISFACTORY

Classical science, with its analytical approach formalized by Descartes in his *Discourse on Method* published in 1637, explained lots of phenomena. But this approach recently failed in different domains (Le Moigne 1990b). The analytical method can be used for the solution of complicated problems but not complex ones[3]. When it is applied to complex problems, it makes them even more difficult to remove.

The analytical approach is based on the four precepts of the *Discourse on Method*_which allows to «search the truth in sciences » (sub-title of the *Discourse*):

"...so, in place of the large number of precepts of which logic is composed, I believed that I would have enough with the following four, provided that I were to make a firm and constant resolution not to fail, even a single time, to observe them.

The first was never to accept anything as true that I did not evidently know to be such: that is to say, carefully to avoid precipitation and prejudice; and to include in my judgments nothing more than that which would present itself to my mind so clearly and so distinctly that I were to have no occasion to put it in doubt.

The second, to divide each of the difficulties that I would examine into as many parts as would be possible and as would be required in order to better to resolve them.

The third, to conduct my thoughts in an orderly manner, by beginning with those objects the most simple and the most easy to know, in order to ascend little by little, as by degrees, to the knowledge of the most composite ones; and by supposing an order even among those which do not naturally precede one another.

And the last, everywhere to make enumerations so complete and reviews so general that I were assured of omitting nothing.

Those long chains of totally simple and easy reasonings of which the geometers are accustomed to make use in order to arrive at their most difficult demonstrations had given me occasion to imagine that all those things which can fall under the knowledge of men follow from each other in the same fashion, and that, provided only that one abstains from accepting any of them as true that not be, and that one always keeps to the order that is necessary in order to deduce the ones from the others, there can be none so remote that one not finally reach them, nor so hidden that one not discover them."

(Descartes, Discourse on Method, 1637, p.35 in the 1994 edition of University of Notre Dame Press).

The first precept points out that the truth and the proof are based on its **obviousness**. The second one advises to decompose the difficulties in as many particles as necessary in order to remove them. Then, it is a question of practicing the **reductionism** (the decomposition) in order to analyze the problems. The third one explains that the comprehension of the

---

[3] According to Le Moigne, a complicated system is made up of many processors connected only by arborescent relationships. (This is worth nothing that Le Moigne prefers the use of the word processor rather than element because the object or the system is active, what's characterized by a behaviour. The word *processor* suggests activity more than the word *element*). As for the complex systems, they are made up of processors, not many necessarily, which keep up not only with potential arborescent relationships, but also feed-back relationship as well.

problem is based on the principle of **causality**. Then the fourth one shows that to explain a phenomenon, it is necessary to make a complete description: this is the precept of **exhaustivity** of the analysis.

Le Moigne harshly criticizes these four precepts and prefers four others that, according to him, seem "to be more adjusted today to the practice of the intelligence" (Le Moigne 1990a). Le Moigne had criticize these four precepts in general terms. Our aim is to look at these precepts with a MIS perspective.

The objective of the following point is to present the alternative for each precept and to examine it from the IR point of view (3.1.). This will result in the proposition of the word *construction* as substitute for the word *analysis* (3.2.).

Critique of the Four Precepts of Descartes' Method

The precept of OBVIOUSNESS, or the negation of representations

What is **obviousness**? Le Moigne (1990b) speaks ironically: to Plato, it was certainly obvious that a society was composed of citizens and slaves. Since any obviousness must be replaced in a given ideology, that is to say in the context of the representations that built it. Can a human thought be impervious to the influence of its social context (which contains ideology)? Mannheim (in Berger and Luckmann 1966) does not think so. A given objective obviousness independent of the observer does not exist. That is why Le Moigne prefers the concept of **PERTINENCE** rather than the one of evidence. This concept allows to relativity:

> *"It is in relation to some finality that our perceptive (and more generally cognitive) intelligence practices. The equal sign does not have the same obviousness for the mathematician writing 2+2=4 than for the computer scientist writing N=N+1, but for both of them, this sign is pertinent in relation to their current project" (Le Moigne 1990a, p.33).*

The problem of the requirements leads us to wonder if the requirements are obvious. Many economists take a positive point of view about the notion of requirement (Albou 1976); according to them, the requirements do exist. They impose themselves on us. And that is how Bernard-Bécharies (1970) states: "Let us consider the act of fulfillment and the need as positive data about which one does not have to wonder". There is no use in wondering! The needs are obvious; they are given. As such, for Bernard-Bécharies as well as for many other economists, the data that the needs represent must "be taken as they are, as one directly understand them in the concrete" (Albou 1976, p.22).

"So, there is objective obviousness, that is independent of the observer…" says Le Moigne (1990b, p.18), after having presented Descartes' four precepts. According to the economists quoted by Albou, the needs are really objective obviousness, independent of the observer. On the contrary, we think that the needs are constructions. If they are built by the subject, they are likely to come not only under the influence of the subject's environment in general, but also particularly under the influence of the subject who tries to gather these needs. So, the needs are subjective data built by the subject according to a complex game of interactions with the environment.

Thus, it becomes difficult to take the needs "as we directly understand them in the concrete". We prefer the precept of pertinence proposed by Le Moigne rather than the one of obviousness. For example, it could be relevant for a selling manager who wants to evaluate his representatives' job, to need an analysis of the turnover realized by each of his representatives. In relation to his project this piece of information seems to be relevant (but not obvious !) because it helps him to accomplish his task.

The maladjustment of the precept of REDUCTIONISM to complex problems

The first difficulties of the analytical approach appeared in the science of the living being, because of the precept of **reductionism,** when it was about to explain the working of live objects, which is governed by interactions between the elements. It was a biologist, Von Bertalanffy, who was the first one to lay down the basis of systems theory.

The application of reductionism in the analytical process needs two conditions:

- first, the interactions between the parts must be non-existent or weak enough to be neglected. Only in that case can the parts really be isolated and then gathered together;
- secondly, the relationships that describe the behaviour of the parts must be identical. Only in that case can the equation of the behaviour of the whole have the same form as the ones of the parts.

Now, as far as the live objects are concerned, these two conditions are not fulfilled. More generally, these two conditions are not fulfilled as soon as one no longer tries to describe a complicated object (which can be analytically decomposable even if it is composed by many varied elements) but a complex object. It is impossible to decompose when the links between the parts are defineable. That means that the behaviour of the object depends essentially on the links between the parts rather than the parts themselves and moreover, that these links unify the whole itself. Therefore, the whole becomes more than the sum of its parts and the global approach should be preferred to the reductionist one. That is why Le Moigne substitutes the precept of **GLOBALISM** for Descartes' precept of reductionism[4]. Should the individual's, society's or group of people's needs as a whole be considered as a simple field? Or, on the contrary, must one envisage the individual's needs as a whole like a system, where the links between the needs are defineable? The pertinence of the application of the reductionist approach depends on the answer to this question. If the field of needs is simple, it becomes possible to study one need independently of the other ones. The needs as a whole can be cut or as Le Moigne says "tied up like a sausage" in particles, without attending to the links between them. On the other hand, if the field of the needs, field of

---

[4] Let's explain that Le Moigne does not reject the principle of reductionism. He only states that it is not adapted to situations with complex problems, but it can be perfectly appropriate in many other situations:

"Considering these complex problems as complicated ones and dealing with them by the analytical methods, they are made even more complex."

"The failures in the processing of complex problems that one tries to model by analytical methods are numerous and cruel. Some present-day examples: juvenile delinquency, road safety, the crisis of agricultural surplus, world hunger, desertification of land, the desperate growth of unemployment, the mastery of nuclear energy..." (Le Moigne 1990b, p.19).

representations is, as we think, a complex field where the elements are neither given nor stable, then the global approach should be preferred to the reductionist one.

When the precept of CAUSALITY does not allow to explain the behaviour of an object by its finality

Le Moigne regrets that the precept of causality linked to the "determinist assumption" which still governs the scientific institution today (Le Moigne 1994), is considered a universal principle. He prefers to substitute for this precept the principle of **TELEOLOGY**, which aims at understanding the object's behaviour thanks to its projects, or more exactly, thanks to the projects that the observer or the modeller assigns to the object, rather than as a result of laws. In other words, to bring us nearer to the understanding of an object, Le Moigne prefers to be connected to the "in order to" rather than to the 'because'[5]:

"The intelligence substitutes then, for the "cause-effect explanation", "the interpretation (or the understanding) behaviour-finality". I substitute the precept of teleology for the precept of causality. According to the precept of teleology, the thought about the finality of an object to be known, is one of the keyholes of the device of rational intelligence." (Le Moigne 1990a, p.39).

This principle of teleology seems to correspond to the process of IR research. One may say that it is *in order* to evaluate his representatives that the sales manager needs the information concerning the turnover realized by each one. More generally, one may say that an entity's IR can be researched according to the finality he desired. This is how one begins to understand an entity's finality before undertaking any research of IR.

The myth of the precept of EXHAUSTIVITY

How can this precept be applied today? How can one create such rigorous enumerations and such general surveys and be assured of not omitting anything? Le Moigne affirms that it is "in practice… impracticable". To lead to the understanding of an object, Le Moigne proposes omission, to select some groups of data, and thus to choose aggregates, so to practice **AGGREGATIVITY.**

Is it possible, as the authors in IR fields recommend, to take a census of the IR as an exhaustive whole? Perhaps the discourse can be moderated according to the studied subject. For example, the problem of exhaustivity can be differently envisaged depending on whether one is interested in the research of a manager's IR who wants to evaluate his subordinates, or if one studies the IR for an automation such as the pay. In the second case, if one only wants to reproduce in an automatized way an activity that has been up to now accomplished in a manual way, then one may possibly admit the use of the word *exhaustivity.* Actually,

5 Let's state that if I write that Le Moigne *prefers* to be connected to the "in order to" rather than to the 'because', it does not mean that he proscribes any research of an object's understanding thanks to the causal explanation. What he rejects is the assumption according to which the causal principle is unique and universal, which he explains with these words: "the new discourse includes the former one without repudiating anything but its pretention to universality and to the monopoly of rationality." (Le Moigne 1990a, p.39).

the exhaustivity is reached when the automatized system allows this accomplishment *strictly* in the same way as the manual process does. Nevertheless, do such situations often happen? Is not automation often the occasion to modify a bit procedure? We think that the principle of exhaustivity is a delusion in as much as the needs are not *strictly conformed* by the reproduction of a manual process with an automatized process. Henceforth, individuals and their interpretation of reality are concerned with this matter (when they are in a schematic way hypothetically absent in a process that aims at reproducing strictly a manual process in an automatized process). When is it possible to say, for the research of the manager's IR who wants to evaluate his subordinates, that an exhaustive list of his need is obtained? We don't have the answer to this question since its formulation itself has no relevance to us. Perhaps it is possible to obtain a list of pieces of information that would satisfy the manager at a given moment, but under no circumstances can one say that an exhaustive list of the manager's needs could have been obtained.

Proposition of substitution: Construction against analysis

All in all, the word analysis is connoted the following way:

> *"[...] there is objective obviousness independent of the observer to which one has access by decomposition or division: the analysis. These stable evidences are connected by cause-effect relationships that one can identify as soon as one proceeds to the exhaustive census closing the model."* (Le Moigne, 1990b, p.18).

Thus, the IR:

- are not obvious, nor given;
- are constructions, in permanent evolution, hence they are not stable;
- are not independent of the method used by the observer to identify them;
- are not independent of the observer's beliefs;
- are not determined;
- cannot be recorded in an exhaustive way.

So it becomes a delicate issue to use the word analysis associated with requirements. What word can be better to use? One should prefer the word research of IR, but this, implies that the requirements are hidden somewhere and that the analyst's task is to find them, such as one can look for a precious metal in a variety of places. The word collection could be chosen. But this one also implies, that the requirements exist independently of the process that leads to writing down in black and white a list of requirements.

We don't think that the requirements are stated in the individual's mind and that the computer scientist's task is to extract them. The computer scientist is not neutral. In the list of requirements he has to write down, his influence and the one of the method used are rediscovered. It is impossible for him and for the method not to have an effect on the final result. That is why we prefer talking about construction of IR. The process of construction is the one that results in a list of IR. In this process, the interviewee and the interviewer work together to elaborate this list.

CONCLUSION

The aim of this article was to discuss the 'real' aspect of the IR. From the literature on IR and from the researchers' discourse, the IR is considered as real data. And that is how the phase of analysis of the IR aims at succeeding in taking the census of the real requirements as a comprehensive whole. To use the words census, comprehensive, and above all real is to believe in the positive aspect of the requirement. After criticizing the real aspect of the IR, we come to the conclusion that the IR can easily be considered as a construction. The IR is constructed in relation to the way the actor interprets the events, that is to say in relation to his or her interpretations. The IR is also constructed in relation to the five constructive factors displayed in the following figure, which proposes a recapitulation:

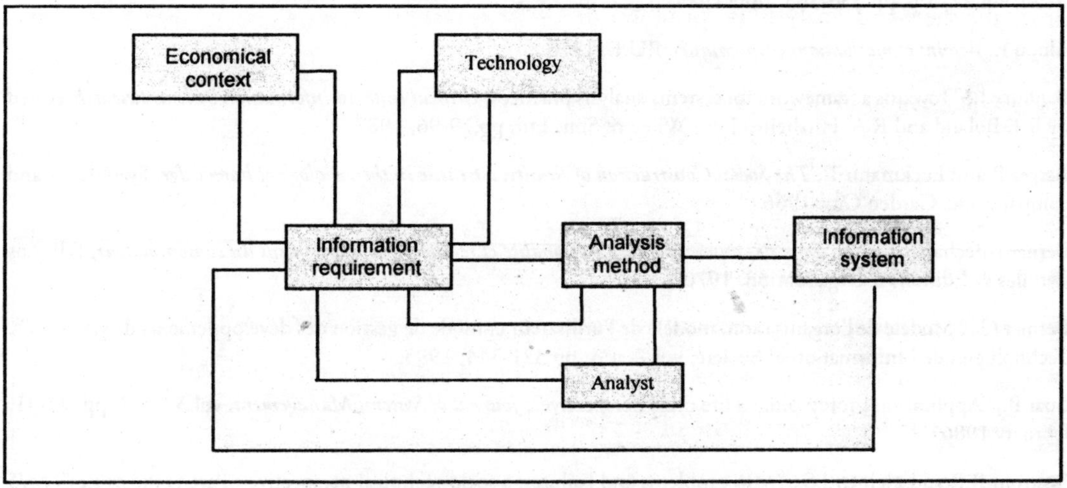

Figure 9: The constructor factors of IR

Now that the requirement is considered as a construction, it is no more possible to use the words exhaustive, census or users' real requirements. The following board shows the differences that have been made between the approach considering the requirement as positive data and the approach considering the requirement as a construction.

	Positivist approach	**Constructivist approach**
Aim of the phase of analysis of IR	To take a census of the users' real requirements as a comprehensive whole.	To build a list of IR that leads to the elaboration of an IS satisfying the users.
The analyst's aim	To remove his or her influence.	To minimize his or her influence.
Terminology chosen	Analysis of IR.	Construction of IR.

Board 1: Differences between the statement approach and the construct one

The last line of the board reveals that in the constructivist approach, the word construction is preferred to analysis in order to qualify the phase of determination of the IR. We dislike the use of the word analysis because of its strong connotation noted by Le Moigne (1990a and 1990b) in Descartes' Discourse on Method. It seems to be inappropriate as soon as the requirement is considered as a construction, not as positive data (positivist approach).

The purpose of this article is not at all to criticize or to modify practices. It only aims at showing that a constructivist epistemology is useful in the problematic of IR. Even if the construction aspect transpires in a lot of authors' talks, they often refer to a positivist epistemology. We think that this paradox can be solved. One has only to explicitly recognize the construct aspect of the IR.

REFERENCES

Alain, *Propos d'économique*, Gallimard, 1934.

Alavi M., "An assessment of the prototyping approach to information systems development", *Communications of the ACM*, vol.27, n°6, pp.556-563, June 1984.

Albou P., *Besoins et motivations économiques*, P.U.F., 1976.

Banbury J., "Towards a framework for systems analysis practice", *Critical Issues in Information Systems Research*, edited by R.J. Boland and R.A. Hirsheim, John Wiley & Sons Ltd, pp.79-96, 1987.

Berger P. and Luckmann T., *The Social Construction of Reality; a treatise in the sociology of knowledge*, Doubleday and company, inc. Garden City, 1966.

Bernard-Bécharies J.F., *Le choix de consommation - Rationalité et réalité du comportement du consommateur*, Editions Eyrolles et Editions d'Organisation, 1970.

Bernier C., "Modèle de l'organisation, modèle de l'utilisateur et mode de gestion des développements de systèmes", Technologies de l'Information et Société, vol.7, n°3, pp.321-344, 1995.

Boar B., "Application prototyping: a life cycle perspective", *Journal of Systems Management*, vol.37, n°2, pp. 25-31, february 1986.

Bostrom R.P. and Heinen J.S., "MIS problems and Failures: a socio-technical perspective - Part 1: the causes", *MIS Quarterly*, pp.17-32, September 1977.

Byrd T.A., Cossick K.L. and Zmud R.W., "A synthesis of research on requirements analysis and knowledge acquisition techniques", *MIS Quarterly*, pp.117-138, march 1992.

Cooper R.B. and Swanson E.B., "Management information requirements assessment: the state of the art", *Data Base*, vol.11, n°2, pp.5-16, fall 1979.

Dagwell R. and Weber R, "System designers' user models: a comparative study and methodological critique", *Communications of the ACM*, vol.26, n°11, November 1983.

Davis G.B., "Comments on the critical success factors method for obtaining management information requirements", *MIS Quarterly*, pp.57-58, September 1979.

Davis G.B., "Strategies for information requirements determination", *IBM Systems Journal*, vol.21, n°1, pp.2-30, 1982.

Davis G.B., Olson M.H., Ajenstat J. and Peaucelle J.-L., *Systèmes d'information pour le management - Volume 1: les bases*, Economica, 1986.

Descartes R., *Discourse on Method,* University of Notre Dame Press, (original title: *Discours de la méthode,* 1637) 1994.

Gilhooley I.A., "A methodology for productive systems development", *Journal of Information Systems Management,* vol.3, n°1, pp.36-41, winter 1986.

Green G.I., "Perceived importance of systems analysts' job skills, roles, and non-salary incentives", *MIS Quarterly,* vol.13, n°2, pp.115-133, June 1989.

Janson M.A. and Smith L.D., "Prototyping for systems development: a critical appraisal", *MIS Quarterly,* pp.305-315, December 1985.

Land F., "Adapting to changing user requirements", *Information & Management,* vol.5, n°2, pp.59-75, June 1982.

Leifer R., Lee S. and Durgee J., "Deep structures: real information requirements determination", *Information & Management,* vol.27, n°5, pp.275-285, November 1994.

Le Moigne J-L., *La théorie du système général. Théorie de la modélisation,* P.U.F., 3ème édition, (première édition: 1977) 1990a.

Le Moigne J-L., *La modélisation des systèmes complexes,* Afcet systèmes, Editions Dunod, 1990b.

Mahmood M.A., "System development methods – a comparative investigation", *MIS Quarterly,* pp.293-311, September 1987.

Malhotra, Thomas, Carroll and Miller, "Cognitive Processes in Design", Journal of Man-Machine Studies, vol.12, pp.119-140, 1980.

Mason R.O. and Mitroff I.I., "A program for research on management information systems", *Management Science,* vol.19, n°5, January 1973.

McKeen J.D., Naumann J.D. and Davis G.B., "Development of a selection model for information requirements determination", *Working Paper,* MISCR Graduate School of Business Administration, University of Minnesota, June 1979.

Mendes K.S., "Structures systems analysis: a technique to define business requirements", *Sloan Management Review,* vol.21, n°4, pp.51-63, summer 1980.

Mouakket S., Sillince J.A.A. and Fretwell-Downing F.A., "Information requirements determination in the software industry: a case study", *European Journal of Information Systems,* vol.3, n°2, pp.101-111, 1994.

Munro M.C., "Determining the manager's information needs", *Journal of Systems Management,* vol.29, n°6, pp.34-39, June 1978.

Murdick R.G., "MIS development procedures", *Journal of Systems Management,* vol.21, n°12, pp.22-26, 1970.

Necco C.R., Gordon C.L. and Tsai N.W., "Systems analysis and design: current practices", *MIS Quarterly,* pp.461-475, December 1987.

Peaucelle J.-L., *Les besoins en information dans les systèmes informatiques de gestion,* thèse, Université de Paris-Sud, 1977.

Reix R., *Systèmes d'information et management des organisations,* Vuibert Gestion, 1995.

Robey D. and Markus M.L., "Rituals in information system design", *MIS Quarterly,* vol.8, n°1, pp.5-15, March 1984.

Rojot J. and Bergmann A., *Comportement et organisation,* Vuibert, 1989.

Analysis and design of information systems, McGraw-Hill, 1984.

Taggart W.M. and Tharp M.O., "A survey of information requirements analysis techniques", *Computing Surveys*, vol.9, n°4, pp.273-290, December 1977.

Telem M., "Information requirements specification I: brainstorming collective decision-making approach", *Information Processing & Management*, vol.24, n°5, pp.549-557, 1988.

Turner J.A., "Understanding the elements of system design", *Critical Issues in Information Systems Research*, edited by R.J. Boland and R.A. Hirsheim, John Wiley & Sons Ltd, pp.97-111, 1987.

Watson R.T., "Influences on the IS manager's perception of key issues: information scanning and the relationship with the CEO", *MIS Quarterly*, vol.14, n°2, pp. 217-231, June 1990.

Watzlawick P., *The language of change*, Basic Books, 1978.

Watzlawick P., "Self-Fulfilling Prophecies", *The Invented Reality. How do we know? What we believe we know? Contributions to Constructivism*, edited and with commentary by P. Watzlawick, W.W. Norton & Company, pp.95-116, (original title: *die erfundene wirklichkeit. Wie wissen wir, was wir zu wissen glauben? Beiträge zum kronstrucktivismus*, 1981), 1984.

Zmud R.W., Anthony W.P. and Stair R.M., "The use of mental imagery to facilitate information identification in requirements analysis", *Journal of Management Information Systems*, vol.9, n°4, pp.175-191, Spring 1993.

2

Financial Innovation Leads to Financial Inclusion: The Case of Sub-prime Lending

FAIZ MOHAMMAD*
JAVED GHAFFAR*
SAIF SAMI*
DR. VALEED A. ANSARI**

Financial inclusion, which is a process of ensuring reasonable access to banks for everybody, is becoming an important policy priority in many countries, as it has been shown to increase income and welfare. The index of financial inclusion is the new comprehensive indicator of the level of financial inclusion in the economy. The index is the amalgamation of three aspects of financial inclusion:

1. Penetration of the banking system.
2. Its availability to users.
3. Its actual usage.

With a score of 0.209, India ranked 21 in the survey of 45 countries by ICRIER indicating a low level of inclusion.

This paper examines the sub-prime lending as a tool for improving financial inclusion in the country, by describing sub-prime lending in the US mortgage market. Sub-prime lending is a relatively new and rapidly growing segment of the US mortgage market that expands the pool of credit to borrowers who, for a variety of reasons would otherwise be denied credit. We also review the demographic and economic profile of households who benefited from the growth of sub-prime mortgage market. Moreover, we analyze the role of securitization and innovative financial instruments like Collateral Debt Obligation and Mortgage Backed Securities in triggering the growth as well as precipitating the decline of the sub-prime mortgage market.

Our findings indicate that because of its complicated nature, sub-prime lending is simultaneously viewed as having great potential and great peril. The potential of sub-

* Research Scholar at Deptt. of Business Administration, Faculty of Management Studies and Research, Aligarh Muslim University, Aligarh, (U.P).

** Reader of Finance at Deptt. of Business Administration, Faculty of Management Studies and Research, Aligarh Muslim University, Aligarh, (U.P).

prime lending is that it can provide opportunity for home ownership to those who were either subject to discrimination or could not qualify for mortgage in the past. The peril lies in the fact that it can also be described as high cost lending, thus carrying greater probability of default by borrowers.

Also, sub-prime borrowers are a disproportionate minority with lower income, older, less well-educated, less financially sophisticated and less likely to search for best interest when applying for mortgage. Finally, the economic value of securitization and risk transfer value of Collateral Debt Obligation has given mortgage lenders greater access to capital markets and spread risk more broadly, thereby increasing the supply of credit to all types of borrowers. But the inherent complexity in these innovative financial instruments also created valuation problems whereby rating agencies underestimated the risk involved in giving loan to a sub-prime borrower.

INTRODUCTION

Financial inclusion, which is a process of ensuring reasonable access to banks for everybody, is becoming an important policy priority in many countries, as it has been shown to increase income and welfare. The index of financial inclusion is the new comprehensive indicator of the level of financial inclusion in the economy. The index is the amalgamation of three aspects of financial inclusion:

- Penetration of the banking system.
- Its availability to users.
- Its actual usage.

Penetration is measured using data on number of bank accounts per capita, while number of bank branches per thousand population indicates availability and the size of bank credit and deposits relative to the GDP indicates usage. A score of 0.6 and 1 indicates a high level of financial inclusion, which has been achieved only by three countries, Switzerland, Denmark and Malta. A score between 0.4-0.6 indicates a medium level of inclusion while all scores below 0.4 indicate a low level of inclusion. If the index is adopted as a policy tool it will enable setting of clear benchmarks for financial inclusion.

With a score of 0.209, India ranks 21 in the survey of 45 countries by ICRIER indicating a low level of inclusion.

Financial inclusion is synonymous with micro finance i.e. setting up of thousands of rural branches, the extension of loans to small farmers and artisans. Moreover, ineffective schemes like Indira Awas Yojana are introduced to provide low cost housing to the poor.

On the other hand, the Indian stock market is growing at a scorching rate. An extremely bullish secondary market for most part of the year with the sensex hovering above 20000, combined with a high return primary market saw 2007 with a record, highest ever mobilization of Rs 45,137 crore through public equity issues, comprising both, initial public offerings (IPO) and follow on public offerings (FPO). An increase of 83% on the previous year which had seen raisings of Rs 24,679 crore.

We also explore the US sub-prime lending and financial innovations of securitization, MBS and CDO to see how they channeled the credit risk of the mortgage lending process to the investors of the stock market thereby improving financial inclusion.

WHAT IS SUB-PRIME LENDING?

Our findings indicate that because of its complicated nature, sub-prime lending is simultaneously viewed as having great potential and great danger. The potential of sub-prime lending is that it can provide opportunity for home ownership to those who were either subject to discrimination or could not qualify for mortgage in the past. The danger lies in the fact that it can also be described as high cost lending, thus having greater probability of default by borrowers.

Sub-prime Lending Defined for Lenders

A type of mortgage that is normally made out to borrowers with very little data on their credit record or lower credit ratings (below 600). As a result of the borrower's lowered credit rating, a conventional mortgage is not offered because the lender views the borrower as having a larger-than-average risk of defaulting on the loan. Lending institutions often charge interest on subprime mortgages at a rate that is higher than a conventional mortgage in order to compensate themselves for carrying more risk. Finally, these loans usually require intensive levels of servicing and collection efforts to ensure timely payment.

Sub-prime Lending Defined for Borrowers

From the borrower's perspective, the primary distinguishing feature between prime and sub-prime loans is that the upfront and continuing costs are higher for sub-prime loans.

Upfront costs include application fees, appraisal fees, and other fees associated with originating a mortgage.

The continuing costs include mortgage insurance payments, principle and interest payments, late fees and fines for delinquent payments, and fees levied by a locality (such as property taxes and special assessments).

Borrowers obtaining mortgages from sub-prime lenders pay higher rates than their prime counterparts-roughly 88% of prime borrowers surveyed reports rates below 9%, while 67% of sub-prime borrowers surveyed pay 9% or more.

Loan purpose comprise of:

- First mortgage (purchase)
- First mortgage (refinance)
- Second mortgage

Loan type consists of:

- Fixed rate
- Adjustable rate.

Factors Determining Sub-prime Interest Rates

Borrower cost associated with sub-prime lending is driven primarily by two factors: credit history and down payment requirements. This contrasts with the prime market, where borrower cost is primarily driven by the down payment alone, given that minimum credit history requirements are satisfied.

Sub-prime interest rate = *f (loan grade, credit score, LTV)*

Where *loan grade*=f (foreclosures, Chapter 7 and Chapter 13 bankruptcies, debt ratio)

Loan Grade

Countrywide reports six levels, or loan grades, in its B&C lending rate sheet: Premier Plus, Premier, A-, B, C, and C-. The loan grade is determined by the applicant's mortgage or rent payment history), bankruptcies (credit history), and total debt-to-income ratio. Table 1 provides a summary of the four underwriting requirements used to determine the loan grade. For example, to qualify for the Premier Plus grade, the applicant may have had no mortgage payment 30 days or more delinquent in the past year (0 x 30 x 12). The requirement is slowly relaxed for each loan grade: the Premier grade allows one payment to be 30-days delinquent; the A- grade allows two payments to be 30-days delinquent; the B grade allows one payment to be 60-days delinquent; the C grade allows one payment to be 90-days delinquent; and the C- grade allows two payments to be 90-days delinquent.

Foreclosure

The requirements for foreclosures are also reduced for the lower loan grades. For example, whereas the Premier Plus grade stipulates no foreclosures in the past 36 months, the C grade stipulates no foreclosures only in the past 12 months, and the C- grade stipulates no active foreclosures.

Chapter 7 and chapter 11 bankruptcies

For most loan grades, Chapter 7 and Chapter 13 bankruptcies typically must have been discharged at least a year before application; however, the lowest grade, C-, requires only that Chapter 7 bankruptcies have been discharged and Chapter 13 bankruptcies at least be in repayment.

Debt Ratio

However, all loan grades require at least a 50% ratio between monthly debt servicing costs (which includes all outstanding debts) and monthly income. Loan grade alone does not determine the cost of borrowing (that is, the interest rate on the loan). Table 2 provides a matrix of credit scores and loan-to-value (LTV) ratio requirements that determine pricing of the mortgage within each loan grade for a 30-year loan with a 3-year fixed interest rate and a 3-year prepayment penalty. For example, loans in the Premier Plus grade with credit scores above 680 and down payments of 40% or more would pay interest rates of 5.65 percentage points, according to the countrywide rate sheet for California. As the down payment gets smaller (as LTV goes up), the interest rate increases. For example, an applicant with the same credit score and a 100% LTV will be charged a 7.50% interest rate. But, note that the interest rate is fairly stable until the down payment drops below 10%. At this point the lender begins to worry about possible negative equity positions in the near future due to appraisal error or price depreciation.

Credit Score

FICO scores summarize borrowers' credit histories, with lower scores representing higher risk:

Scores lower than 620 generally signify higher credit risk.

Scores between 620 and 680 are usually considered marginal risk.

And scores of 680 and above are considered lower risk.

Loan to Value Ratio

LTV is the measure of down payment to be given by the borrower at origination of home loan. The higher the LTV the smaller the down payment.

Table 1: Underwriting and Loan Grades

Credit history	Premier Plus	Premier	A–	B	C	C–
Mortgage delinquency in days	0 x 30 x 12	1 x 30 x 12	2 x 30 x 12	1 x 60 x 12	1 x 90 x 12	2 x 90 x 12
Foreclosures	>36 months	>36 months	>36 months	>24 months	>12 months	>1 day
Bankruptcy, Chapter 7	Discharged >36 months	Discharged >36 months	Discharged >36 months	Discharged >24 months	Discharged >12 months	Discharged
Bankruptcy, Chapter 13	Discharged >24 months	Discharged >24 months	Discharged >24 months	Discharged >18 months	Filed >12 months	Pay
Debt ratio	50%	50%	50%	50%	50%	50%

Source: Countrywide, downloaded from www.cwbc.com on 2/11/05.

Table 2: Underwriting and Interest Rates

		LTV				
Loan grade	Credit score	60%	70%	80%	90%	100%
Premier Plus	680	5.65	5.75	5.80	5.90	7.50
	660	5.65	5.75	5.85	6.00	7.85
	600	5.75	5.80	5.90	6.60	8.40
	580	5.75	5.85	6.00	6.90	8.40
	500	6.40	6.75	7.90		
Premier	680	5.80	5.90	5.95	5.95	7.55

Contd...

	660	5.80	5.90	6.00	6.05	7.90
	600	5.90	5.95	6.05	6.65	8.45
	580	5.90	6.00	6.15	6.95	
	500	6.55	6.90	8.05		
A–	680					
	660	6.20	6.25	6.35	6.45	
	600	6.35	6.45	6.50	6.70	
	580	6.35	6.45	6.55	7.20	
	500	6.60	6.95	8.50		
B	680					
	660	6.45	6.55	6.65		
	600	6.55	6.60	6.75		
	580	6.55	6.65	6.85		
	500	6.75	7.25	9.20		
C	680					
	660					
	600	6.95	7.20			
	580	7.00	7.30			
	500	7.45	8.95			
C–	680					
	660					
	600					
	580	7.40	7.90			
	500	8.10	9.80			

Note: The first three years are at a fixed interest rate, and there is a three-year prepayement penalty.
Source: Countrywide California B&C Rate Sheet, downloaded from www.cwbc.come on 2/11/05.

WHO WERE THE BENEFICIARIES FROM THE GROWTH OF SUB-PRIME MORTGAGE MARKET?

The expansion of sub-prime mortgage lending has made home ownership possible for households that in the past might not have qualified for a mortgage and has thereby contributed to the rise in the home ownership rate since the mid-1990s. In 2006, 69% of households owned their homes; in 1995, 65% did. The increase in home ownership has been broadly based, but minority households and households in lower-income census tracts have recorded some of the largest gains in percentage terms. Not only the new home owners but also their communities have benefited from these trends. Studies point to various ways in which home ownership helps strengthen neighbourhoods. For example, home owners are more likely than renters to maintain their properties and to participate in civic organizations. Home ownership has also helped many families build wealth, and accumulated home equity may serve as a financial reserve that can be tapped as needed at a lower cost than most other forms of credit.

Below we present the demographic profile of borrowers across multiple dimensions of ethnicity, income, age, educational level, and financial sophistication i.e. level of preparation and search criteria:

Ethnicity

The sub-prime borrowers are generally more likely to come from a protected class or undeserved population. Black borrowers account for the disproportionately large share of sub-prime lending: the 16% of sub-prime loans taken out by blacks is more than three times the proportion of prime mortgages going to this group.

Borrower Income

Lower-income borrowers are about twice as likely to obtain mortgages in the sub-prime sector as in the prime sector.

Borrower Age

The sub-prime population tends to be older than the population of the prime borrowers. Only 12% of the sub-prime borrowers are aged 18 to 34 in our survey, while this age group accounts for more than one quarter of the activity of prime borrowers. At the other end of the age spectrum, 30% of borrowers taking out sub-prime mortgages are aged 55 and older, while only 17% of prime borrowers fall into this category.

Educational Level

Sub-prime borrowers also appear to be less educated than their prime counterparts. 62% of sub-prime borrowers did not obtain a college degree, nearly 50% more than the 43 % of prime borrowers who fall into this classification.

By and large sub-prime borrowers appear less financially sophisticated.

Level of Preparation

On the whole, it shows that sub-prime borrowers tend to be somewhat less prepared than their prime counterparts. For instance, 12% of sub-prime borrowers who admit to be unfamiliar with common mortgage terms is double the share of prime borrowers with the same deficit.

Search Criteria

Our focus groups suggested that prime and sub-prime borrowers use quite different search criteria in looking for a loan. Sub-prime borrowers search primarily for loan approval and low monthly payments, while prime borrowers focus on getting the lowest available interest rate.

Thus, sub-prime borrowers are disproportionate minority and lower income, older less well educated, less financially sophisticated and less likely to search for best interest when applying for mortgage.

WHAT WAS THE ROLE OF SECURITIZATION, MORTGAGE BACKED SECURITIES AND COLLATERALIZED DEBT OBLIGATION IN THE GROWTH AND SUBSEQUENT DECLINE IN THE SUB-PRIME MORTGAGE MARKET?

The sub-prime lending industry has grown significantly since the mid 1990s. The industry has gone from representing less than 5% of all originations to 20%. On a dollar volume basis they have gone from $35 billion in 1994 to $625 billion in 2005. A significant share of the increase in home ownership has come from the democratization of mortgage credit that allowed weaker buyers to purchase homes with less financial wherewithal.

The growth of the subprime market has been largely driven by:

(1) Increased investor appetite for mortgage-backed products, which have increased conforming securitization rates from 60% in 2000 to 82% in 2005 and non-conforming securitization rates from 35 to 60% over that same period;

(2) Increased access to securitizations by non-depository lenders; and

(3) Lenders' desire to move these loans off of their balance sheets.

Securitization

Whereas once most lenders held mortgages on their books until the loans were repaid, regulatory changes and other developments have permitted lenders to more easily sell mortgages to financial intermediaries, who in turn pool mortgages and sell the cash flows as structured securities. These securities typically offer various risk profiles and durations to meet the investment strategies of a wide range of investors.

The growth of the secondary market has thus given mortgage lenders greater access to the capital markets, lowered transaction costs, and spread risk more broadly, thereby increasing the supply of mortgage credit to all types of households.

Collateralized Debt Obligations (CDOs)

These derivatives are like a mutual fund that bundles together bonds, loans or swaps. But unlike a mutual fund, a CDO has different tranches that give investors different rights over this portfolio. For example, as interest payments on the underlying bonds come in, they will first be allocated to the senior tranches. Only when these have been paid will the more junior tranches get their share. And if defaults occur, the junior tranches take the first hit.

How MBS became appealing because of CDO

The tailoring introduced by CDOs can turn coarse corporate cloth into investment-grade *haute couture.* Take a bunch of companies, with bonds rated A (not the best credit-rating, but reasonably secure). Assemble them in a portfolio and give one group of securities rights over the first 70-80% of the cash flows from the bonds (and protection against the first 20-

30% of defaults). Since it is highly unlikely that 20-30% of the A-rated bonds will go bust, the rating agencies will give such securities the highest AAA appellation. *In a world where very few individual companies can command such a lofty rating, this transmutation makes such instruments highly appealing.*

Of course, it concentrates the risks in the rest of the portfolio. The lowest-rated securities (the last to get the cashflows and the first to bear the brunt of default) are known as "equity". Although they are not strictly shares, they do tend to offer share-like returns of 15-20% or so. The securities in between the equity and the senior securities are known as mezzanine.

The bottom tiers of these CDOs have been called "toxic waste". But they have been almost nourishing in recent years, thanks to the low default rate on corporate bonds. Their buyers have enjoyed the rewards without seeing much of the risks.

The ongoing growth and development of the secondary mortgage market has reinforced the effect of these innovations.

Finally, the economic value of securitization and risk transfer value of Collateral Debt Obligation has given mortgage lenders greater access to capital markets and spread risk more broadly, thereby increasing the supply of credit to all types of borrowers.

How Mortgage Backed Securities and Collateral Debt Obligations triggered the fall of sub-prime lending

But the inherent complexity in these innovative financial instruments also created valuation problems whereby rating agencies underestimated the risk involved in giving loan to a sub-prime borrower.

Role of MBS

Mortgages and mortgage backed securities are difficult to value.

MBS, like other fixed-income financial instruments, are valued as the present discounted value of expected cash flows. Like most fixed-income investments, MBS are affected by default risk.20 MBS, however, are substantially affected by prepayment risk-that is, the risk that the borrower will unexpectedly pay off the loan early. While a great deal is known about measuring borrower default risk, relatively little is known about measuring borrower prepayment risk. Where default risk is more a function of credit risk, prepayment risk is more a function of market risk; the levels of interest rates, the shape of the yield curve, volatility, seasonality and market competition to name a few. Hence, prepayment risk creates substantial difficulty in estimating the value of an MBS as a function of expected cash flows relative to other financial instruments.

Role of CDO

CDOs add complexity to MBS and other constituent credit instruments.

CDOs aggregate existing securities, which themselves are difficult to value. Furthermore, the term, CDO, comprises a set of very different types of structured finance arrangements, from cash flow CDOs to synthetics. Favoured collateral types for all those arrangements can and sometimes do change rapidly over time. Those features create the potential for high volatility in sectors that rely principally upon CDOs for funding. Thus, Dynamic composition of CDO collateral pool further complicates the task of valuation.

CDOs held a lot of MBS, most of it below AAA ratings

A study by Moody's, a credit-rating agency, of asset-backed CDOs found that, on average, slightly less than half their portfolios were invested in subprime RMBS. But in some cases, the exposure was nearly 90%. Losses will be magnified for investors in the junior tranches. At worst, Moody's says, the vast majority of tranches in such CDOs would be downgraded to junk-bond status.

This CDO funding of MBS was highly leveraged

As we demonstrated earlier, only some 10% or so of a typical MBS financing structure is made up of lower-tier (junior) securities. Those lower-tier (junior) tranches to provide the desired credit support for the higher-tier (more senior) tranches. In other words, the entire MBS structure above the lower-tier (junior) tranche cannot be sold until those lower-tier (junior) tranches are sold.

Highly fragile

Hence, the CDO market purchased more mezzanine MBS in 2005 as was actually issued that year. Furthermore, and crucially, the relatively small amount of MBS purchased by the CDO market provided support for the rest of the $1,193 billion issued in private RMBS during the entire year of 2005. The point, therefore, is that the CDO market adds liquidity to MBS and ABS markets in a highly leveraged fashion by funding lower-tranche MBS securities.

The frenzy of innovation around debt and securitisation got out of hand. Risk was supposed to be bought by those best able to afford it, but often ended up with those seduced by yields they did not understand.

CONCLUSION

Our findings indicate that because of its complicated nature, sub-prime lending is simultaneously viewed as having great potential and great perils. The potential of sub-prime lending is that it can provide opportunity for home ownership to those who were either subject to discrimination or could not qualify for mortgage in the past. The danger lies in the fact that it can also be described as high cost lending, thus carrying greater probability of default by borrowers.

Also, sub-prime borrowers are a disproportionate minority with lower income, older, less well educated, less financially sophisticated and less likely to search for best interest when applying for mortgage. Finally, the economic value of securitization and risk transfer value of Collateral Debt Obligation has given mortgage lenders greater access to capital markets and spread risk more broadly, thereby increasing the supply of credit to all types of borrowers. But the inherent complexity in these innovative financial instruments also created valuation problems whereby rating agencies underestimated the risk involved in giving loan to a sub-prime borrower.

BIBLIOGRAPHY

Mason, Joseph and Rosner, Joshua. "How Resilient are Mortgage Backed Securities to Collateralized Debt Obligation Market Disruptions," *Working Paper*, (2007), Hudson Institute.

Krishnamurthy Ramasubbu, "financial inclusion becoming priority," *The Indian Express*, November 26, 2007, p.17.

Paul Krugman, "*The making of a mess,*" *The Hindu*, December 4, 2007, p.9.

Paul Krugman, "*Blindly into bubble*," *The Hindu*, November 22, 2007, p.9.

Paul Krugman, "*Gone baby gone*," *The Hindu*, October 24, 2007. , p.9.

Paul Krugman, "*Enron's second coming*," *The Hindu*, October 2, 2007, p.9.

Paul Krugman, "Workouts, not bailouts," *The Hindu*, August 18, 2007. , p.9.

C.R.L.Narasimhan, "Factors behind the global market volatility," *The Hindu*, August 13, 2007, p.15.

Edmund L. Andrews, "In reversal, U.S. Federal Reserve approves plan to curb risky lending," *New York Times, December* 20, 2007, p.17.

C.R.L.Narasimhan, "Sub-prime accountability issues to the fore," *The Hindu*, November 26, 2007, p.15.

Ila Patnaik, "Sub-prime mindset," *The Indian Express*, August 18, 2007, p.10.

Chomsisengphet, Souphala and Pennington-Cross, Anthony. "The Evolution of the Sub-prime Mortgage Market,", *Federal Reserve Bank of St. Louis Review*, (jan-feb 2006)

Lax, H., Michael Manti, Paul Raca, and Peter Zorn. "Sub-prime Lending: An Investigation of Economic Efficiency," *Housing Policy Debate* Volume 15 Issue 3 Fannie Mae Foundation (2004).

Gerardi , K., Harvey S. Rosen, and Paul Willen, "Do Households Benefit from Financial Deregulation and Innovation? The Case of the Mortgage Market,"

Public Policy Discussion Papers, Federal Reserve Bank of Boston, (June 2006)

Liz Moyer, "Cost of The Crunch? $2 Trillion, Says Goldman," *Forbes* (November 2007).

Feldman, R., and J.Schmidt, "Why all concerns about subprime lending are not created equal," *fed gazette*, (July99)

Speech Chairman Ben S. Bernanke At the Federal Reserve Bank of Chicago's 43rd Annual Conference on Bank Structure and Competition, Chicago, Illinois May 17, 2007

WEB REFERENCE

www.federalreserve.gov/newsevent/speech

www.mpls.frb.org

www.forbes.com

3

Human Resources Training and Excellence of Universities

MEHDI SHARIATMADARI*
SOMAYEH MAHDI**

Organizational growth, change and success ultimately depend on the actions of human beings. Training and development are the ways in which organization invests in its human capital. Like all investments, the aim is that the organization should receive a benefit from its investment. In the case of investment on human resources training, benefits are reflected in improvement of performance, productivity and efficiency of the Human Resources (HR).

HR training can be defined as a process of formal and informal education based on a set of dynamic objectives and expected results towards individual and organizational effectiveness over time. This education consists of acquiring changes in behaviour by gaining desirable knowledge, attitudes and mental and manual skills.

A sound training programme in an organization is of paramount importance for individual professional development and consequently for the improvement and effectiveness of the organization. The key factor in the success of organizations is improving their HR. In fact, the planning and implementation of HR improvement programmes can develop more productive personnel.

In higher education systems, the goal of HR training, particularly teachers' training and development is to address changing circumstances regarding new knowledge and technology over time and also to improve the quality of education. Undoubted, the survival and growth of the higher education systems as an educational organization depend on growth and development of the teachers as their major human capital. Therefore, training and specially teachers' training is essential.

* Faculty Member and PhD Student, Islamic Azad University, Central Organization, Iran.
** PhD Student, University of Pune, Education Department.

Therefore, considering the importance of HR training and development, there is an inevitable need for training evaluation in order to assess the extent to which an organization is effectively developing new knowledge and competence among their HR.

This paper reviews the findings of PhD dissertation of Mehdi Shariatmadari, which is a comparative analysis of efficiency of two teacher training in-service programmes in two universities: Islamic Azad University of Iran and Pune University of India from the view of administrators. This study addressed the perspective of administrators of the mentioned universities on the role of in-service training in strengthening teachers' job satisfaction, innovation, service quality, professional and job skills and it also studied the efficiency of these trainings in improving joint work and cooperation among administrators and teachers, job growth and promotion and observing work discipline by the teachers. As this paper summarizes a larger study conducted to evaluate teachers training in-service programmes in two developing countries, three factors - teachers' job satisfaction, innovation and their cooperation with the administrators - are taken into consideration. The paper describes the problem, explains procedure of the study, and then presents the findings of the study.

INTRODUCTION

Stepping into the new era of information technology imposes the need to redefine teachers' roles. This has become more complex and demands specialized training and qualifications, which, in turn, lead to changing the paradigms of pre-service and in-service teacher training. Teachers are no longer the only source of information for the students or, indeed, the most important one. What they are expected to be today is to serve as mediators between the students and varied sources of information and to act as counsellors and consultants. They are also responsible for organizing a proper environment for the personnel development of each student and for stimulating the learning and learning-to-learn process, and thus being able to manage the impact of information and technology effectively.

It is obvious that the revolution of science and technology affects the domain of change in the teacher's role. But the prescribed scenarios stating that introducing new technology will lessen the role of the teacher and restrict the need for a teacher in the classroom does not seem likely to happen. There is enough evidence to prove the contrary. In fact, new technologies demand enhancing and strengthening the role of the teacher.

However, in this regard one of the key areas affected by the changes taking place in education is related to teacher training. If teachers are not offered training and education adequate to the new reality, they will not be able to participate effectively in changes taking place. Therefore, active participation in the changes happening in today's world with a view to the tomorrow is an essential issue. Contemporary teacher training has to enable teachers to recognize their new mission and responsibilities when facing the challenges of twenty-first century.

TEACHERS' IN-SERVICE TRAINING

In a society undergoing rapid development there is an ever-increasing need for training and education. The rate of development and the increasing demands with regard to knowledge require extensive flexibility in the workforce, as it has to; on a running basis acquire skills with regard to changing job content- or entirely new jobs. In order to meet these requirements, education and training now has become a lifelong process. However it is not sufficient merely for the individual to be prepared for change and motivated to learn. There is also a need for a fundamental reorganization of educational system.

Among most of the professions the need for training and education and in-service training is increasing; in this regard, teachers are not exceptions. The lifespan of modern information, where the world's collective knowledge is replaced or renewed over a 5-7 year period, will change the need for training, particularly in-service.

However, generally two phases of training in teacher education are considered as two main types of teacher training:

- Pre-service training
- In-service training

Table 1

Types of Training	Description of Activity	Pros
Pre-Service	Formal Teacher Training through Institutes, colleges or universities	• Supports development of untrained teachers • In-depth instruction • Raises profile of teachers • Leads to official certification of teachers and etc.
In-Service	Training of teachers during their service	• Support the development of trained and untrained teachers • More effective as smaller training elements are covered with time to integrate training into classroom practice • Enables teachers to continue teaching • Easier to implement and adapt to meet the needs of the teachers

In this study, the effects of in-service training programmes as short-term training programmes, offered by University of Pune in India and Islamic Azad University in Iran, on teachers' efficiency are investigated; hence this research focuses on teacher training in-service programmes.

The concept of teacher training in-service in higher educatiòn was first developed in west during the boom period of 1970s. A variety of teacher training and development programmes were offered by universities in Europe. Most of these programmes are still being run as short-term training courses to improve the competencies of teachers in university system. The university system in the world has, indeed, made provision for faculty improvement programmes, study leave, seconding to research projects, attending at conferences, etc., as short-term measures for improvement in quality of teaching.

SIGNIFICANCE OF TEACHERS' TRAINING IN-SERVICE

Human beings, as intelligent animals, have unlimited abilities and potential, which can be activated through organized and effective training and education. In recent years, the era of rapid development and changes in technology and sciences, only those systems of higher education can survive and sustain their activities, that their teachers, as one of the most important elements of development, continuously improve their skills and abilities. Indeed, the need for training is increasing day-by-day. Higher education systems that hope to maintain a place in local and global education market are quickly coming to the realization that investments in in-service training are essential to their future competitiveness. Life-long learning is no longer an option; it is now a key part of an education system's continued success. In this way, one of the major and vital duties of management of higher education is teacher's training in universities.

Teachers are typically unprepared to enter the classroom. They usually enter the higher education system after graduation in formal education through institutes, colleges, and universities. As a result, they have to face teaching situations without proper skills and enough knowledge in teaching methods, communication skills and etc. Although they would have good knowledge about their subjects, which is acquired during their education, they are not capable to transfer this knowledge because of lack of requisite skills such as teaching skill, methods, communication, motivating students, monitoring and etc. With all these, training is essential for experienced teachers too. Indeed, training is not limited to a special time or a restricted to a special group of teachers. It means all teachers need life-long and continuous training and retraining in order to improve their efficiency and performance.

In this regard, every university makes attempt to develop new teachers with modern knowledge and prepare them with new technology, sciences and methods by providing effective and fruitful training in-service courses. This fact increases the necessity of in-service training for teachers.

In-service training is seen today as an idea which is both old and new. The idea is already old because it appeared in a number of countries immediately following the war, and in some cases even earlier, and yet new because - in its current form - it is often only slowly becoming established; old again, because it is already necessary to reassess its content in the light of current circumstances, and new because, once the obstacles to its development have been overcome, it is only now that everyone can become involved in making it work effectively. In-service training has become increasingly important in the field of education, thanks to technological advances, the growing demand for quality education, etc.

Since the 80s, the importance of the in-service training in the professional development, and especially in education is accepted by all. In service training is not seen as a remedy for deficiencies in initial training, but as a long-term process and a part of continuing education that makes possible the acquired knowledge in the initial training and that can be defined as "a variety of activities and practices in which teachers become involved in order to broaden their knowledge, improve their skills and assess and develop their professional approach". The in-service training is understood as a tool to professionalize teaching, improve quality and efficiency of the new educational systems and promote the scientific and technological advances and innovations. If we also keep in mind the characteristics of present day society, with present transition, with continuous changes and adaptation to new technological, social, cultural changes... in-service training turns to be the only tool to face these changes, as well as to democratize people's access to culture, to information and work.

In fact, continuous training in today's evolving education scenario is a necessity and good training ensures that teachers' knowledge and skills are managed to the optimum. The world in which teachers operate is changing rapidly. Teachers need new skills and capabilities to respond to a wide range of demands:

Economic: economic globalization is leading to pressure to raise educational standards in order for countries to be internationally competitive;

Social: changes in society are influencing students' home and family environment and mean it is not always possible to address students' educational needs without also considering their social needs and cultural identity;

Knowledge economy/society: technology is bringing about rapid changes to all aspects of life;

Educational: educational research continues to reveal new insights about teaching and learning which teachers need to incorporate in their teaching practice;

Use of information and communication technology in learning: the effective use of ICT in classrooms has the potential to enhance teaching and learning, but only if teachers are adequately trained; etc.

Therefore, teacher training programmes are moving from distinct pre- and in-service concepts to modalities of life-long learning. Teachers' in-service training is one of the most effective ways to train and develop skills and knowledge. This type of training is most effective because the trainee learns and develops skill/skills under actual working conditions while training under an experienced trainer. Rather than dealing with concepts and theories, the trainee teacher learns and develops actual skills in the service. However, unlike schoolteacher training, almost all training of higher education teachers takes place within organization that employs both the trainees and trainers.

The academic and professional training of the teachers has a direct and positive bearing on the quality of their performance and consequently on the achievements of the students, which will lead to improvement of the quality of higher education system. In this regard, the relevant teacher training and development programmes are necessary. In-service training programmes are varied in nature and quality, and only some have undergone formal evaluations to determine effectiveness of different organizational deliveries and the effect on teachers' performance. Effective in-service training programmes that are known to make difference to the quality of teaching support teachers to develop their knowledge, skills and classroom practices. However, these programmes do not always provide adequate linkage and ongoing support with ongoing classroom practices and therefore actual instructional practices or teacher performance are often not changed. Consequently, more research should be conducted in this field to assess and evaluate the training programmes and providing effective training programmes.

FEATURES OF EFFECTIVE TEACHERS TRAINING IN-SERVICE

Effective in-service training programmes for teachers tend to have the following characteristics:

Need Analysis

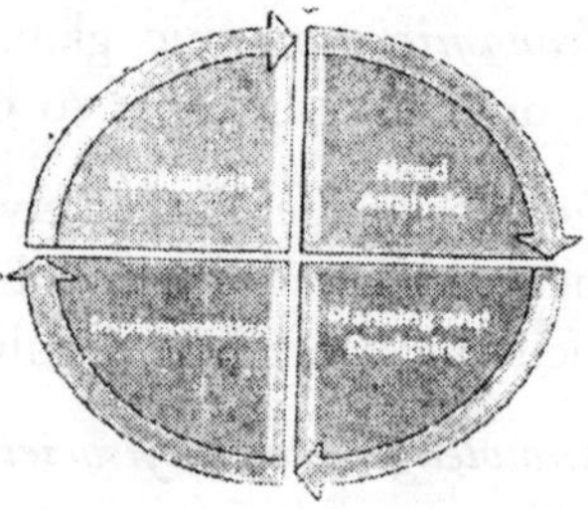

Before designing training programmes, it is essential to determine what are the needs, interests, weaknesses and strengths of teachers. In this stage, it should be ascertained what training the teachers need, what training they already have, will the programmes provide new knowledge and skills needed by the teachers or is it refining already acquired knowledge and skills, etc. This information is important to determine the goals, content, best delivery method, and evaluation of activity.

Planning and Designing

Effective programmes are well planned, and tend to be formal in nature.

Some of these programmes focus on improving the performance skills of individual teacher, some of the programmes emphasize on organizational issues that will affect whole teachers, and some programmes focus on both individual and organizational issues. In this stage, an overall strategic framework for the long-term effort is necessary. The overall planning need to consider how various needs might be met. Thus, adequate time and resources need to be set aside for teachers training programmes.

However, it should be taken into consideration that apart from consultation about their needs, teachers, along with administrators - principals, vice-principals, deans and heads of departments need to be involved in the planning step of training programme. Those programmes that involved participant teachers in the planning of such programmes tended to have greater success in accomplishing their objectives than those without assistance of the participants.

Implementation

Conducting or implementing a training programme requires considerable efforts and coordination. Although every training department conducts courses regularly but preparation for every individual course is essential. Advance preparation not only prevents the omission of important steps; but it makes one feel more confident at the start of the training and helps to create a welcoming learning environment.

Evaluation

Feedback informing facilitators on the modes of presentation, involvement, relevance, adequacy of facilities and trainers, etc. are valuable. However, an effective evaluation must also investigate whether attitudes and practices of participants have actually changed for the better, and whether these changes are manifested in classroom practices and processes. In other words, the performance of the teachers should be evaluated too.

Evaluations of teachers' performance are usually conducted for two purposes: to make judgments about a teacher's performance, and to provide useful information to improve the teachers' instructional practices. A key factor here is the appropriateness of the criteria for the purpose of the evaluation. Peer and self-evaluations are often used to improve teaching proficiency. While supervisor evaluations from principals, vice-principals, heads of departments and other supervisory staff are also helpful in providing development information, these evaluations are also often used as the basis for terminating or retraining and even designing new training programmes.

TEACHERS IN-SERVICE TRAINING IN OTHER COUNTRIES

Teachers' training and development in higher education was taken up seriously in the Western world during the affluent period of late 1970s. Centres of higher education were established in most of the universities to provide some kind of guidance on the professional development of teachers. In the erstwhile Soviet Union and to some extent in China, compulsory training for teachers and academic staff of the university has been in practice for many years. In Germany, Brigitte Berendt and others started a model in 1982. She has identified five approaches to staff development: a) the professional approach which functions within specific context, b) the research-oriented approach that takes up learner-oriented forms of teaching through a linked research programme, c) the personal de-attitudes and teaching to optimize learning, d) the self-help approach for working in groups to exchange experiences for improving the organization of learning and, e) the comprehensive reforms of studies approach to establish a staff development unit to use a strategy to bring about improvement in teaching, research, consultancy and extension.

In the same way, teachers' in-service training has gradually been introduced over the course of last century, and has existed in Finland, Sweden and Germany on a voluntary and relatively informal basis since the end of 19th century. It later developed in other countries in a similar manner before becoming more structured. This type of training has often evolved in two stages (Belgium, Netherlands, Austria, Portugal, Spain, Finland, Sweden and Scotland), the first being informal and voluntary and the second more structured, based on legislations and sometimes compulsory participation. In some countries, teachers' in-service training had a late start. Usually, in-service training has been provided for all levels of education at the same time (Belgium Flemish Community, Germany, Netherlands, Austria, Portugal, Scotland and Norway).

In the last decade, most countries, not only those in Europe, have engaged in educational reform. Wherever this has taken place, the reform of teacher education and training has been one of the key issues. Reasons for focusing teacher training are not difficult to discover. Teacher training is a large enterprise. Large population of student, teachers is to be found in thousands institutions; and their training involves millions of teacher trainers in all over the world. Hence most countries tended to reinforce training in-service programmes along with teacher education programmes in order to achieve proper results in reforming the teacher education and training programmes.

Arrangements for in-service training vary widely between countries depending on factors such as current institutional arrangements, the character and status of the teaching profession, views on curriculum and pedagogy and the relationship between government agencies and schools. In many countries, increasing emphasis is being given to the importance of in-service training and this is leading to the introduction of more structured arrangements.

In the same way, a comparative analysis of teacher training in-service programmes shows a great diversity between and within countries. For example in Bulgaria, Romania, the Russian Federation, Slovakia, Slovenia, teacher training in-service represent an important part of educational policy. This is evident from numerous legislative documents adopted after 1990, several of which contain regulations concerning teacher education and in-service training.

In some of the countries such as Poland, for teacher training in-service purpose and needs, separate institutions have been set up. This tendency has both positive and negative aspects. The emergence of different systems of teacher training in-service indicates awareness of the need to respond to a diversity of situations, coupled with diversity in training of teachers to cope with these situations. It is also proof of the realization that a separate structure could play a different role in education other than existing institutions within the education system. In other words, educational policy meets practice face to face. Some of the negative sides of teacher training in-service relate to the separation of teacher training in-service from initial teacher education teacher training. Particularly where universities are the major institutions for initial teacher education and training, and due to their academic autonomy, there is lack of co-operation and co-ordination between initial teacher education and teacher training in-service.

It could be mentioned that there is no single model of teacher training in-service programmes. In most countries, especially Central and Eastern European countries, teacher training in-service is integrated in different institutions at central, regional or local levels. However, in these countries, in-service training, as a major factor in professional growth, requires further upgrading. Furthermore, lifelong education of teachers is becoming one of the major issues in all Central and Eastern European countries.

However, in many European countries such as UK, France, Germany and so on, there is an on-going debate about entitlement of teachers to teacher training in-service programmes and whether it should be voluntary or compulsory. Most in-service training programmes take place in the teachers' spare time but there is an argument that each teacher should be given an entitlement to a certain amount of retraining throughout his/her career. There is another debate that suggests balance between in-service training and courses organized to meet the needs of teachers. This suggests that the institution based models of training, by providing programmes base on the perceived institutions goals, may neglect the individual needs of teachers. As a result, the wide diversity among the models of teacher training tends to result different countries moving in different directions when engaged in teacher training in-service programmes.

ISLAMIC AZAD UNIVERSITY (IAU)

The Islamic Azad University is a part of an international network of "new generation" universities. These modern institutions are committed to provide relevant courses for today's rapid changing world.

IAU is a non-profit, non-government system of higher education founded in 1982 in response to increasing social demand for specialized and skilled manpower and development. IAU is a dynamic and fast- changing university and its steady expansion is mirrored in the broad range and increased number of its undergraduate and postgraduate courses. IAU has a reputation for innovation and relevance in teaching and research, offering associated Diplomas, Bachelor, Master and Ph.D. programmes in more than 561 courses in its over 357 campuses/branches and centres inside the country and 4 outside of Iran in UK, Emirates, Lebanon and Tanzania.

Human Resources Training and Development Department (HRTDD), Islamic Azad University: Considering the significance of the role of the teachers and also revolution of science and technology, a higher education system that aims to offer a quality education for all young people should be able to count on teachers and staff who are well-trained. Hence, the management of Islamic Azad University, decided to compensate the loss - lack of comprehensive and organized training programmes, by establishing human resources training and development department, which is supported by the Finance Department.

As a result, in 2000, the Human Resources Training and Development Department (HRTDD) established and organized short-term training programmes in the four areas as mentioned below:

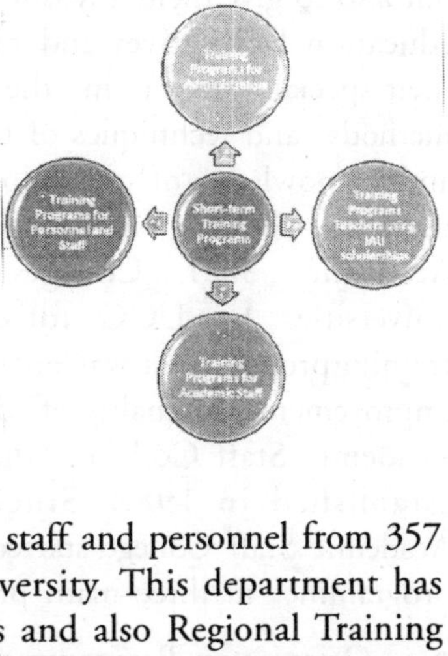

Training Programmes for Administrators (Principals, Vice-Principals, Deans, Head of the Departments)

Training Programmes for Academic Staff (Full Time and Part-Time Faculty Members) Training Programmes Teachers using IAU scholarships

Training Programmes for Personnel and Staff: This department located in the Central Organization of Islamic Azad University in Tehran covers all administrators, academic staff and personnel from 357 campuses and branches in 12 regions of Islamic Azad University. This department has established in- campus Human Resources Training Centres and also Regional Training Centres in order to enhance access and quality of education. The programmes offered by these centres are conducted in three levels: a) In-campus centres level, b) Regional level and c) National level.

UNIVERSITY OF PUNE (UOP)

Established in 1948, the University Pune has since become one of the leading centres for research and teaching in India. The 411 acre campus is located in the North Western part of Pune. The placid environs and state-of-the-art facilities provide its numerous students with an ideal atmosphere to pursue research in various areas of Science, Arts, Commerce and Languages. The university houses 61 departments which provide a wide array of academic programmes. Though a young centre, the university has made a significant impact in various areas of research and teaching, and continues to strive for excellence. At present, the university has 60 departments, schools and centres and 472 affiliated colleges and 270 recognized research institutions, 107 postgraduate centres. Further, the University of Pune also has a "Study Abroad Programme" with foreign universities such as:

- the University of Lausanne, Switzerland
- the University of Sorbonne, France
- the University of Bremen, Germany the University of Tehran, Iran
- and the University of Central Queensland, Australia

ACADEMIC STAFF COLLEGE (ASC), UOP

The tradition in India has been to regard training for college or university teachers as unnecessary. For them, some suitable form of training and orientation are essential, not only to overcome their initial teaching troubles and to create sense of confidence, but also to give them a reasonable understanding of educational objectives and purposes and place of their special subject in the curriculum of new methods and techniques of teaching and learning, and a knowledge of psychology on which good teaching should be based. The starting of Academic Staff Colleges in some selected universities by UGC for conducting teachers' trainingprogrammes was an important step in the improvement of quality of education in India. The Academic Staff College, University of Pune was established in 1987. Since its inception the Academic Staff College started to conduct training programmes in three main programmes:

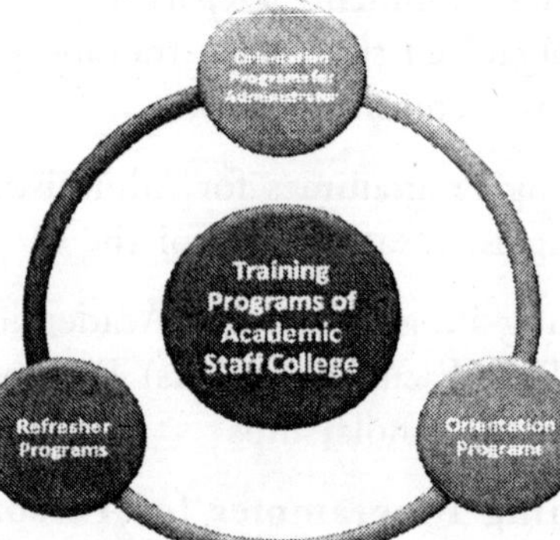

- Orientation Programmes
- Refresher Programmes

- Orientation Programmes for Administrators of
- Higher Education

RESEARCH PROCEDURE AND METHODOLOGY

The present study was predominantly descriptive in nature as its primary aim was to describe the current state of teachers' short-term training programmes in Iran and India and study the effect of these training programmes on improvement of teachers' efficiency and performance. Further, the study also aimed at presenting a model for providing more effective short-term training programmes and making recommendations regarding what should be in place in teachers' short-term training programmes to ensure that prospective teachers are equipped with knowledge and skills required to cope with changing nature of today's education systems. For this purpose, the following hypotheses were asserted:

Main Hypothesis: There is a significant difference between viewpoints of Islamic Azad University administrators and Pune University administrators, regarding the effect of short-term training on improvement of teachers' performance and efficiency.

Null Hypothesis: There is significant difference between viewpoints of Islamic Azad University administrators and Pune University administrators, regarding the effect of short-term training on improvement of teachers' performance and efficiency. Special hypotheses of this study are as below:

1. Short-term training programmes will improve teachers' innovation.
2. Short-term training programmes will reinforce administrators and teachers joint work.
3. Short-term training programmes will lead teachers to observe work discipline.
4. Short-term training programmes will cause teachers' service quality improvement.
5. Short-term training programmes will increase teachers' job satisfaction.
6. Short-term training programmes will improve teachers' professional and job skills.
7. Short-term training programmes will provide bases of job growth and promotion.
8. Short-term training programmes will lead the teachers and organization follow the same direction.

The primary design used in this study was a survey. A survey was the chosen method for this study for two main reasons: (a) the study required collection of data from a large number of persons located over a wide geographical area - therefore, administering survey instruments (primarily questionnaires) to these participants was the most efficient means of collecting required data, and (b) since one of the primary aims of the study was to gather various perspectives to describe and make inferences regarding the state of teacher training programmes in Iran and India, data collection methods used in surveys are especially suited for the type of data required for this study. Both primary and secondary data were used for the study. These sources provide information about the related literature of the study. The primary data for the study was collected through a questionnaire developed by the researcher. The target population for this study encompassed all administrators of Islamic Azad University in Iran and administrators of Pune University in India (including Principals, Vice- principals and Heads of Departments). Administrators were selected for this study because of their knowledge of teachers' performance and efficiency. In addition, they are the leaders in the educational arena; they have the authority to create, accept, fund, and implement new programmes that can greatly influence teacher training.

Considering the expansion of the target population and their geographical spread, a sample group is chosen from all administrators of Islamic Azad University and Pune University. 400 administrators including Principals, Vice-Principals, Heads of departments, of 400 samples, 200 are administrators of University of Pune and 200 are administrators of Islamic Azad University. A two-stage sampling procedure was performed to select the sample for this study: (a) purposive sampling of districts, and (b) randomly selection of study participants-administrators. The target population for this study encompassed all administrators of Islamic Azad University in Iran and administrators of Pune University in India (including Principals, Vice-principals and Heads of Departments). Administrators were selected for this study because of their knowledge of teachers' performance and efficiency. In addition, they are the leaders in the educational arena; they have the authority to create, accept, fund, and implement new programmes that can greatly influence teacher training. In addition, administrators of the universities were selected as a population to be studied for three main reasons:

(1) They play a significant role in providing effective training programmes for teachers by supporting such programmes.

(2) They provide a broad perspective on the effects of short-term training programmes on teachers'efficiency and performance improvement.

(3) They are able to observe and supervise the teachers' performance directly and from a broader perspective.

Therefore, these administrators were a potent data source and equipped with knowledge required to provide data to answer the relevant research questions.

For the purposes of this study, two methods were used to gather data required to answer the research hypotheses: (a) related literature review, (b) self-developed survey instrument. The questionnaire used in this study titled "Administrators Perspective on the Effects of Short-term Training" (APEST) was developed by the researcher. APEST survey's questions were designed to solicit administrators' perspective on the effect of short-term training on teachers' efficiency and performance improvement. Data collected through the questionnaires were analyzed using Statistical Package for Social Science (SPSS version 11.5). The following statistics were used to analyze the data: 1) By use of descriptive statistics, frequencies were tabulated and compared to indicate the effect of short-term training on the teachers' efficiency and performance; 2) Chi-Square test was used to analyze the viewpoints of administrators of Islamic Azad University of Iran and Pune University of India regarding the effects of the short-term training on teachers' efficiency and performance improvement; 3) Spearman Correlation test was also utilized to find out the relationship between the variables of hypotheses.

RESULT AND DISCUSSION

This study declares that there is no significant difference between the perception of administrators of Islamic Azad University, Iran and University of Pune, India. The findings of this study can be summarized as follow.

Figure 1 reflects the emphasis of the administrators in Iran and India on the effects of training in- service programmes on the improvement of teachers' innovation (Hypothesis 1). 63% and 66.5% of the respondents respectively from Iran and India agreed that participating in training in-service courses has improved the teachers' innovation.

Table 2: Descriptive Statistics of Special Hypothesis 1

Variables	Strongly Agree		Agree	Undecided	Disagree				Strongly Disagree		
India	29	14.5%	133	66.5%	23	11.5%	11	5.5%	4	2%	200
Iran	45	22.5%	126	63%	21	10.5%	7	3.5%	1	0.5%	200
Total	74	18.5%	259	64.75%	44	11%	18	4.5%	5	1.25%	400

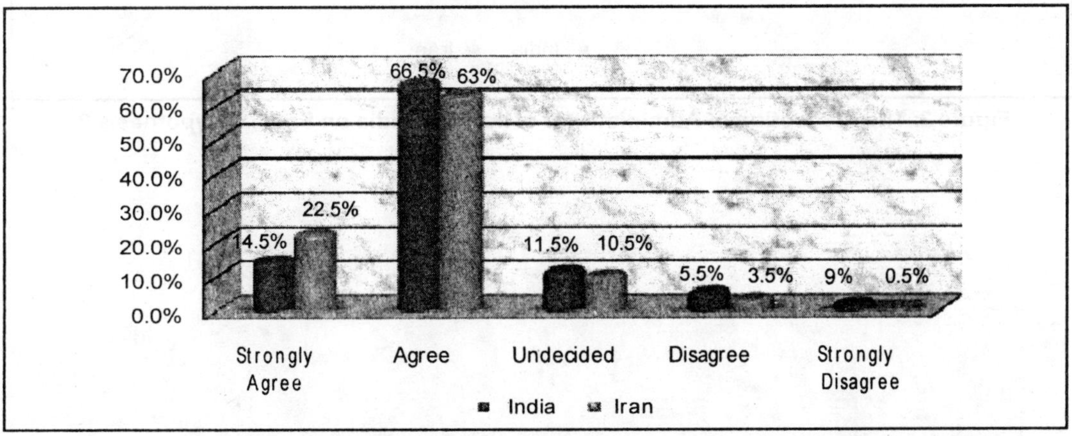

Figure 1: The Perception of Administrators of Iran and India on Special Hypothesis 1

Figure 2 reflects the emphasis of the administrators in Iran and India on reinforcement of administrators and teachers' Joint Work (Hypothesis 2). 62% and 64.5% of respondents respectively from Iran and India agreed collaboration between the teachers and management has increased.

Table 3: Descriptive Statistics of Special Hypothesis 2

Variables	Strongly Agree		Agree		Undecided		Disagree		Strongly Disagree		
India	29	14.5%	129	64.5%	21	10.5%	15	7.5%	6	3%	200
Iran	36	18%	124	62%	17	8.5%	21	10.5%	2	1%	200
Total	65	16.25%	253	63.25%	38	9.5%	36	9%	8	2%	400

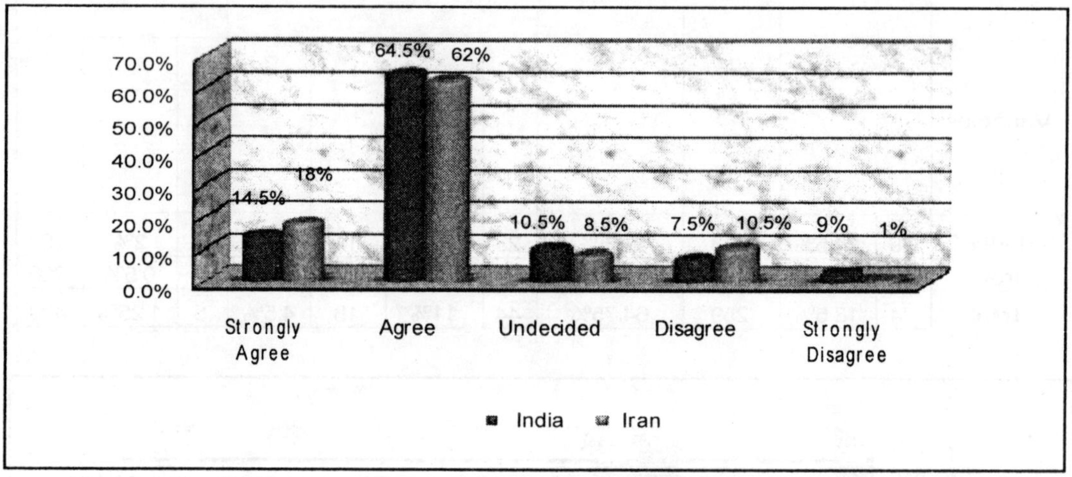

Figure 2: The Perception of Administrator of Iran and India on Special Hypothesis 2

The administrators participating in this study believed that participating in training in-service programmes has increased teachers' job satisfaction. As it is shown in figure 3, 53.5 % of respondents from Iran and 61% of respondent from India agreed to this statement.

Table 4: Descriptive Statistics of Special Hypothesis 5

Variables	Strongly Agree		Agree	Undecided	Disagree				Strongly Disagree		
India	39	19.5%	122	61%	20	10%	16	8%	3	1.5%	200
Iran	48	24%	107	53.5%	15	7.5%	24	12%	6	3%	200
Total	87	21.75%	229	57.25%	35	8.75%	40	10%	9	2.25%	400

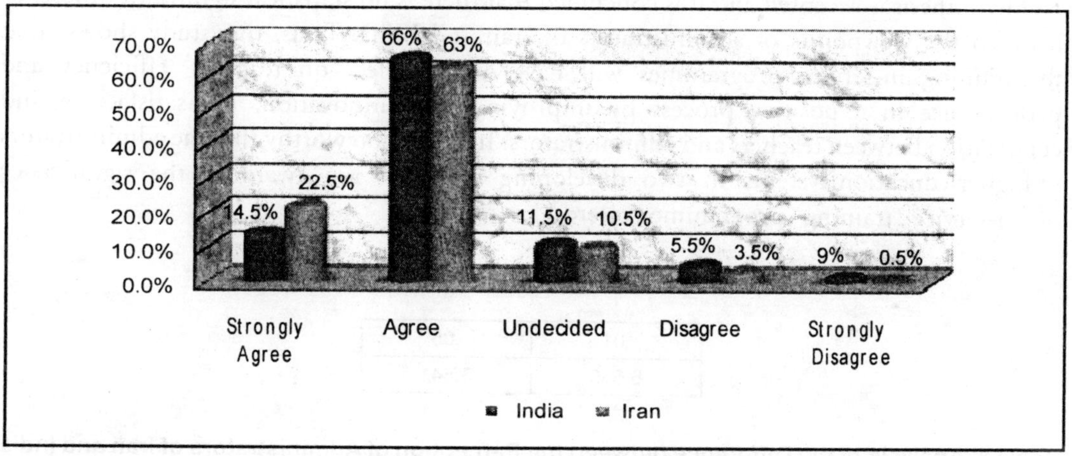

Figure 3: The Perception of Administrators of Iran and India on special Hypothesis 5

Table 6 indicates the computed values of Chi-square and descriptive statistics performed on the hypotheses. This table shows that the calculated chi-square concerning the perceptions of the administrators of Islamic Azad University, Iran on are more than of the table value at .05 and .01 level of significance (see Table 5 & 6). Hence, the three special hypotheses mentioned above are accepted. Similarly, the calculated Chi-square regarding the viewpoints of the administrators of University of Pune, India are also more than the tabulated Chi-square at .05 and .01 level of significance (see table 5 & 6). Therefore, the above-mentioned hypotheses are accepted. Both groups of the administrators believe that training in-service will improve teachers' innovation and job satisfaction. They also emphasize that participating in training in-service programmes has reinforced joint work and cooperation between teachers and administrators.

Table 5: Tabulated Chi-Square (DF=4)

.01	.05
13.277	9.488

Table 6: Analysis of the Perception of Administrators of Iran and India

Variables	India					Iran				
	χ^2	df	Sig	Mean	SD	χ^2	df	Sig	Mean	SD
H1: Teachers' Innovation	268.6	4	.000	3.85	0.76	232.6	4	.000	4.03	0.70
H2: Teachers' and Administrators' Joint Work	256.8	4	.000	3.80	0.85	230.7	4	.000	3.86	0.83
H3: Teachers' Job Satisfaction	189.1	4	.000	3.88	0.81	204.8	4	.000	3.84	0.96

But according to the Chi-square test performed to measure the main hypothesis of the study, there is no statistically significant differences between the viewpoints of the administrators of Iran and India (see Table 8). In other words, the Chi-square calculated to measure the difference between the viewpoints of the administrators of Islamic Azad university and University of Pune are less than the tabulated Chi-square. Therefore, the null hypothesis is accepted and it is concluded that there is no statistical significant difference between the viewpoints of administrators of Iran and India. Thus, this study shows that the training in-service programmes will have salient effect on teachers' efficiency and performance in a positive process by improving their innovation, job satisfaction and cooperation between teachers and administrators. It is also noteworthy that the administrators of higher education systems in two developing countries are aware of the significance of in-service training programmes offered for teachers.

Table 7: Tabulated Chi-Square (DF=1)

.01	.05
6.635	3.841

Table 8: Analysis of the Difference between the Perception of Administrators of Iran and India

Variables	χ^2	df	Sig	Mean	SD
Main Hypothesis	0.269	1	0.604	3.88	0.80
H1: Teachers' Innovation	0.578	1	0.443	3.94	0.74
H2: Teachers' and Administrators' Joint Work	0.711	1	0.399	3.83	0.84
H5: Teachers' Job Satisfaction	0.406	1	0.524	3.86	0.89

CONCLUSION

As a result, it can be concluded that organizational training is fast gaining ground owing to the various benefits that provides to the organization and people serve in it. Continuous training in the today's evolving market scenario is a necessity and good training ensures that people knowledge and skills are managed to the optimum.

Teachers are considered as human capital in higher education organizations and institutions. Considering the revolution of science and technology in recent decades, it seems that many teachers are typically unprepared to enter the classroom and address the needs of the students. This could be caused by lack of skills and knowledge. Therefore, training in-service programmes are required to:

- help teachers to cope with the changes
- transfer information and knowledge to teachers
- equip teachers to translate that information and knowledge into practice with a view to enhancing higher education effectiveness and the quality of education
- advise them on good techniques
- review familiar subject areas and so on.

Obviously, the development of teachers' performance and efficiency, ideally as part of a continuous process of performance management, needs to be tackled at both the organizational and the individual level. It is believed that there are a number of reasons, which may contribute to high-performance and efficiency of teachers at any point of time. One of these reasons, in organizational level, may relate to adequate leadership, efficient management practices or systems. In other words, attaining higher education goals will depend on the ability of teachers to assign the best for their responsibilities and their endeavour to conform with the environment around them. Teachers' efficiency will depend on the management of the system. In fact, the policies and decisions made by the administrators play a significant role in improving the efficiency of the teachers, and therefore the institutions. To cope with the increasingly changing expectations regarding teachers' efficiency and performance, training in- service seems to be vital. Training and retraining in-service cause increase of the efficiency of teachers. In-service training is fast gaining ground owing to the various benefits that provides to the institution and people serve in it.

Continuous training in today's evolving market scenario is a necessity and good training ensures that people knowledge and skills are managed to the optimum. Thus, it is a continuous and organized effort by management for improving teachers' efficiency and performance, and finally for the higher education efficiency and performance.

To consider all above mentioned notes, every university makes attempts to develop their teachers with modern knowledge and prepare them with new technology, sciences and methods by providing effective and fruitful training in-service courses. The administrators play a significant role in activating in-service or short-term training programmes. On the one hand, they may employ the policies and plans which will lead to improve the quality of education and brighten up in-service training programmes; on the other hand they may apply policies and plans which will hinder development of in-service training programmes. In fact, the administrators act as support for short-term training programmes of teachers, by: a) adopting positive policies regarding in-service training; b) providing facilities for conducting training in-service programmes; c) motivating teachers to participate in such programmes; d) monitoring teachers efficiency and performance; e) monitoring training programs and etc.

For any reform to take root, it is necessary to motivate the leaders and decision-makers within the system to accept reform as part of growth and development. For this, the viewpoints of administrators of higher education - the senior administrative staff: heads of departments, principals of colleges - in two developing countries - Iran and India - were studied to find out whether they believe on the effects of short-term training programs on improving teachers efficiency and performance or not.

RECOMMENDATIONS

Considerable research evidence confirms that administrators' viewpoint associated with the effects on the teacher in-service training programmes is positive; in fact they believed that these programmes have improved teachers' efficiency and performance.

The organizational structure and the facilities of the in-service training system are not sufficient to carry out its functions effectively. To solve this problem, administrators in different units of organization and particularly from In-service Training Department, which is responsible for the in- service training of teachers, should become a more practical organization with its central and local units. These departments and centers should be supplied with the necessary personnel and equipment, as well as finances. The staff in those units should be increased in number and have the competencies to plan, administer and implement in-service training programmes by using scientific methods. The university departments', especially the education departments' support should be provided for training the in-service training staff - administrators, trainers and specialists. This, of course, requires increasing the cooperation between the administrators of universities.

In order to plan and implement effective programmes, scientific methods should be used for assessing the training needs, selecting the trainees and evaluating the programmes. For this purpose, specialists are needed to work in the in-service training units of the organization. To make teachers more interested in continuous professional development and increase their attendance at in-service training, some motivating elements should be added to the system. For example, teachers may earn certain credits in the in-service training programmes, and these may help teachers to be promoted through requiring certain standards for the programmes. Apart from this, it is recommended that in-service training activities well become a part of the teacher's working schedule in university. In other words, the teachers may spend certain working hours in a week on in-service training instead of teaching students.

Although the result of this study confirms that administrators of Islamic Azad University and University of Pune believed that in-service training programmes had positive effects on teachers performance and efficiency, many of administrators universities, colleges and other education institutions consider in-service training less important compare to other issues and consequently give it less attention. This fact has caused considerable limitations to the in-service training of teachers. To overcome this problem, administrators should be trained and persuaded about in-service training through seminars, and be helped to develop positive attitudes towards it. Also, they should especially be informed about the objectives, content and implementation of the in-service training.

It is rather difficult to provide continuous and face-to-face in-service training for all teachers because there are a great number of teachers, and financial means for the in-service training of teachers are insufficient. Therefore, distance in-service training of teachers should be increased. For this purpose, as an alternative, a distance education approach could be used. Different kinds of programmes with different purposes could be implemented through the Internet, radio, television, CDs and printed materials. The number of periodicals and publications could be increased; moreover, these materials could be distributed to all teachers.

REFERENCES

Baldwin, T. T., & Ford, J. K. "Transfer of training: A review and directions for future research". *Personnel Review*, 26.3(1988): 201-213.

Best, John W. and Kahn, James V. *Research in Education*. New Delhi: Pearson Prentice, 2006.

Blackburn, V., & Moisan, C. *The In-service Training of Teachers in the Twelve Member States of the European Community*, Maastricht: Presses interuniversitaires européennes, 1987.

Bramley, P. *Evaluating training effectiveness*. Maidenhead: McGraw-Hill, 1996.

Chalam, K.S. *Academic Staff Development in Higher Education*. Calcutta: K.P Bag chi & Co.,1991.

Goldstein, I. *Training in organizations*: Needs assessment, development, & evaluation. Monterey. CA: Brooks-Cole, 1993.

Goldstein I.L. and Ford J.K. *Training in Organizations*. (4th Ed). CA: Wadsworth, 2002

Information Communication Technology. Islamic Azad University: www.ict.iau.ir

LeClercq, J. "*Teachers in a context of change in Central and Eastern Europe*", Proceeding of Educational Reforms in Central and Eastern Europe Symposium. Prague, Strasburg: Council of Europe, 1995.

Lynton, R.P. and Pareek, U. *Training for Development*. (16th Ed.). New Delhi: Vistaar Publication, 2005.

Murillo, P. *El aprendizaje del profesorado y los procesos de cambio*. Sevilla: Mergablu, 1999.

Phillips, J. J. *Handbook of training evaluation and measurement methods*. (2nd ed.). Houston, TX: Gulf, 1991.

Perron, M. "*Vers un continuum de formation des enseignants: elements d'analyse*". Recherche et formation. 10 (1991): 137-152.

Rao, Digumarti Bhaskara. *European Education and Teachers*. New Delhi: Discovery Publishing House, 2003.

Rossi, P.H., Freeman, H. E., & Wright, S. R. *Evaluation: A systematic approach*. Beverly Hills, CA: Sage, 1979.

Sagar, Krishna, (2005), *ICTs and Teacher Training*, Authors press, New Delhi

Shariatmadari, Mehdi. "Study the Effects of Short-Term Training in Improvement of Teachers' Efficiency from the Viewpoint of Islamic Azad University and Pune University Administrators. Dissertation submitted in University of Pune in partial fulfillment of PhD Degree in Education, 2008.

Shariatmadari, Mehdi. *Theories and Patterns of Human Resources Training in Organization*. Tehran: Yekan Publishing, 2003.

Shariatmadari, Mehdi. & Mahdi, Somayeh. "*The Role of In-Service Training in Human Resources Development*", SMART3.2 (2007): 9-14.

Sharma, Sita Ram. Teacher Education: *A Manual for In-service Teachers Education Institutions*. Jaipur: Mangal Deep Publications, 2003.

UNESCO, International Commission on Education for the Twenty-first Century. Report of the Commission: Preliminary Synthesis. Paris: UNESCO, 1995.

4

Globalization and the Revolutionary Cultural Change Imperative of African Organizations

CONSTANTINE*
IMAFIDON*
TONGO*

In order to cope with the demands of globalization, African organizations must take proactive steps in dealing with issues that pertain to their cultures. This means that national cultures that are inimical to organizational effectiveness must be done away with. Consequently, the current thinking in the field of organizational theory and behaviour which states that organizational cultures are subservient to and circumscribed by their national cultures is bound to collapse in the very near future. This paper, therefore, concludes that in this dispensation of globalization, the African work organization would serve as the most instrumental agent of cultural change in the whole continent. This is because it is more prone to the vagaries of global capitalism than other social institutions.

INTRODUCTION

In a series of study based on the functioning of organizations, Etzioni (1964) asserted that our societies are organizational societies. We are born in hospitals, educated in schools, employed by business firms and government agencies; we join trade unions, sleep in hotels and are laid to rest in churches. In sickness and in health, at work and play, life in modern industrial society is increasingly conducted in organizational settings (Haralambos and Heald, 1980). The organization is not a new invention. As far back as pre-industrial times, organizations were created to pursue specific goals. For example, in ancient Egypt, a very large organization consisting of several thousands of skilled workers was formed to build the pyramids of Egypt (Haralambos and Heald, 1980).

However, the most striking difference between the organizations of the 21st century and their pre- industrial counterparts, is the degree of vulnerability of both categories of

* Lecturer, Department of Business Studies, College of Business and Social Sciences, Covenant University, Ota, Ogun State, Nigeria.

organizations to certain distant forces or factors, (which are hundreds and hundreds of miles away) in contemporary and pre-industrial times respectively. Globalization, which is the main carrier of these distant forces, is fast becoming a buzzword in the world of business today. It is bringing about a social re-engineering of both societies and organizations. Consequently, any present study or research carried out to understand the behaviour of organizations in societies, must of necessity incorporate the ways by which globalization is currently affecting both social entities, i.e. organizations and societies.

According to Iyayi (2003), one of the major properties of the conventional accounts of organizations is that, there is a relationship between the level and form of social development of each society and the culture of organizations, characteristic of such societies. Organizations do not only represent an important class of institutions in society, but in fact determine to a large extent how society is actually constructed. A major implication of this, is that the study of the culture of a society not only becomes a basis for developing a model of organizational forms; more importantly, it draws attention to the argument that an analysis of the culture of a society's work organizations can also provide an adequate basis for understanding the culture of the entire society (Iyayi, 2003). As Hofstede (2001) observed from his monumental cross-cultural study:

> *... organizations are culture-bound. This applies not only to the behaviour of people within organizations and to the functioning of organizations as a whole; even the theories developed to explain behaviour in organizations reflect the national culture of their author, as do the methods and techniques that are suggested for the management of organizations. In the management literature, there are numerous unquestioning extrapolations of organizational solutions beyond the border of the country in which they were developed. This is especially true for the exportation of management theories from United States to the rest of the World, for which the non-United States importers, are at least, as responsible as the United States exporters. However, the empirical basis for American management theories is American organizations; and we should not assume without proof that they apply elsewhere. This assumption is found not only in the popular literature: in scholarly journals - even in those explicitly addressing an international readership - the silent assumption of universal validity of culturally restricted findings is frequent....*

If organizations are culture-bound, it then follows that to be adequate, any explanation of organizational functioning, within as well as between societies must be constructed out of an analysis of the differential impact of culture as a variable (Iyayi, 2003). Hofstede's analysis becomes even more important, when we consider the case of work organizations in Africa and other developing nations. What has been observed over the years is that, there is little or no attempt by these organizations to build up distinct cultures of their own. These African organizations, passively import the beliefs and values of their underdeveloped societies. For instance, Jaeger and Kanungo (1990), have opined that within organizations in developing nations, human capabilities are often viewed as more or less fixed with limited potentials. Hence career planning and progression are extremely limited. The adherence to such an assumption on human capabilities did not arise from a vacuum. Inadvertently, there must have been a diffusion of the beliefs and values of the larger underdeveloped societies into these organizations. African indigenous organizations are characterized by collectivism, high power distance, favouritism, fatalism, and political decision-making (Jackson, 2004). These cultural particulars have hampered the ability of the African indigenous organization to compete favourably well in the present global economy.

In this paper, it is believed that the available theorizing on the organizational and national culture interface has paid little or no attention to the effects of globalization on this interface. With the dissolving of national boundaries, shrinking of the global market and the transfer of beliefs and values across nations, via globalization; it is expected that work organizations, especially those of African nations would proactively evoke cultures different from those in which they are domestically domiciled, in order for them to become globally competitive. Consequently, it is the objective of this paper to pre -empt scholars of organizational culture to envisage the possibility of the emergence of a revolutionary paradigm; which would upset the current thinking on the restrictive influence of national culture on organizational culture.

NATURE OF ORGANIZATIONAL CULTURE

Managers and scholars are giving increasing attention to organizational culture, and this popularity of organizational culture reflects mainly three different concerns or purposes. First, it introduces a major new metaphor for thinking about organizations, adding to the prior ones of an organization as a machine or an organism. The cultural metaphor promotes attention to the generation, function, and consequences of meaning. A second use of the idea is to provide an umbrella term, under which many ideas for organizational understanding can be gathered and related. Thirdly, organizational culture is seen by some as either the means or the target for changes that have major commitment, control, productivity, or even bottom line consequences.

Schein (1985), who is one of the most referred commentator on organizational culture defines organizational culture as a pattern of basic assumptions, invented, discovered or developed by a given group as it learns to cope with its problem of external adaptation and internal integration - that has worked well enough to be considered valuable and therefore to be taught to new members as the correct way to perceive, think, and feel in relation to those problems.

Organizational culture can be defined as a pattern of shared values and beliefs that help individuals understand the organizational functioning, and thus provide them with the norms for behaviour in the organization.

According to Iyayi (2003), apart from the fact that most of these definitions are too general, it is also apparent that each says and yet leaves out something about culture and that it is the synthesis of all statements that a complete understanding of culture is to be found. For these reasons, we find those discussions, which differentiate between different levels of culture to be the most adequate in providing an understanding of organizational culture.

Consequently, Schein (1988), differentiates between three levels of culture: these are (i) core beliefs and basic assumptions (ii) values and (iii) artifacts and creations.

Core Beliefs and Assumptions

These are beliefs about the world. They deal with both 'espoused theory' and 'theory in use'. They are thus not only about what people assume works in the real world but also about the actual beliefs used in action. The importance of beliefs for reality creation is no more eloquently captured today than in the popular saying that: "seeing is not believing; believing is seeing". Believing is characterized by a set of assumptions about the world. Especially assumptions about reality and human nature. Cole (1997)" sees this level of organizational culture as the "implicit culture, probably closer to reality, which resides in the assumptions made by management and staff about what really is important. For example, an organization can claim to be an equal opportunities employer in its job advertisements (explicit culture) and yet in reality women and racial minorities fail consistently to get promotion and men are rarely considered for posts typically held by women (cashiers, secretaries etc.). In this case, the implicit culture predominates over the explicit and public culture (Cole, 1997).

Values

Values are social principles, philosophies, and standards considered to have intrinsic worth. They help to arrange the various beliefs in some order of priority and importance. If basic assumptions deal with the" is proposition" and indicate what the world is like, values deal with the "ought proposition", and act as tie breakers in the world of action and decision. Organizational values refer to principles that underlie patterns of behaviour and norms.

The values of top management are an essential element in explaining the behaviour and performance of a business. These values affect the management style, the structure, the approach to the market, and the strategies for success employed by the business. Values thus contain and convey expectations about how individuals will behave in the given context against the background of a shared understanding of what is important. They act as tie-breakers in defining moments when individuals have to choose between two or more sets of beliefs that apply to the situation. Values thus enable beliefs and assumptions to be arranged in a hierarchy.

Artifacts and Creations

This is the visible aspect of organizational culture. Artifacts result from the context of values and assumptions. They describe and present the constructed physical and social environment, its written and spoken language, artistic productions and the overt behaviour of its members. They also describe productivity levels, the quality of products and services provided and the type of social relationships constructed within and among group members. Finally too, they help describe the attitudes and hence behaviour of group members towards such issues as individual responsibility and achievement, the purpose of life and related matters.

ORGANIZATIONAL AND NATIONAL CULTURE IN A NON-GLOBALIZED CONTEXT

The national culture in which a work organization is situated has been found to have an immense influence on its organizational culture. The impact of national culture on organizational culture has in fact been stressed increasingly by several writers (Deal and Kennedy, 1982). These writers have maintained that the interests in organizational culture must be distinguished from the many comparative studies that have been forced to confront the obvious cultural differences that exist from country to country and their effect on and in the organizations of these countries. It would be commonplace to observe that organizations differ in their cultural systems according to their country of origin or presence. Less commonplace is to find those factors that remain impervious to these differences.

For example, the fact that the West and East, and more specifically, the United States and Japan have vastly different cultural values, is well acknowledged. The U.S. is characterized by such values as assertiveness, decisiveness, innovativeness, and risk taking, which stem from its frontier-conquering history (Hall and Hall, 1990). The U.S. culture is also characterized by individualism - the belief in the power and autonomy of the individual (Yeh, 1995).

For instance, Easterners, particularly the Japanese, complain that Americans are too legalistic and less willing to be flexible (Thorton, 1993). Hence, Japanese firms, as compared to U.S. firms, are more likely to have cultures characterized by flexibility and people and detail orientation. Possibly, these cultural factors are the driving force behind the success of Japanese firms. That is, Japanese firms may rely heavily on the virtues of flexibility, people orientation, detail orientation, and team orientation to achieve greater business performance and customer satisfaction. And relative to Japanese firms, U.S. firms are more likely to have cultures characterized by innovation, outcome orientation, and aggressiveness. Further, these cultural values that characterize the U.S. firms are likely to impact on their performance, because their business strategies and the resulting successes are attributable to their cultural values. Just as Japanese firms utilize the cultural values that characterize them to achieve greater performance, U.S. firms will exercise the characteristics of innovation, outcome orientation, and aggressiveness as their competitive weapon to achieve greater business performance and customer satisfaction. Thus, it is expected that the relationships between organizational values and outcomes (both customer satisfaction and business performance) should vary across national cultures. Hofstede (1994) alluded to this when he pointed out that the academic community has been relatively slow in accepting that not only management practices, but also the validity of organizational culture theories may stop at national boundaries.

AFRICAN ORGANIZATIONS AND THEIR NATIONAL CULTURES

In sub-Saharan Africa, the extended family (with grandparents, uncles, aunts, cousins, the father's additional wives and their children) is an economic unit that has to care for itself.

Families are collectives sharing a common kinship lineage, living and collaborating in a village for common security in the face of threats by nature and man. Village compounds provide the safe context for life-long learning of crafts, social behaviour and survival techniques (Iguisi, 1994).

Kingship groups extend from the past over the present to the future. Only some members are currently alive, others are dead (ancestral spirits) and countless are still to be born. Naming children after their grandparents stands for linking generations. This keeps the family context constant and also signifies a circular perception of time.

The strong family loyalty also supports ethnic and religious loyalty. African societies are "We" societies and "We" opposes "them". On the culture dimension of individualism versus collectivism identified by Hofstede (1980), African societies scored strongly on collectivism. All Western countries scored strongly on individualism.

In the African cultural pattern, there still tends to be a strong emphasis on the settling of disputes. The goal is to keep personal relationships as harmonious as possible. If a dispute cannot be solved by the parties, elders will try to mediate. In certain cases, in order to resolve some disputes, ancestral spirits were consulted, and they reveal their response through oracles (Iguisi, 1994).

In a survey by Iguisi (1994), it was found that the national cultures of Nigeria and the Netherlands, as measured by the work values and desires of the employee populations are different. Nigeria is higher on collectivism than the Netherlands. Power distance, which is the degree of inequality between subordinates and superiors that people consider normal was higher in Nigeria, like elsewhere in Africa. The larger power distance obtainable in Nigeria means that respect and authority are based on position, experience and seniority. The ideal African manager is a benevolent paternalist. In collectivist society, in-groups are superior to out-groups in terms of recognition. This leads to favouritism. Individualization has not progressed to a level where kinship and tribal background have stopped playing a role in how subordinates are treated in organizations. Work and private life have not become separate spheres like in industrialized countries. This also means that African managers and non-managers alike will at times let private interests prevail over their obligations to the company. The African manager proudly retains the inheritance of his or her culture, but at the same time thinks he can function effectively in a global competitive market.

An implication of the African mindset, is that most African work organizations function at a low level of efficiency, and according to the survey report of Iguisi (1994), one-third of the workers considered themselves dedicated and satisfied, but not motivated - a correlation hardly recognized in the comparable Dutch company.

In a comparative study of the United States, Indian, Japanese and Nigerian cultures, Obisi (1993) found that whereas the American and Japanese were of the belief that: individuals can influence the world around them and help to determine the future of their countries; an individual can make a difference in the achievement of organizational goals, and differences of opinion cannot make persons disagreeable and unwanted. On the other hand, the Nigerian culture and civilization tend towards determinism - which assumes that all things in life are tied to destiny (Obisi, 1993).

Hofstede (1980), in his study of African values found that wisdom is more important than knowledge in the African context. Wisdom comes from experience and time, not from education. Attributed wisdom that is not based on knowledge and education is a dubious foundation for the development of any country (Hofstede, 1980).

It is also important to note that the reliance of African societies on family and ethnic ties as the key social network reduces their members' ability to share new information and learn. Family and ethnic ties generally create closed networks with rigid sets of norms and define "in group" boundaries. This hampers the inflow and dissemination of information that may conflict with prevailing thoughts and values within the family and ethnic communities (Kuada, 2007).

As can be seen, the foregoing depicts a rather negative, disturbing and depressing view about Africans and their culture, that is, the African ethos. The unquestioning mind of the average African militates against the economic, social and political advancement of the nation.

Adopting Schein's (1988) discussion of the different levels and areas of cultural reality; Iyayi (2003), in a dialectical manner, explains the crucial imprint of national culture on organizational behaviour. According to him, a dialectical understanding of culture would enable us delimit what he termed cultural universals and cultural particulars. The objective of such delimitation would be to permit organizational comparisons across cultural contexts and, at the same time, enable us capture specific cultural particulars.

Cultural Universals according to him, are the sets of questions that are posed in each area of cultural reality at the level of core beliefs and assumptions. They include questions about who we are and whether we believe that the environment is subject to human control. Other questions are whether the members of the society believe that they can: dominate nature, creatively rearrange their environment, and be certain about the future.

Cultural particulars reflect the unique constellation of answers that each society provides to the sets of questions in each area of cultural reality. It then follows that organizational cultures vary between different national cultures, as a result of the differences in the answers that are provided by members of society to the questions that are posed in each area of cultural life (Iyayi, 2003). He identified three organizational forms: the underdeveloped, transitional and the developed, and these have their correlates in three types of societal contexts. Specifically, the underdeveloped society is characterized by the underdeveloped organization. Consequently, organizations in African nations can be termed underdeveloped. These organizations generally carry the following cultural particulars: people are not sure about who they are; nature and environment are not subject to human control; individuals cannot creatively rearrange their lives; reality is neither objective nor verifiable; truth is established on the basis of tradition, feel and intuition, luck, background, contacts and politics are the basis for achievement; individuals do not need autonomy and freedom for personal growth; and it is impossible to achieve perfection (Iyayi, 2003). Contrarily, the developed organizations in developed societies, hold that: people are sure about who they are; nature and environment are subject to human control, individuals can creatively rearrange their lives, reality is objective and verifiable, truth is established on the basis of scientific researches, individuals need autonomy and freedom and personal growth, and it is possible to achieve perfection (Iyayi, 2003).

At the level of organizational artifacts, developed and underdeveloped organizations also vary. For instance, there are differences between organizations established and managed by people in Africa, like Nigeria, and those that are established and managed by foreigners in Nigeria from Western societies (Europeans and Americans).Taking the example of the use of space, it is readily apparent that the European or American organization in Nigeria, establishes and operates by quite a higher standard of quality than Nigerian organizations. Nigerians are often amazed at not only how the European enterprise creates housing estates that are equipped with all the needed infrastructures, but also at the fact that these infrastructures often work at same or nearly the same level of efficiency as may be found in European societies. By contrast, the Nigerian organizations that establish housing estates often adopt a haphazard approach; the infrastructures are often never always comprehensive and if they were established by some European group of companies as part of a turnkey project, the infrastructures often break down shortly after the departure of the first European occupants. These and other observable differences in organizational artifacts are explicable not simply in terms of the fact that one housing estate was established by Westerners and the other by Nigerians. The differences are explicable in the underlying sets of beliefs and values that characterize the Western organization in Nigeria and the Nigerian organization in Nigeria (Iyayi, 2003).

ORGANIZATIONAL AND NATIONAL CULTURE IN A GLOBALIZED CONTEXT

There is no doubt that the foregoing discussions have been able to assert that a limitation does exist for organizational culture transcending the boundaries of national culture. This is as a result of the unfettered influx of the beliefs and values of a nation state into its internal organizations; and the inability of these organizations to create cultures different from those of their national culture.

However, those who have previously made such assertions on the organizational/national culture interface did not take into cognizance the emerging global economy, during the time of their theorizing. Hofstede specifically did not pay much attention to this, perhaps because global human resource strategies were much less developed in the 1970s when he carried out his research. These previous researchers only x-rayed organizational cultures from the standpoint of national culture, leaving behind the diverse global cultural linkages that are being brought by globalization. This is a major flaw in their analysis.

Giddens (1990) has described globalization as the intensification of worldwide social relations that link distant localities in such a way that local happenings are shaped by events, occurring many miles away and vise versa. Organizational activities and relationships are being uprooted from local origins and cultures by globalization (Gray, 1999). Information technology has now created the possibility and even likelihood of a global culture. The Internet is sweeping away cultural boundaries. Global entertainment companies now shape the perceptions and dreams of individuals and organizations, wherever they live. The sum effect of all of these happenings is that, the cultural boundaries of most nation states are being dissolved, and there is presently a transfer of foreign beliefs and values into indigenous work organizations. Consequently, in this globalization process, there is a built-in dialectical tension between global and local cultures. Today's competitive organizations are now forced to meet with global standards rather than local standards. Thus the supposedly reactive posture taken by previous organizational/national culture interface theorists, which posits that organizations must derive their cultures from those prevailing in their respective national boundaries, may soon become a thing of the past. As Castells (2001) has noted, business organizations that are organized around networks of production, management and distribution, must respond quickly to changes in the global business environment. In other words, they must first of all, take up the initiative of transforming their own organizational cultures to conform with standards presented by the global economy, irrespective of the culture of the nations in which they are domiciled. For one thing, any form of national culture transformation is a onerous task and can take as long as many dozens of years. Therefore, business organizations cannot afford to wait for such a long time before they themselves can become culturally transformed. Contrarily, we hold the opinion that business organizations, in this dispensation of globalization, would be the most instrumental agent of cultural reformation in modern nation states.

Japanese business organizations currently serve as empirical examples for the envisaged cultural revolution which is expected to occur in the future. Presently in Japan, business organizations have entered a new cultural phase. They are changing their personnel practices by eliminating employee positions. This runs counter to a cultural foundation of Japanese business practices that has emphasized the importance of group harmony, stability, and consensus decision making (Schmidt, 1996).

As in a successful Japanese family, the goal has always been harmony within the group. Individuality became second in importance to peace in the family. Although the father of the family made the major decisions, the other family members were expected to discuss potential activities among themselves and decide courses of action without conflict. The family as a group took the agreed upon action. After the Japanese male left the closely knit family unit of his youth, the work organization assumed the primary support role for him. Group harmony, with its stability and continuity, combined with consensus decision-making became the pillars of the "Japanese Management style" envied by the rest of the industrial world. Just as a family provides a lifetime of association, Japan's successful business organizations provided life-long association through employment for their professional and managerial employees. In Japan the job is the society, and the society is the job (Schmidt, 1996).

The Japanese management techniques are primarily based on trust between varied parties e.g. employer vs employee, buyer vs supplier etc. However, the existence of the "sudden death syndrome" and the high rate of suicides among Japanese managers is a testimony to the human and social costs of the Japanese model (Rafferty, 2001). Recent recession and unprecedented "lay offs" have also pointed to the possible fragility of the paradigm (Rafferty,

2001). It is now becoming necessary for many Japanese firms to build upon the integration of rational economic activity to produce new forms of institutional economics in their cultural frames of reference (Rafferty, 2001).

Consequently, the culture of Japanese work organizations is gradually being changed. For example, the life-long employment provided by Japanese work organizations is almost a thing of the past. Traditionally, if a person's long-term performance record was poor, Japanese work organizations would consider him for early retirement, even as early as his late 40's. However, some organizations in Japan have begun to demote incompetent managers based on the organization's performance evaluation system (Schmidt, 1996). Up till now, groups of Japanese employees hired together were treated similarly with salary increases, job assignments, and promotions for training and development that often lasted 10 to 15 years. Frequent job changes within the same age group to broaden career backgrounds softened the importance of slightly higher assignments. Social events within the organization even included an annual celebration of the group joining the organization. Now individual performance measurements for promotion, retention, and merit pay have introduced competitive factors between employees (Schmidt, 1996). This is the Western style of business that had not been considered before in the Japanese policy of group cohesiveness and harmony. In the past, Japanese have viewed competition between workers as undesirable. Personnel tests after World War II showed that Japanese worker performance deteriorated under competitive conditions (Schmidt, 1996). Emphasis was placed on developing and improving on individual's skills, rather than on competition with each other. But globalization has engendered a situation whereby corporate merit competition has shifted the emphasis to individual performance and away from employee group success.

The reason for this shift from collectivism to individualism in Japanese organizations is not far fetched. Past research supports a relationship between individualism versus collectivism and task-related versus contextual work goals. Individuals with strong collectivistic values place particular importance on contextual job attributes such as working conditions and human relations, whereas individuals with strong individualistic values place particular importance on task-related job attributes such as responsibility and autonomy (Gomex, 2003).

Therefore, since the task-related job attributes is likely to impact more directly on employee job performance and perhaps overall organizational performance, than the contextual job attributes; it behooves organizations in the 21st century to embrace individualistic values, in order to survive in the global economy. Modern organizations would need to pay more attention to the invisible hand of Adam Smith, which is competition. Competition, which is anti-thetical to trust, breeds individualism, rather than collectivism.

THE REVOLUTIONARY CULTURAL PARADIGM FOR AFRICAN ORGANIZATIONS

The above analysis of the cultural shift in Japanese work organizations, first of all, suggests that work organizations all over the world must now strive to align with a global competitive culture, in order to survive in this present competitive global economy. Secondly, it shows that work organizations really do not have to rely on the transformation of their own national cultures, before they can become culturally transformed. Thirdly, it can be predicted that after work organizations have been able to shift away from their own national cultures to the required global competitive culture; they will serve as the most instrumental agent of cultural change in the societies in which they are domiciled. As with the Japanese experience, it is expected that after some time, the individualistic culture that is currently being nurtured by its work organizations would gradually diffuse into the larger Japanese society. This cultural diffusion would later lead to an attenuation of the "collectivist" values that make up her national culture. For example, research on Hispanic acculturation has noted that as Hispanics (Latin Americans) who are high on collectivism become more acculturated into organizations in America, that are uniquely individualistic in nature; the strength of certain dimensions of the value of 'familialism', or an individual's strong identification with his/her family decreases (Sabogal, et.al., 1987).

We are, therefore, tempted to ask two fundamental questions. Is it possible for African organizations to take up the initiative of transforming their own national cultures? If this is possible, what are the factors that can help the African organizations attain this transformation process? In order to answer these questions, it will be useful at this juncture to recall a central argument in the materialism thesis of Karl Marx. According to Marx, the economic organ of a society is the most important part of any society. The value system of any society is fundamentally derived from its economic organ. Therefore, since work organizations are within this economic organ and are currently prone to the vagaries of global capitalism, they will, therefore, serve as the most vital instrument of cultural change in any society. The other agents of socialization, which includes; the peer group, family and educational systems (schools) are less important in this age of globalization, because they exist outside or are only tangentially attached to this economic organ.

Consequently, the African work organization in this globalized competitive economy becomes very important, as an agent of cultural change in her societies. This is due to the fact that African employees are constrained by the necessity to secure their jobs to gradually internalize the beliefs and values of their work organizations. This situation becomes very critical in the African context, considering the very large mass of the unemployed and the relatively few work organizations ready to absorb them. Therefore, individuals employed by the African work organization would be forced at the initial stage of the revolutionary cultural change occasioned by globalization to quickly embrace the new beliefs and values of their organizations, in order to retain their jobs. However, with the passage of time, these new beliefs and values would become fully internalized by them. This internalization process would be made possible through the administration of rewards to those employees who are conforming to the new culture. These rewards will serve as positive reinforcers for the new patterns of behaviour required by the organization.

Following the internalization of the new beliefs and values of the African work organization, the working class in these societies would in turn influence the non-working class towards embracing the newly internalized beliefs and values. This influence would take place as a result of the dependence of the non-working class on the working class for economic survival. If this process continues, the current cultures of most African nation states may be transformed with time.

However, indigenous work organizations in Africa are yet to sufficiently recognize the need for this envisaged cultural change. The reason being that little or no attention has been given to the study of the organizational/national culture interface in African nations. The paucity of empirical research on the subject matter, compounds the naivety of the managers of African work organizations, with respect to how organizational culture can add unquantifiable value to their businesses. We therefore recommend that for African work organizations to fully align with the cultural demands of globalization, their management researchers must first of all, initiate a research agenda towards generating sufficient empirical evidence to ascertain the full impact of national culture on organizational performance. We do believe that when this happens, it will serve as a catalyst for business organizations domiciled in Africa to experience a revolutionary shift from the core beliefs and values operating in their local business environments, which are presently inimical to their businesses, to the most ideal beliefs and values suitable for business performance in the global competitive economy. Subsequently, they will then become poised to effectively compete with their American and European counterparts.

With this happening, the institutional arrangement of national culture would no longer have any meaning, as an ideal model for organizational culture. Theorists of organizational culture would then have to change their present acclamations on the impossibility of organizational culture transcending the boundaries of national culture. Organizational behaviour researchers in Europe and America, may continue to hold tenaciously to their own postulations concerning the restrictive power of national culture on their organizations. The reason being that, European and American societies are presently the architects or manufacturers of the values and beliefs of the global competitve economy. Therefore a strict adherence to these beliefs and values by their work organizations would only make them remain competitive in the global economy, at least for the present. However, for organizations in African nations, there must be a persistent struggle towards downturning the current theoretical framework that assesses the relationship between organizational and national cultures, by breaking away from national beliefs and values, which stifle their competitiveness in the global economy. We envisage that the culturally transformed African organization of the future, would depart from collectivism to individualism, high power distance to low power distance, favouritism to meritocracy, fatalism to the use of scientific enquiries, and political decision-making to rational decision-making; in its modus operandi. In other words, there will be an adoption of the Western individualistic and rational management models by African organizations.

It is also believed that the proposed revolutionary cultural shift for the African work organization would be potent enough to trigger off changes in organizational artifacts; like marketing strategies, communication patterns between staff, boss-subordinate relationships, productivity of employees, the use of available space, and other visible aspects of organizational culture. Consequently, it will then become imperative for managers of the supposedly transformed African organization to carefully screen these organizational artifacts on a routine basis, to avoid cases of misalignment between them and the underlying core beliefs and values of their work organizations.

Finally, we do hope that in adopting organizational cultures that fit into the demands of the global competitive economy, indigenous work organizations in Africa would serve as the most instrumental agent of cultural change in the whole continent.

CONCLUSION

Apart from the family units and schools, which serve as prime initiators of individuals into their national cultures; the work organization has been perceived as another social institution, in which employed individuals can learn and imbibe certain beliefs and values that are akin to those of their national cultures. Scholars of organizational behaviour have opined that the culture of a work organization is nothing, but a mere derivative or microcosm of the wider national culture. However, with the current cultural revolution occasioned by globalization, it is believed that some indigenous work organizations (especially business enterprises), resident in Africa and other underdeveloped regions of the world, would be forced to disengage from traditional beliefs and values of these regions, which are presently inimical to their ability to compete favourably well in the global economy. This revolutionary shift would help them proactively evoke cultures that are completely different from those of the societies in which they are domestically domiciled; and this in turn would ultimately help in reconfiguring the beliefs and value system of individuals employed by such work organizations. Consequently, an incoming upset of the existing paradigm in the literature of organizational/national culture interface, which refutes the possibility of organizational culture transcending the boundaries of national culture becomes inevitable.

When this upset becomes a reality, a new theory of the organization that sees organizations as cultural change agents in societies would be born. Though many images, metaphors, paradigms and theories have been propounded in time past to understand the workings of organizations; for instance, Morgan (1998) had developed eight of such images that analyze how the organization functions; however this new organizational theory should be particularly invaluable in understanding the cultural implications of managing organizations in a period of globalization.

REFERENCES

Castells, M. (2001). 'Information Technology and Global Capitalism' in Hutton, W. and Giddens, A. (eds). *On The Edge, Living With Global Capitalism,* London: Vintage.

Cole, E. (1997). *Personal Management: Theory and Practice*, London: Letts Educational Publishers.

Deal, T. and Kennedy, A. (1982) *Corporate Cultures*, Reading, M.A: Addison-Wesley.

Etzioni, A. (1964). *Modern Organizations,* Englewood Cliffs: Prentice- Hall.

Giddens, A. (1990). *The Consequences of Modernity*, Stanford: Stanford University

Gomex, C. (2003). 'The Relationship Between Acculturation, Individualism/Collectivism, and Job Attribute Preferences for Hispanic MBAs' *Journal of Management Studies,* Vol 40, No 5:1090-1105.

Gray, J. (1999). *False Dawn. The Delusion of Global Capitalism,* London: Granta.

Hall, E. and Hall, R.(1990) *Hidden Differences: Doing Business with the Japanese,* New York: Doubleday Anchor Books.

Haralambos, M. and Heald, R. (1980). *Sociology: Themes and Perspectives,* New Delhi: Oxford University Press.

Hofstede, G. (1980). *Culture's Consequences: International Differences in Work Related Values,* Newbury Park CA: Sage.

Hofstede, G. (1994). 'Cultural Constraints In Management Theories', *International Review Of Strategic Management,* Vol.5: 27-48.

Hofstede, G. (2001). *Culture's consequences: Comparing Values, Behaviours, Institutions, and Organizations Across Nations,* London: Sage publications, second edition.

Iguisi, O.(1994). 'Appropriate Management in an African Culture' *Management in Nigeria,* January –February Issue:18.

Iyayi, F. (2003). 'Culture, Societal Contexts and Organizational Forms' *being an unpublished paper, in the Department of Business Administration,* University of Benin, Nigeria.

Jackson, T. (2004). *Management and Change in Africa,* London: Routledge.

Jaeger, A. and Kanungo, R.(1990). *Management in Developing Countries,* London: Routledge.

Kuada, J. (2007). "Cultural Impacts on Employee Goals and Behaviour in Africa" in Okpara, J. (ed). (2007). *Management and Economic Development in sub- Saharan Africa: Theoretical and Applied Perspectives,* pp28- 43, London: Adonis and Abbey Publishers Ltd.

Morgan, G. (1998). *Images of Organization,* London: Sage Publications.

Obisi, C. (1993) 'Human Resource Management', *Journal of the Institute of Personnel Management of Nigeria,* Vol 111, No 1:17-24.

Rafferty, J. (2001). 'The Synthesis of Economic Organization and the Management of Change: Intercultural Transferability and the Japanese Paradigm', *Journal of Management History,* Vol 39, Nos 5 and 6: 415-419.

Sabogal, F.; Marin, G.; Otero- Sabogal, R.; Mari, B.; and Perez, E. (1987).'Stable, Hispanic Familism and Acculturation: What Changes and What does'nt'?.' *Hispanic Journal of Behavioural Sciences,* Vol 9: 397-412.

Schein, E. (1985). *Organizational culture and Leadership,* San Francisco: Jossey- Bass.

Schein, E. (1988). *Organizational Culture and Leadership: A Dynamic View,* San Francisco: Jossey Bass Publishers.

Schmidt, R. (1996) 'Japanese Management Recession Style', *Business Horizons,* March-April, edition, 1996, pp16-24.

Thorton, E.(1993). 'Thailand: Japan vs the U.S.', *Fortune,* Vol. 128: 145-149.

Yeh, R.(1995) 'Downward Influence Styles In The Cultural Diversity Settings', *International Journal of Human Resource Management,* Vol. 6: 625-641.

5

Implication of Balanced Scorecard on Customer Perspective in Service Organisations with Special Reference to Audit Firms

DR.S.USHA NANDHINI *
T.M.VENKATESWARAN**

Quality Service is the motto of any service organization. Quality is a basic tool used for retaining any existing customer in the service industry. In today's context, retaining an existing customer is much more difficult than acquiring a new customer. For an audit firm, which is in knowledge industry, the retention of customer base is a vital phenomenon to ensure smooth running and growth in all the areas. The basic measures of any scorecard are derived from an organization's vision and corporate goals. Balanced Scorecard is a tool used for measurement of performance as well as implementation of corporate strategies. A Balanced Scorecard consists of four perspectives; viz. Financial Perspective, Customer Perspective, Internal Business Process Perspective, and Learning & Growth Perspective. The objective of this study is to analyze the strategies used for Customer Retention Measures by Audit Firms, out of the four perspectives of BSC. The core measurement group includes measures of Market Share, Customer Retention, Customer Acquisition, Customer Satisfaction, and Customer Profitability. Primary data were directly collected from randomly selected 50 audit firms in Tamil Nadu. Appropriate statistical tools used for analyzing the data. The outcome of the analysis is expected to establish a direct impact of Balanced Scorecard as a strategic tool for customer retention in audit firms.

Keywords: Quality, Balanced Scorecard, Customer Retention, and Audit Firm

INTRODUCTION

The ever changing needs of a customer in a service industry can be met out only by constant improvement in the performance of the partners and employees of the service provider according to the need of the situation. Many a times the customer may not be

* Senior Lecturer, Department of Management Studies National Institute of Technology, Tiruchirapalli, Tamil Nadu.
** Doctoral Research Scholar, Department of Management Studies National Institute of Technology, Tiruchirapalli, Tamil Nadu.

aware about the seriousness of the situation or his obligation towards law. Every service industry needs to take care of customers for two types of situations viz, regular maintenance and emergency situation. Regular maintenance is a kind of preventive measure. It may be for periodic service of a car or discharging statutory a obligation. For example, filing of tax returns is a regular duty for every citizen applicable according to the law of each country. Emergency situation may arise because of non-regular maintenance or from unforeseen circumstances also.

An audit firm or a consultancy group needs to strive its best to ensure that its clients do not fall into emergency situations due to non-compliance of periodic tax obligations. "Caveat Emptor" (let the buyer be beware) concept is not applicable for an audit firm. The client is not aware of the law and that is the reason they approach us. The multi-dimentional needs of customers vary from industry to industry. And in today's situation audit firms do not practise income-tax law alone. Clients want everything under one-roof pattern, so that an audit firm can take care of all the legal requirements or obligations of their organisation. So, every audit firm needs to follow a set of strategies to cater the needs of various clients. The strategies required are for maintaining the reputation of the firm among clients as well as other competitors, customer satisfaction, monetary growth of the firm, abreast knowledge of the partners and employees of the firm, employee retention, etc. A perfect scorecard is required to execute any strategy to ensure the achievement of the desired result.

A new approach to strategic management was developed in the early 1990's by Dr. Robert Kaplan (Harvard Business School) and David Norton. They named this system as 'balanced scorecard'. To overcome some of the weaknesses and vagueness of previous management approaches, the balanced scorecard approach provides a clear prescription as to what companies should measure in order to balance the financial as well as non-financial perspectives. Balanced Scorecard can be used to measure as well as manage any system. Measurement of the existing situation is a pre-condition to establish and manage any policy and strategy. In order to transform any strategy into action proper management tools are to be used. Balanced Scorecard(BSC) is one such tool which can be used for proper implementation of any goal or strategy. Major thrust in BSC is given for getting an instant feedback from the employees/customers of the organisation at the implementation stage itself, so as to ensure smooth translation of strategy into an action programme.

Balanced Scorecard as a management tool envisages four areas or perspectives. They are discussed below:

1. ***Employee Perspective:*** This perspective is also called "Learning and Growth Perspective". Retaining an experienced employee is the most difficult task in today's world at all the levels of an organisation. Mentors and tutors are required inside an organisation to motivate the employees to learn and grow. Proper orientation on the job is to be provided before anything is expected out of an employee. Employee's problems are to be addressed online so that their morale is well-maintained. Establishment of suitable communication mode among the employees as well as with their higher authorities will ease the employee relationship and also will help in higher employee

productivity as well as retention. This perspective of Balanced Scorecard can be used as a strategy to solve lot of issues from the employees and for the employees.

2. *Internal business process perspective:* Innovations in the existing process, reducing cost, saving time and energy, improved performance with the existing resources are areas of thrust under this perspective. This perspective measures the progress in various processes achieved in the day-to-day activities. The effects of learning curve are measured here. This perspective refers to effectively internal business activities. Metrics based on this perspective help managers to organize their everyday activities effectively to ensure quality improvement and better performance in the internal process.

3. *Customer Perspective:* Customer satisfaction and customer growth are the main areas under this perspective. Every organization can grow well with a list of reputed customers as well as their loyalty for the products and brand name. In the same way, unsatisfied customers will destine the products and the organization for eventuality. Customer focus and targeted group of customers will help the organization to stabilize as well as grow financially in the future. This perspective ensures a proper system of customer feedback and a planned course of action for improved activities in all the areas of the organization so as to avoid customer dissatisfaction in future.

4. *Financial Perspective:* Finance is the bottom line for every organisation. Quality, customer satisfaction, employee morale, etc. are all concentrated to achieve the financial stability and growth. It is not only the earnings but the earning capacity of every organisation in all areas is to be improved, to sustain competition in the market. Financial results and key indicators are to be reported to the right person at the right time in the organisation. Every activity in an organisation involves some financial implication. Understanding the right financial effect is very much important to decide whether to continue or discontinue a project or an activity. Net income, return of investment, return on capital employed are some of the key indicators under this perspective.

WHY BALANCED SCORECARD..?

Modern performance measurement systems in general and Balanced Scorecard in particular attempt to address a key management issue of converting strategy into action at all the levels of an organization. But having good strategies alone is not enough to be successful. Various stages and processes of implementation will decide the success of a strategy. Operational excellence is also needed to execute them. To achieve and maintain high levels of productivity, quality, and customer service, comprehensive operations or process measurement systems are needed to manage processes, departments and work units. These systems would include the measures that are strategically important, but those measures alone are insufficient for effectively managing operations.

Kaplan and Norton believed the best approach for implementing a new strategy for the development of a business unit is to use the Balanced Scorecard methodology in conjunction with its four perspectives. Balanced Scorecard performance systems have an established record of success, but it needs a disciplined way of building and implementing the system to ensure that business strategies get executed and that the necessary organization culture change gets implemented. One framework that is becoming an international "best practice" is the Balanced Scorecard Institute's Nine-Step Methodology for developing strategic themes, business strategies, strategic goals, strategy maps, performance measures, targets, and new initiatives. The result is a strategic management system that is comprehensive, logically sound, responsive and supported by the whole organization. Balanced Scorecard does not assure that all strategies will work, but the measures will provide timely feedback about how well they are working so timely corrective action can be taken regarding the strategies or their execution. Without these measures, a company's strategy and finances could get substantially off-track before any problem is even recognized.

This paper proceeds in the following way. The first section reviews the literature on evolution of Balanced Scorecard. The second section presents data sources, followed by the third section that describes methodology. Thereafter, the fourth section deals with analysis using statistical tools. The fifth section portrays the key findings.

OBJECTIVES OF THE STUDY

This paper is based on the following research questions:

1. To understand the implication of Balanced Scorecard in service industries.
2. To analyse the customer perspective of Balanced Scorecard in audit firms.
3. To provide suggestions to audit firms with respective Client Retention.

REVIEW OF LITERATURE

According to Kaplan and Norton (2001) the Balanced Scorecard is a performance measurement tool used to translate an organisation's long-term goals into financial and non-financial performance measures. Unlike formula-based measures, the Balanced Scorecard is based on subjective weightage to aggregate the various financial and non-financial measures in order to determine the overall performance of an organization. The Balanced Scorecard contained four categories of financial and non-financial performance measures that intended to measure both quantitative and qualitative aspects at all levels of the organization. The Balanced Scorecard measure is required in a performance measurement system to communicate in both directions, evaluate and reward the better performing managers. Kaplan and Norton (1997) also stated that the firms have to develop customized scorecards to fit the strategic goals within the context of overall organizational strategy. The cutomised scorecards pave a better platform for managers to identify and set targets for the employees. The ultimate aim of using any performance measure is to accomplish the strategic goals. The Institute of Management Accounting (IMA) in the US found that many managers feel that existing performance measurement system is highly inadequate in explaining efficiency of the organization. The main reason for the popularity of the Balanced Scorecard measure is not only limited to financial indicators and also focusing on non-financial parameters and the organization's objectives. Kaplan and Norton developed the Balanced Scorecard measure to overcome the in-built shortcomings in existing performance measurement system based on financial indicators.

Feltham and Xie (1994) acknowledged that, consistent with the Balanced Scorecard concept, theoretical work on performance evaluation using multiple signals in agency settings indicates that financial measures along may not provide the most efficient means to motivate the managers to act in the manner desired by the firm's owners. According to Kaplan and Norton (1996), the Balanced Scorecard provides financial as well as non-financial mechanism for linking long-term strategic objectives with annual action plan. The Balanced Scorecard aids the managers to develop a strategic plan around the organization's vision and mission. It also helps managers to communicate the long-term strategy throughout the organization. Further, it is a vital tool to integrate strategic and financial plans in order to allocate the resources and set priorities. Finally, it proved to be an excellent strategic feedback system and allowing the organization to rectify their wrongly chosen strategic objectives. Many surveys have been conducted to analyse the usefulness of Balanced Scorecard measure in the US, to indicate the relative strength of this measure in comparison with other traditional performance measures.

According to Ittner et al. (1997), US firms now use both financial and non-financial measures to determine employees' annual bonus contracts. They also found 36% of US firms adopted a comprehensive Balanced Scorecard measure for revising the Chief Executive's annual compensation. Banker et al. (2004) indicated that any bonus contract should include any performance measure that provides incremental information about desired managerial actions in order to efficiently motivate the managers. Knut H Mikalsen (2003) felt that through Balanced Scorecard the problems of the company were identified and the corporate vision and strategic objectives were clarified. Objectives and targets at corporate, departmental and technology level have been developed to increase overall performance.

Emilio Boulianne (2006) stated that the Balanced Scorecard has received a great deal of attention as a comprehensive model of performance that takes into account both financial and non-financial measures. With reference to content validity, internal consistency reliability and factorial validity, results show that BSC, with measures grouped into its four dimensions, is a valid performance model.

Gregory Weghmann (2007) indicated that Balanced Scorecard can be used for strategic control approach as well as a knowledge management tool that can be used as a relevant management instrument that can drive the firm's objectives. William B Taylor (2007) felt that managers who are involved in selecting strategic initiatives perceive those initiatives as having been more successful than managers who are not involved in the initiative-selection process (holding constant actual scorecard performance). The effects of motivated reasoning are mitigated by giving managers responsibility for the selection of scorecard measures; but this mitigation occurs only if the balanced scorecard is framed as a hypothesized causal chain of performance.

RESEARCH

Hypothesis

H1: There is no significant relationship between Customer Retention and Firm Performance

Data Collection

The data used in this paper is derived from a standard questionnaire developed by researchers. A questionnaire has been developed to represent the customer perspective of the Balanced Scorecard as suggested by Kaplan and Norton, who are the pioneers in the concept of Balanced Scorecard. The questionnaire contained 10 non-standard questions to represent the customer perspective of Balanced Scorecard. The survey has been conducted in fifty audit firms in Tamil Nadu during November 2007.

Research Methodology

This section deals with variables taken up for this study. There are three variables used to analyse the implication of Balanced Scorecard on quality in Service organizations with special reference to audit firms. Three variables being used such as independent, dependent variables. Customer perspective of Balanced Scorecard developed by Kaplan and Norton used as independent variables.

Dependent Variable

Customer Perspective

Independent Variables

S.No	Variables	Description
1	Competitiveness	How far your firm is competitive..?
2	Client Retention	The firm's ability to retain the clients
3	Threat	Removal of statutory requirements
4	Place of Service	Firm's premises/ Premises of the client
5	Reception	Warm reception at the firm's premises
6	Target Group	Ensuring 100% coverage of the targeted group
7	Customer Relationship	Firm efforts to maintain effective relationship with customers
8	Image of the firm	Customer's reputation about the firm
9	Reliability of Customers	How far the customer's make the work easy for the firm
10	Follow up	Follow up with the customers after the service is over

DATA ANALYSIS

This section deals with statistical tools applied in this paper. The Multiple Regressions analysis would also throw light on impact of the 10 factors into the overall customer perspective of the Balanced Scorecard.

Reliability Statistics

Cronbach's Alpha	Cronbach's Alpha Based on Standardized Items	No of Items
.837	.845	10

Cronbach's alpha is the most common form of internal consistency reliability coefficient. Alpha equals zero when the true score is not measured at all and there is only an error component. Alpha equals 1.0 when all items measure only the true score and there is no error component.

Interpretation: Cronbach's alpha can be interpreted as the percentage of variance the observed scale would explain in the hypothetical true scale composed of all possible items in the universe. Alternatively, it can be interpreted as the correlation of the observed scale with all possible other scales measuring the same thing and using the same number of items.

Multiple Regression

Model	R	R Square	Adjusted R Square	Std. Error of the Estimate
1	.898	.806	.756	.331

The model summary table shows R-Square for this model is .806. This means that 80.6 % of the variation in overall Customer Perspective (dependent variable) can be explained from the ten independent variables. The table also shows the adjusted R-square for the model as.756.

Any time another independent variable is added to a multiple regression model, the R-square will increase (even if only slightly). Consequently, it becomes difficult to determine which models do the best job of explaining variation in the same dependent variable. The adjusted R-Square does just what its name implies. It adjusts the R-square by the number of predictor variables in the model. This adjustment allows the easy comparison of the explanatory power of models with different numbers of predictor's variable. It also helps us decide how many variables to include in our regression model.

Coefficients

Model		Unstandardized Coefficients		Standardized Coefficients	t	Sig.
		B	Std. Error	Beta		
1	(Constant)	-.333	.320		-1.039	.305
	To what extent profession is subjected to competition	.038	.071	.054	.531	.598
	Client Retention Ratio	.201	.067	.221	3.007	.005 *
	Profession is under any threat from unforeseen situation	.090	.116	.094	.782	.439
	% of clients is to be serviced at their place	.191	.075	.269	2.544	.015 *
	Reception are you ensuring for your clients	.072	.051	.123	1.414	.165
	Customers are actual targeted group	.100	.067	.156	1.482	.146
	Own measures of customer relationship	.075	.085	.095	.880	.384
	Perception of image firm is enjoying with clients	.192	.077	.260	2.486	.017 *
	Customers are ready to share their actual financial position	.136	.064	.197	2.104	.042 *
	Follow up with customers after the service is over	.051	.134	.054	.381	.705

Dependent Variable: Overall Customer Perspective

To determine if one or more of the independent variables are significant predictors of overall performance of customer perspective, we examine the information provided in the coefficient table. In the above ten independent statements, only four statements are significant at 0.05%. The remaining six variables are not significant at 0.05% level. The statements are (1) Client Retention Ratio, (2) % of clients are to be serviced at their place, (3) Perception of image firm is enjoying with clients, (4) Customers are ready to share their actual financial position.

The standardized coefficient beta column reveals that client retention ratio has a beta coefficient of .221 which is significant (.05). Similarly, the percentage of clients to be serviced at their place, perception of image firm is enjoying with clients, customers are ready to share their actual financial position have beta coefficients .269, .260, .197, respectively (Sig. Level of .05). The above mentioned four statements are strong predictors of customer perspective.

In the above model, the percentage of clients is to be serviced at their place have maximum beta value 0.269, which contribute maximum towards customer perspective.

The Multiple Regression equation is formed as,

Customer Perspective = -0.333 + (0.269)A+(0.260)B+(0.221)C+(0.197)D + 0.331 (standard error of estimate)

A - Per cent of clients to be serviced at their work place

B - Image of the firm with clients

C - Client Retention Ratio

D - Customers sharing actual financial position

Inference: for every unit that 'Per cent of clients to be serviced at their work place' increases the customer perspective will increase by 0.269 times.

The relationship between Customer Perspective and 'Clients to be serviced at their Place' is positive and moderately strong compared with the remaining three factors.

FINDINGS AND DISCUSSION

Reliability test Cut-off criteria: Cronbach's alpha test result is 0.837. By convention, a lenient cut-off of. 60 is common in exploratory research; alpha should be at least .70 or higher to retain an item in an "adequate" scale; and many researchers require a cut-off of. 80 for a "good scale."

MULTIPLE REGRESSION EQUATION

In the above model, the percentage of clients is to be serviced at their place have maximum beta value 0.269, which contribute maximum towards customer perspective.

The Multiple Regression equation is formed as,

Customer Perspective = -0.333 + (0.269)A+(0.260)B+(0.221)C+(0.197)D + 0.331 (standard error of estimate)

A - Per cent of clients to be serviced at their work place

B - Image of the firm with clients

C - Client Retention Ratio

D - Customers sharing actual financial position

Inference: for every unit that percentage of clients to be serviced at their work place' increases the customer perspective will increase by 0.269 times. Similarly, for every unit that '% of 'image with customer' increases the customer perspective will increase by 0.260 times, for every unit that 'client retention ratio' increases the customer perspective will increase by 0.221 times, and for every unit that 'customers sharing their actual financial position' increases the customer perspective will increase by 0.197 times.

CONCLUSION

Balanced Scorecard has proved to be more effective management tool for service industries especially for audit firms, where customer's requirements are to be addressed without any error. In our study, we have analyzed the 10 variables of customer perspective of Balanced Scorecard and found that out of the 10 variables, 4 variables are more influential compared to other 6 variables. Our survey results also indicate that Quality Service is the major phenomenon for an audit firm which is in the service industry. In order to improve the customer perspective of an audit firm more thrust should be given on the major four factors viz, Client Retention Ratio, servicing clients at their work place, improving the image of the firm with clients, ensuring that actual financial position of the clients are obtained. Also, modern customers of an audit firm want to be serviced at their workplace where the auditor can see the actual happenings and provide proper consultation to the client, instead of the clients coming to the office premises of an audit firm in order to explain themselves. With the above suggestions we feel that an audit firm in the service industry can grow along with its clients.

REFERENCES

Kaplan, R.S. & Norton, D.P. (1992). The balanced scorecard—measures that drive performance. *Harvard Business Review*, 70 (1), 71-79.

Kaplan, R.S. & Norton, D.P. (1996). The balanced scorecard: translating strategy into action, Boston: *Harvard Business School Press.*

Lipe M.G. and S.E.Salterio (2000), The Balanced Scorecard; Judgmental effects of common and unique performance measures , *The Accounting Review,* 75 (3) 283-298.

Lerner J.S. and P.E. Tetlock, (1999), Accounting for the effects of Accountability, *Psychological Bulletin,* 125 (2); 255 – 275.

M.Meyer (2003), Subjectivity and the weighting of performance measures; evidence from a Balanced Scorecard, *The Accounting Review,* 78(3), 725-758.

'Developing the Balanced Scorecard', a report by Best Practices LLC, Chapel Hill, NC (1998).

Lawton, Robin, "Using Measures to Connect Strategy with Customers", *Journal for Quality and Participation* (2000).

"*Balanced Scorecard as a strategic management tool; The Case of Seagull AS*" by Knut H Mikalsen (2003).

"*Empirical analysis of reliability and validity of Balanced Scorecard*" by Emilio Boulianne (2006).

"*Balances scorecard as Knowledge Management Tool: a French experience*" by Gregory weghmann (2007).

"*The Balances Scorecard as a strategy-evaluation Tool : The effects of responsibility and casual chain focus*" by William B Taylor (2007).

W. & Thierry, H. (1996), 'Vroom's expectancy models and work-related criteria: a meta-analysis', *Journal of Applied Psychology*, 81, 575-586.

6

Can IT Act as a Catalyst in Development of SMEs?

NAVNEET U DUBEY*

Growth of small and medium enterprises (SME) is very important for any economy. It generates a large employment pool for skilled and semi-skilled workforce. In India, SMEs contribute a significant percentage to the entire GDP. Hence, a focused approach targeted towards developing this sector at a faster rate is of prime importance. This paper deals with the contributing factors for development of SME segment and how information technology can help this segment to grow. The paper aims at proposing a four dimensional model for development of SMEs leveraging on IT. Firstly, IT can act as a strong medium for integration of the scattered SMEs. Knowledge and the exchange of information are too very important elements of growth. Within SME clusters, which are scattered all over the country, all companies face similar type of issues in development and integration. Integration within clusters can lead to development of the whole cluster. Secondly, ERP is catching up with all the industries but it is costly for any small company to go for ERP independently. IT can help in developing an ERP system that will help all the companies improve their processes like demand forecasting, order processing, HRM and customer relationship jointly. This can also help all companies to improve on efficiency by implementing supply chain management, contributing towards vertical integration of the industry. The proposed system will have information sharing but with the concept of federalization incorporated in it. This system will be deployed as different versions for different companies so as to cater to company specific requirements. Thirdly, mobilizing capital is sometimes a bottleneck in developing SMEs. Here, if the companies can reach out to the financial institutions and venture capitalists (VC), not just in one location but throughout the country, it will prove to be instrumental in deciding the future of SMEs. The need is to develop a common platform, which brings on board various SMEs and financial institutions/ VCs and helps them in reaching out to each other. Finally, the training and development programs in equipping workers with the requisite expertise in computer skills and skills used in the industry is a key aspect in development. With

* Student, SP Jain Centre of Management, Dubai/Singapore.

concepts like development centres coming up, IT can plug itself here and promote such development centre for related industries. Again, taking into consideration the cost factor for SMEs, it will be feasible to go for a centre that is not solely owned by a company, but by companies of related business needs.

Key words: SMEs, IT, Industry integration, ERP in SME.

INTRODUCTION

The IT industry has grown at a commendable rate over last three years. The overall size of the domestic market, comprising hardware, software and services (IT-BPO), grew by an impressive 29 % in FY2006, and is forecasted to reach USD 15.9 billion in FY2007 (Indian IT Industry Factsheet Feb. 2007 by NASSCOM).

This market is led by MNCs currently, but as projected SMEs will be present in this market in the years to come as Indian firms will increase their IT adoption. But looking at the growth statistics, one can easily say that the major portion of growth in the IT sector is attributed to exports.

The IT services sector (in 2004), saw revenue of 10.4 billion out of which 7.3 billion came from exports.

In 2006, out of the total of 17.8 billion, 13.3 billion came from exports. Similarly, in the ITES-BPO sector, out of the total 7.2 billion, only 0.9 billion came from the domestic market in India. For Engineering Services and R&D, Software Products in 2006, out of a total revenue of 5.3 billion, exports amounted to 4 billion.

All the figures given above clearly suggest that the domestic market for IT is very small in India. Though the exports have been increasing, there is one point, on which views of the industry have converged. Cost arbitrage is not a strong enough justification for outsourcing to India, the IT service providers need to clearly articulate their value proposition and relate it to business benefits (Domestic Services-IT 2007, published by NASSCOM).

As pointed by the report released by NASSCOM, it clearly defines the role of IT companies in India "IT services vendors should be able to assist the CIOs to focus on generating business value from IT investments, by offering total solutions and end-to-end services."

This is very clear because arbitrage of any type will not continue for a long-term as the markets will settle down into an equilibrium state. So, even if Indian IT sector may continue to attract outsourcing in future (at a reduced rate) based on the value proposition; it will have to focus more on our domestic market.

So, what are the alternatives when it comes to investing in the domestic market? Though there are various alternatives available, this paper will look at SMEs segment as one of the potential investment options.

SME market will play an instrumental role in a holistic progress of the Indian economy. Growth of small and medium enterprises (SME) is very important for any economy. It generates a large employment pool for skilled and semi skilled workforce. In India, SMEs contribute a significant percentage to the entire GDP. Hence, a focused approach targeted towards developing this sector at a faster rate is of prime importance.

The paper will look at various options associated with business development of the SMEs. It will try to carve out a roadmap for the IT companies to take up strategic actions in the progress of the SME segment in India. Basically, the scattered location of SMEs will be targeted. Also, approaches that will unite/integrate the SMEs to leverage on IT thereby reducing overall cost and improving effectiveness will be considered.

HYPOTHESIS DEVELOPMENT

The future survival of the IT sector will have to depend on value proposition. Development of IT domestic market will help in overall development of the Indian economy as a whole. If value proposition is going to be the formula of success when there is no cost arbitrage advantage in the Indian products; the same has to apply to the Indian market as well. The cost of software development is going up in India, partly because of increasing salaries of developers and partly due to the falling dollar against the rupee. Though it means more revenue in the short run from foreign projects, the Indian IT sector still needs to look at the market that is completely available to it and is not being paid proper attention to.

There is a huge market in India waiting for IT to turn its fate. Because IT is not just a service anymore but a catalyst in the overall development of the country's economy; IT should focus on the Indian market. If you look at the breakup of how revenues were generated by the IT sector (NASSCOM report, 2006); you will find that most of it comes from BSFI and manufacturing. Two of the most growing fields are still very low i.e. retail, and communications and media. Though BSFI generates a major chunk of revenues, still there is a tremendous scope of capturing this market as well. Also, looking at the report of software sector in India released by NASSCOM, it is evident that most of the revenue comes from exports and the domestic market still remains to be tapped in a big way.

Based on above two points, it becomes very obvious why the IT sector should place more importance on the domestic market. The points discussed above pertain to the existing market and identified sector of demand. But there is one sector that is more or less neglected in terms of all IT related developments and has a huge potential not just in providing business in India but also contributing in a big way to the Indian Economy as a whole. This sector is the Small and Medium Enterprise (SME) segment.

In India, small and medium industries play a vital role in the growth of the economy. Small industries have a 40% share in industrial output, producing over 8,000 value-added products. They contribute nearly 35% in direct exports and 45% in the overall exports from the country.

However, SMEs in India, which constitute more than 80% of total number of industrial enterprises and form the backbone of industrial development, suffer from the problems of sub-optimal scale of operation and technological obsolescence. Indian SMEs are facing tough competition from their global counterparts due to liberalization, change in manufacturing strategies and turbulent and uncertain market scenario. Innovation has always been the hallmark of small and medium enterprises. SMEs that integrate innovation can reap significant benefits. Studies conducted by US Department of Commerce, revealed that since World War II, 50% of all innovations and 95% of radical innovations, have come from new and smaller firms.

The purpose of the paper is to chart out a way for capturing this particular segment in India and making it more competitive and achieving overall economic progress in the country.

H0: IT sector can act as a catalyst in the development of small and medium enterprises in India.

But what should be the process to go about it? What should be the policies to tap the domestic market in India? The paper aims to propose a four-dimensional model for development of the SMEs segment. It takes into consideration an integrated approach for development of not just one company but an entire cluster of SMEs located in an area or related business. It also proposes a model for bridging the gap between venture capitalist and project finance options and small companies, who are in need of cash. The paper also analyses how training and development for SMEs can be facilitated by IT.

LITERATURE REVIEW

In her paper on "Overcoming Barriers to Innovation for Indian SMEs", Stuti Kacker (Joint Secretary, Government of India, Ministry Small Scale Industries, 2004) points out how important it is to focus on the development of SMEs in the country. It provides employment to about 30 million people in the country. In a study (Jeona,, Hanb and Lee, 2006) on determining factors for adoption of e-business for SMEs in Korea, the most important factors that come out are (i) the CEOs knowledge of IT /e-business (ii) relative advantage and benefit from implementing e-business (iii) governmental support (iv) globalization strategy and (v) the factors specific to North Korea. The same framework can be applied to all the SMEs in any country. The basic way of operation in any SME is more or less same and the issues faced by them is also similar. In addition to all these factors, certain factors that are identified with the SMEs in India (Kacker, 2004) are managerial barriers, financial barriers and technological barriers. As analysed in her report, the driving element in an SME is innovation. Of all innovations, 50% have come from small companies and this is a figure convincing enough to suggest the innovation is the most important element in the survival of the SMEs.

Further in the paper, the barriers will be analysed in detail and approaches that can be adopted will be proposed. It is estimated that there are more than 400 modern small scale industries (SSE) and more than 2000 rural SSEs in India. These account for more than 60% total manufacturing exports of India. Some clusters of SSEs are so large that they produce about 80% total exports in that segment. This is just an example of the potential of the small scale industries in India. It also shows how the small scale industries are operating in India. They generally are located in clusters and the entire business of a cluster is independent. As the paper progresses, it will be seen how this can act to the advantage of the IT companies if they go for integrating these clusters. This cluster factor can also be helpful in easing the integration process of the entire industry.

Tanabe, Watanabe in their paper (Tanabe, Watanabe, 2005) discuss how SMEs are benefiting from the growth in the IT field. They point out that the advantage of SME lies in their organizational flexibility, efficiency and their subsequent qualified services management. This study conducted in Japan shows how SMEs have improved their competitiveness by maximizing the benefits of tie ups with the external institutes for assimilating external knowledge to improve on their services. They suggest that the dramatic improvement in business performance is not achieved because of technological innovation but through better services management by the small companies. The stress is given on R&D of the SMEs and the study also suggests that the distinguishing factor of a SME that has performed exceptionally and the one which has not, lies in their R&D initiatives. The expenditure on R&D by high performing companies is around 3% of total sales as against below 2% of poorly performing companies. They also point out that tie ups with external institutes has yielded very high results for the SMEs. As is evident that in an industrial age, where the economies of scale was a major factor for good performance of large companies, the scene is different in service oriented economies. India is no exception to this case, hence, SMEs have a greater advantage as against the larger companies in using efficient information integration, optimization of market mechanism and less organizational inertia. As the SME segment will grow the need for information technology will keep on increasing. With increase in capacity and expansion the need of automation also increases. "ICTs enabled solutions to networking and communication needs can explain SME growth in some instances whilst the act of growing itself heightens the need for strategic ICT use" (Paul Matthews, 2006)

Taking into consideration all the facts mentioned above, this paper will propose a four dimensional model for development of SMEs in India, while leveraging on the strength of IT. It is apt of SMEs to take up this path if they have to compete with large companies in a services oriented economy. As Matthews discusses in his paper "...governments continue to work to promote an environment for growth, the need for support in ICTs will likewise grow. This will present useful opportunities, not only for governments and industry bodies, but also for the ICT service sector." Therefore, the growth of SMEs is not just important for the SME segment alone but for the benefit of the entire country as a whole. Even the information and communication field will benefit a lot from this development.

DISCUSSION

The key point here is to boost the induced consumption of IT services, which is already on an upward trend due to various government policies. The need is to strengthen the domestic demand in the IT sector. As discussed in the earlier sections, this is required for overall development of the SMEs and IT sector as well. It is a conventional belief that IT is mere cosmetic change in the progress of an organization. But this perception needs to change, because IT has entered into the phase of ERP, CRM and business intelligence, which place a company strategically on a vantage point. Technological orientation will have a significant direct effect on product newness to customers (Salavou, 2005).Technological orientation will have a significant indirect effect through learning orientation on new product uniqueness (Salavou, 2005).

Slowly the trend world over suggests that companies view IT as a strategic device now. But, still the perception needs to change in India. Companies should realize that IT can define the entire future of a company. The domestic market for IT in India is not encouraging by any means. Looking at the projected figures for IT industry (Table 1), it can be inferred that the focus is changing from just "ITfication" to IT Consultancy. CRM, ERP and various other value added products are taking the centrestage even in India.

Table 1: Indicates the trend of Indian IT sector over next three years

Breakups	2004	2005	2006	2007	2008	2009	CAGR
IT Consulting	4748	5669	6775	7774	9109	10674	17.4
System Integration	34011	42979	51900	62065	72960	85399	20.2
Application Development	13997	17115	19852	22586	25113	27924	14.8
End-to-end outsourcing	6328	8221	10247	12343	14344	16850	21.6
Discrete outsourcing	16731	21055	25819	31401	36262	41509	19.9
Deploy and support	23631	28321	32907	37651	42510	48186	15.3
IT Education and training	4126	4879	5609	6534	7260	8067	14.3
Grand Total	103606	128239	153109	180354	297559	238607	18.2

Companies have to realize that in a service-oriented economy, it is IT that is going to provide them an edge. The concept of economies of scale that was a dominant factor in the industrial economy is no more applicable. Also, small companies have an advantage over the larger ones in terms of reaping the benefits of this. Due to their relatively less complex system and ability to embrace changes in the system, they stand to gain more from IT as compared to larger companies. Right from system integration to planning and estimation, every aspect of IT is yet another value addition for a business. Any industry that competes on cost has to realize the importance of this. IT can help businesses leverage a great deal by capitalizing on cost reduction due to optimization of their processes. CEO's knowledge of Information Technology, relative benefits from implementing e-business, governmental support and globalization strategy are major factors for progress of SMEs in Korea (Jeon, Han and Lee, 2006).

Unfortunately, IT penetration in the Indian market has not been very high. One of the major restrictions is imposed by growth in other industries and the scales at which they operate.

As far as the developed sectors are concerned IT has already reached them and will capitalize on them in future as well. But, IT needs to go beyond that and look at what it has not captured yet.

SME Market in India

As was discussed in the introduction part regarding the SME market in India and its potential in holistic progress in the Indian economy; it becomes obvious point to pay due attention to development of this sector in India.

There are some basic questions that will prove as a guiding factor for this study. First, what is it that should be targeted to capture in SME market i.e. what is the value proposition of IT sector to the SME segment?

Industrial integration in terms of knowledge sharing or product exchange is a very important criterion for development of the industry. It is difficult for an SME to survive in a market without integration with the industry. It does not have enough resources, capital or infrastructure to develop a market on its own. So, one aspect that needs to be addressed by IT is: integration of SME sector in India.

Innovation has always been the motive force of small and medium enterprises (Kacker, 2004). SMEs that integrate innovation can reap significant benefits. Studies conducted by US Department of Commerce, revealed that since World War II, 50% of all innovations and 95% of radical innovations, have come from new and smaller firms (Pavitt K., 1990).

So, one of the most important criterions for growth and sustainability of the SME sector is innovation. But, due to years of protective trade practices, the risk taking ability has been killed in this industry (Kacker, 2004). Any kind of innovation in this sector is considered to be risky. The risk that this industry has to take is in terms of two major categories in which IT can be a catalyst:

a) Process innovation

b) Organizational innovation

Process innovation is defined as new ways of producing and delivering services that lead to cost effectiveness. On the other hand, organizational innovation deals with development of new business process to provide competitive advantage.

As the IT industry has already come of age and started looking at value added features, it can act as a catalyst in the growth of SMEs in a big way.

Risk Sharing and Innovation

Although Indian SMEs realize the importance of technological innovation, most of the Indian SMEs still believe in importing technology, rather than developing them in-house or through/ in association with national Research and Development (R&D) centres. Indian SMEs, over the years, have largely ignored their R&D and have mostly not embarked on new product development and technological upgradation. This is despite the fact, that India has the third largest pool of technologically trained manpower (Kacker, 2004).

SMEs are strictly risk averse and their complacence needs to be broken now. The IT industry in India should take a lead ahead and share their risk and mutually try to develop products targeted at process and organizational changes. This provides two advantages:

- Capturing Indian SME market and leading them to a faster growth path through innovation and,
- This opportunity will not only help IT industry in this market, but will also provide them with an insight into global SME market.

The focused approach will be able to develop business models that would be innovative and could cater to markets in the other countries as well. This way the companies can also capitalize on a new product selling and the underlying SME could earn from patent revenues. There are products designed by SAP especially for the SMEs, which have enabled 25,000 small and medium customers grow on the world stage. SAP might be a costly capital expenditure for small companies in India, but Indian software companies can definitely cater to this segment by providing cheaper and customized products. Developing a business model from SMEs, which can be implemented in other countries, is one aspect on which IT companies can capitalize. This has been a rather unexplored area.

IT, even today works to deliver a customized/ready product to any industry. As is the case for business solutions in any industry, IT companies build upon their knowledge base and keep improving on their product and make a valuable product that can be offered to big players. This case can also be implemented in the case of SMEs. SME segment is a major contributor not just in India but in most of the countries. Many of these markets might be unexplored and hence can be tapped to advantage.

As the cycle continues, India will keep losing its attractiveness as a development centre or outsourcing centre for software development. Along with that, the markets that IT companies cater to now, will also keep shifting from one country to another.

It is not the case that IT industry has matured in India; it also needs to keep growing and innovating and exploring new prospective markets. Dealing with SMEs is going to provide a lot of value addition to this sector.

There are various factors that are plaguing the industry. The coming of many multinational companies in India has forced the competition to a very high degree. These multinational companies are very old companies with a highly mature business models. Added to this, they have long years of experience. When these companies pitch against Indian IT companies, they are bound to get an upper hand. Since the development cost in India was very low many companies came to India and now the scene is that it has created a fierce competition in the country. Further factor is the rising development cost for IT companies.

It is becoming increasingly evident that India does not have much of a cost advantage because the developers are reaching a level that is at par with the developers in the other countries. So, if the companies have to go for quality, the costs are bound to shoot up. The third factor that is aggravating the condition will complete a vicious cycle of cost arbitrage.

IT was the sector that enabled India to stand in a strong position on the global stage. The country became the centrestage for IT development projects. Most of the projects that these companies had were from the United States. Hence, as the current scene is, the dollar is falling drastically against the Indian rupee. This has led to a dramatic reduction in the revenues of most Indian software companies. Due to this, companies are hiking their billing rates. Also, some companies are thinking of going for billing in terms of Indian currency. All these factors have contributed in eliminating, though not completely yet, the cost arbitrage factor. But, the future seems difficult for the IT sector, if it does not take appropriate measures to diversify this risk.

Hence, the focus of these IT companies should turn towards developing SMEs in the country. It is evident that IT is not a 'one time' cost but it is more of a recurring cost for any country. Development of small companies, will secure a bright future for the IT companies as well.

Taking the viewpoint form the SMEs side, as was discussed before that in case of industries in Japan, the R&D adoption played a major role in their performance. Moreover, the companies that went for R&D as tie ups, got to benefit more than the ones which did not do it. IT can play a major role in helping small companies to partner with R&D centres in the country in developing more innovative means of improving production. The software product market is small in the country and IT companies can develop products that will help the R&D organizations to better use their resources.

Role of Knowledge Management (KM) in an R&D organization

KM is one of the fastest developing fields of IT related services. In any R&D organization, the wealth is what lies in the knowledge of the company. Be it the tacit knowledge or the explicit knowledge in the organization, IT can act in a big way in developing platforms, which can make the best use of this resource to optimize productivity. There are many organizations in the country which are not integrated in terms of knowledge management. This leads to lot of rework and delayed outputs. Interaction amongst the people in the organization to share information is one of the key features of KM. IT can act as an instrumental medium in helping these organizations leverage on knowledge that they have. So, though indirectly, IT can help SMEs achieve in a big way while exploiting the R&D activities and innovation. There are various ways in which the IT can come together and help SMEs in developing portals, which can help in capturing and presenting their hard earned knowledge capital to other employees. The SME segment does not have enough of money to keep spending on training and development of employees and with such portals taking the centrestage, the employees will stand to benefit in a big way. The low skill workers also are slightly away from internet, with such an initiative they can be brought close to the world network. They will also become available to a vast amount of resources spread all over the world.

Partnering in Growth and Innovation

The SMEs and the IT industry should come together and develop processes that are globally competitive. Though SMEs will not take risk all alone, but coupled with the IT industry they can take initiative to go to the frontiers of innovation. Taking an example in this case: Consider a simple cloth manufacturing industry in the district of Tiruppur. Some figures that will stress on this fact are present below:

- Tiruppur is one of the largest foreign exchange earning towns in India. Last year, the export turnover from the town was more than Rs 5,000 crore (Rs 50 billion). There are some 7,000 garment units in the town that provide employment opportunity to close to one million people.
- The first spot of any international buyer for Indian garments is Tiruppur. Buyers from 35 countries frequently visit Tiruppur. Tiruppur can deliver customized samples in less than 12 hours; half a million pieces in a matter of days.
- 56% of Indias' total knitwear exports come from Tiruppur. The Export-Import Policy of 2002-2007 makes laudable tribute to Tiruppur for its contribution to the export efforts and calls it a 'Town of Export Excellence.

It is a huge industry and is a major supplier of cloth in the country and also a major exporter. This provided tremendous opportunity for IT companies in terms of business integration and other business solutions. There are a large number of these industries, which thrive only on their traditional channels. IT can play a very important role in these industries because they are very old companies and might need process changes to compete with the global markets. Also, these companies do not have any presence on the web and hence are restricted to a large extent in their reach. Though, they might provide cloth at a very cheap cost and might end up capturing a bigger market, they still dwell at traditional levels. The IT industry needs to capture this segment and nurture the growth potential of new business processes.

Integrating Different SME Clusters

It is estimated that there are 400 modern SSEs and 2000 rural and artisan based clusters exist in India. These contribute to 60% of India's manufacturing exports. Some of the clusters are so big that they produce 70 to 80% of the total volume of that particular product produced in India. For example, Panipat produces 75 % of the total woolen blankets produced in the country; Tiruppur produces 80% of the country's cotton hosiery (Kacker, 2004).

The concept of cluster development offers new insights into the potential role of SMEs, in enhancing their access to new technology. Characteristics of a successful cluster are inter-firm cooperation and cooperation coupled with competition.

There are various factors that are distinct to these clusters and help the clusters to be successful. First of all, the inter-firm co- operation is one of the most important elements. These companies, though competing with each other, are very cooperative when it comes to a common goal. If these companies are integrated on one platform, it will be very advantageous for them. The communication will ease out to a great extent and will help in information exchange between all the companies. Some other factors that are common to these clusters are the importance of local value systems, flexibility and innovative capacity, geographic proximity, sectoral specialization, a local pool of skilled labour and the presence of a large number of firms. It also includes willingness to work together to resolve potential clashes of interest, widespread entrepreneurial spirit and ability, promotion of a social compromise.

IT industry can integrate these scattered clusters of industries. This will not just bring together the competitiveness of this sector but will also give them the necessary strength to stand against the technological changes in the global market. And as these industries grow, the growth potential of the IT industry in this segment will improve. The integration can be in terms of developing a platform where all these companies can share their resources, interact and have basic facilities like mails, document archives, news related to the industry. It can also act as a source of posting specific needs of some company. There are cases when one company is in need of some resources, which is available to the others but is not in use. These companies can come together and help each other out in such situations. There are various such reasons where the integration of these companies on one platform can change the way they function.

Developing Innovative Business Models

IT consultancy is the future formula for this industry. A new association with SMEs will provide a much needed input for developing innovative business models. SME sector is a huge segment in not just India but world over and by developing innovative models it can capture those markets as well.

The basic assumption of growth of IT industry as seen in the earlier sections is that there has to be development in other sectors as well. It is the induced consumption where the potential of IT lies. This becomes a cyclic process then; IT helps in growing the developing businesses at a faster pace and then again capitalizes on their growth and addresses their future expansion plans.

At any stage, IT has to take a lead and provide other sectors with cutting edge technology in terms of business models and organizational models. Here, views from both the IT industry and the SMEs are considered. Consultancy is one business which needs to be close to the SMEs. With SMEs facing so many issues and learning more from their mistakes, it will be to the collective advantage of all such companies to go for consultancy. Times are changing today and the conventional business models would not prove to be very useful. Hence, IT can plug itself here and try to bring these small companies at par with their contemporaries on the world stage. Developing innovative business models and then applying them to these small companies could prove to be very beneficial.

Integration with Financial and Infrastructure Institutions

The SME segment in India is also one of the major consumers of finance and infrastructure. For any future growth this is inevitable. The government has started some initiatives in this respect to extend support to SMEs in terms of IT related developments. The Ministry of Small Scale Industries, Government of India has been promoting the use of IT in SMEs, as a part of the overall effort towards enhancing SME competitiveness, in the context of globalization. The Small Enterprises Network (SENET) project was launched for ensuring electronic delivery of services, to SMEs through dynamic web based applications and e-enabling SMEs. It primarily does this through a knowledge portal for SMEs, which is also the front end for delivery of services. The Ministry of SSI has also recognized various IT enabled services such as medical transcription, call centres, back-office processing, as well as software development by SMEs in the services sector. This recognition enables such SMEs easier access to land, infrastructure and credit.

But, this initiative has not caught the fancy of IT industry as such and hence is not a success in India. On one hand, this allows IT in enabling the SMEs to compete globally in the foreign markets. On the other hand, with this kind of integrated development, it can solve the issues of land, infrastructure and credit lending for SMEs. This could be a market where financial institutions will be interest in coming to. Credit or project finance is one of the major concerns of many small and medium enterprises in India. There are various reasons for this and one of them is an improper integration between small industries and the financial institutions. IT can help in bridging the gap between the two. There are so many venture capitalists in the country, who are looking for attractive avenues to invest in. Similarly, there are many SMEs, who are scouting for funds to grow in the future.

Many a times it so happens that the companies which are located in one area are financed by some financial institution in that area. And if the company is already leveraged, even if it can give high future cash flows for new projects, the banks might not provide them the needed funds. Though the banks perceive it as high risk investment, the question here is whether or not the risk can be taken against the profits that can be achieved. There are many VCs in the country or even abroad, who would be willing to finance such projects. IT can bring together these two and help the SMEs to grow in a big way. Common platforms can be formed, where both parties can come together and interact. Using the web for purpose of project finance can act as a great advantage for the SMEs.

One more advantage here is that in the process of providing this development feature for the SMEs, IT industry can also capitalize on its markets of banking and finance.

The BFSI sector in India is growing at a commendable pace and growth figures for BFSI industry validate this phenomenon. But, IT is currently providing solutions in the traditional fields. Through this new association with the SMEs, various new ways of doing business can be unleashed. There is a huge potential for developing new ways and models of financing and infrastructure development.

Microfinance is one of the fields, which is drawing the attention of various financial institutions in a big way. Therefore, IT can again take a lead here and help them chart out new business models to capture this market and develop infrastructure that will make it more attractive. The major concern in this category is cost effectiveness, as microfinance runs on the principle of low cost. IT can help in developing systems that can be utilized to reach a wider segment of market with a very low cost involved. There exists also the potential of developing various cost effective products, for making this an attractive proposition. Because of the low cost involved, it is very difficult for any institution to have offices, or even ATM-type stations in these areas. The need is to develop such business models and technologically viable products that will enable the institutions to enter these markets with confidence.

Supporting SMEs in growth

SMEs find it difficult to match the wage rate, job security and career development opportunities, available in larger organizations and therefore are not in a position to hire skilled and competent manpower. Often, as a result, a bottleneck develops in the SME organization, which may result in just one or two people controlling the organization, whether at the decision making level or at the operational level.

Even in moderately large sized firms employing several hundred workers, these bottleneck points seem to exist. The decision- makers at the bottleneck points are obviously busy people. They must handle many day-to-day problems that demand immediate attention, e.g., payroll, inventory, finances, personnel, suppliers, and customer demands. These problems must be solved quickly, or the company will be unable to function. Clearly, there is little chance for them to think about making major changes or risk taking, which is essentially required for innovation process.

Therefore, there is a great potential for IT to pitch in here in terms of providing ways of improving efficiency for the SME sector.

Concept of development centres: The first area that requires attention is the individual's growth in the SME sector. Due to their restrictions they are not able to promote career opportunities to a great extent. IT can act as a great facilitator here, linking the industry that excels in required skills and the one that needs them. There can be 'development centres', which provide various means of development individual skills of a person. This can be technical expertise as well as managerial training. These development centres might be constructed on a network basis, where many companies can come together and fund this centre. This will help them leverage the benefits of a greater good after investing little amounts of their profit every year. IT can take the entire infrastructure development, planning, designing, maintenance, support and if necessary linkage with source industry and the destination. IT can tap the possibility of business consulting here, when the source training institutes want to get into such markets. Small and medium enterprises do not have excess cash on hand to invest in development of an employee or help people in the company develop some skills. Companies of related business will more or less have the same kinds of demand in terms of skills and expertise. Even the managerial issues faced by most of the companies located in one cluster or in one particular business domain will be same. Since, these SMEs individually cannot afford to have training centres, an approach can be taken of an integrated training centres.

Companies can come together and pool in money to provide facilities in the development centres that will be required for the development of a particular skill required in that industry. IT can help in developing web portals, which will help in knowledge management of these companies as well. Generally, these small companies are run by heroes in the projects. This is to say that there are certain people in the company who are experts in their fields and they drive the show in the company. Once they retire or leave the company, the company begins to collapse. IT can help in forming web portals, which will be used for knowledge transfer in the organization. This approach will have a federal way of distribution. All the companies will have their identity, and employees in one company will be able to view the contents that will be applicable to that company alone. This will also help in keeping the 'cooperation blended with competition' formula alive in the clusters, which is one of the characteristics for overall development of any cluster.

Operational Efficiency: The second part is operational efficiency of the SMEs. How can this be improved due to interaction with the IT sector? IT can play a big role in business consulting here. As of today, business consulting is a fancy word that applies to large businesses. It helps in their expansions, integrations and future developments. Why can't the same logic apply to the SME sector? This is the sector that needs most of such guidance. IT can leverage on this potential opportunity. The SME segment has never seemed so attractive to the entire software development class.

But the point is if everyone targets the same set of customers, who are already better off, losing-out on some is inevitable. First, it will neglect the development of the much-needed SME sector in the country, which can really benefit from such an initiative. Second, it will end up saturating the target segment because; this segment has got its own limitations, and will not be able to generate revenues regularly for a longer time in future. The attitude has to be of one looking at alternatives and if there are no such alternatives, IT has to help identify the potentials and develop them into such prospective businesses.

Enterprise Systems

Today the enterprise systems have proved to be instrumental in the growth of any industry. These systems have also entered the small and medium enterprises in a big way. SAP and many other companies also have many products that cater specially to the small and medium enterprises. Microsoft has products which cater to the small enterprises grow while leveraging on the IT expertise and business consultancy. Indian SMEs do not have that kind of money that is required for adoption of such business suites.

While there is definitely a cost advantage of developing software products in India, this factor can be used to the advantage of the SMEs. The IT companies can tailor their ERP products to the need to small and medium enterprises. These products might be costly, but there is a place for a new concept here. Typically, any ERP system tries to break the silos of functional departments in any organization and integrates into one process. The same concept can be used in developing the enterprise systems for the small and medium size companies. Also, the old and outdated business model of functional departments can be renewed. These two can be merged and a platform can be developed, that can help more than one company to come together on one platform and adopt this ERP software.

The proposal here is to apply enterprise system design in the reverse way. The enterprise systems break the silos and create an integration of processes. Here, the silos are to be created! This is to say that the systems are provided with such security features that they do not interact with each other. This restriction can be imposed on operational part or management part of the business. One aspect that can and should be made common is the supply part of the business. In small companies

(especially in clusters), the suppliers are more or less same and there is hardly any product difference between the materials they offer. These suppliers can be brought together on one platform and can be integrated with the companies. The entire process of purchase, order management and delivery management systems can be integrated on this platform. The companies can also have a federal approach in having a forecasting systems in place. This will help them in better planning their resources. Based on the models that they have, new systems can be developed that can help them in the forecasting. Even if they go for a complete vendor product, they can still weak their forecasting procedures to fit in the enterprise models. After all, the enterprise system reflects the collective wisdom of the entire industry.

Central to all this is 'the best practices of the industry', which forms the core of any enterprise system. Many small companies keep going in one direction for a long time and making the same kinds of mistakes. With best practices, they will be able to charter out new ways of doing business, which are advantageous for their company.

INTEGRATED APPROACH

After going through the discussion in the previous section, a model is proposed for the development of SMEs in the country leveraging on the IT sector.

The approach is broken down into four dimensions viz.

- Industry integration
- Training and development
- Project finance options
- Integrated Enterprise systems

The development of the SMEs will be explained with a four dimensional model. First of all, the industry needs to be integrated. The SMEs are scattered all over the country and it needs to be consolidated for overall development of the clusters. The resources in one cluster are more or less of the same type. The markets that they cater to are also the same and related issues they face reflect in the same way in the entire cluster.

With integrated industry, many problems can be sorted out. Secondly, the SMEs cannot have training and development facilities on individual basis. It involves a huge cost and is difficult for companies to support with the kind of revenues they make.

The model proposes to adopt the concept of development centres where many companies in related business can install training facilities or skill development facilities. This will not only help companies in developing their skills but will also help in retaining employees by providing a path for their development.

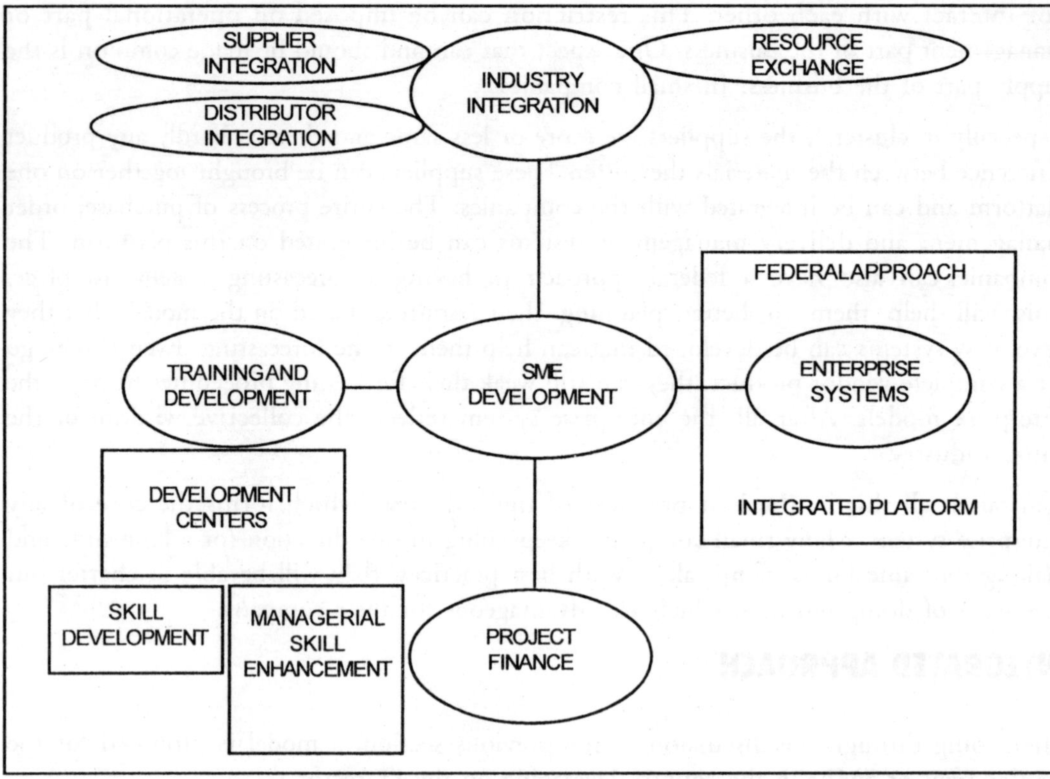

Thirdly, SMEs face a big challenge of project finance for their growth. There are many venture capitalists in the country, who are looking for good projects in the country. By bringing these two communities on one platform, the needs of one can be mapped on to the other. The biggest issue with the funding of projects can be eliminated using this medium. Finally, the adoption of ERP systems can lead to a dramatic improvements in the functioning of the companies. But, this option is too costly for the companies. The proposed model looks at a platform that can allow more number of companies to jointly develop an ERP system. This can be developed with a federal approach and certain functions that are unique to a company can be restricted from other companies. The details of all these aspects are discussed in the previous sections. Using this four dimensional model, SMEs can aim at a higher rate of growth in the future. This will also help IT sector to grow in the domestic market.

CONCLUSION

The SMEs segment contributes in a big way in the total GDP of the country and its development is very essential for the development of the economy. The IT sector will also avail of the much needed option of creating a high growth domestic market in the country if the SME segment grows. Leveraging on the IT sector the SME segment can develop based on the four dimensional model proposed in the paper. The growth will focus on aspects of industry integration, training and development, project finance and implementation of enterprise system. Taking into consideration all the aspects of the model proposed, the SME segment can look at a sector that is integrated not just in the way they do business but also in terms of entire supply chain that they have. IT can help these small companies integrate their entire supply chain and manage their resources in a better way. The future of any industry lies in optimization of the way it does business and IT can certainly help them improve on that dramatically.

REFERENCES

Paul Matthews, "*ICT Assimilation and SME Expansion*", Overseas Development Institute, London (2006).

Helen Salavou "*Do customer and technology orientation influence product innovativeness in SMEs? Some new evidence from Greece*", Athens University of Economics & Business(2004).

Bang Nam Jeon, Kyeong Seok Han and Myung Jin Lee ,"*Determining factors for the adoption of e- business: the case of SMEs in Korea*", (2006).

Koji Tanabe and Chihiro Watannabe,"*Sources of small and medium enterprises: excellent business performance in a service oriented economy*" (2004).

Stuti Kacker ,"*Overcoming Barriers to Innovation for Indian SMEs*", IAS, Joint Secretary, Government of India, Ministry of Small Scale Industries,(2004).

Pavitt K.,"What we know about strategic management of technology", *California Management Review* (1990).

"*Indian IT Industry Factsheet*", NASSCOM, (2007).

"*Domestic Services-IT*", NASSCOM, (2007).

"*Textile industry factsheet*", Edelweiss (India equity research, (2007).

7

Study of Adverse Events-effective in Adoption of Agricultural Products Insurance: A Case Study of Kurdistan, Iran, Dec. 2007

ER.ABDOLALI BAHRAMI*
BEHROOZ SHAHMORADI**

Crop insurance is an effective method that is being practiced by farmers in all economic sectors at all seasons in an effort to minimize risk. Crop insurance is being considered as a proper mechanism for protecting financial resources of producers in the agriculture sector. The objective of this study is to study climatic changes which are effective in the application of crop insurance in Kurdistan - Iran.

The required data were obtained through 200 questionnaires that were completed by sample insured farmers in the year 2005-2006 from Kurdistan province in Iran.

The result of the study showed that the average for application of crop insurance in the group with low degree of adoption was 30% of their entire under cultivation land while the figure was 47% and 67%, for the group with the medium and high degree of adoption respectively.

The regression analysis showed that forecasting the possibility of climatic changes such as cold weather, frost, floods and drought display in total 56.7% of the variance for the application of agricultural products insurance.

Keywords: Adoption, Risk, Adverse Events, Agricultural Products Insurance

INTRODUCTION

Nowadays, the place of agricultural section as compared to other economic sections, with a view of assuring, the required food of growing population in the world has an important

* Ph.D Scholar, DOS in Science, University of Putra, Malaysia.
** Faculty Member of Kurdistan University, Iran, and Ph.D Scholar, DOS in Economic University of Mysore, India.

role. The general view is that in agriculture, there is a lack of certainty (Ezat. A, & Najafi, 2002).

One of the main problems that make it difficult to achieve greater agricultural development and achieve rural targets is the presence of variables of risk that are natural. In agriculture, the degree of dependence on nature is too high, which causes such risk variables to gain a firm foothold and uncertainty in the production of crops.

Undoubtedly, one of the most important barriers in attracting private investment in agriculture are damaging natural events and incurable hazards that always menance the agricultural products in a country. Existence of many natural risks in a country lead to farmers continuously facing many problems. It also will discourage them from investing in this sector in the coming years. Also, decreasing agricultural investment leads to decrease in agricultural output and therefore, society faces food insecurity (Matlabi. 2001).

The most obvious aspect of rural life is uncertainty. They don't have security because from one side, natural factors mostly threaten them with reduction in the quantity of their crops and from another side they are faced with fluctuation of prices in market (Kerchegali 2001).

Product too, in agriculture and livestock, has many basic differences. Its activities are faced with large scale of natural and unnatural risks. Thus work and activities in this section are connected to a high degree of risk. (Anderson.J.R,&J.L.Dillon, 1992).

From the point of view of E.J. Baker (1990), agricultural product insurance is a measure that encounters problems at the stage of entry in rural communities. FAO researchers reveal that nearly 70% of hazards and risks in investment emanate from cultivation. Avoidance of repayment is common. The lower rate of return on investment can also be traced to the occurrence of natural events (Nori S. 1999).

According to Krabasi A., in order to attract corporations to agriculture, agricultural beneficiaries have to be drawn to the acceptance of agricultural insurance. In this respect, the efficient factors in sustaining demand should be identified, while also arriving at an estimation of the demand function (Krabari A., 1999).

BACKGROUND

Ghadirian and Abiar have derived from in their study on efficient factors on tendency for Soya's insurance from Golestan province in Iran that factors like age of beneficiaries, farm scale, diversity of product, level of insurance other crops, and previous records of risk in Soya's farms have a negative influence on propensity and elasticity of farmers related to Soya insurance. While the amount of credits, which have been received from farmers, had a positive effect on propensity of farmers to purchase of insurance (Ghadirian and Abiar 1995).

Efficient factors on demand for agricultural product insurance in FARS province (IRAN), show that land proprietorship, amount of wheat produce in the previous year, age and literacy, farmer's capital, risk taker, previous record for facing risk, have a positive relationship with demand for wheat insurance. But other factors like land value, land rotation and number of truck land have a negative relationship with the demand for wheat insurance (Torkamani and Nikoee, 1991).

According to Ghorbani and act, in their research work around the efficient factors on adoption of agricultural crops insurance, increasing the level of insurance and examination of efficient factors for decision-makers will have an important role for knowing the strengths or weaknesses and potentials of insurance adoption processing (Ghorbani and act 2000).

Bouquet and Smith, in their studies on wheat producers of the American state of Montana connected to agricultural insurance have that shown factors like previous recording facing risk, amount of debt to credit institutions and banks, variations of output product quantity, literacy of farmers and rate of insurance, are important for acceptance of wheat insurance (Boquet, A & V. Smith, 1996).

Baker in his study, has examined the demand for rainful insurance in half dry areas. The results of obtained from this project show that the knowledge of farmers related to advantages and significance of rainful insurance, have had a positive impact on their propensity for acceptance of insurance (Baker.E.J, 1990).

According to Ridant, high degree of adoption of agricultural products insurance adoption in central America depends on the existence of probable hazards in agriculture, insurance expenditures which farmers should pay, feeling of satisfaction from getting insurance and other factors like; psychological and social factors. (Tiraee.y.n, 2002).

These high expenditures not only reduce the profitability of agricultural activities, but also pose problems in the matter of achievement of development goals in this sector. The reduction of risk in agricultural activities and increase in the coefficient of investment security in this sector depend upon the level of our knowledge of the ideas of risk management, practical methods and profitability that risk management advocates and bring forth, in order to face and deal with risk inherent in situations.

This study focused on the examination and identification of the most important factors of risk in the case of accepting agricultural products insurance in the Kordistan (Iran) province. With this assumption, the prediction of the possibility of risks or natural hazards occurring hinges on the rate of acceptance of insurance of agricultural products.

In this paper, agricultural products insurance is considered as one of the efficient techniques which can reduces the coefficient of agricultural activities risk and increase investment security in this section.

METHODOLOGY

The present research is applied in the case of goals and their attainment, because it looks to the development of applied knowledge in special cases population of insurance and its development. Also, in the case of data collection method, it contains descriptive researches.

Research method

The research method applied in this study is cross-sectional, using a lot of surveys. Also, on the basis of research goal, has used correlation method for analyzing relationship between variables and estimated and expressed variation of dependent variables by using independent variables. Then the correlation technique applied for analyzing the relationship between independent and dependent variables, and also by using multiple regressions for estimated and expressed variation of dependent variables with including dependent variables.

Farmers forecast from occurring risk, is one of the main factors that can be useful in the field of applying suitable methods, for meeting risk. The pertinent question here is what kind of risk or natural events can influence on adoption of insurance by farmers? In other words, what kind of risk (flood, harsh winter, etc.), has more effect on adoption of insurance?

Therefore, in order to find answers to these questions, an examination of the above variables is very important. In order to ascertain the deeply-herd beliefs and attitudes of farmers and to predict each one of the above risks, the five-point Likert Scale (questionnaire) is used as follows:

1. very high
2. high
3. medium
4. low
5. too low

According to this questionnaire, rank 1 is for those people who can predict the risk properly and 5 for those people who cannot predict the risk.

Research Findings

Descriptive section: Collected data show that a total of 32% of the respondents couldn't predict the occurring cold weather, 19% were in two minds and 49% could predict it, and considered it as a serious threat to their products.

Near the 49% of respondents, didn't take flood as a serious risk for their product and had weak predicated for probability of occurring it. 20.5% of them were in two minds, and 30.5% of them could predict the occurring flood. Also, collection of data shows that near the 45% of respondents, consider the probability of occurring frost, 27% were uncertain and 27% could not predict it. In the case of drought display, 18% could not predict it, 60% in this category were in two minds and 52% predicted its occurrence and considered it as a serious threat to their products (Figure 1).

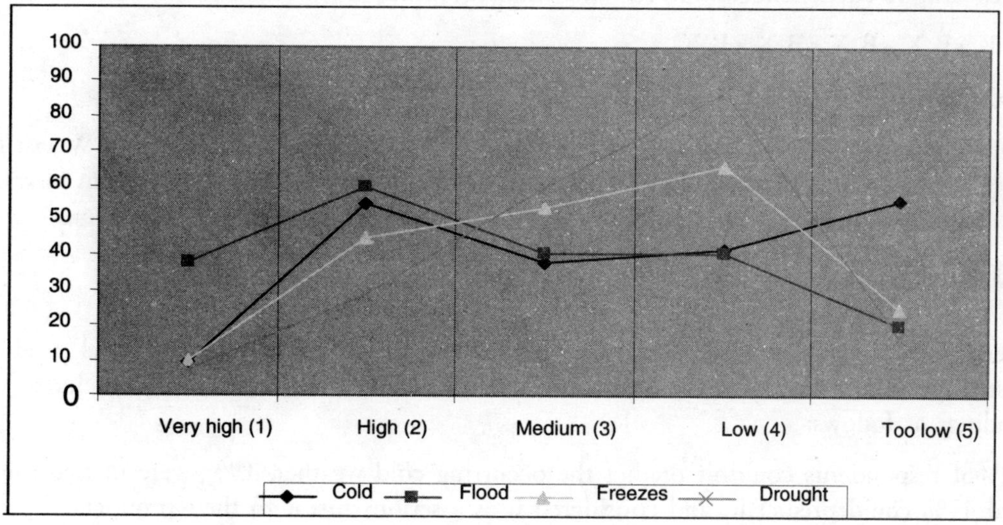

Figure 1: Estimation of frequency distribution of occurring risk

Multiple Regression Analysis: For determining linear function between independent variables set with dependent variable, this study has used from step-wise multiple regressions. In this method, the most effective variables enter one by one, in such a manner that significant test error reach 5%. In other words, variables enter into the function according to magnitude partial correlation with dependent variables. In the following part, we explain the results of last step.

In this stage, results of variance analysis and sum of F calculated (63.928) in this level significant. Therefore, with 99% probability, in total, 56.7% of dependent variables variance, with the use of four variables including forecasting the possibility of climatic changes such as cold weather, frost, floods and drought display has been expressed (Table 1).

Table 1: Coefficients variables entered into regression function

Sig	T	Beta	SEB	B	forecasting	Dependent variable
0.000	9.434	0.534	0.007	0.067	X_1= occurring cold	Adoption level of product insurance
0.000	4.529	0.254	0.008	0.037	X_2= occurring frost	
0.022	2.304	0.111	0.006	0.014	X_3= occurring flood	
0.028	2.216	0.105	0.008	0.018	X_4= occurring drought display	
0.397	0.849		0.037	0.032	Fixed amount	

According to coefficients and fixed value counted, multiple regression function is as follows:

$Y=B_0+B_1X_1+B_2X_2+B_3X_3+B_4X_4$

$Y=32\%+67\%+37\%+14\%+18\%\ X_4$

For examining the existence of serial correlation in the final model, from D.W test has been used in which the amount of 1.99 was near 2 and showed that the problem of values estimated in the final model, does not exist; so suitable estimation has carried out.

CONCLUSION

Here, according to examine the factors influencing on adoption of agricultural products insurance in Kurdistan province, on the base of obtained results, we will concluded our findings as follows:

32%of respondents couldn't predict the occurring cold weather, 19% were in two minds and 49% could predict it, and considered it as a serious threat to their products.

Near the 49%of respondents, didn't take flood as a serious risk for their product and had weak predict for probability of occurring it.20.5% of them were uncertain, and 30.5% of them could predict the occurring flood. Collection data too shows that near the 45% of respondents, consider the probability of occurring frost, 27% uncertain and 27% could not predict it. In the case of drought display, 18% didn't predict drought display, 60% were in two minds and 52% predicted its occurrence and considered it as a serious threat to their products.

Results of the study showed that the average for application of crop insurance in the group with a low degree of adoption was 30% of their entire under cultivation land while the figure was 47% and 67% for the groups with the medium and high degree of adoption respectively.

56.7% of independent variable variances are expressed, with the use of a linear composition of four variables: forecasting occurring of drought display, frost, flood and cold weather ($R=0.753$, $R^2=0.567$).

Finally on the base of obtained results, we can say that the main part of dependent variable variances, are explained by natural variables (natural events) and another part too, is influenced by unnatural factors (economical, social, cultural and so on).

In fact, these research findings show challenges and problems which affected agricultural activities. Findings in this study are close to results which were achieved by Farming Agricultural Organization (FAO).

SUGGESTION

For correct and efficient use of the results of this study, some suggestions on the basis of obtained results from descriptive and inferential part have been given. In additional, on the basis of direct observation in this investigation and results obtained from conversation with farmers, some advice has been given to them related to use of more agricultural products insurance.

Regarding descriptive results, with the view of 49%of respondents (cold weather occurring probability), 49.5% (اس آل يس ان) occurring probability), 30.5% (flood occurring probability), 45%(frost occurring probability) and 52%(drought display occurring probability) have predicted and consider them as a great threat to their products. Also, from one side there is a significant and positive correlation(1%) between four first variables and adoption of agricultural products insurance and also(5%) between drought display and dependent variable. On the other side in the multiple step-wise regression analysis, the variable of (cold weather occurring probability), with 67% positive coefficient, the variable of (frost occurring probability), with 67% positive coefficient, the variable of (flood occurring probability), with 67% positive coefficient and the variable of (drought display occurring probability), with 67% positive coefficient has set in the final regression function. Therefore, in the field of risks covered by insurance (insurable risks) it has been suggested that in the field study and same areas, adjusted and optimized agricultural products insurance should be carried. And the above variables should be used as main priorities of covered the risks of agricultural products insurance.

Finally, in this study, for better application of the findings of this research, the following suggestions have been given.

- For developing the insurance culture, is necessary that farmers increase their knowledge through better and meaningful relationship with insurance agents.
- One of the important factors that can influence the adoption of agricultural products insurance is the previous risk record in farms. Therefore, identification of different types of risks and the effects of each one on agricultural products and covering them by insurance can be effective in the case of increasing agricultural products.
- Prepare suitable ways for farmers co-operation and their contribution with experts in a way that they can forecast damages and estimate compensations.
- Suitable methods should be applied for forecast damages and estimate compensations. In this case, determining the damages measurement indexes and using professional experts in the cultivation field are very important.
- Government support through guarantee of price increasing of agricultural products and effective use of applied methods can encourage them to adopt enhanced insurance measures.
- The study suggests that compensation of damage, should be restricted only to real damages till the culture of using insurance becomes congenial with rural culture.

REFERENCES

Anderson.J.R, & J.L.Dillon,(1992), *Risk Analysis in Daryaland Farming System*, FAO, Farm System Management, Series 2,Rome.

Baker.E.J, (1990), *Demand for rain full insurance in the semi-arid tropics in India*, FAO, Farm System Management, series 2, Rome.

Boquet, A & V. Smith, (1996), Demand for multiple peril crop insurance: Evidence from Montana wheat farms, *American Journal of Agricultural Economics*, vol. 78, pp. 189-201.

Ezat. A, & Najafi, (2002), examine the possibility of future markets on the reducing price fluctuations in agricultural products in Iran, case study of pistachio market, *Iranian Journal of Agricultural Economics Society*,vol.41-42,Iran

Food and Agricultural Organization, (1991), *FAO crop insurance compendium*, Rome.

Ghadirian. & act, (2002), *Efficient Factors to Tendency for Soya from Golestan province*, papers presented in the meeting of agricultural products insurance development and investment protection, Iran.

Gorbani. & activities,(2000), *Efficient factors on adoption of agricultural crops insurance*,Bimeh insurance and agriculture Keshavarzi, Iran.

Grean.J, & activities, (1998), *Managing risk on your small farms program*, 162 Morrison Hall, Cornell University, Itheca.

Kerchegali.(2001), *Agricultural products insurance, guarantee and food security*, Payame Jahade Keshavarzi Journal, first year, vol 2, Tehran.

Krabasi.A.(1999), *Examine attitude of farmers and effective factors on agricultural products insurance*, papers presented in the meeting of Agricultural Products Insurance Development and Investment Protection, Iran.

Matlabi.(2001), *Agricultural products insurance and its role in investment guarantee and food security*, Monthly Domesticated animal, cultivation, industry, second year Tehran

Mishra. P, (1996), *Agricultural Risk, Insurance and Income: A study of the impact and design of India's comprehensive crop insurance scheme*. Avebury Publishing, Alddershot, UK.

Nori.S.(1999), *Insurance and its role in agricultural development*, papers presented in the meeting of Agricultural Products Insurance, Development and Investment Protection, Iran.

Turkamani. J, & act, (2002), *Final reports of plan efficiency of wheat insurance, planning research and agriculture*, Economic Institution of Agricultural Department, Iran.

Tiraee.y.n, (2002), *Study of the characteristic factors influencing adoption of agricultural products insurance in Khozestan province*, thesis submitted for the master's degree, Tehran.

8

An Interactive Possibilistic Linear Programming Approach For Multiple Objective Transportation Problems

DR. CELAL HAKAN KAGNICIOGLU*

Transportation models are very important for the supply chain management activities of the companies especially for minimizing the costs and time. Due to incompleteness and/or unavailability of required data over the mid-term decision horizon, critical parameters (such as transportation cost and demand) are assumed to be imprecise in nature. This paper deals with the solutions of multiple objective transportation problems with fuzzy coefficients in the objective functions and fuzzy parameters on the right hand side of the constraints by possibilistic linear programming approach. In this study, the transportation model has one imprecise objective function: minimization of transportation costs and one precise objective function: minimization of transportation time. The fuzzy objective function is substituted by three crisp functions: minimizing the most possible value of the imprecise total costs, maximizing the possibility of obtaining lower total costs, and minimizing the risk of obtaining higher total costs. Furthermore, triangular possibility distribution is used to represent each of these fuzzy parameters. Demand and supply quantities are constructed based on the three prominent data: the most pessimistic value, the most possible value and the most optimistic value. The imprecise constraints are then converted into crisp ones by Lai and Hwang's weighted average method. After specifying the linear membership functions for all of the objective functions, Zimmermann's fuzzy programming method for solving multiple objective linear programming called max-min approach is applied for achieving an overall satisfactory compromise solution. In order to find a satisfactory solution to the transportation problem and an overall degree of decision maker satisfaction with determined goal values, results are modified interactively by adjusting the linear membership functions and related model parameters. Finally, an example is given to illustrate the solution of transportation model by possibilistic linear programming approach.

Keywords: Multiple objective transportation problems, possibilistic linear programming, fuzzy sets.

* Assistant Professor, Anadolu University ESYO Yunusemre Kampusu 26470 Eskisehir/TURKEY.

INTRODUCTION

Transportation problem (TP) is an important linear programming that has taken a lot in the literature. There are many applications of the model including job scheduling, production inventory, production planning, production distribution, allocation problems and investment analysis. The classical transportation problem is one of the subclasses of linear programming problem in which all the constraints are equality type. Initially, Hitchcock (1941) and Kantorovich (1960) developed a transportation model and solved it by simplex method.

Efficient algorithms have been developed for solving the transportation problem when the cost coefficients and the supply and demand quantities are known exactly. However, these parameters are not always in a precise manner. The unit shipping cost may vary in a timeframe can be an example of it. The supplies and demands may be uncertain due to some uncontrollable factors. To deal quantitatively with imprecise information in making decisions, Bellman and Zadeh (1970) and Zadeh (1978) introduce the notion of fuzziness.

Since the transportation problem is essentially a linear program, fuzzy linear programming techniques are applied to the fuzzy transportation problem. Luhandjula (1986) deals with the problem of incorporating possibilistic data into a multiple objective linear programing approach. Bazaraa et al (1990) uses the parametric analysis in large-scale linear programming, where one finds a direction along which the objective function is perturbed and then seeks to move along this direction. When the current point is still maintaining optimality, the range of this direction is also obtained. With respect to the techniques for solving a linear programming problem with imprecise coefficients in the objective function, Rommelfanger (1996) states that a fuzzy objective function should be interpreted as a multiobjective demand. Tanaka et al (1984) adopt a weighted average as a substitute for the fuzzy objective with a special crisp compromise objective. The extreme values of the parameters will have an impact on the effect of the weighting sum. Sakawa and Yano (1989) proposes an a-Pareto-optimal solution that restricts the fuzzy coefficients to a-level-sets. Lai and Hwang (1992) referred to portfolio theory and converted the fuzzy objective with a triangular possibility distribution into three crisp objectives.

Verma et al (1997) apply the fuzzy programming technique with some non-linear membership functions to solve a multiobjective transportation problem as vector minimum problem. Hussein (1998) deals with the complete set of a-possibly efficient solutions of multiple objective transportation problems with possibilistic coefficients of the objective functions. The parametric analysis is used to characterize the set of all a-possibly efficient solutions. Hsu and Wang(2001) constructed a possibilistic linear programming model to determine appropriate safety stocks of materials, regulation of forecast demands and the numbers of key machines. They transformed the possibilistic linear programming model into a crisp multiple objective linear programming model. Liu and Kao (2004) formulated a pair of two-level mathematical programs for calculating the a-cuts of the fuzzy total transportation cost based on the extension principle. Islam and Roy (2005) introduced a fuzzy multiobjective mathematical programming problem with generalized fuzzy number costs in objective function and a multiobjective entropy transportation problem with an additional restriction is considered. El-Wahed and Lee (2006) present an interactive fuzzy goal programming approach to determine the preferred compromise solution for the multiobjective transportation problem.

This paper deals with solution of the multiple objective transportation problems by an interactive possibilistic linear programming approach. In this transportation problem, there are two objective functions, which are minimization of transportation cost and minimization of transportation time. Transportation costs are imprecise in nature and they are fuzzy coefficients with triangular possibility distribution. Transportation times are assumed to be crisp in the model. The demand and supply values are also fuzzy numbers with triangular possibility distribution. Therefore, in this study a possibilistic linear programming model is constructed to determine the quantity to be transported from any origin to any destination. The possibilistic linear programming model is then transformed into a crisp multiple objective linear programming model. Finally, Zimmermann's (1978) fuzzy programming method is applied to obtain a composite single objective.

MATHEMATICAL MODEL

In a typical transportation problem, a homogeneous product is to be transported from several origins (sources) to numerous destinations in such a way that the total transportation cost is minimum. Let us suppose that there are m origins O_i (i =1,2,...,m) and n destinations D_j (j =1,2,...,n). The sources can be production facilities, warehouses, etc. and the destinations can be warehouses, sales outlets, etc., and at each origin O_i let a_i be the amount of a homogenous product, transported to n destinations D_j to satisfy the demand for b_j units of the product there. A penalty C_{ij} is associated with transporting a unit of the product from origin i to destination j. The penalty could represent transportation cost, delivery time, distance, quantity of goods delivered under used capacity or many other criteria. The decision variable X_{ij} represents the quantity to be transported from origin O_i to destination D_j.

In real life situations, TP usually has multiple, conflicting and incommensurate objective functions and it is called multiobjective transportation problem. The mathematical model of the multiobjective transportation problem can be stated as follows:

$$\text{Minimize } Z_k = \sum_{i=1}^{m}\sum_{j=1}^{n} C_{ij}^{k} X_{ij}, \quad k=1,2,\ldots,K$$

subject to

$$\sum_{j=1}^{n} X_{ij} \le a_i, \qquad i=1,2,\ldots,m,$$

$$\sum_{i=1}^{m} X_{ij} \ge b_j, \qquad j=1,2,\ldots,n,$$

$X_{ij} \geq 0,$ for all i and j.

The subscript on Z_k and superscript on C_{ij}^k denote the kth penalty citerion. It is assumed that $a_i \geq 0$ for all i, and $b_j \geq 0$ for all j, and $C_{ij} \geq 0$ for all i and j. Besides, $\sum_i a_i \geq \sum_j b_j$.

INTERACTIVE POSSIBILISTIC LINEAR PROGRAMMING MODEL

Most practical decisions made to solve multiobjective TP usually consider total costs and transportation times. The total costs are the sum of transportation costs of all products transported from origins to destinations. The related cost coefficients in the objective function frequently are imprecise in nature since some information is incomplete or unobtainable in a medium time horizon. The second objective function, which is the Transportation Times (TT), are assumed to be crisp. These values are known precisely. Accordingly, two objective functions of the model are as follows:

$$\text{Minimize } Z_1 = \sum_{i=1}^{m}\sum_{j=1}^{n} \tilde{C}_{ij} X_{ij},$$

$$\text{Minimize } TT = \sum_{i=1}^{m}\sum_{j=1}^{n} T_{ij} X_{ij},$$

where $\tilde{C}_{ij}$ is imprecise coefficient with triangular possibility distribution and T_{ij} which is the transportation time of a product from origin i to destination j, is precise.

$$\sum_{j=1}^{n} X_{ij} \leq \tilde{a}_i, \quad i = 1,2,\ldots,m,$$

$$\sum_{i=1}^{m} X_{ij} \geq \tilde{b}_j, \quad j = 1,2,\ldots,n,$$

The amount of supply at origin i is ai and the amount of demand at destination j is bj. Both of these coefficients are imprecise, owing to uncertain supply and demand with triangular possibility distribution.

According to the first constraint, the supply of an origin must be equal or greater than the amount transported to all destinations. For the second constraint, the demand of a destination must be equal or smaller than the amount transported from all origins.

$X_{ij} \geq 0,$ for all i and j.

The last constraint is the non-negativity constraint, which shows that all of the decision variables are zero or greater than zero.

MODEL DEVELOPMENT AND SOLUTION

This study assumes that all imprecise coefficients have the pattern of triangular possibility distribution. The possibility distribution can be stated as the degree of occurrence of an event with imprecise data.

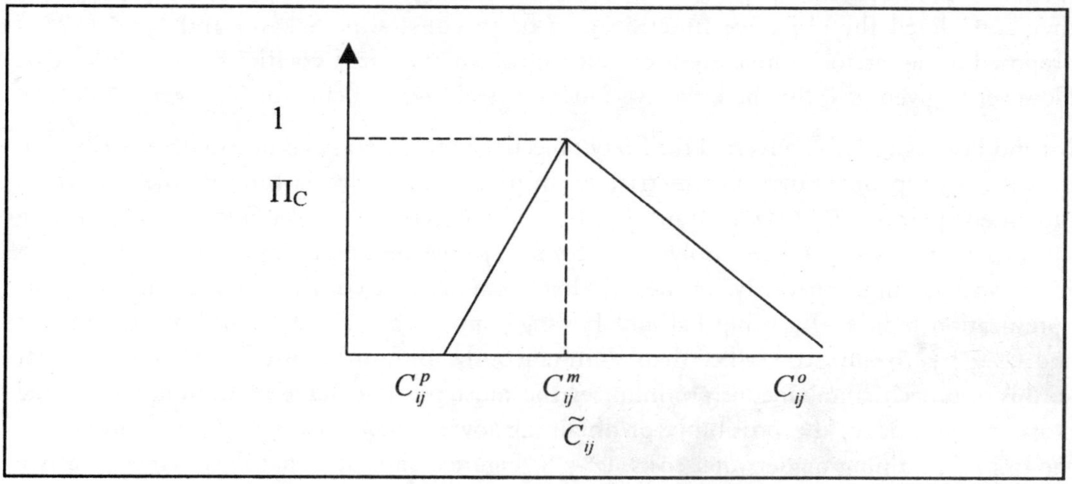

Figure 1: The triangular possibility distribution of $\tilde{C}_{ij}$

$\tilde{C}_{ij} = (C_{ij}^{p}, C_{ij}^{m}, C_{ij}^{o})$, where $C_{ij}^{p}, C_{ij}^{m}, C_{ij}^{o}$ are the most pessimistic value, the most possible value, and the most optimistic value of $\tilde{C}_{ij}$ estimated by a decision-maker. Figure 1 presents the triangular possibility distribution of imprecise number $\tilde{C}_{ij} = (C_{ij}^{p}, C_{ij}^{m}, C_{ij}^{o})$.

$\tilde{a}_i = (a_i^{p}, \tilde{a}_i^{m}, \tilde{a}_i^{o})$ and $\tilde{b}_j = (\tilde{b}_j^{p}, b_j^{m}, \tilde{b}_j^{o})$ are the parameters having triangular possibility distributions.

Generally, the triangular possibility distribution of $\tilde{C}_{ij}$ can be constructed based on the three prominent data, as follows (Wang and Liang, 2005).

1. The most pessimistic value (C_{ij}^{p}) that has a very low likelihood of belonging to the set of available values (possibility degree = 0 if normalized)

2. The most possible value (C_{ij}^{m}) that definitely belongs to the set of available values (possibility degree = 1 if normalized)

3. The most optimistic value (C^{o}_{ij}) that has a very low likelihood of belonging to the set of available values (possibility degree = 0 if normalized)

With respect to the techniques for solving a linear programming problem with imprecise coefficients in the objective function, Rommelfanger (1996) states that a fuzzy objective function should be interpreted as a multiobjective demand. Generally, an ideal solution to this problem does not exist. Tanaka et al (1984) proposed a method to obtain a compromise solution and adopted a weighted average as a substitute for the fuzzy objective with a special crisp compromise objective. Besides, when the goal of the objective can be given, they considered the objective function as a fuzzy constraint. Sakawa and Yano (1989) proposed an a-Pareto-optimal solution and restricted the fuzzy coefficients to a-level-sets. However, a given goal for the objective function is always difficult for managers to decide.

Lai and Hwang (1992) converted the fuzzy objective with a triangular possibility distribution into three crisp objectives. Geometrically, imprecise objective is fully defined by three prominent points (z^p, 0), (z^m, 1) and (z^o, 0). This objective can be minimized by pushing the three points toward the left. Solving the fuzzy objective becomes the process of minimizing z^p, z^m and z^o simultaneously. However, there may exist a conflict in the simultaneous optimization process. By using Lai and Hwang's approach, z^m and (z^o-z^m) are minimized and (z^m-z^p) is maximized, rather than simultaneously minimization of z^p, z^m and z^o. That is, this approach simultaneously minimizes the most possible value of the imprecise total costs, z^m, maximizes the possibility of obtaining lower total costs, (z^m-z^p), and minimizes the risk of obtaining higher total costs, (z^o-z^m). Figure 2 indicates that these three objective functions guarantee the minimization of the imprecise objective function. Therefore, this imprecise objective function is transformed into three new crisp objective functions with the other objective function, which is the minimization of the transportation times, as follows:

$$\text{Min } Z_1 = Z^m = \sum_{i=1}^{m}\sum_{j=1}^{n} C^m_{ij} X_{ij} ,$$

$$\text{Max } Z_2 = Z^m - Z^p = \sum_{i=1}^{m}\sum_{j=1}^{n} (C^m_{ij} - C^p_{ij}) X_{ij} ,$$

$$\text{Min } Z_3 = Z^o - Z^m = \sum_{i=1}^{m}\sum_{j=1}^{n} (C^o_{ij} - C^m_{ij}) X_{ij} ,$$

$$\text{Min } Z_4 = TT = \sum_{i=1}^{m}\sum_{j=1}^{n} T_{ij} X_{ij} .$$

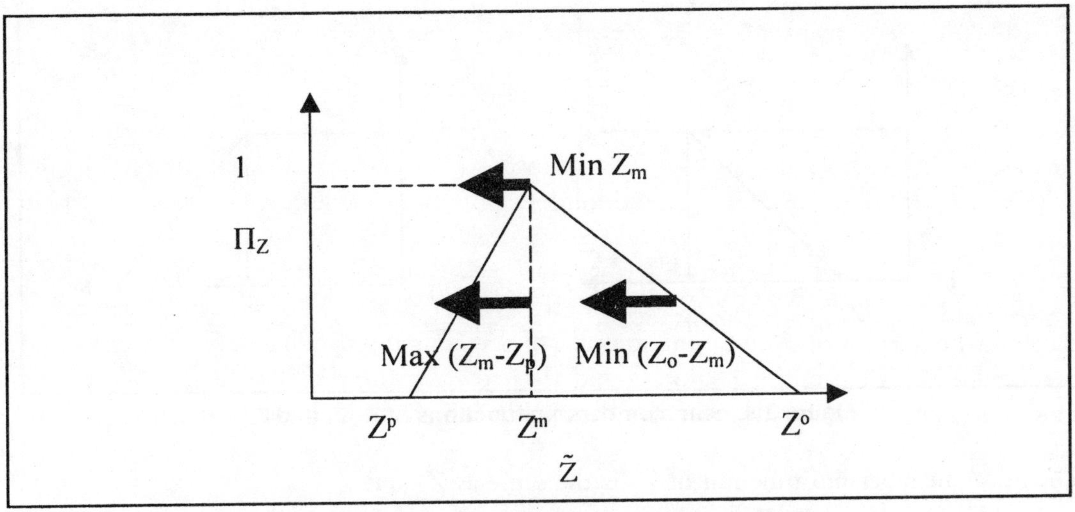

Figure 2: The strategy to minimize the total costs

Furthermore, this auxiliary multiobjective linear programming problem can be solved by converting into an equivalent single goal linear programming problem by using the Zimmermann's (1978) fuzzy programming method. At first, the positive ideal solutions (PIS) and negative ideal solutions (NIS) of the three objective functions should be obtained (Lai and Hwang, 1992).These are

$$Z_1^{PIS} = \text{Min } Z^m, \qquad Z_1^{NIS} = \text{Max } Z^m,$$
$$Z_2^{PIS} = \text{Max } (Z^m - Z^p), \qquad Z_2^{NIS} = \text{Min } (Z^m - Z^p),$$
$$Z_3^{PIS} = \text{Min } (Z^o - Z^m), \qquad Z_3^{NIS} = \text{Max } (Z^o - Z^m).$$
$$Z_4^{PIS} = \text{Min TT}, \qquad Z_4^{NIS} = \text{Max TT}$$

The linear membership function of these objective functions shown in Figure 3 can be computed as

$$f_{1(3)}(Z_{1(3)}) = \begin{cases} 1, \dots\dots\dots Z_{1(3)} < Z_{1(3)}^{PIS}, \\ \dfrac{Z_{1(3)}^{NIS} - Z_{1(3)}}{Z_{1(3)}^{NIS} - Z_{1(3)}^{PIS}}, \; Z_{1(3)}^{PIS} \le Z_{1(3)} \le Z_{1(3)}^{NIS}, \\ 0, \dots\dots\dots Z_{1(3)} > Z_{1(3)}^{NIS}, \end{cases} \quad f_2(Z_2) = \begin{cases} 1, \dots\dots\dots Z_2 < Z_2^{PIS}, \\ \dfrac{Z_2 - Z_2^{NIS}}{Z_2^{PIS} - Z_2^{NIS}}, \; Z_2^{NIS} \le Z_2 \le Z_2^{PIS}, \\ 0, \dots\dots\dots Z_2 > Z_2^{NIS}, \end{cases}$$

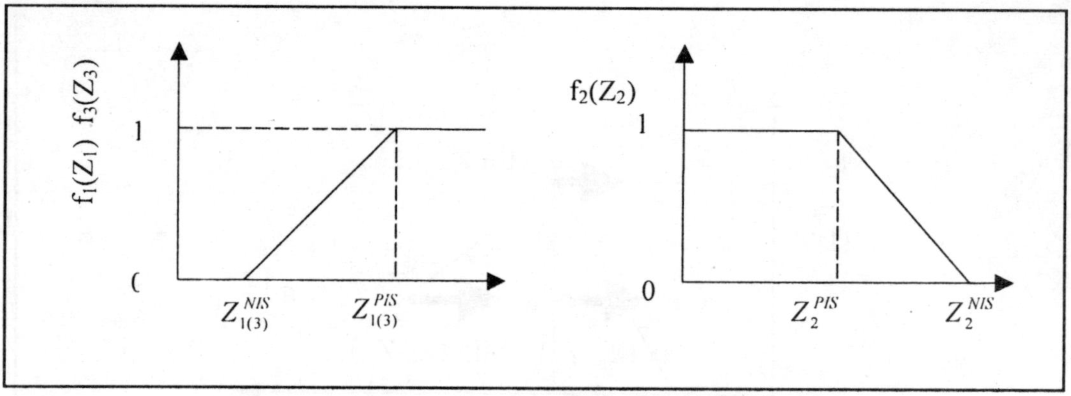

Figure 3: Linear membership functions of Z_1, Z_2 and Z_3

The linear membership function of Z_4 is the same as Z_1 and Z_3.

Both of the constraints about demand ($\tilde{a}_i$) and supply ($\tilde{b}_i$) are imprecise right-hand sides, and they have triangular possibility distributions with the most possible and least possible values. In real life, a possible interval for imprecise demand and supply can be estimated based on experience, intuition and knowledge. The crisp representative number for the imprecise demand and supply can be obtained by Lai and Hwang's (1992) weighted average method. If the minimum acceptable possibility, β, is given, then the auxiliary crisp equality constraints can be presented as follows:

$$\sum_{j=1}^{n} X_{ij} \leq w_1 a^{p}_{i,\beta} + w_2 a^{m}_{i,\beta} + w_3 a^{o}_{i,\beta}, \qquad i = 1,2,\ldots,m,$$

$$\sum_{i=1}^{m} X_{ij} \geq w_1 b^{p}_{j,\beta} + w_2 b^{m}_{j,\beta} + w_3 b^{o}_{j,\beta}, \qquad j = 1,2,\ldots,n.$$

where $w_1 + w_2 + w_3 = 1$ and w_1, w_2, and w_3 denote the weights of the most pessimistic, most possible and most optimistic value of the imprecise demand and supply, respectively. Although these weights can be determined subjectively by experience and knowledge, most of the time $w_1 = w_3 = 1/6$ and $w_2 = 4/6$ are taken, since most likely values here is that the most possible values usually are the most important ones, and thus should be assigned more weights.

Finally, after having the crisp constraints for the TP, Zimmerman's equivalent single objective linear programming model is applied to obtain the overall satisfaction compromise solution.

Max L

s. to

$L = f_1(Z_1)$

$L = f_2(Z_2)$

$L = f_3(Z_3)$

$L = f_4(Z_4)$

$$\sum_{j=1}^{n} X_{ij} \leq w_1 a_{i,\beta}^{p} + w_2 a_{i,\beta}^{m} + w_3 a_{i,\beta}^{o}, \qquad i = 1,2,\ldots,m,$$

$$\sum_{i=1}^{m} X_{ij} \geq w_1 b_{j,\beta}^{p} + w_2 b_{j,\beta}^{m} + w_3 b_{j,\beta}^{o}, \qquad j = 1,2,\ldots,n.$$

$0 = L = 1,$

$X_{ij} = 0$ for all i and j,

where $f_i(Z_i)$ is the satisfaction degree of the ith objective function.

Algorithm

The algorithm for solving the TP is as follows.

1. Model the imprecise coefficient $(\tilde{C}_{ij})$ and right-hand sides $(\tilde{a}_i, \tilde{b}_j)$ of the formulated multiobjective TP model using triangular possibility distribution.
2. Three new crisp objective functions for the imprecise objective function are developed. These three new objective functions minimize the most possible total cost value, maximize the possibility of obtaining lower costs and minimize the risk of obtaining higher costs, respectively.
3. Given the minimum acceptable possibility, β, imprecise constraints are converted into crisp ones by the weighted average method.
4. After having PIS and NIS of the objective functions separately, linear membership functions are specified for all the objective functions, and then the auxiliary multiobjective TP is converted into an equivalent linear programming model by the method of Bellman and Zadeh (1970) and Zimmermann's (1978) fuzzy programming method.
5. The model is solved and linear membership function is modified interactively until the solution is satisfactory. When the solution is accepted as satisfactory, it is stopped.

ILLUSTRATIVE EXAMPLE

An example is given to illustrate how this method is applied to transportation problems. The presumed company has six production facilities (PF) and six warehouses (W) in different parts of the country. The company produces just one type of product and finished products are transported to the warehouses. Transportation cost of one product from facilities to the warehouses and demand of the warehouses and supply of the production facilities are given in Table 1. As is shown in Table 1, all of these values are imprecise numbers with triangular possibility distributions.

Table 1: Transportation costs, supply and demand data

	W1	W2	W3	W4	W5	W6	Supply (000)
PF1	(20,25,28)	(28,33.36)	(19,23.25)	(22.26.28)	(14,17.19)	(30.34.39)	(35,37,40)
PF2	(13,16.20)	(9.12.16)	(18,22,25)	(11,14,16)	(10,13,15)	(22,24,25)	(62,64,67)
PF3	(36,38,39)	(23,25.26)	(14,16,19)	(37,40,45)	(37,40,42)	(34,36,39)	(38,40,41)
PF4	(64,66,70)	(56,59,64)	(37,40,44)	(45,47,50)	(34,36,40)	(21,24,26)	(37,39,40)
PF5	(44,46,50)	(53,56,60)	(25,28,31)	(46,49,53)	(34,37,39)	(26,28,31)	(40,43,45)
PF6	(67,69,73)	(34,37,41)	(23,26,28)	(33,36,38)	(43,46,50)	(18,21,25)	(22,24,28)
Demand(000)	(20,24,26)	(55,60,63)	(17,19,22)	(15,17,20)	(33,37,40)	(50,54,56)	

Transportation time (minute) of a product from production facilities to warehouses are shown in Table 2. These values are precise values.

Table 2: Transportation time data

	W1	W2	W3	W4	W5	W6
PF1	35	34	46	70	28	44
PF2	45	33	54	27	60	38
PF3	28	47	42	37	48	27
PF4	67	19	35	45	60	46
PF5	86	41	32	38	52	29
PF6	39	32	52	66	39	40

Given data (Tables 1 and 2) of the example, transportation problem is formulated according to the multiobjective linear programming model described above. The imprecise data is modelled by triangular possibility distributions. There are two objective functions of the model. While one of the objective functions is precise (transportation time), another one is imprecise as shown in Table 1. Three new crisp objective functions are developed for the imprecise objective function. Therefore, the model has four objective functions. Since right-hand side of the constraints (demand and supply) are imprecise, auxiliary crisp constraints are formulated by using weighted average method at $\beta = 0.5$.

Four crisp objective functions of the auxiliary multiobjective linear programming problem presented in the example are solved using the crisp single-goal linear programming model, and shown in Table 3.

Table 3: Solutions of single-goal linear programming models

Objective function	Min Z_1	Max Z_2	Min Z_3	Min Z_4
Z_1	4151.5			
Z_2		871.2		
Z_3			356.2	
Z_4				5832.7

According to these solutions in Table 3, the corresponding PIS and NIS of the initial solution are specified in Table 4.

Table 4: PIS and NIS of the objective functions

	Z_1	Z_2	Z_3	Z_4
PIS_1, NIS_1	4000,20000	900,600	300,600	5500,10000
PIS_2,NIS_2	4100,10900	880,470	350,1100	5500,14500

By using different set of PIS and NIS of the objective functions, the corresponding linear membership function of all the objective functions can be defined. These membership functions will be prepared according to Figure 3 and formulation given above Figure 3. Two different set of PIS and NIS values are used for the solutions as it is seen in Table 4. Then, the complete equivalent single-goal linear programming model for the multiobjective linear programming model can be formulated using the fuzzy decisions of Bellman and Zadeh (1970) and Zimmermann's fuzzy programming method.

The initial model (PIS_1, NIS_1) and the improved model (PIS_2,NIS_2) is solved by Lingo 8 computer software and the results are given in Table 5.

Table 5: Initial and improved solution for the example

X_{ij} (000)	Initial solution	Improved solution
X_{11}	0.0	22.7
X_{12}	34.3	14.3
X_{13}	2.8	0.0
X_{14}	0.0	0.0
X_{15}	0.0	0.0
X_{16}	0.0	0.0
X_{21}	0.0	0.0
X_{22}	0.0	31.2
X_{23}	0.0	0.0
X_{24}	27.1	29.9
X_{25}	16.3	0.0
X_{26}	20.8	3.0
X_{31}	23.8	1.0
X_{32}	0.0	0.0
X_{33}	0.0	0.0
X_{34}	0.0	0.0
X_{35}	16.1	36.0
X_{36}	0.0	1.9
X_{41}	0.0	0.0
X_{42}	5.9	14.2
X_{43}	0.0	0.0
X_{44}	0.0	0.0
X_{45}	0.0	0.0

Contd...

X_{46}	33.0	24.6
X_{51}	0.0	0.0
X_{52}	0.0	0.0
X_{53}	16.3	25.7
X_{54}	0.0	0.0
X_{55}	0.0	0.0
X_{56}	0.0	0.0
X_{61}	0.0	0.0
X_{62}	19.7	0.0
X_{63}	0.0	0.0
X_{64}	0.0	0.0
X_{65}	4.5	0.0
X_{66}	0.0	24.2
Objective value L	**0.44**	**0.70**
Z_1(000)	6368.0	6147.9
Z_2(000)	768.1	809.4
Z_3(000)	473.1	601.6
Z_4	8191.0	8288.8

Since transportation cost (Z_1)is imprecise and has a triangular possibility distribution, it is calculated by ($Z_1 - Z_2$, Z_1, $Z_1 + Z_3$). Therefore, the initial transportation cost is imprecise and has a triangular possibility distribution of (5599.9, 6368.0, 6841.1), and transportation time (Z_4), is 8191.0 minutes. The improved solution is also imprecise and has a triangular possibility distribution of (5338.5, 6147.9, 6749.5), and transportation time is 8288.8 minutes. As it is seen in Table 5, overall satisfaction degree of the objectives increased from 0.44 to 0.70 by the improved solution.

In the multiobjective transportation problem, the values of Z_1, Z_3 and Z_4 are attempted to be minimized and the value of Z_2 is attempted to be maximized. However, when the values of the objective functions are compared in the initial and improved solution, Z_3 and Z_4 values of the improved solution are greater than the initial solution. It is because of the structure of the TP model. Since TP is not balanced (supply = demand) due to imprecise values, the number of products transported in the improved solution ($\sum x_{ij}$ = 228.7) is greater than in the initial solution ($\sum x_{ij}$ =220.6). So, when the number of products transported increase, the cost and time of the transportation increase, as well. Thus, this indicates why the overall satisfaction degree of the objective functions for the improved solution (0.7 > 0.44) is bigger than the initial solution while some cost values higher than the initial one. Besides, although more number of products transported in the improved solution, the possibilistic distribution of the costs shifted to the left as it is required, shown in Figure 4.

Changes in the PIS and NIS of the objective functions are very effective on the value of the overall satisfaction degree of the objectives (L). Changes in PIS and NIS values increase the value of L sharply (from 0.44 to 0.70), but because of the explanations above, the total cost slightly decreases. The value of L, which is the overall satisfaction degree of the objectives, 0.70, can be a sufficient value for the multiobjective TP models with imprecise and precise objective functions. The decision-maker will decide on it, if it is acceptable or not. If not, then different values of PIS and NIS can be used for the membership functions to fýnd a more satisfying compromise solution. If the solution is L = 1, then each goal is fully satisfied, stop. If 0<L< 1, then all of the goals are satisfied at the level of L, and if L =0, then none of the goals are satisfied.

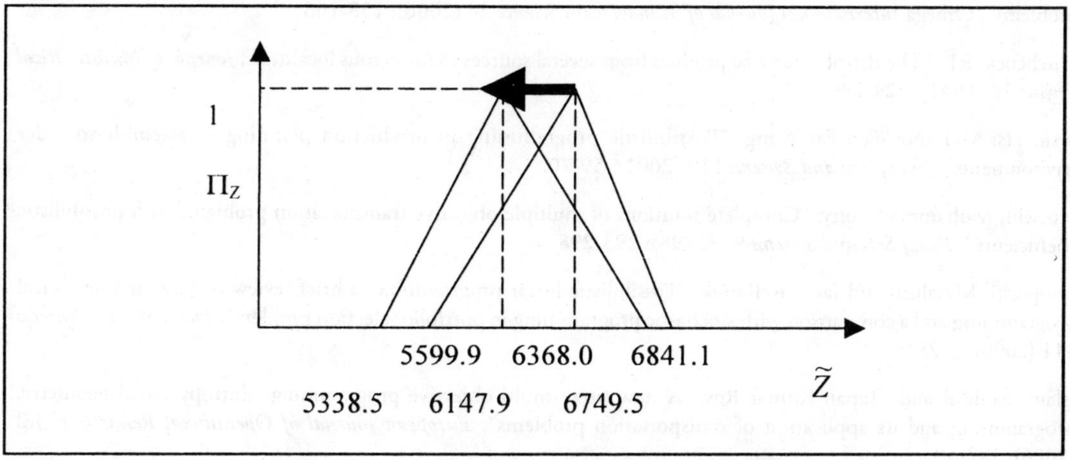

Figure 4: The possibilistic distribution of the costs

CONCLUSION

The transportation model is a special class of the linear programming problem. The parameters and cost coefficients of this model are usually imprecise in real life. This approach helps to solve most of the real life transportation problems with multiobjective and imprecise and precise parameters through an interactive decision-making process. This work aims to present an interactive possibilistic linear programming problem approach for solving multiobjective transportation problems with imprecise cost, demand and supply. By this approach, simultaneously the most possible value of the imprecise total costs are minimized, possibility of obtaining lower total costs are maximized and the risk of obtaining higher total costs are minimized.

The application of this approach is easier than stochastic programming models because of inefficiency and difficulty in the computations of stochastic problems. This approach is more efficient and flexible than the stochastic problem models.

The numerical example shows the effect of PIS and NIS values for the overall satisfaction degree of the objectives. Changing these values and solving the problem interactively gives the decision-maker flexibility in accepting the values of the decision variables. Besides, it gives the decision-maker to make trade offs among the alternatives (interactive solutions) according to all interior and outer conditions. Decision-maker can modify the imprecise parameters until finding a satisfactory solution according to all environmental conditions.

Finally, it can be said that the proposed approach yields an efficient compromise solution for transportation problems with multiple objective and imprecise objective functions and right-handsides.

REFERENCES

Belman, R.E. and L.A. Zadeh. "Decision making in a fuzzy environment," *Management Science* 17 (1970): 141-164.

El-Wahed, Waiel F. Abd and Sang M Lee. "Interactive fuzzy goal programming for multi-objective transportation problems", Omega *International Journal of Management Science* 34 (2006): 158-166.

Hitchcock, F.L. "The distribution of a product from several sources to numerous localities", *Journal of Mathematical Physics* 20 (1941): 224-230.

Hsu, Hsi-Mei and Wen-Pai Wang. "Possibilistic programming in production planning of assemble-to-order environments", *Fuzzy Sets and Systems* 119 (2001): 59-70.

Hussein, Mohammad Lofty. "Complete solutions of multiple objective transportation problems with possibilistic coefficients." *Fuzzy Sets and Systems* 93 (1998): 293-298.

Inuiguchi, Masahiro and Jaroslav Ramik. "Possibilistic linear programming: a brief review of fuzzy mathematical programming and a comparison with stochastic programming in portfolio selection problem", *Fuzzy Sets and Systems* 111 (2000): 3-28.

Islam, Sahidul and Tapan Kumar Roy. "A new fuzzy multi-objective programming: Entropy based geometric programming and its application of transportation problems", *European Journal of Operational Research* 173.2 (2006): 387-404.

Kantorovich, L.V. "Mathematical methods of organizing and planning production (in Russian)", English translation in *Management Science* 6 (1960): 366-422.

Lai, Y.J. and C.L. Hwang. " A new approach to some possibilistic linear programming problems", *Fuzzy Sets and Systems* 49 (1992): 121-133.

Liang, Tien-Fu. "Distribution planning decisions using interactive fuzzy multi-objective linear programming", *Fuzzy Sets and Systems* 157 (2006): 1303-1316.

Liu, Shiang-Tai and Chiang Kao. "Solving Fuzzy Transportation problems based on extension principle", *European Journal of Operational Research* 153 (2004):661-674.

Luhandjula, M.K. "Multiple objective programming with possibilistic coefficients", *Fuzzy Sets and Systems* 18 (1986): 15-30.

Rommelfanger, H. "Fuzzy linear programming and applications", *European Journal of Operations Research* 92 (1996): 512-527.

Sakawa, M. and H. Yano. "Interactive fuzzy satisficing method for multiobjective nonlinear programming problems with fuzzy parameters", *Fuzzy Sets and Systems* 30 (1989): 221-238.

Sounderpandian, Javayel and Bala Balashanmugam. "Multiproduct, multifacility scheduling using the transportation model: a case study." *Production and Inventory Management Journal* 32.4 (1991): 69-73.

Tanaka, H., K. Ichihashi and K. Asai. "A formulation of linear programming problems based on comparison of fuzzy numbers", *Control Cybernet* 13(1984): 185-194.

Torabi, S.A. and E Hassini. "An interactive possibilistic programming approach for multiple objective supply chain master planning", *Fuzzy Sets and Systems* 159 (2008): 193-214.

Verma, Rakesh, M.P.Biswal, and A.Biswas. "Fuzzy programming technique to solve multi-objective transportation problems with some non-linear membership functions", *Fuzzy Sets and Systems* 91 (1997): 37-43.

Wang, Reay-Chen and Tien-Fu Liang."Applying possibilistic linear programming to aggregate production planning", *Int. Journal of Production Economics* 98 (2005):328-341.

Zadeh, L.A. "Fuzzy sets as a basis for a theory of possibility", *Fuzzy Sets and Systems* 1 (1978): 3-28.

Zimmerman, H.J. "Fuzzy programming and linear programming with several objective functions", *Fuzzy Sets and Systems* 1 (1978):45-56.

9

Role of Anxiety in Employee Burnout

M.VASUKI*

Every organization is made up of people of different temperaments. It is a challenge for any organization to coordinate and manage human resources for its survival. There has been a tremendous change in the concepts like long-term loyalty and a sense of corporate community among the employees as the employers expect more and more from their employees but offer little security in turn. The work load has increased considerably in the last twenty five years that leads to performance culture where employees are subjected to 360' appraisal. This competitive work environment produces anxiety and stress among the employees. Anxious and stressed out employees often land up in depression -it is not the mental depression but the job depression which can also be called "job burnout". Any person from junior recruit to seniormost can be a victim of burnout.By maintaining the work life balance, one can break the vicious circle of burnout. Irrespective of whether the source is the job or personal life, burnout is a trap that affects the person both physically and psychologically. Work life balance helps to meet the challenge of managing human resources by streamlining ineffective human capital issues like job burnout. Therefore, an attempt is made to study the relationship between burnout and anxiety among corporate employees. The sample consisted of 60 employees including both males and females of equal number. Simple random sampling was used to select the sample. The research design adopted for the present study was ex post facto in nature. The tools - Job burnout Inventory and STA! (Charles D. Spielberger, 1983) were used to collect the data. Collected data was tabulated and subjected to statistical analysis.

INTRODUCTION

Effective human engagement is possible when the organization creates a work environment that develops an emotional bond. When this emotional bond is broken, the employee undergoes emotional turmoil leading to job burnout. An engaged employee, as opposed

* Counselling Psychologist,ICFAI Business School, Chennai.

to one who is just satisfied, not only stays with the business but actively contributes to business success through human capital excellence. The focus on engagement, the opposite of burnout, promises to yield new perspectives on strategies to alleviate burnout. A proper match between the job environment and the individual promotes employee engagement whereas misfit leads to burnout. A committed employee will be more involved in the organizational activities and thrive for excellence.

Employees of Indian BPO sectors are often faced with Burn-Out Stress Syndrome (BOSS). Severe fatigue, sleep disorders, complete change in the rhythm of the body, and gastrointestinal problems are some of the symptoms of this syndrome. According to UNITES (Union for Information Technology & Enabled Services Professionals) 20% of BPO professionals seek counselling for high work stress, while 30% have problems of a skewed work-life balance for whom walk-in counselling and e-counselling were provided (The telegraph, November 05).

The research findings of Bakker, Arnold B. et al (2006) confirmed that team-level burnout and work engagement are related to individual team members' burnout (i.e., exhaustion, cynicism, and reduced professional efficacy) and work engagement (vigor, dedication, and absorption). Saar Langelaan et al (2006) predicted that burnout would correlate negatively with temperament traits (strength of excitation, strength of inhibition, and mobility), whereas work engagement would correlate positively with them. These findings indicate that there is a correlation between human burnout and employee engagement that has an impact on HC productivity which in turn affects the company's financial position. Therefore, burnout must be minimized to improve the company's productivity.

Concept of Burnout

Burnout occurs when the individual reaches a saturation point due to various reasons like unrealistic expectations, prolonged exposure to unhealthy work life, monotony in the work, and absence of job satisfaction. This state of exhaustion affects the physical, emotional and mental well-being of an individual. Invariably it leads to work stress, which causes frustration, hopelessness and fear of failure in the individual. This in turn adversely affects productivity, human capital, relationships and health.

One may be prone to burnout if:

- One identifies too strongly with work
- One lacks a reasonable balance between work and personal life
- One tries to be all-in-all in an organization
- One has a heavy work load
- One's job is monotonous
- One works in the helping professions, such as the medical profession, counselling, teaching or politics.

Symptoms of Burnout

The symptoms of burnout are that one

- finds oneself being more cynical, critical and sarcastic at work
- has lost the ability to experience joy
- drags oneself to work and has trouble getting started on arrival
- becomes more irritable and less patient with co-workers, customers or clients
- feels that one faces unrealistic barriers at work
- feels the lack of energy needed to be consistently productive
- no longer derives satisfaction from achievements
- feels directionless about the job
- finds that sleep habits and/or appetite have changed
- suffers from headaches, neck pain or lower back pain

Causes of Burnout

One needs to identify the causes in order to overcome burnout. Some of the factors could be:

1. ***Lack of control:*** The employee experiences a lack of control when he/she is unable to influence decisions that affect his/her job, such as which hours he/she will work or which assignments he/she would get. Sometimes he/she is unable to control the amount of work that comes in.
2. ***Unclear job expectations:*** The employee faces uncertainty over the degree of authority he/she has and does not have the necessary resources to do his/her work.
3. ***Unhealthy workplace relationships:*** It is stressful if one is working with an office bully, being undermined by colleagues or has a boss who micromanages one's work.
4. ***Incompatibility in values:*** If the employee's values differ from the way the company does business or handles employee grievances, it will wear out the employee.
5. ***Job mismatch:*** Working in a job that poorly aligns with one's interests and skills can become more and more stressful over time.
6. ***Monotony or chaos in job routine:*** When a job is always monotonous or chaotic, one needs a great deal of energy to remain focused. This energy drain can eventually lead to burnout.
7. ***24/7 Workplace:*** Working round the clock without any break is exhausting for most people and leads to imbalance in mind, body and spirit, and affects work life balance, leading to burnout.

8. *Family/ Personal issues:* Family problems or unresolved personal issues can interfere with focus on work, affect productivity and cause great stress.

Strategies to Prevent, Reduce or Heal Burnout

To prevent and reduce burnout, one can make the following changes to improve one's physical, emotional and social well-being.

- *Healthy eating:* Cultivating healthy eating habits such as taking more fruits and vegetables and making sure meals are taken regularly and on time in order to remain energetic throughout the day.
- *Getting enough exercise:* Ensuring regular and adequate exercise through activities such as stretches, walking and yoga.
- *Taking adequate rest:* Making sure to get the sleep and rest that the body needs.
- *Consulting a psychologist:* Having a complete health check-up to rule out symptoms of burnout and having a talk with the doctor.
- *Maintaining equanimity:* Physical health is affected by a disturbed mind. Techniques like meditation can ensure a healthy mind-body connection and restore and maintain equanimity.
- *Learning coping skills:* One can develop coping skills for dealing with stress such as relaxation techniques, visualization and affirmations..
- *Enhancing self-awareness:* Understanding one's strengths and weaknesses can help one learn better ways to deal with day-to-day stress.
- *Developing emotional competence:* Becoming aware of one's own emotions and channelizing them is very essential.
- *Learning time management:* It helps to plan one's work day with adequate intervals between tasks and delegate tasks if necessary.
- *Setting goals:* Setting short- and long-term goals that are achievable and working towards them gives one a sense of purpose.
- *Having time for oneself:* It is important to regularly set aside time to be alone, to do something one enjoys, and explore hobbies and to recognize oneself.
- *Making a list:* Of each action according to the preference or priority and taking five to ten minutes at the end of each day to review the list will give one a head start for the next day.
- *Spending quality time with family and friends:* This will help restore energy and counter the harmful effects of burnout.

Studies have shown that happier employees are more productive and more loyal. More productivity leads to a healthier bottom line. Also, employers must realize that work/life balance is different for everyone. Work/life balance enables a company to retain the best candidates in their original positions, increasing productivity even further. In short, it is a win-win situation for both the employer and the employee. More and more employees are attempting to strike a balance between work and family by gaining satisfaction in both their personal life and their work. It is better if a company reviews the work-life balance of their employees on a regular basis. Employers can provide individual development plans for employees or mentoring by colleagues in order to monitor progress and satisfaction in the workforce. Guidelines to handle problems should also be established so that business and personal needs can be met. By implementing such strategies in the organization, job burnout is alleviated and work/life balance is achieved, which in turn, improves human capital performance, employee commitment and the company's productivity.

According to Workplace Stress: A Survival Guide prepared by Donato, Mary (2006) one should avoid the constant feeing of anxiety by developing his/her creative thinking. Avoiding anxiety in the workplace setting would in turn help to remove the negative effects of stressful situations. A research study done on "Staff burnout"(Corrigan et al 1994) in a psychiatric hospital shown that burnout in staff members is significantly associated with state anxiety. Therefore a need arises to study the relationship between anxiety and employee burnout.

METHODOLOGY

The objectives of the present study were

1. To investigate the relationship between the state anxiety and employee burnout.
2. To investigate the relationship between the trait anxiety and employee burnout.
3. To determine whether gender has any effect on the state and trait anxiety of employees.
4. To determine gender differences with reference to burnout among employees.
5. To determine whether age has any association with the burnout of employees.

The following hypotheses was formulated based on the objectives of the present study.

1. There will not be a significant relationship between state anxiety and employee burnout.
2. There will not be a significant relationship between trait anxiety and employee burnout.
3. There will not be a significant difference between male and female employees in their state anxiety level.
4. There will not be a significant difference between male and female employees in their Trait anxiety level.
5. There will not be a significant difference between male and female employees in their burnout level.
6. There will not be a significant association between age and employee burnout.

Research Design

The research design adopted for the present study was ex post facto in nature. Using simple random sampling, 60 employees consisting of both males and females of equal number were selected for the present study.

Sampling Design

The sampling design is presented below:

a) Sample characteristics

The sample consisted of employees ranging from 30 to 50 years currently working in different organizations. Both the genders were equally represented in the sample - 30 males and 30 females - from the organizations.

Schematic Representation of the Sample

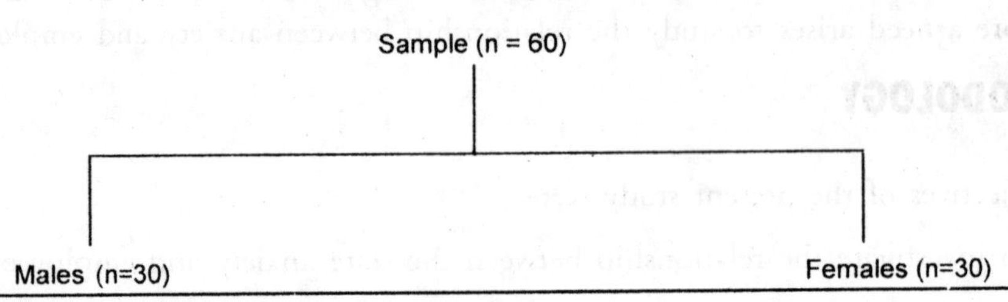

Figure 1

Tools Used

Standardized tools were used to gather data required for the research. The tools AFMC Job Burnout Test developed by the Armed Forces Medical College, Pune and State Trait anxiety Inventory (STAI, Charles D. Spielberger, 1983) were used to collect the data.

Processing and Analysis of Data

The collected data was subjected to a number of statistical operations. The data was classified, tabulated and statistically analyzed using SPSS (Ver.11). The statistical techniques that were applied to analyze the data included unpaired't' test and product moment correlation.

Results

This section deals with the outcome of the data analysis. The hypotheses are tested and interpreted following which appropriate discussions are presented.

Table 1: Relation between State Anxiety and Burnout

Variables	N	Mean	SD	correlation	Level of significance
State Anxiety	60	50.950	17.308	0.925**	0.01
Burnout	60	41.950	11.804		

From the above table, the correlations between the state anxiety and burnout were found to be significant. The co-efficient of correlation was 0. 925 which is significant at 0.01 level. Therefore, the hypothesis 1, "There will not be a significant relationship between state anxiety and burnout of employees" is rejected.

Table 2: Relation between Trait Anxiety and Burnout

Variables	N	Mean	SD	Correlation	Level of significance
Trait Anxiety	60	39.850	4.758	.075	NS
Burnout	60	41.950	11.804		

From the above table the correlations between the traits anxiety and burnout were found to be non-significant. The co-efficient of correlation was 0.075 which is significant at 0.01level. Therefore, the hypothesis 2, "There will not be a significant relationship between the traits anxiety and burnout of employees" is accepted.

Table 3: Gender and State Anxiety

Groups	N	Mean	SD	SE	't' Ratio	Level of significance
Males	30	48.0667	17.1543	3.13194	1.298	NS
Females	30	53.8333	17.2628	3.1517		

The above table shows the 't' analysis for difference between males and females in their level of state anxiety. The mean scores indicate there is a difference between two groups. But the non-significant t value implies that the state anxiety of the two groups does not differ significantly. Therefore the hypothesis 3 "There will not be a significant difference between male and female employees in their state anxiety level" is accepted.

Table 4: Gender and Trait Anxiety

Groups	N	Mean	SD	SE	't' Ratio	Level of significance
Males	30	41.1333	4.3050	0.7859	2.153	NS
females	30	38.5667	4.9108	0.8965		

The above table shows the 't' analysis for difference between males and females in their level of the trait of anxiety. The mean scores indicate there is a minimal difference between two groups. But the non-significant t value implies that the trait anxiety of the two groups does not differ significantly. Therefore the hypothesis 4 "There will not be a significant difference between male and female employees in their trait anxiety level" is accepted.

Table 5: Gender and Burnout

Groups	N	Mean	SD	SE	't' Ratio	Level of significance
Males	30	40.4000	11.485	2.096	4.046**	0.01
Females	30	47.9005	12.181	2.224		

The above table shows the 't' analysis for difference between men and women employees in their burnout level. The mean scores indicate there is a difference between the two groups. This is substantiated by the significant t value ($t=4.046$; $P<0.01$) which implies that the burnout of the two groups differs significantly. Therefore, the hypothesis 5 "There will not be a significant difference between male and female employees in their burnout level" is rejected.

Table 6:Age and Burnout

Age	Burnout				Chi-value
	No burnout	Moderate burnout	Severe burnout	Total	
30-40	9	20	5	34	0.007
41-50	5	6	15	26	
Total	14	26	20	60	

It can be seen from the Table 6 that the association between educational qualification and decision-making styles is significant as the chi-value, 0.007, obtained for the correlation is less than 0.05. Therefore the hypothesis 6, "There will not be a significant association between age and employee burnout" is rejected.

DISCUSSION

On the whole, burnout can be prevented or healed by developing self-awareness and emotional competence, and cultivating and maintaining a healthy relationship with oneself and others. It is always important on the part of the employee to realize that he/she is burning out or burnt out and address it in time. If necessary it can be expressed to their employer too. Responding to the call of the employee and doing the needful will help to heal burnout in the employee in order to improve human capital, productivity and work life balance.

Work life balance helps the employers not only to protect the health and safety of their employees, to promote their welfare, but also to have better labour relations with their employees. It also depends on the quality of work life prevalent in the organization and the degree of importance given by the employers to working conditions and the well being of the employees. The notion of 'working conditions' is usually extended to the design of the workplace, working methods and the work environment. The concept of well-being means that work should be adapted to the person, that monotonous and repetitive work should be avoided, and that the worker should be able to influence the rhythm of work, which in turn enhances human capital performance and productivity. Also, employees will become more committed. The more committed they are, the more they act to find resolutions to problems they face in the organizations.

The results of the present study imply that there is a significant association between state anxiety and burnout among employees. This is in line with the findings of Corrigan et al (1994), who has shown that burnout in staff members is significantly associated with state anxiety. State anxiety describes the present feelings best. A safe work environment provides the base for an employee to enjoy working. Work should not create any health hazard for the employee. The employer and employee, aware of their risks and rights, could achieve a lot in their mutually beneficial understanding. This will help the employee to stay calm and relaxed in the workplace. An unsafe work environment induces anxiety that inturn leads to burnout. People who are non anxious generally (trait anxiety) are prone to burnout as they become anxious (state) at the workplace. This is applicable for both men and women.

According to the present research, women easily become burnt out than their counter parts. Though India is a strange combination of numerous religions and communities of people, the basic values and systems of family life remain similar. For instance, a woman, whether she is working or not, shoulder the major part of the household responsibilities, like raising the children and imparting values to them, taking care of elders in the family is expected to be accomplished. This makes a working woman become burnt out faster than male employees.

It is also interesting to note that senior people become more burnt out than the young employees. Initially, one will find his job wonderful. As he has boundless energy and enthusiasm and all things seem possible. One believes that the job will satisfy all the needs and desires and solve all the problems. Once this phase wanes, the awakening stage begins with the realization that one's initial expectations were unrealistic. The job isn't working out the way one thought it would. It doesn't satisfy all the needs; one becomes unsatisfied with the co-workers and the organization and rewards and recognition are scarce.

As disillusionment and disappointment grow, one becomes confused. One starts working even harder to fulfil one's desires. But working harder doesn't change anything and one becomes increasingly tired, bored and frustrated. One doubts one's competence and ability and start losing one's morale and in turn becomes indecisive, and productivity drops. This gradually leads to burnout. This may be the reason for senior employees to have higher levels of burnout.

CONCLUSIONS

The following conclusions were arrived from the results of the present study

- State anxiety is directly related to employee burnout.
- Trait anxiety is not related to employee burnout.
- Females and males are found to have the same level of state anxiety.
- Females and males are found to have the same level of trait anxiety.
- Women employees are found to be more burnout than their counterparts.
- Senior employees are found to have higher burnout level than junior employees.

Implications of the present study

- As the state of anxiety is an important contributor to burnout an understanding of the relationship between state anxiety and burnout will help to identify the individuals who need training. Interventions and counselling can be planned accordingly to alleviate anxiety, which in turn help the individual to improve his work life balance.

- As senior employees get burnt out faster, the management can make a direct attempt to address the issue of the anxiety-provoking experiences and develop senior employees' capacity to respond to anxiety in a psychologically healthy way. Management must acknowledge the ability of its employees and provide support to deal with anxiety and other distress.

REFERENCES

Bakker, Arnold B.·van Emmerik, Hetty, Euwema, Martin C. (2006) *Crossover of Burnout and Engagement in Work Teams, Work & Occupations*, Vol. 33 Issue 4, p464-489.

Corrigan, Patrick W.; Holmes, E. Paul; Luchins, Daniel; Basit, Abdul; Parks, Joseph J.; Buican, Brett(1994) Staff burnout in a psychiatric hospital: a cross-lagged panel design, *Journal of Organizational Behavior*, Vol. 15 Issue 1, p65-74, 10p.

Donato, Mary (2006) Workplace Stress: A Survival Guide, *Sales & Marketing Management*, Vol. 158 Issue 9, p24-24, 1p, 1c.

HR.com (2006) *Work-Life Experts Launch New Web-Based Training to Help Employers Battle the Costs of Stress and Build a Resilient Workforce.*

Saar Langelaan, Arnold B. Bakker, Lorenz J.P. van Doornen and Wilmar B. Schaufeli (2006) Burnout and work engagement: Do individual differences make a difference? *Personality and Individual Differences, Volume 40, Issue 3.*

www.telegraphindia.com

10

Innovative Quality Circle for Quality Assurance: A case study at GFT Technologies (India) Pvt. Ltd.

R. NEIL SAMSON*
DR. S.R. DEVADASAN**
S. VINODH***

One of the facets of total quality management (TQM) philosophy is to achieve continuous quality improvement through total employee participation. Numerous researches have established that total employee participation leads to continuous improvement. Time and again, several models for effecting 'total employee participation' have emanated in literature. Despite the emergence of many models, the quality circle programme (QCP) that emanated in Japan during the early 1960s had been a platform for effecting employee participation. Quality circle is a group of employees of an organization who volunteer to assemble regularly for discussing the quality improvement oriented problems and proposing solutions to the management. The concept of quality circle was introduced by the quality guru Ishikawa during the 1950s which subsequently found wide adoptions throughout the world.

The main contribution of quality circle concept is the involvement of employees at all levels to share theoretical and practical knowledge for achieving continuous quality improvement. Such a creditable concept is currently adopted in organisations only to a lesser extent because of many reasons. One of the reasons is the absence of innovation-promoting tools and techniques in the conventional framework of quality circles. Hence it becomes necessary to bring out a model that would integrate both innovation management and quality circle concepts that would be acceptable to the practicing managers. The research work described in this paper has attempted to overcome this research and practice gap. For this purpose, Innovative QC was designed and test implemented in GFT, which is a software developing company. Generally, in the software developing company, quality of the products is maintained or quality is assured in life cycle approach with the help stages mentioned in Software Development Life Cycle (SDLC). The outcome of Innovative QC

* Sr. Quality Associate, GFT Technologies (India) Pvt. Ltd, Trichy, India.
** Professor, Department of Production Engineering, PSG College of Technology, Coimbatore.
*** Research Scholar, Department of Mechanical Engineering, PSG College of Technology, Coimbatore.

implementation was presented to the top management personnel of GFT. Subsequently, feedback of the competent personnel was gathered. These feedbacks indicated the possibility of successfully applying Innovative QC in software companies and its quality can be assured by involving the stages of SDLC.

INTRODUCTION

One of the facets of total quality management (TQM) philosophy is to achieve continuous quality improvement through total employee participation (Hill, 1997; Sumukadas, 2006). Numerous researches have established that total employee participation leads to continuous improvement (Bhuiyan and Baghel, 2005). Time and again, several models for effecting 'total employee participation' have emanated in literature (Dimitriades, 2000; Dale et al, 2001). Despite the emergence of many models (Hill, 1997), the quality circle programme (QCP) which emanated in Japan during early 1960s (Goh, 2000) had been a commonly used technique for effecting employee participation (Markey et al., 2002). In this context, QCP is viewed as a powerful vehicle using which opportunities are created for participation of employees in the TQM journey of an organization (Randeniya et al., 1995; Forster et al., 2000). An unique aspect of QCP is that it encompasses systematic problem solving methods (Hill, 1997). There are a number of reports in literature which establish the contribution of QCP through its systematic problem solving approach in attaining higher degree of quality.

Today's competitive world is expecting innovation in products, processes and services rather than just solving the problems (Martensen and Dahlgaard, 1999a, 1999b; Denton, 1999; Drejer, 2002; Massa and Testa, 2004; Ehigie and McAndrew, 2005). In fact, along with quality, innovation is considered as competitive weapon (Ehigie and McAndrew, 2005). The traditional QCP does not meet this requirement. Since the QCP is found to be acceptable to both management and employees (Coates, 1988), its existing framework shall be improved to make it to offer innovative solutions. In this background, during the research being reported here, the basic theories of innovation management (IM) principles have been infused with the QCP to design a model called innovative QC. This model was subjected to implementation study in an Indian software developing company by name GFT Technologies (India) Pvt. Ltd. The details of pursuing this research are presented in this paper.

INNOVATION MANAGEMENT (IM)

This research began by gathering literature covering three fields namely IM, TQM and Quality Circles. Then these literatures were reviewed to establish the linkage of IM with TQM and Quality circles. The findings of the literature review are presented in this chapter.

According to the Chambers Twentieth Century Dictionary 'innovative' means

- to introduce something new;
- to introduce novelties;
- to make changes.

Main categories of innovation are as follows (Kanji,1996)

- *Product innovation:* improvement or development of new products, e.g. the first fully automatic washing machine by Hitachi 1961.
- *Process innovation:* improvement in the process for product manufacturing, e.g. reduction in cycle time or reduction in the number of process steps.
- *Application innovation:* the application of existing or new ideas or the development of new methods of new design concepts, e.g. fuzzy logic based pattern recognition, fuzzy logic control of automatic washing machines.
- *System innovation:* a new system to integrate a variety of subsystems, involving product, process and application innovations, e.g. in a system the electrical subsystem, the control subsystem and the computer subsystem were combined to construct a new integrated electrical (control) computer system.
- *Core competence innovation:* design, fabrication testing and manufacturing innovation needed to achieve competence innovation, e.g. the development of micro-controllers for use in manufacturing industries, electrical appliances, information processing, automobiles, etc.
- *Horizontal transfer innovation:* achieved by introducing various innovations in application areas, using horizontal transfer to core competence.

Idea Generating Tools

The heart of IM rests on idea-generating tools. The idea-generation tools (Smith and Ainsworth,1993) illustrate various processes to generate ideas. These techniques are used not only for idea-generation but also for opportunity generation.

The processes used for idea generation are:

- Slip/card writing
- Brainstorming (and variations)
- Semantic processes (idea stretch and idea growth matrices)
- Excursion techniques

Slip/Card Writing

Slip writing is used for collecting a large number of ideas in just a few minutes. No one knows who offered each idea. In slip writing, a pile of ideas can be produced in a form that allows fast sorting into categories for action planning. Everyone at a meeting is given a pad of paper or cards. The problem statement in 'how to' form is presented by the teacher. The importance of holding back judgments is explained by the teacher and each person is asked to write down as many answers to the question as the time period allows. A separate slip or card is used to answer each question. After the explanation has been made, the time allotted for the task need only be 4 or 5 minutes.

Each person must be provided with a pad of slips and a specific method must be prepared for collecting the slips. Boxes or cartons placed at strategic points can be used as idea banks. The participants should write each idea on a separate slip.

The basic rules are:

- The 'how to' problem must be kept as specific as possible.
- Keep the pace up

Slip writing method need not be limited to 'how to' questions.

Variations of slip card writing include the transfer of slips from one person to another.

Brainstorming

Brainstorming is a generic term used to describe any sort of meeting in which individuals are encouraged to offer ideas on a particular situation. In other words, everyone's ideas will be heard and recorded.

Brainstorming sessions seem to work probably to some degree because:

- All ideas are recognized with receptiveness and are provided reinforcement.
- The idea generation is increased because of the stimulating effect of people voicing ideas in groups increases.
- Basic rules for brainstorming:
- Brainstorming session has no part for evaluation
- Brainstorming encourages quantity without reference to quality.
- Brainstorming session looks for combinations and linking of ideas and improvements.
- The ideas offered are recorded without censoring

Variations to Brainstorming:

- In this technique, the discussion is started by the leader with some of the concepts basic to or closely associated with the discussion. The discussion is stimulated by the leader and the true situation is revealed when the group is close to a satisfactory solution.
- *Cascade sessions:* One of the ideas so far generated is given to each group, and asked to write new ideas silently triggered by the one being given. After three minutes, each person is asked to hand over his pad to his neighbour, who uses these top of the page ideas as triggers to generate some more new ideas.
- *Catalogue technique:* The source for ideas used is a commercial catalogue such as telephone book or yellow pages. In turn, these may suggest more ideas, or trigger new approaches.

Semantic Processes

This method makes use of idea stretch matrix and idea growth matrix. These 'matrices' are called as opposed to 'checklists' since they can be used in groups and individuals' reactions can be recorded in the available spaces. The gap in the matrix can be contributed by anyone and not all the gaps are to be filled. The idea growth and idea stretch matrices can be used in pairs before involving the entire group is a useful process and the pairs seem to force each other to provide answers.

Both the idea growth and idea stretch matrices are simple. The question series have produced some novel ideas and the following illustrates such a novel idea. Self-drawing curtains: At the end of the curtain rod, a special self-recoiling unit is provided which withdraws the curtains when they are pulled slightly. This was a response to the question 'where else can I use it' for a group investigating retractable electric power leads.

Excursion Techniques: When the satisfactory results cannot be achieved with the normal processes of idea building one or another form of excursion from the problem may be developed. An excursion is used to stimulate divergent thinking, which is hard to do when we are concentrating on the point where we are stuck.

Excursion techniques are not difficult to use. Excursion techniques can be used with new product development and with problems in marketing, administration, cost-reduction, personnel, etc.

TOTAL QUALITY MANAGEMENT (TQM)

TQM is about continuous performance improvement of individuals, groups and organizations. What differentiates TQM from other management processes is the emphasis on continuous improvement. Total quality is not a quick fix, it is about changing the way things are done-forever.

Seen in this way, TQM is about continuous performance improvement. To improve performance, people need to know what to do and how to do it, to have the right tools to do it, to be able to measure performance and to receive feedback on current levels of achievement. TQM provides this (see Kanji & Asher, 1993) by adhering to a set of general governing principles. They are:

- Delight the customer;
- Management by fact;
- People-based management;
- Continuous improvement.

Each of the principles can be used to drive the improvement process. To achieve, this each principle is translated into practice using core concepts, which show how to make the principle happen. These concepts are:

- Customer satisfaction
- Internal customers are real
- All work is a process
- Measurement
- Teamwork
- People make quality
- Continuous improvement cycle
- Prevention.

Elements of TQM

Following are the elements of TQM:

- Top management commitment and involvement.
- Customer involvement - Quality Function Deployment (QFD).
- Design products for quality.
- Design production processes for quality.
- Control production processes for quality - PCI.
- Develop supplier partnerships.
- Customer service, distribution and installation.
- Building teams of empowered employees - Quality Circle.
- Benchmarking and continuous improvement.

QUALITY CIRCLE

Quality Circle is one of the employee participation methods. It implies the development of skills, capabilities, confidence and creativity of the people through cumulative process of education, training, work experience and participation. It also implies the creation of facilitative conditions and environment of work, which creates and sustains their motivation and commitment towards work excellence. Quality Circles have emerged as a mechanism to develop and utilize the tremendous potential of people for improvement in product quality and productivity.

Quality Circle is a small group of 6 to 12 employees doing similar work who voluntarily meet together on a regular basis to identify improvements in their respective work areas using proven techniques for analysing and solving work-related problems coming in the way of achieving and sustaining excellence leading to mutual upliftment of employees as well as the organisation. It is "a way of capturing the creative and innovative power that lies within the work force".

Quality Circle is a people - building philosophy, providing self-motivation and happiness in improving environment without any compulsion or monetary benefits. It represents a philosophy of managing people specially those at the grassroots level as well as a clearly defined mechanism and methodology for translating this philosophy into practice and a required structure to make it a way of life. It is bound to succeed where people are respected and are involved in decisions, concerning their work life, and in environments where peoples' capabilities are looked upon as assets to solve work-area problems.

The Quality Circle philosophy calls for a progressive attitude on the part of the management and their willingness to make adjustments, if necessary, in their style and culture. If workers are prepared to contribute their ideas, the management must be willing to create a congenial environment to encourage them to do so.

The concept of Quality Circle is primarily based upon recognition of the value of the worker as a human being, as someone who willingly activises on his job, his wisdom, intelligence, experience, attitude and feelings. It is based upon the human resource management considered as one of the key factors in the improvement of product quality and productivity. Quality Circle concept has the following three major attributes:

a. Quality Circle is a form of participation management.

b. Quality Circle is a human resource development technique.

c. Quality Circle is a problem solving technique

Following are the characteristics of Quality Circles:

1. *Change in Attitude:* From "I don't care" to "I do care". Continuous improvement in quality of work life through humanisation of work.

2. *Self Development:* Bring out 'Hidden Potential' of people. People get to learn additional skills.

3. *Development of Team Spirit:* Individual vs Team - "I could not do but we did it". Eliminate inter departmental conflicts.

4. *Improved Organisational Culture:* Positive working environment. Total involvement of people at all levels. Higher motivational level. Participate management process.

LINKAGE BETWEEN TQM AND IM

The main purpose of both TQM and innovation is to delight the customers with the help of continuous improvement', which can be achieved either by an evolutionary or revolutionary process using TQM principles. The linkage between innovation and TQM can be where each type of innovation goes through the TQM process for successful innovation. If we accept that successful innovation depends on the TQM process, then the continuous improvement strategy of TQM and innovation will open the door for organizations to develop their management understanding for future growth and competitiveness.

In reality, to develop innovative work, one must deal with the various characteristics of innovation. For example, to deal with the problems of rapid technological obsolescence, one must adopt new competencies as well as new products. In order to reduce the concept-to market cycle time and provide wider opportunities, organizations must adopt strategic alliances. Further, for globalization of design, research, production and marketing, organizations must develop an integrated management process. Here, design competence is one of the most critical aspects of creating and sustaining competitiveness, which is a common goal for both TQM and innovation. The crucial link between innovation and TQM is therefore the long-term and short-term quality strategies, which integrate the action of today with the vision of tomorrow.

To understand the linkage between TQM and innovation, one must also consider the horizontal transfer innovation. In general, horizontal transfer of innovation provides an opportunity to integrate technology and market information. This information exchange helps shop floor workers to develop rapid problem-solving skills through quality circle and kaizen (i.e. TQM method and principles) techniques, which in turn help the organization to manage its business successfully.

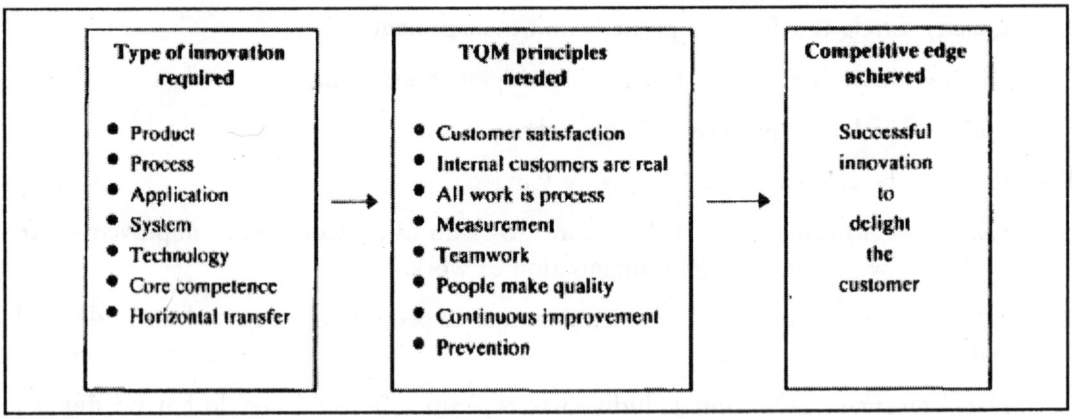

QUALITY ASSURANCE IN SOFTWARE

Quality assurance (QA) is the activity of providing evidence needed to establish quality in work, and that activities that require good quality are being performed effectively. All those planned or systematic actions necessary to provide enough confidence that a product or service will satisfy the given requirements for quality.

For products, quality assurance is a part and consistent pair of quality management offering supposedly fact-based external confidence to customers and other stakeholders that a product meets needs, expectations, and other requirements. QA claims to assure the existence and effectiveness of procedures that attempt to make sure - in advance - that the expected levels of quality will be reached.

QA covers all activities from design, development, production, installation, servicing to documentation. It introduced the sayings "fit for purpose" and "do it right the first time". It includes the regulation of the quality of raw materials, assemblies, products and components; services related to production; and management, production, and inspection processes.

Software Development Life Cycle (SDLC)

The SDLC is a conceptual model used in project management that describes the stages involved in an information system development project, from an initial feasibility study through maintenance of the completed application. Various SDLC methodologies have been developed to guide the processes involved, including the waterfall model (which was the original SDLC method); rapid application development (RAD); joint application development (JAD); the fountain model; the spiral model; build and fix; and synchronize-and-stabilize. Frequently, several models are combined into some sort of hybrid methodology. Documentation is crucial regardless of the type of model chosen or devised for any application, and is usually done in parallel with the development process. Some methods work better for specific types of projects, but in the final analysis, the most important factor for the success of a project may be how closely the particular plan was followed.

In general, an SDLC methodology follows the following steps:

- The existing system is evaluated. Deficiencies are identified. This can be done by interviewing users of the system and consulting with support personnel.
- The new system requirements are defined. In particular, the deficiencies in the existing system must be addressed with specific proposals for improvement.
- The proposed system is designed. Plans are laid out concerning the physical construction, hardware, operating systems, programming, communications, and security issues.
- The new system is developed. The new components and programs must be obtained and installed. Users of the system must be trained in its use, and all aspects of performance must be tested. If necessary, adjustments must be made at this stage.
- The system is put into use. This can be done in various ways. The new system can phased in, according to application or location, and the old system gradually replaced. In some cases, it may be more cost-effective to shut down the old system and implement the new system all at once.
- Once the new system is up and running for a while, it should be exhaustively evaluated. Maintenance must be kept up rigorously at all times. Users of the system should be kept up-to-date concerning the latest modifications and procedures.

DESIGN OF INNOVATIVE QC

The research being reported was begun by designing Innovative QC. For this purpose, the principles of both traditional QCP and IM were studied. These principles were carefully linked to meet strategic requirement. This work progressed through three stages. First, the Innovative QC was defined. Followed by that, its organizational structure was developed and the power and authorities of the personnel were defined. Finally, the methodology of running Innovative QC was developed. The details of the work carried out during these stages are briefly described in the following three subsections.

Defining Innovative QC

The beginning of designing Innovative QC was marked by formulating the following definition: "Innovative QC is a small group of employees from the same work area who meet for an hour each week to identify not only solutions to the problems but also innovations using idea generation techniques and make recommendations to the management". This definition has been coined by referring to the conventional definition of quality circle (Tang et al, 1993; Goulden, 1995; Millson and Kirk-Smith, 1996; Ehigie and McAndrew, 2005) and integrating it with the core principles of IM (Smith and Ainsworth, 1993). As envisaged in this definition, the members of Innovative QC shall be required to orient towards creating innovations. For this purpose, the Innovative QC members shall be exposed to idea generation techniques and innovation principles.

Organizational Structure

Organizational structure of the Innovative QC has been designed by linking that of the QC (Udpa, 1990) with IM principles (Smith and Ainsworth, 1993). The hierarchy of innovative QC organizational structure is depicted in below Figure 1. The authority and responsibilities of the personnel in Innovative QC organization are enumerated in the following subsections.

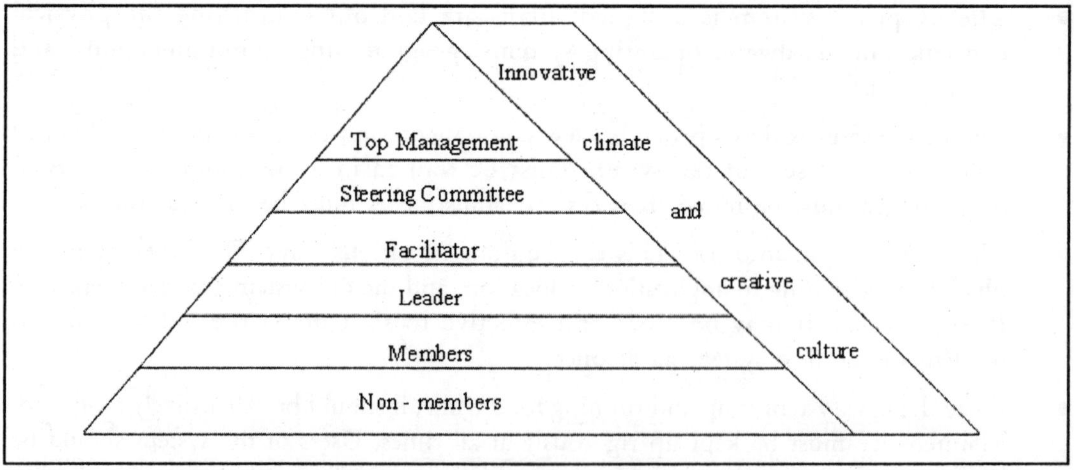

Figure 1: Innovative QC organizational structure

Top management: Top management is committed to provide necessary resources and environment, conducive for continuously evolving innovation and improving quality by generating ideas and stimulating creativity among the members. For this purpose, the top management shall address the employees and indicate the evidence of accepting innovative continuous quality improvement ideas which emerge from Innovative QC members.

Steering committee

Steering committee is composed of senior management personnel such as heads of departments and other senior functionaries employed in the administrative department. Responsibility of this committee is to provide necessary guidelines for bringing out innovative climate and continuous quality improvement culture throughout the organization and to bring out ideas from the members and inculcate creativity among them. The steering committee shall take up the responsibility of popularizing techniques facilitating innovative continuous quality improvement techniques. The steering committee shall prepare a manual and magazine which would provide guidelines and appreciate the Innovative QC members for their contributions towards innovative continuous quality improvement.

Facilitator

Facilitator plays a foundational role in an Innovative QC. He shall be a senior officer of the department. Three to four Innovative QCs shall function under one facilitator. The management nominates him/her. His/her responsibility is to act as a bridge between the management and members and identify the training needs of the members on new idea generation techniques and creativity that would lead to innovative continuous quality improvement. He/she is required to evaluate the innovative idea on the basis of the factors that would lead to continuous quality improvement and the weighting factors recommended by the management.

Leader

A leader is a member of the Innovative QC who has the basic responsibility of convening the weekly or fortnightly meetings. The leader shall possess the aptitude and attitude towards innovative continuous quality improvement. Besides, while conducting the meetings, he/she is required to make sure that all members in the Innovative QC get equal opportunity to take part in discussions. He/she is also required to identify the triggers that are required to generate creativity and innovative ideas among the members that would lead to continuous quality improvement.

Members

Members are the basic elements of the organizational structure of Innovative QCs. Employees working in the same work area or engaged in similar type of work shall voluntarily become members of Innovative QCs and participate to evolve innovations infused continuous quality improvement solutions. Members shall be exposed to both innovation and continuous quality improvement tools and techniques by conducting both educational and training programmes. Such programmes shall be so interesting that it shall facilitate the members to acquire, aptitude for creativity and bringing out innovations that contribute towards the attainment of continuous quality improvement strategies.

Non-members

While conducting the proceedings of Innovative QCs, situations may arise to seek the help of experts to evolve innovations infused continuous quality improvement solutions. In those situations, such kind of personnel may be invited to become non-members. Those non-members shall have exhibited their capabilities in bringing out innovation infused continuous quality improvement solutions. They will be associated with the Innovative QCs only when their contributions are solicited.

Operational Features of Innovative QCs

The steps to be followed to operate Innovative QCs have been designed by adopting the problem solving procedure followed in traditional QCs and linking them with IM principles. The operational features of innovative QCs are depicted in Figure 2.

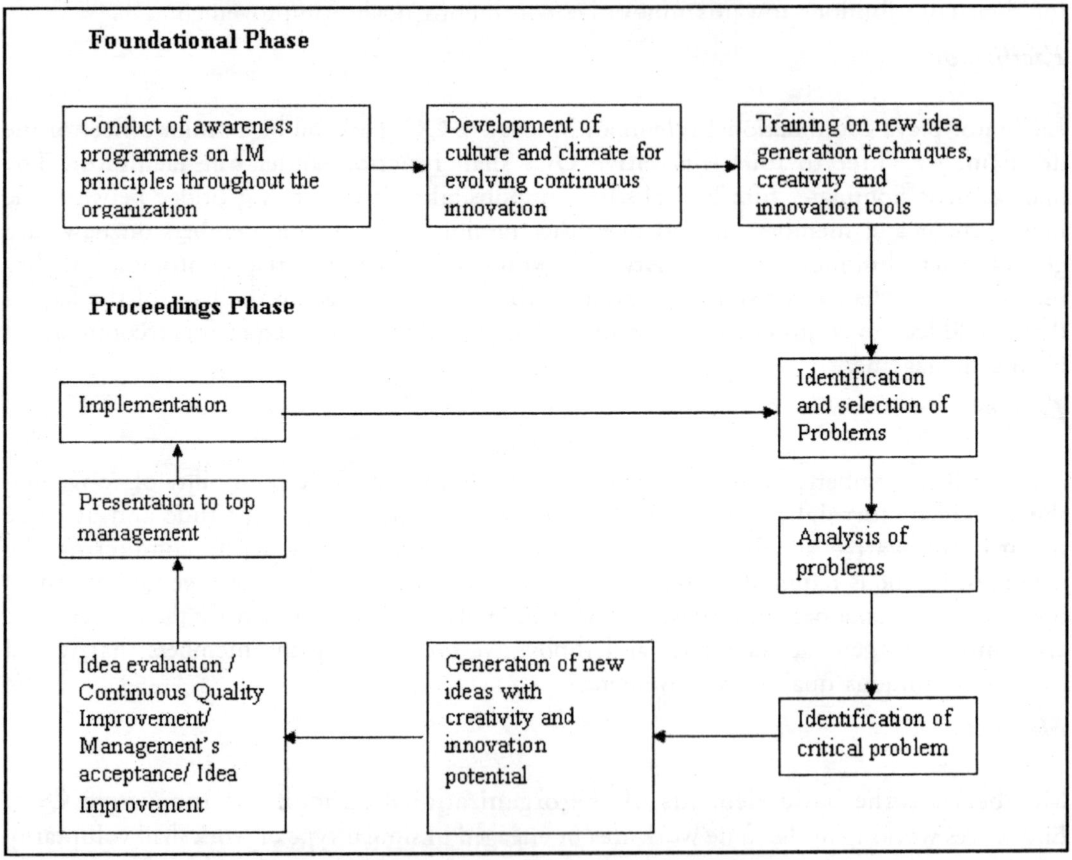

Figure 2: Operational features of Innovative QCs

As shown, the operation of Innovative QC shall pass through two phases. Those phases are named as 'foundational phase' and 'proceedings phase'. The activities to be carried out under these phases are briefly described in the following two sub-sections.

Foundational phase

As shown in Figure 1, the foundational phase shall pass through three stages. These stages shall be carried out only once and shall not be repeated since they are the foundational elements of Innovative QC. However, these foundational elements have to be sustained for a prolonged period of time. Even though these activities are carried out only once in an organization, their importance cannot be underestimated since they play the ultimate role in ensuring the success of Innovative QC.

During the beginning of foundational phase, the management must promote IM awareness programmes throughout the organization over a period of one to two years. During the conduct of these programmes, the management must commit its interest in receiving innovations which would arise from all personnel and other sources of the organization. The success stories of companies, which have adopted innovations, may also be deliberated during the conduct of these programmes. Followed by this, the management shall develop a culture and climate for evolving innovations in a continual manner. During this stage, the management shall introduce rewards and promotional schemes based upon the innovations evolved by the individual employees or groups (Davis and Moe, 1997; Martins and Terblanche, 2003). The management shall also publish the contributions of those innovative employees by releasing newsletters and special circulars. In order to systematically develop an innovative culture and climate in a sustained manner, scientific efforts are required to be exerted. For this purpose, employees shall be trained in the idea generation techniques and creativity and innovation tools such as slip/card writing, brainstorming, semantic processes etc (Smith and Ainsworth, 1993; Roffe, 1999).

Proceedings phase

After the completion of the foundational phase, the proceedings phase of Innovative QC shall be started. Unlike the foundational phase, the activities of proceedings phase are to be cyclic. In other words, the proceedings phase shall be on a continual basis and subjected to continuous improvement. As shown in the figure, one cycle of proceedings phase has to pass through seven stages. The first stage begins with the identification and selection of problems. In the case of Innovative QC, the problem to be identified and selected shall not be restricted to those that cause disturbances such as production stoppage and increased rejection rate. Rather, the problems in Innovative QC shall be identified and selected based on the higher benchmarks than the existing.

During the second stage, the importance of the problems shall be analyzed by referring to the various factors, which will include the market condition and the company's performance status. During the third stage, appropriate ranking method shall be followed to identify the critical problems. During the fourth stage, idea generation techniques shall be deployed to generate new ideas with innovation potential. During the fifth stage, those ideas shall be evaluated from the point of view of their contribution in continuous quality improvement journey and willingness of the management to accept them. If found necessary, ideas shall be modified to improve their effectiveness. During the sixth stage, the consolidated form of the above ideas shall be presented to the management. During the seventh stage, approval from the management shall be obtained and the above new ideas generated by conducting Innovative QC shall be implemented. This stage marks an important tenet of IM, as innovation calls for successful implementation of new ideas, which leads to the development of new solutions for succeeding in the market place (Cumming, 1998).

IMPLEMENTATION STUDY

The implementation features of innovative quality circle principles were studied at GFT. GFT is one of the leading technology companies for integrated e-Business Solutions in Europe. As a partner of established and long-term clients, they implement intelligent business models and innovative Information Technology (IT) solutions - from Design to Application Management - that are based on most advanced technologies.

Launched over 15 years ago, as a technology pioneer with innovative product solutions, their extensive portfolio of products and services today covers the entire digital value chain. Over 1,000 highly qualified business and IT specialists at 21 locations around Europe and in India, develop IT solutions for their clients specially turned for the challenges they face. Be it to initiate innovative business models, to conceptualize complex IT architectures or to implement advanced technologies, we can rely on the competence and project experience of one of Europe's most experienced IT and web service providers.

Specialists in technology, business, strategy and design are the core of their competence. Unique personalities with varying areas of expertise and from different cultures colour their identity, their style, and the way the work.

The Indian Office was established in December 2000 with the aim of providing software product development, support and project services, GFT India, the former E-quadriga Software Private Limited was taken over by GFT Technologies A.G. as 100% subsidiary in October 2003. Based in the southern Indian city of, Trichy, the company has highly qualified staff members with special expertise in the field modern Internet technologies. In the past three years, Indian software developers have programmed e-learning products for the Klett publishing house, Germany's leading provider of teaching material for schools science and education in Germany.

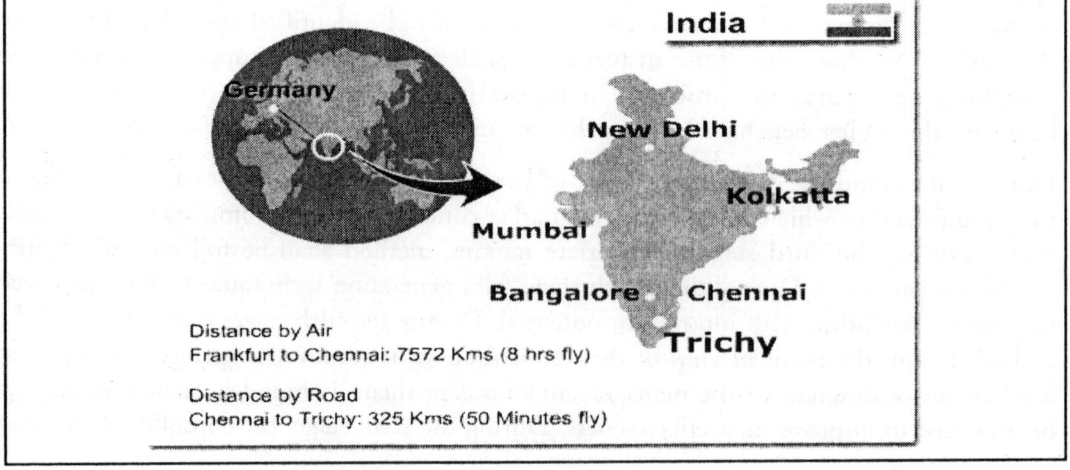

In addition to the onsite - and near share units of GFT Europe in Spain and Hungary, GFT India is a strategically important element of the integrated GFT production network. In mixed teams with the European staff, they focus on offshore application development and application management. GFTs perform interactive projects combined with local proximity through front ends in Europe.

GFT India is supported by the following foundation stones:

1. Strong German front end.
2. Working with German clients for past 7+ years.
3. Competence in latest technologies.
4. Intercultural training imparted to all employees.
5. People who can converse in German.
6. Qualified architects, graphic designers, developers and testers.

The organisational structure is depicted in Figure 3.

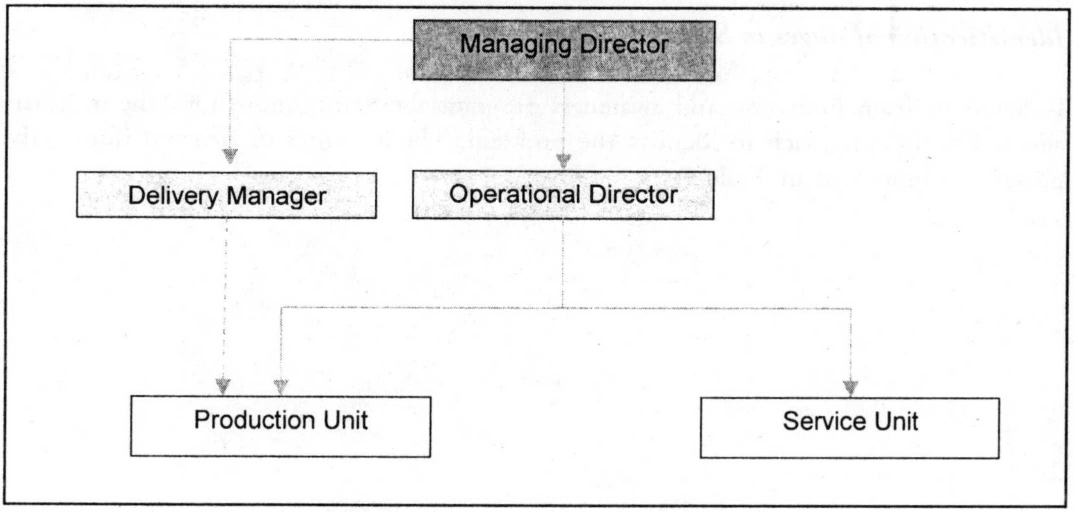

Figure 3: Organisation structure of GFT

Generally when we split the organization structure, there are mainly five sectors\departments in GFT. Administration, Finance, Development, Testing (Quality Control), Networking.

The administration department consists of top level personnel and human resource management, finance department works with numbers and budget, networking department has to set up hardware and software. Personnel in these departments works indirectly for software production and development.

The personnel from the development and training department are directly involved in softwares development. Therefore, personnel from testing and development department will play an important role in the implementation study.

Initial Work

As the first stage, personnel from all five departments were called to attend the awareness programme. But due to the tight schedule of their individual work, this did not happen. Since the personnel in the development and testing are directly involved software development, the innovative quality circle was formed with members from testing and development. These personnel were explained the important phases of IM. During this phase, these members came to know about the method of generating innovative solutions. Three sessions on awareness were carried out. During this awareness program testing department members participated enthusiastically. Due to huge work pressure, attendance of development department personnel was less. Also, during the first presentation session it was found that personnel had mental blocks and their views were not wide open. This is due to the reason that, GFT being a software development company the term "Innovative QC" was totally new to them. Personnel from development struggled over it. Since the testing department have a meeting called QA formal weekly once, this concept was accepted by them. At the end of third session, this concept was almost accepted by personnel from development department too. It was conducted with power point presentation.

Identification of stages in SDLC

Followed by team formation and awareness program about Innovative QC, the members adopted SDLC approach to identify the problem. The activities carried out during the phase are enumerated in Table 1.

Table 1: Activities carried out during SDLC

Phase Number	Phases in SDLC	Description
1	Curtain Raiser	Products should be user-friendly, They should have place in the market although they are engineered using the best and recent technologies.
2	Market Research	Assumptions should be realistic and can cause a nosedive in the entire venture.
3	Research and Development	The R&D group making possible value additions in the product.
4	System/ Information Engineering and Modelling	As software is always of a large system (or business), work begins by establishing requirements for all system elements and then allocating some subset of these requirements to software.
5	Software Requirement Analysis	This is also known as feasibility study. In this phase, the development team visits the customer and studies their system. To understand the nature of the program(s) to be built, the system engineer ("analyst") must understand the information domain for the software, as well as required function, behaviour, performance and interfacing.
6	System Analysis and Design	The software's overall structure and its nuances are defined. In terms of the client/server technology, the number of tiers needed for the package architecture, the database design, the data structure design etc are all defined in this phase.
7	Code Generation	The design must be translated into a machine-readable form. The code generation step performs this task. If the design is performed in a detailed manner, code generation can be accomplished without much complication.
8	Testing	Once the code is generated, the software program testing begins. Different testing methodologies are available to unravel the bugs that were committed during the previous phases. Different testing tools and methodologies are already available.
9	Maintenance	Software will definitely undergo change once it is delivered to the customer. There are many reasons for the change. Change could happen because of some unexpected input values into the system.

Selection of Problems

After the completion of SDLC phases, as the third phase two brainstorming sessions were conducted to identify and to select the problems. These proceedings of this session are enumerated in Table 2.

Table 2: Problems identified by conducting brainstorming sessions

Serial Number	Phases in SDLC	Problems
1	Curtain Raiser	Product identified not user friendly
		The roles and responsibilities should be defined
		Risk and mitigation
		Budget, release and communication plan
		Resource identification (hardware and software (CM) human)
2	Market Research	Lack of comparison skills with existing competitive products
		Unrealistic assumptions
		Lack of knowledge about the product for market survey
3	Research and Development	No value additions from the personals
		Lack of technological support
		Misunderstanding of the customers requirement
4	System/ Information Engineering and Modelling	Requirements are not clear/or no requirements
5	Software Requirement Analysis	Feasibility study is not done
6	System Analysis and Design	Architecture is not perfect
		Design is not scalable (future enhancement and performance)
		No review for design (requirement missing, mismatch)
		Security should be handled
		Ambiguous design (B4 and after this phase)
		Framework should be perfect and correct
7	Code Generation	Selection of compilers, interpreters, and debuggers is not up to mark
		No documentation
		No standards
		No unit tests
		No code review
		Inefficient coding
8	Testing	Version to testing environment is not in time.
		Duration for testing life cycle is less.
		Frequent change request – particularly at the end of phase
		Unavailability of hardware/software resources
		Test plan not according to scenario – not intelligent
		Ineffective Test Case
		QC team does not have control over release of version – to test team and to customers
		QC was forced to test the version in short duration.
		No documentation of QC activities
		No baseline of requirements
		Poor apprise of organizational process
		No QA activity
		Objective of test cycle not defined

Contd...

		No escalation of process deviation.
		Attitude towards QC team
		Issues not accepted when it is raised by testers
9	Maintenance	Acceptance test should be carried out
		No CR plan
		No impact analysis on CR
		No debugging efficiency

During these two sessions testing department members participated enthusiastically.

Since testing phase of SDLC holds numeral problems, testing phase is base-lined for problem analysis to derive its solution. Two brainstorming sessions were conducted to derive solution. These proceedings of this session are enumerated in Table 3.

Table 3: Proceedings to identify the Solutions

Serial Number	Problems	Solutions
1	Version to testing environment is not in time.	Code freeze should be achieved irrespective of the bugs with respective to the build. Deviation schedule should be escalated.
2	Duration for testing life cycle is less.	Schedule should be planned perfect.
3	Frequent change request – particularly at the end of phase	Impact analysis on CR (resources, schedule, budget..) should be given to customers. This is called change request management.
4	Unavailability of hardware/software resources	Budget should be planned by the management during the project kick off.
5	Test plan not according to scenario – not intelligent	Should be created with PLM, PLT and PL (QC) for effective test plan.
6	Ineffective Test Case	1. Test case should be designed thought freezed requirement and proper use case. 2. Test case review should be done along with domain expert. 3. Experienced testers should write test case.
7	Quality Control team does not have control over release of version – to test team and to customers	1. Based on the recommendations from Quality Control, management should decide on version release. 2. Quality Control team activity has to be independent

Contd...

8	Quality Control was forced to test the version in short duration.	High priority test case should be checked and escalated to customers.
9	No documentation of quality control activities	TL should document all the activates in prior.
10	No baseline of requirements	Both customers and management should sign a contact for base lining.
11	Poor appraisal of organizational process	Process in the Quality Control activity has to be improved with other phases of SDLC
12	No Quality Assurance activity	1. Assessments like CMMI, ISO etc should be performed. 2. There should be Quality Assurance manager.
13	Objective of test cycle not defined	Related to test plan.
14	No escalation of process deviation.	Process should be monitored and should be escalated to team.
15	Attitude towards Quality Control team	Top management should take care.
16	Issues not accepted when it is raised by testers.	Anyhow it should be logged into the bug tracking system.

The problem occurred and the solution derived during the brainstorming session in the testing SDLC phase is projected to the top management. Also, to check the understanding and interest of quality circle member, feedbacks were sought. The feedbacks were listed below.

Feedback

After the conduct of innovative QC by including SDLC approach, the feedbacks on its outcome were gathered from the competent personnel of GFT. The feedback expressed by them in their own words are presented in the following two sections.

Feedback from Innovative Quality Circle member

Feedback from Balasundaram V, Sr. Quality Associate (& Sr. Quality Circle Member), GFT Technologies (India) Private Limited is as follows:

Feedback about awareness programme in TQM and innovation management

Awareness programme on TQM and innovation management is informative.

Awareness programme helped us to improve the quality of the product.

Structure and innovative process models were identified during the programme.

Knowledge gained on TQM innovation management

The objective of TQM is to eliminate the product defect completely. Defect occurs at every phase. It should be identified and eliminated in the same phase itself.

It is a structured approach to an organization that seeks to improve the quality of product and services through refinements in response to continuous feedback. It is a continuous process. The feedback of the every phase is reviewed and fixed in the successive phases.

TQM is based on quality management from the customer's point of view. Satisfying customer's need is the main aim of TQM.

TQM processes are divided into four sequential categories: plan, do, check, and act (the PDCA cycle).

About current organisation structure

In the current organization structure, the activities are done based on current requirements and needs. It should be structured, organized and planned.

Possibility to restructure the current organization, structure to innovative quality circle

Planning to create a quality circle team in the organization.

Quality circle is a volunteer group composed of employees.

This team meets at regular intervals to consider the problems related to the quality outputs of a process and to make correction of such problems or to the improvement of increase quality.

About brainstorming session

During brainstorming session problems are discussed during meeting. For each problem more than one solution are recorded. Among the solutions, optimum solution is identified and given for implementation.

Exchange of ideas between the participants strengthens the team co ordination. Knowledge is shared among the team members.

Conclusion

With the implementation of TQM process, the company can increase the satisfaction level of customers. These processes lessen the overall time and cost.

Feedback from top management

Feedback from Leo Ananth J, Operational Director, GFT Technologies (India) Private Limited is as follows:

This work has created awareness among the employees regarding TQM and Quality Circle and about the benefits they could bring to our organization. This has also pointed out the areas which could be improved.

The management will take necessary steps to improve the current state and do the needful to get maximum benefit. We will arrange for regular periodic meetings for members of the

Quality Circle to exchange ideas and discuss problems faced during their regular work.

All necessary facilities will be provided to improve the teams' knowledge on these areas. If required, an external consultant will be hired for training and consultancy.

The current team size can also be increased, based on the work load and planned activities. R&D and innovation has to form an integral part of the team and no compromise will be made on these areas.

A knowledge bank and component repository will be created to ensure efficient reuse of skills and technology. Every process in unsuccessful and successful projects will be documented and studied to see areas which could have been handled in a better manner.

The current SDLC cycle followed in the company is based on the requirements of the parent company and the necessity that the offshore unit in India was primarily created to cater to the needs of internal projects and support the onsite units in R&D and presales activities. However, the quality circle has to be ensure the quality, of not only the end product, but should begin from scope document itself.

Radical changes in organization structure or processes are not needed to improve the current state of the organization. Investments are also not necessary. All that is required is that every member understands the project expectations and gives his best for the overall interest of his team and his project. Everyone should be accountable for his actions and take responsibility for their deeds.

Everyone in the quality circle should be aware of the latest tools and techniques and be well versed in their respective domains, be it be quality planning, quality assurance or quality control. Environment and organization factors should also be taken into consideration.

I am happy that this project work was a first step to meet the management's expectations from the quality circle.

Indication Discernable From the Feedback

The feedback given by the competent personnel of GFT indicates that innovative QCs can be implemented in software companies with high success rate.

CONCLUSION

Till the 1980s, management professionals were devoting their expertise and time on implementing TQM. During this time, this practice was highly appreciated in companies. At one point of time, companies of all types were implementing TQM in different forms. However, this condition began to change from the 1990s. From this period, customers began to expect companies to go beyond ensuring quality of their products. One among those additional expectations is the innovation infused products. As a consequence of this trend, some researchers have worked on linking TQM with IM field. However, there had been very little work carried out on linking IM with QC concepts. The research reported in this paper has attempted to overcome this research and practice gap. For this purpose,

Innovative QC was designed and test implemented in GFT, which is a software developing company. The outcome of Innovative QC implementation was presented to the top management personnel of GFT. Subsequently, feedback of the competent personnel was gathered. This feedback indicated the possibility of successful applying Innovative QC in software companies; quality of the products is maintained or is assured in the life cycle approach with the help stages mentioned in SDLC.

Limitation and direction for future research

The Innovative QC model had to be reoriented to suit its application to GFT. Since GFT is a software company, this reorientation may not work well in other types of companies, to indicate the exhaustive validity of Innovative QC. Hence, in future, researchers may apply Innovative QCs in different companies and study those implementation experiences. This kind of researches may lead to the development of several models, which would be used by different types of companies to evolve innovation with quality in the solutions they offer to the customers. This will help those companies to acquire core competencies and thereby, quality can be assured and the firm can compete in the market.

REFERENCES

Bhuiyan, N. and Baghel, A. 'An overview of continuous improvement: from the past to the present', *Management Decision*, Vol. 43, No. 5, pp.761 – 771 (2005).

Dimitriades, Z.S. 'Total involvement in quality management', *Team Performance Management: An International Journal*, Vol. 6, No. 7/8, pp.117 (2000).

Cumming, B.S. 'Innovation overview and future challenges', *European Journal of Innovation Management*, Vol. 1, No. 1, pp.21 – 29 (1998).

Dale, B.G., Elkjaer, M.B.F., van der Wiele, A. and Williams, A.R.T. 'Fad, fashion and fit: An examination of quality circles, business process re-engineering and statistical process control', *International Journal Production Economics*, Vol. 73, pp.137-152 (2001).

Dimitriades, Z.S. 'Total involvement in quality management', *Team Performance Management: An International Journal*, Vol. 6, No. 7/8, pp.117 – 121 (2000).

Drejer, A 'Situations for innovation management: towards a contingency model', *European Journal of Innovation Management*, Vol. 5, No. 1, pp.4 – 17 (2002).

Ehigie, B.O. and McAndrew, E.B. 'Innovation, diffusion and adoption of total quality management (TQM)', *Management Decision*, Vol. 43, No. 6, pp.925-940 (2005).

Gopal K. Kanji. "Can total quality management help innovation?" *Journal of Total Quality Management*, 3-9 (1996).

Goh, M., 'Quality Circles: Journey of an Asian Public enterprise', *International Journal of Quality & Reliability Management*, Vol. 17, No. 7, pp.784 – 799 (2000).

Goulden, C. 'Supervisory management and quality circle performance: an empirical study', *Benchmarking for Quality Management & Technology*, Vol. 2, No. 4, pp.61-74 (1995).

Hill, F.M. 'Enroute to TQM: Organizational learning through quality circles', *Training for Quality*, Vol. 5, No. 2, pp.84-87 (1997).

Kanji, G . K . & Asher, M . Total quality management process: a systematic approach. *Total Quality Management*, 4, Suppl 1993.

Massa, S. and Testa, S. 'Innovation or imitation? Benchmarking: a knowledge-management process to innovate services', *Benchmarking: An International Journal*, Vol. 11, No. 6, pp.610-620 (2004).

Metaxiotis, K., Psarras, J. and Samouilidis, E. 'Integrating fuzzy logic into decision support systems: current research and future prospects, *Information Management & Computer Security*, Vol. 11, No. 2, pp.53-59 . (2003).

Smith, N.I., and Ainsworth, M. *Managing for innovation*, Viva Books Private Limited, New Delhi 1993.

Sumukadas, N. 'Employee involvement: a hierarchical conceptualisation of its effect on quality', *International Journal of Quality & Reliability Management*, Vol. 23, No. 2, pp.143-161 (2006).

Udpa, S.R. *Quality Circles in India: Participation for progress*, NewDelhi:Tata McGraw Hill, 1990. BMC Software white paper by title "*A Lifecycle Approach to Software Quality – Venturing Beyond the QA Imperative*", May 2006.

11

Social Sensitivity of Management Students - An Empirical study on the Effectiveness of Intervention Programmes

MANOJ MATHEW*
SAM THOMAS**
JAMES T ANTONY***

The current socio-economic scenario in our country calls for the emergence of more and more youngsters in different walks of life with socially and ethically upright values guiding them. Business schools and business education all over India have a great responsibility of moulding young managers with greater social responsibility and appropriate ethical values.

The present study was conducted in a leading business school in Kerala where students from diverse social, economic, political and geographic backgrounds come for their post-graduation in management. During the initial phase of their first semester, the students are exposed to a week long Social Sensitisation Programme in a remote rural area. The main objective of this unique training programme is to transform the future managers into socially sensitive individuals with the capability to creatively address social issues.

The study was designed in two stages: The first stage of assessment identified the level of social sensitivity of students at entry level. This was done at the time of students leaving the campus for the programme. In the second stage of assessment, the level of social sensitivity of the participants was reassessed immediately after the Social Sensitisation Programme. Both these studies were conducted with standardized questionnaires among 132 management students.

The data was analyzed to find out the variation in the level of social sensitivity of the students as a result of the intervention process. The variation in the sensitivity scores of the participants were analyzed in relationship with other relevant demographic variables.

* Lecturer, Rajagiri School of Management, Rajagiri College of Social Sciences, Ernakularm, Kerala.
** Associate Professor, Rajagiri School of Management, Rajagiri College of Social Sciences, Ernakularm, Kerala.
*** Lecturer, Rajagiri School of Management, Rajagiri College of Social Sciences, Ernakularm, Kerala.

This study threw light on the need and possibilities of designing various intervention programmes to improve the social sensitivity of management graduates. Business schools all over India should give more emphasis in their course curriculum to programmes which can positively create an impact on the social outlook of business management students.

INTRODUCTION

Management education in India is going through its most exciting stage of transition as the number of institutes recognised by AICTE is skyrocketing as we reach the first decade of 21st century. Increase in mere numbers is going to be a major cause of apprehension if the authorities concerned do not take appropriate steps in improving the quality, to suit both national and international corporations' requirements.

The impact of business organisations in the socio-politic fabric of the country is often surpassing its impact on the economic environment. Unlike the pre LPG period, where the government had a major say in the socio-economic direction of industrialisation, the post LPG era requires the corporations to be more involved in addressing the concerns of all the stakeholders in their macro economic environment. This is a major shift in the business focus of organisations, and serious efforts are taken by leading business houses like the Tatas, Aditya Birla Group, Infosys, Wipro, ITC etc in promoting their CSR initiatives to reach out to the larger society in their area of operation. It is worth mentioning in this context the work of Prof. C.K.Prahalad highlighting the importance of focusing on the 'Bottom of the Pyramid' to make more business sense in 21st century.

The current emphasis on developing economic models for furthering inclusive capitalism in the country is gaining momentum among political, economic and management thinkers and practitioners. If the country wants to get into the big league of developed nations in the near future, what it requires is a new generation of young and dynamic entrepreneurs and professional managers imbued with the right blend of business and social sensitivity.

The present study was conducted in a leading business school in Kerala where students from diverse social, economic, political and geographic backgrounds come for their post-graduation in management. During the initial phase of their first semester, the students are exposed to a week long social sensitisation programme in a remote rural area. The main objective of this unique training programme is to transform the future managers into socially sensitive individuals with capability to creatively address social issues.

The study was designed in two stages: The first stage of assessment identified their level of social sensitivity. This was done before the programme. In the second stage of assessment, the level of social sensitivity of the participants was reassessed immediately after the Social Sensitisation Programme. Both these studies were conducted with standardized questionnaires among 132 management students.

The data was analyzed to find out the variation in the level of social sensitivity of the students as a result of the intervention process. The variation in the sensitivity scores of the participants were also analyzed in relationship with other relevant demographic variables.

RATIONALE FOR THE STUDY

In the recent era, many management schools believe and proclaim diversity as an integral part of their curriculum. Diversities within the curriculum can be measured by the sheer number of courses and it is a component or central focus. At the first glance, it appears in the curriculum as an academic strategy. But, it has coupled with an additional curricular approach that frames students to explore social sensitization before they graduate. Historically, the issues of intercultural explorations, ethical implications of knowledge and action, and social sensitivity are dealt only at the realm of sociology and social work. As an alternative of the more typical formal requirements for graduation, a few management schools have identified social sensitization as an integral part of their curriculum. These business schools attach their students to well established NGOs all over the country for a period ranging from couple of days to a month. The main objective is to sensitise students to social reality along with a hands on experience to managing the operational issues of running an NGO. These initiatives should enable the students to understand real life situations and help them to empathize with the marginalized people in the society. By exposing students to social sensitivity, it helps the students to see, "the powers and limits of each field." By providing curricular space for students to explore their own culture and compare it with at another culture will acquire a deeper understanding of how "thoughts and actions are influenced by culture and history."

An exposure to social reality through a formalized environment will always have its limitations in terms of developing the competencies required for a socially sensitive manager in a high context culture like India. Issues like personal adjustments in diverse groups, effective functioning in an acute situation of resource crunch etc are some of the most significant learning one can have in his/her way to transforming himself/herself into a socially sensitive human being.

The idea of paying special attention to "the poor and mean and lowly" has been emphasised throughout human history by noble souls like Jesus Christ and in recent times by Mahatma Gandhi and Mother Teresa. Yet it is something that is consistently forgotten by most of us. 'Vulnerability' and 'marginalization' can mean different things to different people. The range of individuals who are sometimes described as 'vulnerable', or 'marginalized', by service providers is large. However, whether or not a group is perceived or perceives itself as vulnerable or marginalized will probably depend on its context at any given time. People become vulnerable and marginalized for a reason. Sometimes the causes are subtler than we at first realise. Tackling the causes once they are identified may mean re-examining some of the fundamental beliefs behind our institutions. Involving vulnerable and often marginalized groups is therefore likely to be a challenge for all, both inside and outside research. Ultimately, this should empower all involved, even if the process of getting there is difficult and perhaps uncomfortable. Apart from material support, society needs spirit; the vital ingredient that makes the difference between living life and merely existing; its power to generate mass passion, where innumerable hearts throb as in unison; its ability to draw people together irrespective of differences in race, religion, gender or caste. Unity of spirit and purpose is ultimately what builds bridges between diverse cultures.

Social sensitivity refers to emotional factors and intellectual responses. Some of the emotional factors are feeling, sympathy, aversion and attitude of approval or disapproval. Social sensitivity is voluntary. It involves an idea that it is better to be proactive towards a problem rather than be reactive to a problem. Social responsibility means eliminating corrupt, irresponsible or unethical behaviour that might bring harm to the community, its people, or the environment before the behaviour happens. For the present study, the researchers have identified dimensions like attitude towards marginalised people, gender, good citizenship, casteism and religion to be the factors constituting social sensitivity.

Even though subjects like ethics and environmental management are part of the course curriculum of MBA programme; organised, activity-based interventions are not so common among the business schools in India. Documented evidence of the effectiveness of such type of intervention programme is not often quoted in the academic literature available.This study threw light on the need and possibilities of designing various intervention programmes to improve the social sensitivity of management graduates. The fact that the profile of MBA graduates in the present context is being dominated by students from metropolitan and urban areas again highlight the need for such an exposure to management students, which in turn will enable them to empathise with the marginalized on a later day when they reach positions of decision-making. Business schools all over India should give more emphasis in their course curriculum to programmes which can positively create an impact on the social outlook of business management students.

Thus, the current socio-economic scenario in our country calls for the emergence of more and more youngsters in different walks of life with socially and ethically upright values guiding them. Business schools and business education all over India have a great responsibility of moulding young managers with greater social responsibility and appropriate ethical values.

OBJECTIVES OF THE RESEARCH

General Objective

1. To study the effectiveness of the intervention programme on the level of social sensitivity of management students .

Specific Objectives

1. To analyse the level of Social sensisivity of management students at entry level of their MBA programme .
2. To analyse the variation in the level of social sensisivity of management students after the social sensitisation programme / intervention.
3. To analyse the variation in the level of social sensitivity of management students after the social sensitisation programme, across the different demographic variables.

SCOPE OF THE STUDY

The four elements characterizing the scope of the study are defined as below:

Population: Management students at the entry level of the MBA programme with business schools located in major cities in India.

Place of study: The study was conducted in Rajagiri School of Management, Cochin.

Time period of the study: The period of study was in August 2007.

Data sources: Primary data collected from the participants.

DETAILS OF THE EXPERIMENT

Social Sensitisation Programme is a flag ship co-curricular activity of Rajagiri School of Management right from the time of its initiation of Management courses in 1986. The programme had gone through periods of evolution before reaching its present framework. The Social Sensitisation Camp- 2007 was a massive live-together exercise for the 132 first year management students in a remote village of Idukki district in Kerala known as Kattappana. The students took up the challenge of widening a two metre-wide mud road to a six metre-wide one for a length of two kilometres. More than the construction of a road, the experiment had gone into fine tuning the social fabric required for making the localities sacrifice their land and effort for a common purpose.

The intervention process went through different stages, namely, off site and on site. Off site, the students were oriented by a one day theory input, so as to equip themselves with the theoretical frame work for social analysis. An expert in the area of social work handled this session. In the day-long process the participants oriented themselves to experience the social realities. After the day-long process, a series of short interventions were made by the team of faculty co-ordinators who accompanied them to the camp site. These interventions were based on their visit to the camp site in advance, so as to plan the activities.

The basic management functions of the camp like planning, organising, directing and controlling were carried out through various committees and groups. A core committee of four students elected by the entire participants was in charge of overall camp activity. Different committees namely project, food, transportation, finance, implements etc were assisting the core committee in micro-level management. All students were divided into seven groups so as to ensure their participation in all aspects of camp life spanning from cooking, cleaning, social survey to project implementation. Evaluation and improvisation, the key aspects of on-site stage, were carried out all through the activities and all through the day. Mostly, the evaluative interventions were done by the students and the faculty intervention was kept to minimal, so as to develop student leadership in assessing and evaluating the situation.

Afternoons were set apart for the socio-economic familiarization of the area. Students were sent in small group to houses of local people in different locations to have hands on experience of the rural realities of life. They could observe and assess the situation with the frame work given to them at the time of orientation.

In the evenings, the campers organized cultural programmes involving students as well as the local people. The main objective of cultural evenings, apart from the entertainment, was to make the students appreciate the lifestyle, culture and customs of the local community.

The evaluation process included scanning of the environment, learning points, observations, differences noticed, lifestyle changes, customs and cultural variations etc. Students were encouraged to approach every situation without any bias or prejudice. The daily evaluation took place at the end of the day involving all the campers. The core group, different committee heads, group leaders and few other campers made their evaluation or the observation of the day's activities. They were complemented and supplemented by other campers. Through the process of evaluation the participants could share their learning experiences, personal realisations, contribution to the locality etc .

RESEARCH DESIGN

The study is trying to establish the causal relationship between the intervention programmes and the social sensitivity characteristics of MBA students in India. This type of study falls under experimental designs. There are many categories of experimental designs. We have used the 'one group pre-test - post-test' design. Social sensitivity characteristics of the students were measured just before the commencement of the social sensitization camp. The post-test measure was taken on the day they returned from the camp.

Enough precautions were taken to control the impact of the extraneous variables that may affect the validity of the study.

History: History refers to specific events that are external to the experiment but occur at the same time as the experiment. In this case, the first observation was made immediately before the students left for the camp and the second measurement immediately after they returned. Since all the events occurred during this period is treated as part of the experiment, the impact of history can be ignored.

Maturation: Is an extraneous variable attributable to changes in the test units themselves that occur with the passage of time. Since the experiment lasted only one week and the observations were made just before and after the experiment, maturation is not likely to impact the results.

Testing effects: Refers to a case where the prior observation affects the later observation. In this study, though the same tool was used for the pre and post-measurements, the order in which items were presented in the tool was changed to minimize the testing effect.

Instrumentation: It is an extraneous variable involving changes in the measuring instrument or in the observers or scores themselves. In this study, the same tool and scoring methods were used for both observations. Data was collected through a self-administered questionnaire without any intervention from the researchers.

Selection bias: An extraneous variable attributable to the improper assignment of test units to treatment conditions. In this study, all the participants were exposed to the same treatment without any exemptions.

Mortality: Is an extraneous variable attributable to the loss of test units while the experiment is in progress. It is not applicable in this case.

SAMPLING DESIGN

The experimental design requires a fixed sample on which repeated measurements can be taken. Since the sample had to be subjected to a one week camp, it was difficult to select students across colleges. Hence the study had to be restricted to one b school. First-year MBA students of Rajagiri School of Management were taken as the sample for the study.

TOOLS OF THE DATA COLLECTION

Questionnaire method was used for data collection. The form was handed over to the respondent with a covering note requesting him/her to fill it. Necessary instructions regarding the filling up of the questionnaire were also mentioned.

Following the established practices of instrument development, Fr. P T Mathew SJ has developed and empirically tested a valid and reliable measure of social sensitivity. His final instrument has 18 statements covering the following dimensions of social sensitivity.

- Attitude towards gender
- Attitude towards good citizenship
- Attitude towards marginalized people
- Attitude towards religion and caste

The respondents were asked to indicate their level of agreement with each of these statements on a 5-point Likert scale (strongly disagree, disagree, neither disagree nor agree, agree and strongly agree). 7 items were phrased positively and 11 items negatively so that strong agreement in the former and strong disagreement in the latter resulted in a higher score in favour of social sensitivity. The two-page questionnaire consisted of two parts. Six demographic questions about gender, type of schooling, prior exposure to organized bodies of social action, source of family income, place of upbringing and work experience constituted the first part. The 18 statements relating to social sensitivity formed the second part. Space was provided beside each statement to mark the preference in the five-point Likert scale. The questions were jumbled and arranged in a random order in the questionnaire.

DATA SET

The data was collected from all the 132 participants in the programme. The demographic details of the participants are presented below:

Table 1: Gender profile of the participant

Gender	Number	Percent (%)
Male	61	46.2
Female	71	53.8
Total	132	100.0

Table 1shows that the participant had more or less equal representation from both the genders.

Table 2: The schooling background of the participants

Type of school attended	Number	Percent (%)
Government School	23	17.4
Government aided school	24	18.2
Private School	85	64.4
Total	132	100.0

As seen, majority of them were educated in private schools.

Table 3: Family income details of the participants

Major source of family income	Number	Percent (%)
Salary	92	69.7
Business	25	19.7
Agriculture	4	3.0
Others	11	8.3
Total	132	100.0

Almost 70% of the participants came from salaried class. The representation of students from agriculture families was very minimal at 3%.

Table 4: Place of upbringing of the participants

Born and brought up in	Number	Percent (%)
Metropolitan city	17	12.9
Urban Area	63	47.8
Semi Urban area	34	25.8
Rural area	18	13.6
Total	132	100.0

Over 60% of the students had an urban upbringing. Only 13.6% of the participants came from rural areas.

Table 5: prior exposure to organized bodies of social action

Had previous exposure	Number	Percent (%)
Yes	95	72
No	37	28
Total	132	100.0

Most of the participants had no previous exposure to similar programmes.

Table 6: Previous work experience

Work experience	Number	Percent (%)
Less than 1 year	97	73.5
More than 1 year	35	26.5
Total	132	100.0

Most of the participants were either fresher or graduates with less than one year's experience.

GENERATING THE SOCIAL SENSITIVITY SCORES

As mentioned earlier, the researchers have used the tool developed by Fr. P T Mathew SJ for measuring the level of social sensitivity of the participants. Since the four dimensional structure of the tool has been identified and validated, the next step is to generate appropriate scores to represent these factors for further statistical analysis. For an instrument whose validity, reliability and dimensionality have been proven, summated scales are recommended (Hair et al 2000) from the following considerations. (a) these scales are easily replicated across studies. (b) They are easy to interpret. (c) They represent multiple aspect of the concept under measure.

The researchers have used summated scales for this study. The responses to the negative statements are recorded for uniformity. The score is calculated for each social sensitivity dimension by taking the average of all items included under that dimension. Each of these scores will vary from 1 to 5 where high score indicates high social sensitivity.

DATA ANALYSIS AND INTERPRETATION

Paired-Samples T Test was used to check for variation in the level of social sensitivity of the participants after the camp. Paired-Samples T Test procedure compares the means of two variables for a single group. It computes the differences between values of the two variables for each case and tests whether the average differs from 0. The paired T test has a basic assumption that the differences in the entire population follow a Gaussian distribution though it is not very critical for big samples as in this case.

If pairing is effective, the before and after measurements should vary together. This can be checked by calculating the Pearson correlation coefficient (r). If the pairing was effective, r will be positive and the p value will be small (less than 0.05 for 5% significance level). This means that the two groups are significantly correlated, so it made sense to choose a paired test.

In all the paired T test analysis discussed below, Pearson correlation coefficients were seen to be positive and P values were less than 0.05. Hence the T test results can be interpreted.

Table 7 shows the results of the paired t test on the total group.

Table 7: Paired T test on the total group

Dimension	Mean change	SD	t- value	Sig (2-tailed)
Total score	0.1433	.35743	4.605	.000**
Gender	0.2083	.94109	2.543	.012**
Good citizenship	0.0348	.64890	.617	.538
Marginalized people	0.3320	.49934	7.638	.000**
Religion and caste	0.1086	.81745	1.527	.129

** items are significant at 5% level

As seen, the group showed a statistically significant increase in their overall social sensitivity score after the camp compared to the level before the camp. The significant increase was also seen in the following dimensions of social sensitivity - attitude towards gender and attitude towards marginalized people.

Separate Paired-Samples T Tests were performed on each of identified demographic categories to see whether all these categories are amenable to such an experiment. These results are presented in the tables below.

Table 8a: Paired T test on male participants

Dimension	Mean change	SD	t- value	Sig (2-tailed)
Total score	0.2351	.3412	5.381	.000**
Gender	0.2541	.9157	2.167	.034**
Good citizenship	0.0393	.5748	.535	.595
Marginalized people	0.4789	.4606	8.119	.000**
Religion and caste	0.1048	.8041	1.017	.313

** items are significant at 5% level

Table 8b: Paired T test on female participants

Dimension	Mean change	SD	t- value	Sig (2-tailed)
Total score	0.0644	.35443	1.530	.130
Gender	0.1690	.96712	1.473	.145
Good citizenship	0.0986	.70417	1.180	.242
Marginalized people	0.2058	.49979	3.469	.001**
Religion and caste	.1120	.83440	1.131	.262

The tables 8a and 8b show that male participants showed significant increase in the overall score as well as in the gender and marginalized people dimensions, whereas for female participants, the increase was seen only in the case of marginalized people. Thus, male participants are seen to be more amenable to such intervention programmes than women.

Table 9a: Paired T test on urban class

Dimension	Mean change	SD	t- value	Sig (2-tailed)
Total score	0.1904	.35060	4.947	.000**
Gender	0.2711	.97936	2.522	.014**
Good citizenship	0.0193	.64891	0.271	.787
Marginalized people	0.3606	.49526	6.633	.000**
Religion and caste	0.0363	.78448	0.421	.675

** items are significant at 5% level

Table 9b: Paired T test on rural class

Dimension	Mean change	SD	t- value	Sig (2-tailed)
Total score	0.0565	.34986	1.165	.249
Gender	0.1058	.85941	0.887	.379
Good citizenship	0.1231	.62892	1.411	.164
Marginalized people	0.2767	.49718	4.014	.000**
Religion and caste	0.1629	.87254	2.173	.074

** items are significant at 5% level

Table 9a and table 9b respectively give the results of the paired T test on participants with an urban background and participants with a rural background. The change in the level of social sensitivity is more significant and pronounced in the case of participants who hailed from urban areas. This can be attributed to the fact that the rural students already had enough exposure to the realities of rural life and hence the incremental learning from the camp may be limited compared to their urban counterparts.

Table 10a: Paired T test on private school educated participants

Dimension	Mean change	SD	t- value	Sig (2-tailed)
Total score	0.1289	.37981	3.130	.002**
Gender	0.3059	.96700	2.916	.005**
Good citizenship	.0494	.67887	0.671	.504
Marginalized people	0.2788	.52727	4.875	.000**
Religion and caste	0.0939	.82791	1.045	.299

** items are significant at 5% level

Table 10b: Paired T test on government school educated participants

Dimension	Mean change	SD	t- value	Sig (2-tailed)
Total score	0.1748	.31454	2.665	.014**
Gender	0.0652	.88297	0.354	.727

Contd...

Good citizenship	0.1304	.46557	1.344	.193
Marginalized people	0.4943	.45247	5.240	.000**
Religion and caste	0.0157	.79953	0.094	.926

** Items are significant at 5% level

Although schooling was not seem to be a very significant issue affecting the variation, the participants with private schooling reported significant changes in more dimensions of social sensitivity compared to the participants who had schooling in government schools (tables 10a and 10b). This can be read along with the findings on the urban rural participants. Most of the government school educated students would have come from rural areas and hence the findings may be similar.

Table 11a: Paired T test on salaried class

Dimension	Mean change	SD	t- value	Sig (2-tailed)
Total score	0.1629	.36125	4.326	.000**
Gender	0.2717	.94175	2.768	.007**
Good citizenship	0.0174	.63152	0.264	.792
Marginalized people	0.3651	.53688	6.523	.000**
Religion and caste	0.1485	.83231	1.711	.090

** items are significant at 5% level

Table11b: Paired T test on business class

Dimension	Mean change	SD	t- value	Sig (2-tailed)
Total score	0.0731	.35576	1.047	.305
Gender	0.1923	.84943	1.154	.259
Good citizenship	0.1692	.73906	1.168	.254
Marginalized people	0.2346	.36857	3.246	.003**
Religion and caste	0.0381	.73872	0.263	.795

** items are significant at 5% level

The paired T test results on the salaried class and business class are presented in tables 11a and 11b respectively. The students coming from salaried class are seen to be more favourably changed in their social sensitivity levels compared to students hailing from business families.

Table 12a: Paired T test on work experienced

Dimension	Mean change	SD	t- value	Sig (2-tailed)
Total score	0.0943	.35629	2.620	.010**
Gender	0.1071	.91169	1.163	.248
Good citizenship	0.0531	.63865	0.822	.413
Marginalized people	0.2802	.47013	5.900	.000**
Religion and caste	0.1665	.81308	2.028	.045

** items are significant at 5% level

Table12b: Paired T test on non work experienced

Dimension	Mean change	SD	t- value	Sig (2-tailed)
Total score	0.2844	.32612	5.085	.000**
Gender	0.5000	.97701	2.984	.005**
Good citizenship	0.0176	.68467	0.150	.881
Marginalized people	0.4812	.55611	5.045	.000**
Religion and caste	0.0582	.81902	0.415	.681

** items are significant at 5% level

The paired T test results on participants with and without experience (tables 12a and 12b respectively) show similar results except that the magnitude of change in the social sensitivity scores is more for fresher than participants with prior work experience.

CONCLUSIONS AND RECOMMENDATIONS

The study gave an empirical direction to the researchers theoretical understanding of the usefullness of adopting such social sensitisation camps in real life settings. It also threw light on the possibilities of extending this experiment to other business schools all over the country as a higher level alternative to academic discourse on social sensitivity. Classroom discussions or seminars at the most can sensitise the students to social issues at a peripheral level, whereas a real life exposure to rural realities will enhance the scope of developing relevant 'competencies' which will go a long way in social transformation through management professionals.

The result also threw light on the limitations of the programme design in imparting sensitivity on some of the dimensions of social sensitivity like attitude towards good citizenship, religion and casteism. But the overall improvement shown in the level of social sensitivity is a positive signal to the academic community to work with more rigorous research methods to fine tune such intervention programmes customised to the requirements of each Institute. The result also gives an optimistic picture through the significant improvements shown in the level of attitude towards marginalised people and gender from all participants through a real life exposure to realities of life.

The current family system emerging in the metro cities of India puts a limit to the extent of social exposure to the youngsters. The mass media or other NGOs are also not able to do justice to bridge this information and experience gap that has developed among the youth in the country. This ever-widening gap need to be bridged through all possible interventions from all the stakeholders. Social sensitisation programme again is a golden opportunity for the rural people to get aquainted with a different set of realities through their close encounters with the management students that can go a long way in shedding their wrong notions what-so-ever about the educated and better endowed new generation. As Stephen Covey, author of 'Seven Habits of Effective People' argues, the paradigm shifts in life can happen through real life encounters with realities of life.

The researchers suggest looking into the possibilities of further extending this study through a longitudinal approach by studying the variation in the level of social sensitivity of the same group of participants at different stages of their course and later at their job.

REFERENCES

Cooper, C. *Individual Differences*, London: Arnold, 1998.

Faris,E.L. Robert (Ed.). *Handbook of Modern Sociology*, Rand Mcnally & Co,1964.

Giddens, Anthony. *Sociology*, Polity Press,1997.

Hair, J.F., Anderson, R.E., Tatham, R.L.,& Black, W.C.. *Multivariate Data Analysis*, New Jersey: Prentice-Hall International, USA. 1998.

Malhotra, K. Naresh. *Marketing research: An applied orientation*, Pearson Education, 2003.

Pervin, L. & John, O. (Eds.). *Handbook of personality: theory and research*, New York: Gilford,1999.

Prahalad, C.K. *Fortune at the Bottom of the Pyramid; Eradicating Poverty through Profits*, Pearson Education, 2005.

Watson,J.Tony .*Sociology work and industry*, Routledge,1995.

12

Effectiveness of Celebrity and Non-celebrity Print Advertisements on College Students in Erode Town (T.N.)

C. RANGANAYAKI*
DR. S. SANKARANARAYANAN**

The study was conducted among the college students in Erode town (T.N.). In this study, three mobile companies' (Aircel, Airtel and BSNL) advertisements were used. It was conducted to measure the message effectiveness, impact of credibility on consumers purchase intension and overall effectiveness of celebrity and non-celebrity advertisements of cell phone service companies. In the current scenario, the competition is tough; hence the companies have to design and provide the stimuli in the form of advertisements. All the companies want to sustain in the market and so they are in need of using celebrities and or non-celebrities in the advertisements. The research was conducted among the target group (college students as cell phone users) in the study area (Erode town). The respondents considered for the study are college students in different age groups, gender and educational programs in Erode town of Tamil Nadu. The structured questionnaire was used for data collection. In the questionnaire a semantic differential scale with fifteen items is used to measure the effectiveness of celebrity and non-celebrity advertisements. The researcher has considered only students studying in Arts and Science co-educational colleges. A total number of 250 students (50 from each college) with cell phone subscription are considered for survey. Convenient sampling method was used to select the students. Before filling the questionnaire two types of advertisements (celebrity and non-celebrity) of three cell phone service companies (Aircel, Airtel and BSNL) total six advertisements appeared in the newspapers (in the months of January, March, May, June, and October, 2006) were shown to the respondents. To avoid bias in showing the advertisements, the sequencing of the six advertisements was changed every time and shown to the respondents. Collected data were classified into suitable tabular forms for analysis and interpretation. Statistical tools like Correlation and ANOVA methods were used. This study concluded that the celebrity advertisements of cell phone service companies are more effective than the non-celebrity advertisements among the college students in the study area.

* Research Scholar, Bharathiar School of Management and Entrepreneur Development, Bharathiar University, Coimbatore.
** Lecturer, Bharathiar School of Management and Entrepreneur Development, Bharathiar University, Coimbatore.

INTRODUCTION

Marketers use advertisements with both celebrities and non-celebrities, but advertisements that use celebrities give better results among buyers. A celebrity is a famous person who has mass attraction in public. If the same person (celebrity) comes in the advertisement the people are more enthusiastic and are easily influenced by that advertisement. Many products are promoted through advertising as status symbols; consumers are led to believe that purchasing particular product may enhance their personal status. Using a celebrity (athlete or film personality) endorser is a popular strategy in advertising to promote or communicate the status of a product. Celebrity endorsement is used to enhance the image of the company, product, or brand and to sell corporate products or services.

Research studies comparing the impact of advertisements with and without celebrity endorsers have found that those featuring celebrities were rated more positively. In the grown up stage, the same companies prefer non-celebrities. They are not willing to afford more amounts for the advertisements. So non-celebrity advertisements are produced at lesser cost than celebrity advertisements. It enables remembrance about the products among the customers. One of the biggest differences between the celebrity and non-celebrity advertisement is the appearance of the spokesperson. Other than these factors, both celebrity and non-celebrity advertisements perform the same process.

NEED FOR THE STUDY

To make human life more comfortable and easy, many innovations are coming up in the world almost every day. Use of cell phones has become an essential part of human life in the modern age and advertisements are required to stimulate the subscription of cell phone services. In the current scenario, the competition is tough; hence companies have to design and provide the stimuli in the form of advertisements. All companies want to sustain themselves in the market and so they are in need of using celebrities and or non-celebrities in their advertisements. The research is conducted among the target group (college students as cell phone users) in the study area (Erode town). The reason behind selecting the target group is that students are very eager in communicating with their friends and they are the potential and more frequent users of cell phones. Moreover, the target group is easily attracted towards the celebrity advertisements.

OBJECTIVES OF THE STUDY

- To measure the message effectiveness of celebrity and non-celebrity advertisements.
- To measure the impact of credibility of celebrity and non-celebrity on consumers' purchase intentions.
- To measure the overall effectiveness of celebrity and non-celebrity advertisements of cell phone service companies.

REVIEW OF LITERATURE

Many studies have been conducted in the field of effectiveness of celebrity and non-celebrity advertisements.

Mark R. Forehand and Andrew Perkins (2005) revealed that a positive relationship between celebrity and brand attitude was observed regardless of celebrity identification. The disassociation between the explicit and implicit results suggested that resetting requires explicit evaluation. *Friedman and Friedman (1979)* revealed that a celebrity relative to a non-celebrity spokesperson would be more effective for products high in psychological or social risk, involving such elements as good taste, self-image, and opinion of others. They suggested effectiveness of celebrity for products high in psychological or social risk.

Atkin et al (1983) indicated that the ads featuring celebrity figures produce more favourable ad evaluation ratings and product image, but not believability of the ad or the likelihood of actually purchasing the product. *Kahle et al (1985)* studied three factors manipulated which include celebrity-source physical attractiveness, celebrity-source likeability, and consumer product involvement. Attitudes and purchase intentions are found to change due to celebrity-source attractiveness, but not celebrity-source likeability. The results are interpreted as supporting social adaptation theory.

McCracken (1989) concluded that the image of the celebrity must fit or be congruent with the product. As the congruence is considered one of the major factors in celebrity advertising effectiveness, this issue was examined from a theoretical perspective, using a social cognition framework. *JongWoo Jun and SangMi Lee (2001)* indicated that mobility/convenience and multimedia service were positively related to attitudes toward mobile advertising and lead to favourable behavioural intentions. *Mohan et al., (2001)* found the results from this study did not support the view that using celebrity advertising was more believable or effective than non-celebrity advertising for the brands tested in their study. Consumers generally feel that celebrities are more attractive than non-celebrities; something that may draw initial attention to the advertisement.

Jenny Kriens and Weiqin Zhao (2001) suggested that American and Chinese consumers' perceptions of endorser usage differ and while celebrities attract attention to advertisements from both consumers group, this did not constitute effectiveness. *C. L. Knot and M. St. James (2004)* suggested that as situations change or evolve, the model can be easily updated to capture new information. This allows for celebrities' ratings to change over time and be more accurate, given all available information.

RESEARCH METHODOLOGY

The respondents considered for the study are college students in different age groups, gender and educational programmes in Erode town of Tamil Nadu. The data had been collected only from primary sources. The structured questionnaire was used for data collection. The researcher has considered only students studying in Arts and Science co-educational colleges. A total number of 250 students (50 from each college) with cell phone subscription were considered for the survey. Convenient sampling method was used to select the students. The questionnaire was printed and distributed to the respondents. Before filling the questionnaire, two types of advertisements (celebrity and non-celebrity) of three cell phone service companies (Aircel, Airtel and BSNL, only these three companies are considered for the study because of the usage among the target group.) total six advertisements appeared in the newspapers (in the months of January, March, May, June, and October, 2006) are shown to the respondents. Then the respondents are requested to fill up the questionnaire. To avoid bias in showing the advertisements, the sequencing of the six advertisements was changed every time and shown to them. Collected data were classified into suitable tabular forms for analysis and interpretation. Statistical tools like Correlation and ANOVA methods were used to test the formulated hypothesis.

RESULTS AND DISCUSSION

In this study, the effectiveness of celebrity and non-celebrity advertisements was measured by seven points semantic differential scale developed by Mohan K. Menon et al (2001). The data was used to analyze the message effectiveness, impact of credibility of celebrity and non-celebrity advertisements on purchase intention and overall effectiveness of celebrity and non-celebrity advertisements for cell phone service companies.

The formulated hypotheses were tested through Correlation analysis and One Way Analysis Of Variance (ANOVA). The results were presented in the following tables.

Message Effectiveness of Celebrity and Non - Celebrity Advertisements

The message effectiveness of celebrity and non-celebrity advertisement was analyzed based on the tabulated factors. The respondents had given their ratings to those factors and the mean score values were presented in the following table. It is also shown in figures.

Table 1: Message effectiveness of Celebrity and Non - celebrity Advertisements (Mean Score Values)

Factors	Celebrity Advertisement			Non-Celebrity Advertisement		
Companies	Aircel	Airtel	BSNL	Aircel	Airtel	BSNL
Conveys the message	2.30	1.90	1.86	1.61	1.38	1.30
Informative	1.90	1.40	1.54	1.16	0.95	1.00
Express expertness	1.50	1.17	1.29	0.64	0.76	0.56
Suitable for the ad	1.88	1.20	1.34	0.97	0.62	0.57
Believable	1.51	1.31	1.30	0.75	0.73	0.67
Knowledgeable	1.42	1.24	1.07	0.85	0.63	0.64
Trustworthy	1.48	1.28	1.24	0.78	0.77	0.54
Popularity	2.17	1.72	1.70	0.92	0.80	0.69
Overall Mean score	1.77	1.40	1.42	0.96	0.83	0.75

It can be seen from the above table that in Celebrity advertisements, the overall mean score value of Aircel (1.77) is higher than those of Airtel and BSNL celebrity advertisements.

Further, it is inferred from the above table that in Non-Celebrity advertisements, the overall mean score value of Aircel (0.96) is higher than those of Airtel and BSNL non-celebrity advertisements.

When celebrity and non-celebrity advertisements of each company are compared, the overall mean value for the message effectiveness in Aircel celebrity advertisement (1.77) is higher than its non-celebrity (0.96) advertisement, followed by Airtel celebrity advertisement (1.40) is higher than its non-celebrity (0.83) advertisement and BSNL celebrity advertisement (1.42) is higher than its non-celebrity (0.75) advertisement.

It is concluded that the message in celebrity advertisements are more effective than non-celebrity advertisements.

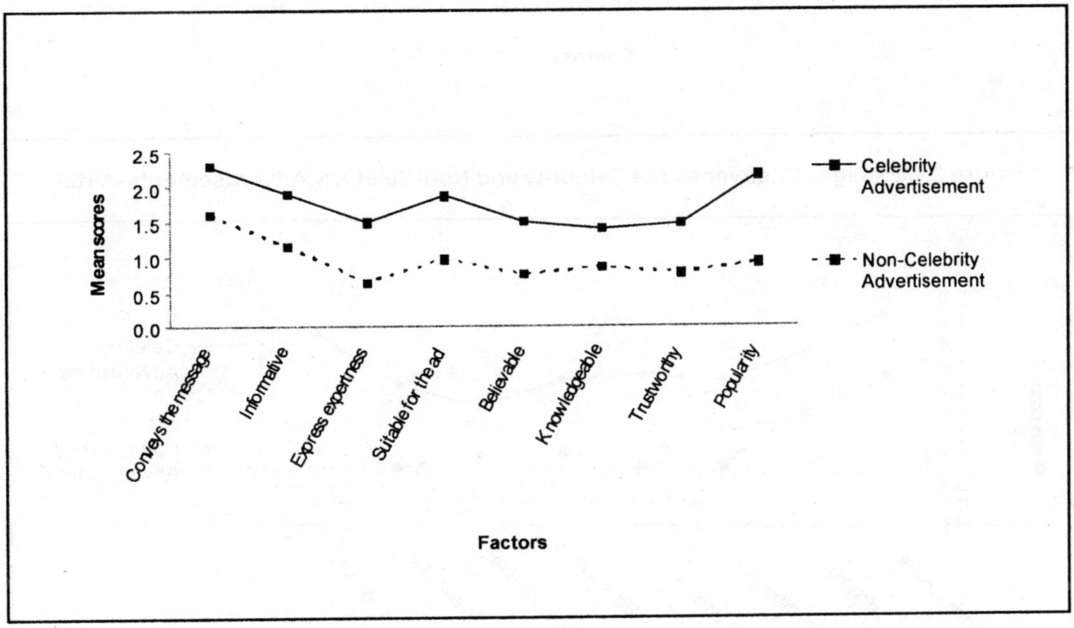

Figure 1: Message effectiveness of Celebrity and Non-Celebrity Advertisements-Aircel

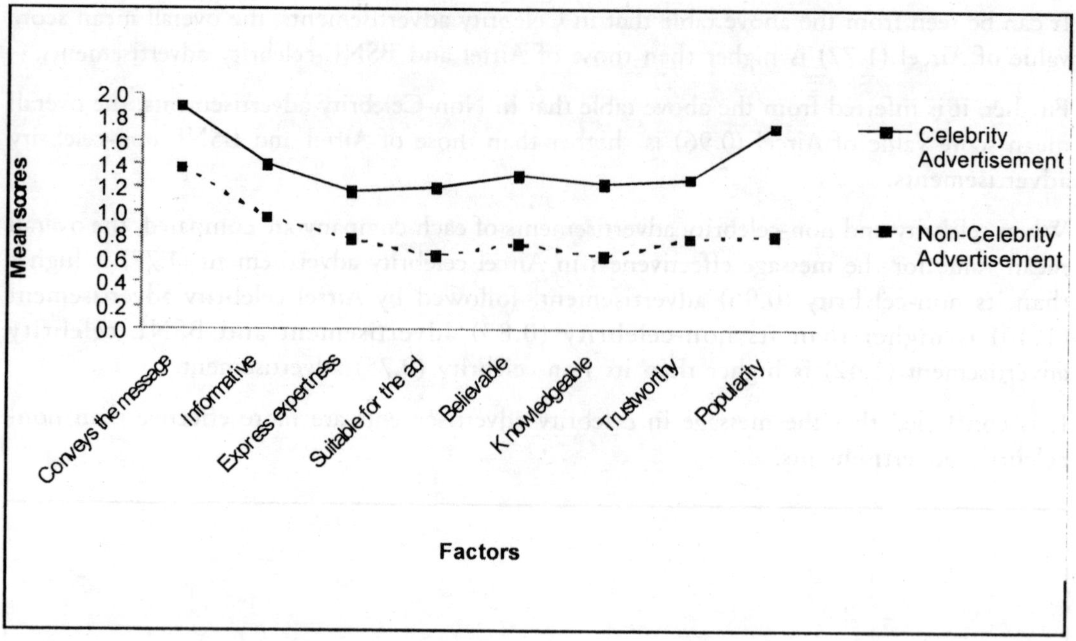

Figure 2: Message effectiveness of Celebrity and Non-Celebrity Advertisements-Airtel

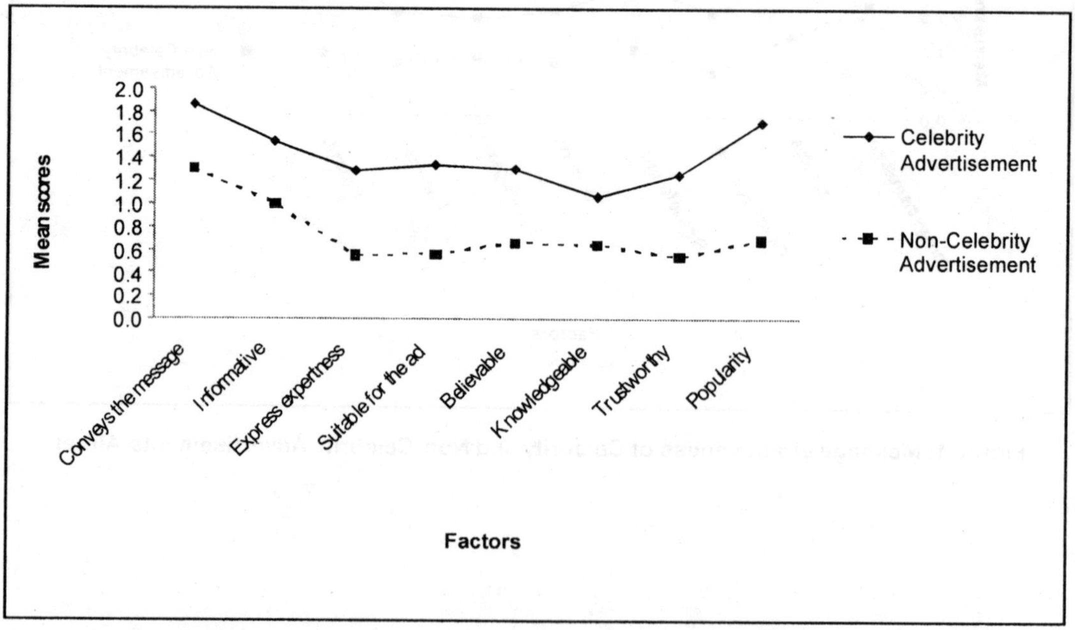

Figure 3: Message effectiveness of Celebrity and Non-Celebrity Advertisements-BSNL

Impact of Credibility of Celebrity and Non-Celebrity Advertisements on Consumer's Purchase Intention

To find out the impact of credibility of celebrity and non-celebrity advertisements on consumers' purchase intention, the mean scores of the six factors shown in the following table were considered. And the results are diagrammatically presented in the following pages.

Table 2: Impact of Credibility of Celebrity and Non-Celebrity Advertisements on Consumer's Purchase Intention (Mean Score Values)

Factors	Celebrity Advertisement			Non-Celebrity Advertisement		
Companies	**Aircel**	**Airtel**	**BSNL**	**Aircel**	**Airtel**	**BSNL**
Suitable for the ad	1.88	1.20	1.34	0.97	0.62	0.57
Convincing	1.65	1.36	1.30	0.84	0.72	0.77
Easy recall	1.64	1.31	1.29	0.74	0.59	0.51
Recommendable	1.57	1.30	1.29	0.81	0.64	0.65
Trustworthy	1.48	1.28	1.24	0.78	0.77	0.54
Popularity	2.17	1.72	1.70	0.92	0.80	0.69
Overall Mean score	1.73	1.36	1.36	0.84	0.69	0.62

It can be seen from the above table that in Celebrity advertisements, the overall mean score value of Aircel is (1.73) higher than those of Airtel and BSNL celebrity advertisements.

Further, it is known from the above table that in Non-Celebrity advertisements, the overall mean score value of Aircel (0.84) is higher than those of Airtel and BSNL non-celebrity advertisements.

It is also known from the above table that the mean scores for the impact of credibility of celebrity and non-celebrity advertisements on consumer's purchase intention Aircel celebrity advertisement (1.73) is higher than its non-celebrity (0.84) advertisement, followed by Airtel celebrity advertisement (1.36) is higher than its non-celebrity (0.69) advertisement and BSNL celebrity advertisement (1.36) is higher than its non-celebrity (0.84) advertisement.

By considering the overall mean scores of ratings from the above table, it is concluded that the impact of credibility on consumer's purchase intention is more in celebrity advertisements than in non-celebrity advertisements.

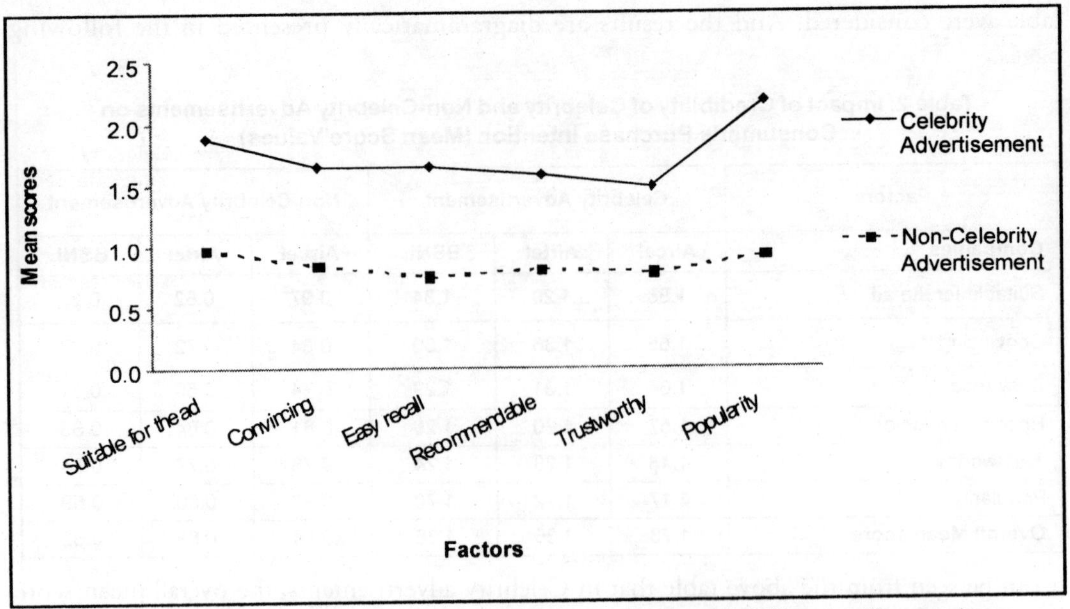

Figure 4: Impact of Credibility of Aircel celebrity and Non-celebrity advertisements on consumers purchase intention

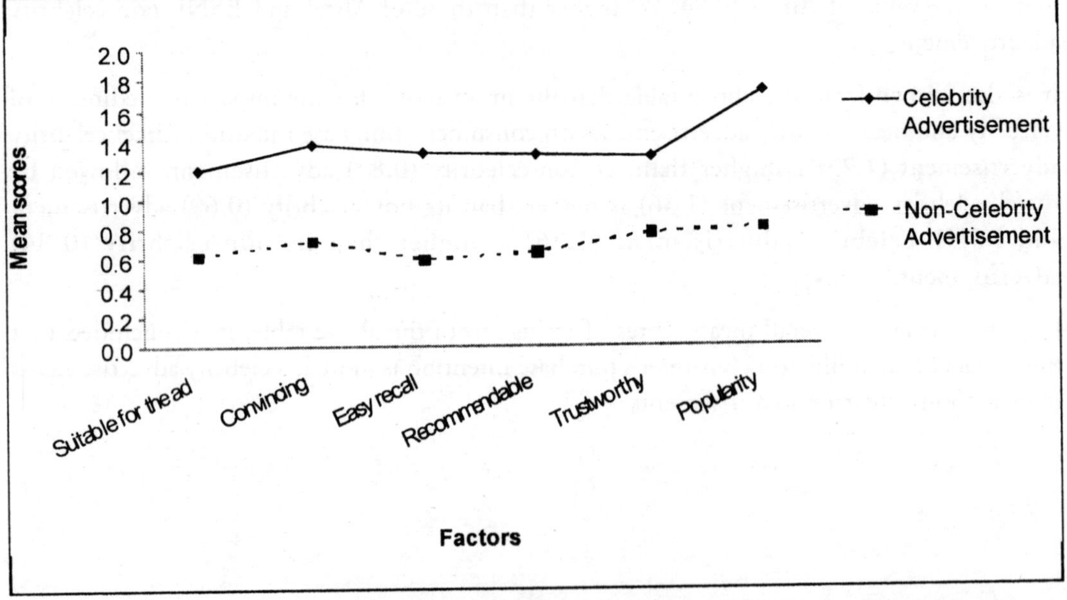

Figure 5: Impact of Credibility of Airtel celebrity and Non-celebrity advertisements on consumers purchase intention

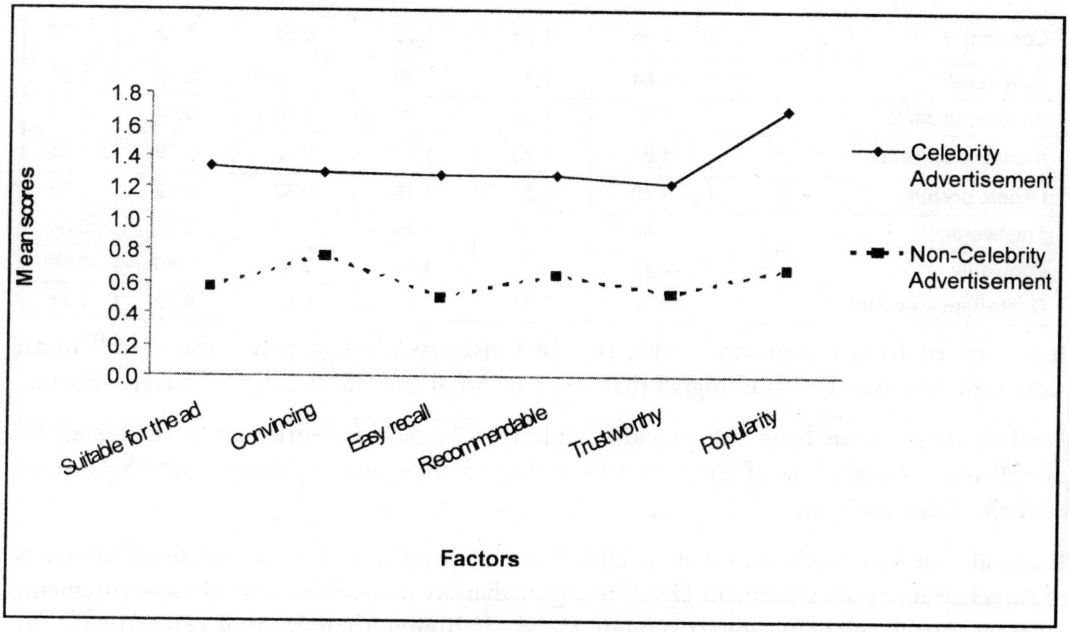

Figure 6: Impact of Credibility of BSNL celebrity and Non-celebrity advertisements on consumers purchase intention

Overall Effectiveness of Celebrity and Non-Celebrity Advertisements for the Cell Phone Service Companies

The following table shows the factors that are influencing the overall effectiveness of celebrity and non-celebrity advertisements for the cell phone service companies and the ratings given by the respondents for the tabulated factors. And the results are diagrammatically presented in figures.

Table 3: Overall Effectiveness of Celebrity and Non-Celebrity Advertisements for the Cell phone Service Companies (Mean Score Values)

Factors	Celebrity Advertisement			Non-Celebrity Advertisement		
	Aircel	Airtel	BSNL	Aircel	Airtel	BSNL
Conveys the message	2.30	1.90	1.86	1.61	1.38	1.30
Informative	1.90	1.40	1.54	1.16	0.95	1.00
More colorful	1.87	1.48	1.56	1.14	0.89	0.77
Attractive costume	1.80	1.38	1.40	0.86	0.82	0.74
Express expertness	1.50	1.17	1.29	0.64	0.76	0.56
Suitable for the ad	1.88	1.20	1.34	0.97	0.62	0.57
Believable	1.51	1.31	1.30	0.75	0.73	0.67
Knowledgeable	1.42	1.24	1.07	0.85	0.63	0.64

Contd...

Convincing	1.65	1.36	1.30	0.84	0.72	0.77
Easy recall	1.64	1.31	1.29	0.74	0.59	0.51
Recommendable	1.57	1.30	1.29	0.81	0.64	0.65
Attractive presence	1.69	1.33	1.17	0.82	0.79	0.55
Likable posture	1.48	1.32	1.15	0.72	0.72	0.68
Trustworthy	1.48	1.28	1.24	0.78	0.77	0.54
Popularity	2.17	1.72	1.70	0.92	0.80	0.69
Overall mean score	1.72	1.38	1.37	0.91	0.79	0.71

It is inferred from the previous table that in Celebrity advertisements, the overall mean score value of Aircel (1.72) is higher than those of Airtel and BSNL celebrity advertisements.

Further, it is known from the previous table that in Non-Celebrity advertisements, the overall mean score value of Aircel (0.91) is higher than those of Airtel and BSNL non-celebrity advertisements.

It can also be seen from the previous table that the mean score for the overall effectiveness of Aircel celebrity advertisement (1.72) is higher than its non-celebrity (0.91) advertisement, whereas Airtel celebrity advertisement (1.38) is higher than its non-celebrity (0.79) advertisement and BSNL celebrity advertisement (1.37) is higher than its non-celebrity (0.71) advertisement.

Hence it is concluded that the celebrity advertisements are more effective than non-celebrity advertisements.

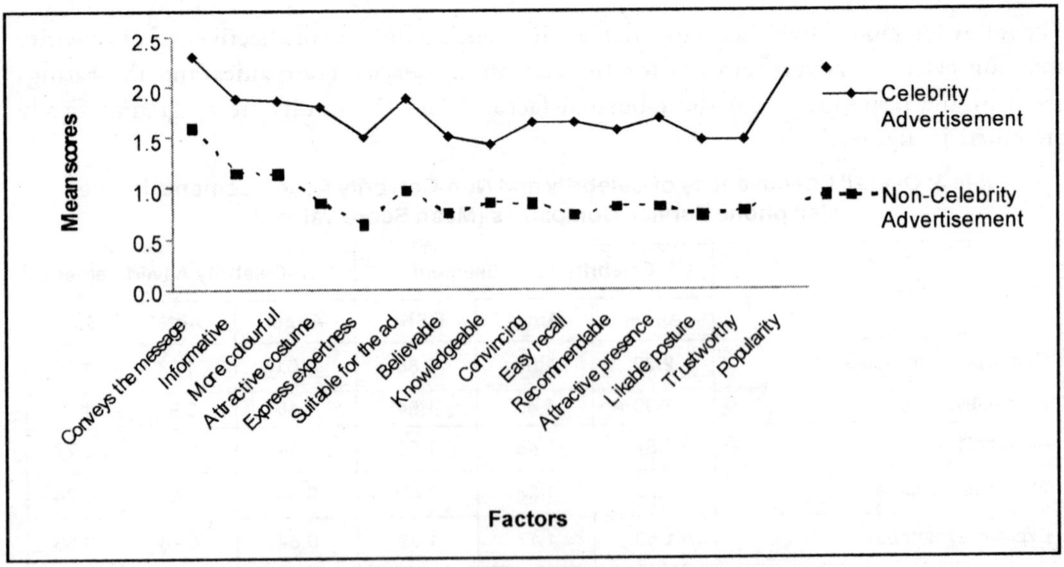

Figure 7: Overall advertising effectiveness with respect to Aircel

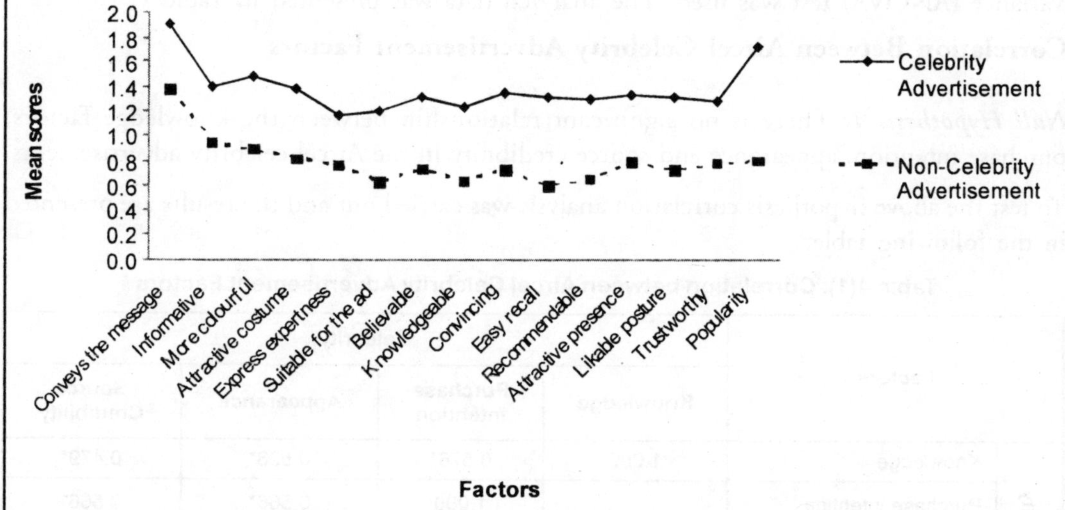

Figure 8: Overall advertising effectiveness with respect to Airtel

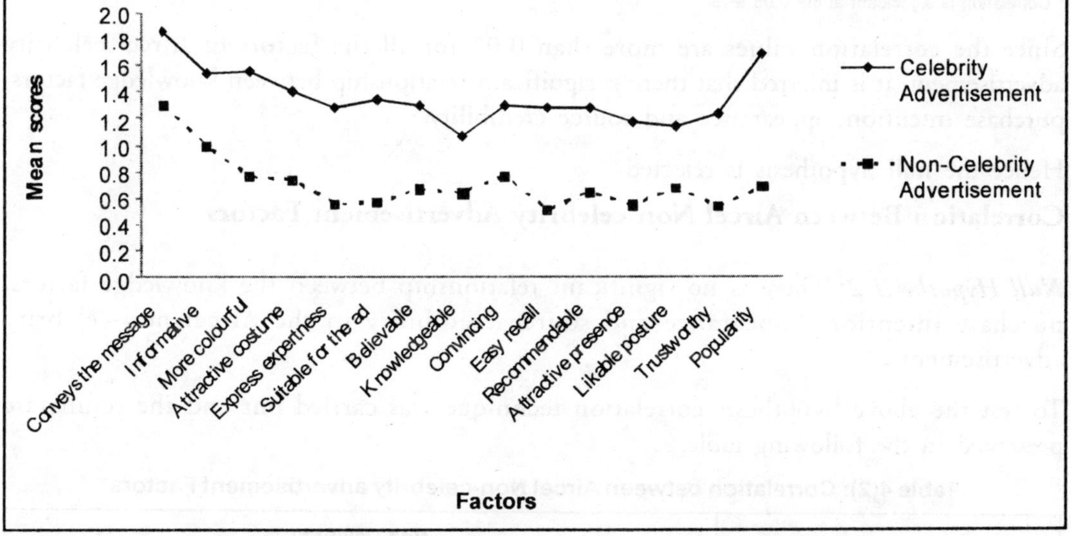

Figure 9: Overall advertising effectiveness with respect to BSNL

HYPOTHESIS TESTING

To find the interrelationship between the knowledge factors, purchase intention, appearance and source credibility in the celebrity and non celebrity advertisements of cell phone service companies, correlation technique is used. The results are presented in the tables (Table 4 to Table 6). To find out the significant difference between the celebrity advertisements and non celebrity advertisements of the cell phone service companies One Way Analysis Of Variance (ANOVA) test was used. The analyzed data was presented in Table 7.

Correlation Between Aircel Celebrity Advertisement Factors

Null Hypothesis 1: There is no significant relationship between the knowledge factors, purchase intention, appearance and source credibility in the Aircel celebrity advertisements.

To test the above hypothesis correlation analysis was carried out and the results are presented in the following table.

Table 4(1): Correlation between Aircel Celebrity Advertisement Factors

Factors		Celebrity			
		Knowledge	Purchase intention	Appearance	Source Credibility
Celebrity	Knowledge	1.000	0.576*	0.528*	0.479*
	Purchase intention		1.000	0.566*	0.566*
	Appearance			1.000	0.556*
	Source Credibility				1.000

* Correlation is significant at the 0.05 level

Since the correlation values are more than 0.05 for all the factors of Aircel celebrity advertisement, it is inferred that there is significant relationship between knowledge factors, purchase intention, appearance and source credibility.

Hence the null hypothesis is rejected.

Correlation Between Aircel Non-celebrity Advertisement Factors

Null Hypothesis 2: There is no significant relationship between the knowledge factors, purchase intention, appearance and source credibility in the Aircel non-celebrity advertisements.

To test the above hypothesis correlation technique was carried out and the results are presented in the following table.

Table 4(2): Correlation between Aircel Non-celebrity advertisement Factors

Factors		Non Celebrity			
		Knowledge	Purchase intention	Appearance	Source Credibility
Non Celebrity	Knowledge	1.000	0.662*	0.705*	0.673*
	Purchase intention		1.000	0.669*	0.706*
	Appearance			1.000	0.734*
	Source Credibility				1.000

* Correlation is significant at the 0.05 level

Since the correlation values are more than 0.05 for all the factors of Airtel non-celebrity advertisement, it is inferred that there is significant relationship between knowledge factors, purchase intention, appearance and source credibility.

Hence the null hypothesis is rejected.

Correlation Between Airtel Celebrity Advertisement Factors

Null Hypothesis 3: There is no significant relationship between the knowledge factors, purchase intention, appearance and source credibility in the Airtel celebrity advertisements.

To test the above hypothesis correlation technique was carried out and the results are presented in the following table.

Table 5(1): Correlation between Airtel celebrity advertisement Factors

Factors		Celebrity			
		Knowledge	Purchase intention	Appearance	Source Credibility
Celebrity	Knowledge	1.000	0.640*	0.674*	0.581*
	Purchase intention		1.000	0.617*	0.552*
	Appearance			1.000	0.644*
	Source Credibility				1.000

*Correlation is significant at the 0.05 level

Since the correlation values are more than 0.05 for all the factors of Airtel celebrity advertisement, it is inferred that there is significant relationship between knowledge factors, purchase intention, appearance and source credibility.

Hence the null hypothesis is rejected.

Correlation Between Airtel Non-celebrity Advertisement Factors

Null Hypothesis 4: There is no significant relationship between the knowledge factors, purchase intention, appearance and source credibility in the Airtel celebrity advertisements.

To test the above hypothesis correlation technique was carried out and the results are presented in the following table.

Table 5(2): Correlation between Airtel Non Celebrity Advertisement Factors

Factors		Non Celebrity			
		Knowledge	Purchase intention	Appearance	Source Credibility
Non Celebrity	Knowledge	1.000	0.643*	0.699*	0.708*
	Purchase intention		1.000	0.715*	0.692*
	Appearance			1.000	0.751*
	Source Credibility				1.000

*Correlation is significant at the 0.05 level

Since the correlation values are more than 0.05 for all the factors of Airtel non-celebrity advertisement, it is inferred that there is significant relationship between knowledge factors, purchase intention, appearance and source credibility.

Hence the null hypothesis is rejected.

Correlation Between BSNL Celebrity Advertisement Factors

Null Hypothesis 5: There is no significant relationship between the knowledge factors, purchase intention, appearance and source credibility in the BSNL celebrity advertisements.

To test the above hypothesis correlation technique was carried out and the results are presented in the following table.

Table 6(1): Correlation between BSNL Celebrity Advertisement Factors

Factors		Celebrity			
		Knowledge	Purchase intention	Appearance	Source Credibility
Celebrity	Knowledge	1.000	0.544*	0.494*	0.550*
	Purchase intention		1.000	0.600*	0.543*
	Appearance			1.000	0.530*
	Source Credibility				1.000

* Correlation is significant at the 0.05 level

Since the correlation values are more than 0.05 for all the factors of BSNL celebrity advertisement, it is inferred that there is significant relationship between knowledge factors, purchase intention, appearance and source credibility.

Hence the null hypothesis is rejected.

Correlation Between BSNL Non-celebrity Advertisement Factors

Null Hypothesis 6: There is no significant relationship between the knowledge factors, purchase intention, appearance and source credibility in the BSNL non-celebrity advertisements.

To test the above hypothesis correlation technique was carried out and the results are presented in the following table.

Table 6(2): Correlation between BSNL Non-Celebrity Advertisement Factors

Factors		Non Celebrity			
		Knowledge	Purchase intention	Appearance	Source Credibility
Non Celebrity	Knowledge	1.000	0.687*	0.705*	0.693*
	Purchase intention		1.000	0.656*	0.632*
	Appearance			1.000	0.764*
	Source Credibility				1.000

* Correlation is significant at the 0.05 level

Since the correlation values are more than 0.05 for all the factors of Aircel celebrity advertisement, it is inferred that there is significant relationship between knowledge factors, purchase intention, appearance and source credibility.

Hence the null hypothesis is rejected.

Difference in Ratings Between Celebrity Advertisements and Non Celebrity Advertisements of the Cell Phone Service Companies

Null Hypothesis 7: There is no significant difference in the ratings of the celebrity advertisements and non-celebrity advertisements among the cell phone service companies.

To test the above hypothesis Analysis Of Variance (ANOVA) test was carried out and the results are presented in the following table.

Table 7: ANOVA - Celebrity and Non-Celebrity advertisements of Aircel, Airtel and BSNL advertisements

Type of Advertisement	Aircel		Airtel		BSNL	
	Mean	S.D	Mean	S.D	Mean	S.D
Celebrity	1.724	0.262	1.380	0.194	1.367	0.709
Non-Celebrity	0.907	0.242	0.787	0.192	0.709	0.205

Service providers	Type of Advertisement	Sum of squares	F value	F. p value
Aircel	Celebrity	5.002	78.842	0.012
	Non-Celebrity	1.776		
Airtel	Celebrity	2.634	70.825	0.037
	Non-Celebrity	1.041		
BSNL	Celebrity	3.241	73.877	0.024
	Non-Celebrity	1.228		

Significance p value $\leq$ 0.05

It can be observed from the previous table that all the p values of three cell phone service providers are less than 0.05, meaning that there is significant difference between the celebrity advertisements and non-celebrity advertisements of all the three cell phone service companies (Aircel, Airtel and BSNL).

Hence the null hypothesis is rejected.

RECOMMENDATIONS AND CONCLUSION

The main feature emerging from the study is that college students are using cell phones mainly for communicating with their friends. Moreover, they are easily attracted towards celebrity advertisements. From the findings, Aircel company is sustaining its customers and trying to attract new customers through celebrity advertisements at all the stages. Though the Airtel company used celebrity advertisements at the beginning stage it switched over to sales promotion strategy subsequently. As far as BSNL is concerned, celebrity advertisement is found to be more effective than non-celebrity advertisement, even though the ratings are low compared to its competitors. Like Aircel, these two companies (Airtel and BSNL) must also try to use celebrity advertisements effectively to sustain their existing customers and attract new customers.

The above study clearly shows that the celebrity advertisements of cell phone service companies are more effective than the non-celebrity advertisements among the college students in Erode town. However, first the customers are attracted by celebrity advertisements than other factors such as coverage, customer service, offers, etc., while buying any brands from the market. Therefore, the cell phone service companies must concentrate on using the celebrity advertisements for attracting the new customers and sustaining the same customers with them.

REFERENCES

Anastasi, *Scaling Techniques*, New Delhi, Tata McGraw- Hill, 1985.

Atkin, Charles and Martin Block, "Effectiveness of Celebrity Endorsers," *Journal of Advertising Research*, Vol. 23, (57-61) February/March, 1983.

C. L. Knot and M. St. James, USA International Transactions in Operational Research, "An alternate approach to developing a total celebrity endorser rating model using the analytic hierarchy process", Volume 11 Issue 1 Page 87-95, (January 2004)

Friedman H.H and Friedman. L, "Endorser effectiveness by product type", *Journal of Advertising Research*, (63-71) 1979.

Jenny Kriens and Weiqin Zhao, University of Nebraska-Lincoln, "*Celebrity Endorsement in Cross-Cultural Advertising*", Association for Education in Journalism & Mass Communication, Student paper, (2001).

JongWoo Jun and SangMi Lee, University of Florida, "*Mobile Media Use and Its Impact on Consumer Attitudes Toward Mobile Advertising*", Association for education in journalism & Mass Communication, Student paper, (2001).

Kahle, Lynn R. and Pamela M. Homer, "Physical Attractiveness of the Celebrity Endorser: A Social Adaptation Perspective," *Journal of Consumer Research*, Vol. 11, (954-961) March, 1985.

Kothari C.R., *Research Methodology*, New Delhi, New Age Internal (P) Ltd., 2004.

Mark R. Forehand & Andrew Perkins, "Implicit assimilation and explicit contrast: A Set/Reset Model of response to celebrity voiceovers", *Journal of Consumer Research*, (Dec 2005).

McCracken, "the effectiveness of the endorsement process". *Journal of Consumer Research*", (p.312-316)1989.

Mohan K. Menon, Louis E. Boone, Hudson P. Rogers, "Celebrity Advertising: An Assessment of Its Relative Effectiveness". *Small Business Institute Journal*, 2001.

Philip Kotler., Marketing Management, Delhi, Pearson Education (P) Ltd., 2005.

Rajan Saxena, "Marketing Management", Tata McGraw- Hill, 2004.

Websites

www.ebsco.com

www.google.com

www.wikipedia.com

www.exchange4media.com

13

Rural Retailing: Is Rural Mall Feasible in Puri District?

BALAVISHWAKUMAR.S*
MAINAK DAS*
NAVEEN URMESE*
SATYA SUDIPTA PADHIARY*

The opportunity provided by rural market is tremendous. The incomes of rural population have been rising and their lifestyles have also undergone a marked change. Thus, the rural market has been growing steadily over the years and is now bigger than the urban market in various sectors. There are at least as many middle income households in the rural areas as there are in urban. Also, with cut-throat competition in urban India, many industries are driven to chalk out new strategies for targeting the rural consumers in a big way. A number of companies have thus begun eyeing the rural market for their retailing operations through setting up of rural mall. A classic and well-known example of a successful rural mall is ITC E-choupal.

But there are various aspects to be considered before venturing into setting up of rural mall in a village. This paper takes villages in Puri district to study these aspects. Puri district is a fast growing district located about 40 km from Bhubaneswar. It has about 1,800 villages, which are predominantly involved in agriculture. However these villages lack a rural mall. This paper studies various factors to be considered before setting up a rural mall in these villages. Primary data on these various factors were collected through survey in the villages of Puri district. Then this primary data was studied with help of various research techniques like cluster and factor analysis. Feasibility is determined based on the results of these analysis and various recommendations are made on setting up of rural mall in villages of Puri district. This paper thus shows the direction for systematic study to check the feasibility of rural malls in rural India.

INTRODUCTION

The purpose of the rural mall is to cater to the needs of population residing in the rural and backward areas outside the retail and distribution network of manufacturing companies.

* Students, Xavier Institute of Management, Xavier Square, Bhubaneswar, Orissa.

The envisaged malls would be based on an amalgamated model of supermarket and discount store and would offer substantial savings over the goods as compared to the local conveniences stores by implementing direct to customer business model and doing away with the intermediary distribution channel thus saving on the margins. The proposed facility would be a geographic concentration of shopping and warehousing space, eating joint, facilitation cell and other amenities of specific and generic use. The rural malls would offer one-stop shop solutions and a unique integrated shopping experience to the rural population and would specifically address the needs and utilizing tendency of these. The malls would act as a two way supply chain. Apart from selling goods to the farmers it would also double up as selling market and would assist the farmer by purchasing their agriculture production at a competitive market price thus providing true value of their produce.

Organized rural retail is comparatively a new trend in India. At present, 85% of the organized retailing takes place in India's urban areas. But the good thing is that the retail focus has already shifted to the rural areas. The Indian rural market with its vast size and demand base offers great opportunities to marketers. Two-thirds of country's consumers live in rural areas and almost half of the national income is generated here. 70% of India's population lives in 6,27,000 villages in rural areas. According to the NCAER study, there are almost twice as many 'lower middle income' households in rural areas as in the urban areas. The rural market for FMCG is growing as fast as its urban counterpart. When organized retail first made its presence felt in rural India, it wasn't a pure retailing operation targeting the rural masses. Companies like DSCL and Godrej who had significant agri-business interests, set them up to meet the needs of farmers in a store's catchments area. These stores are one-stop shops meant to meet the occupational needs of farmers by providing agri-inputs and fertilizers. These stores tend to be located in small towns that function as procurement hubs where the farmers come to sell their produce. These stores tend to target farmers with all sizes of holdings.

However, the concept of rural mall has been pioneered in the country by the tobacco major ITC Ltd. by opening up "Choupal Sagar", the first rural shopping mall of the country at Sehore in Madhya Pradesh. The concept has gained significant success from the start as average foot count recorded at the store was around 600 - 700 on weekdays and increases to around 900 on weekends. E-choupal has been most successful initiative to wire rural India and to involve the farmers in learning. ITC has envisaged on various plans to replicate the success achieved to other states and expand the services offered to other commodities like spices. ITC has also identified E-choupal as an important driver for exports, which are targeted at $ 400 million by 2005.

E-choupal has also attracted attention from the renowned academicians, since E-choupal has managed to innovate the supply-chain, and model applied by ITC has enough potential to be replicated in the under-developed and developing countries. The initial estimated per day sales at the store was around USD1555 - USD1778. The concept has validated C.K Prahalad's famous hypothesis that fortune lies at the bottom of the pyramid. Many other players have been trying to replicate the experience. Ruchi, the largest player in soyabean exports, has made a beginning with 15 villages. The Tata group too has stepped in with its own plans and that too with dual foray, one by the Tata Chemicals the other by Rallis India. Both these Tata group companies have their own set of Kisan Kendras, which total to around 200-plus across various villages. Tata Kisan Kendras (TKK) set up earlier, have roped in the National Remote Sensing Agency (NRSA) for using its satellite imagery service, to be known as 'precision farming'. The service combines the use of information technology along with satellite mapping techniques to advice farms to adopt farming practices that maximizes agricultural yields. NRSA will supply to the TKK satellite images for soil patterns and crop distribution while the TKK's will in turn interpret the data and superimpose it on the digitized image of the village maps. Tata group has also taken up farm management services at Chitradurga in Karnataka to support pomegranate growers and according sources, plans are in the pipeline to undertake contract farming for fruits and vegetables in Andhra Pradesh, wheat in Madhya Pradesh and Basmati rice in the northern states.

But there are certain bottlenecks in establishing rural retailing like rural mall, one of them being the infrastructure. Lack of infrastructure-roads, electricity and personal transport can prove to be a hindrance in establishing the rural mall. There is also the issue of displaced workers, traders and middlemen who would lose their employment in this process. The recent protest against Reliance Fresh in certain states by traders' union is a glaring example of how difficult it is to establish these malls. The cost of setting up "Choupal Sagar" by I.T.C was Rs.5 crores, the availability of seed capital and the feasibility of break even in a particular geographical location is yet another deterrent in setting up the rural mall. The gigantic task of setting up strong and robust supply chains and a localized basket of offerings has also to be undertaken. The quality and the competitive cost factor have to be taken care of. [4] Moreover, a change of mindset and preferences of the target segment to switch over from traditional convenience store to retail mall has to be initiated.

Under these circumstances, our study is to make an effort to study the feasibility of rural malls, with an objective approach. With many companies eying rural retailing, this study will provide an insight into various factors to be considered while setting up rural mall and also would provide a systematic approach to test its feasibility.

METHODOLOGY

The research was to find whether rural mall is feasible in Puri district. Rural mall is defined to be feasible if people of Puri district are willing to procure from rural mall. The first step in this research was to identify the variables/factors affecting the feasibility. Then the factors were measured using questionnaire. Response was obtained from residents of two villages namely Kumudia and Nathapur. From the measured factors, the feasibility of rural mall is decided.

Variable Analysis

The chosen variables and sub-variables for the research are as shown below:

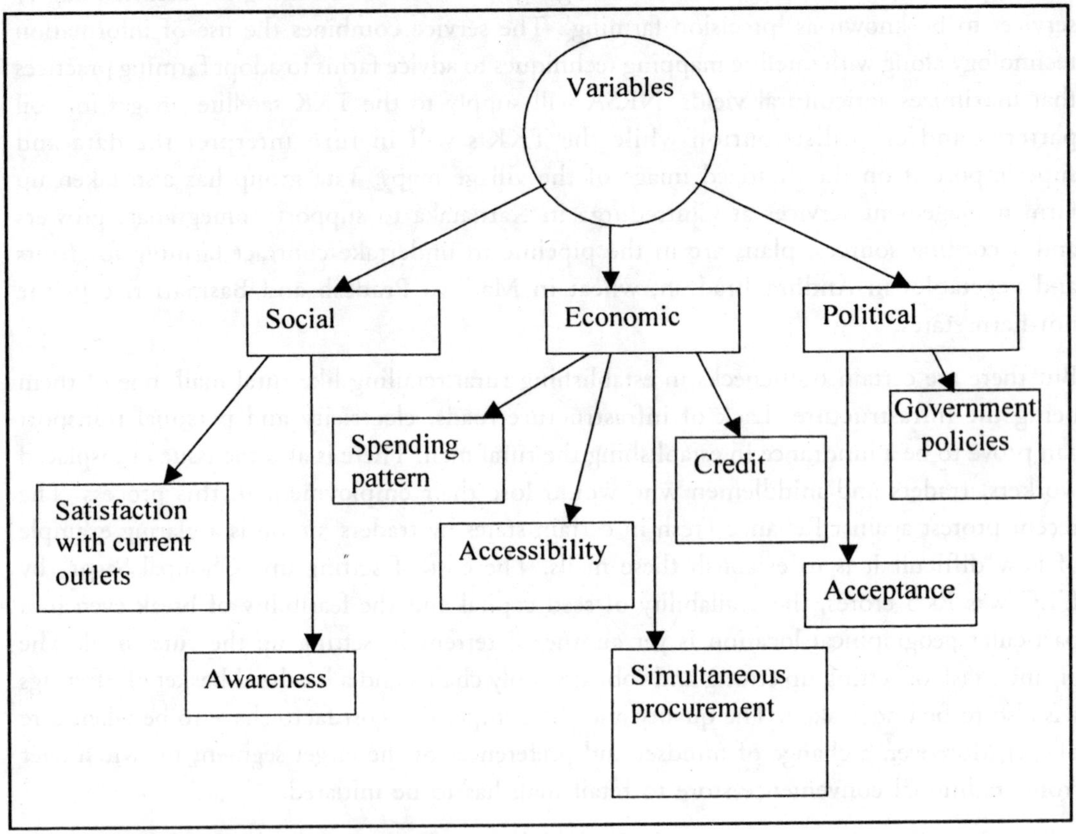

The variables chosen are explained below:

1. *Social:* Society is the most important factor affecting general human behaviour. The present conditions in the society as a whole guide the behaviour of the people who constitute the society. So a study of the social factors that would influence the behaviour of our target population to the idea of a rural mall was very crucial. After thinking over several factors that have social influence on the behaviour of the population, we inferred that there were two sub-aspects of the social variable that can have measurable influence on the feasibility of the rural mall in our target area. These sub-variables are:

   a. *Satisfaction level of people with the current retail facilities:* The people of the rural areas must be obtaining their required items from the local 'kirana' shops. The kirana shops must provide the basic needs. For the items not available in the local shops the people would go to the local 'haat' and if none stock the needed item, his only recourse is a journey to the city. The level of satisfaction with the current retail facilities depends on the extent to which the local shops and 'haats' satisfy a person's needs. With rising levels of income the needs of the people must have become more diversified. If the local shops can't cater to the new needs of the population, the satisfaction of the people will fall. This creates an opportunity for a rural mall to take advantage of.

b. *Awareness of retail mall:* The extent to which people of a place have access to information about a new product or service determines the ease with which that product or service can achieve penetration in a virgin market. A greater awareness of the concept of a mall among the target population would greatly help in creating a favourable opinion about the mall and reduce promotion costs too. A greater awareness can lead to a curiosity factor which can create a pull for the mall, among the rural population.

2. ***Economic:*** Economic health of the target population has a major influence on the possibility of a mall achieving financial profitability, which is a long-term objective of setting up the rural mall. Therefore the economy of the location and of the people in the location will have an impact on the success of the rural mall. The various sub-variables of the economic aspect are:

   a. *Spending pattern of households:* The households in rural areas usually spend maximum amount on food. But depending on the location and the amount of disposable income the spending on other item varies. This is helpful information in determining whether the varieties of item that a rural mall intends to keep have a market.

   b. *Accessibility of the mall:* Location of a mall is a key factor that would determine the repeatability of purchases from a mall. A centrally located mall, which is not too far away from any place in the target area is most suitable. If a person can easily reach the mall with minimal travel he/she will be more willing to go to the mall again and that too in a very short time. So this is a crucial sub-variable.

   c. *Availability of credit for purchases:* A great amount of shopping from rural areas usually happens on credit. Most people in rural areas don't have a regular monthly income. They usually are farmers who sell their produce either once or twice a year. So they may not have ready cash available at all times for their purchases. If the target population feels the need of presence of credit facilities, providing the same with necessary safeguards would help to attract them.

   d. *Need for agricultural produce procurement centre at the mall:* The local 'mandi' where farmers go to sell their produce is one of the most visited places by the rural people, most of whom are farmers. A simultaneous procurement centre can boost the attractiveness of the rural mall. This will generate greater footfalls, which in turn, will generate greater revenues. A procurement centre provides spending power to the people, which can be favourably channeled into greater spending in rural malls.

3. *Political:* Political factors have a major influence on the feasibility of setting up a rural mall. The sub-variables that can politically influence the success of a rural mall are:

   a. *Acceptance of rural mall among the local people:* As it can be clearly seen from the plight of Reliance Retail in different states, creating animosity among the target population by aggressive steps is not always suitable. The acceptance level of the usefulness of rural malls among the local people is a very important criterion that has to be considered in making a decision on setting up a rural mall, which is a long-term investment decision. A greater acceptance level would imply lesser risk of popular revolt as faced by Reliance Retail.

   b. *Government Policy:* In a country like India, the government's role and policies have to be taken into account in any decision. The government policies refer to those by central government, state government as well as the local bodies. Their policies may be favourable to the setting of a rural mall by providing tax relief, etc., which would make profitability easier to achieve. Also, these policies may regulate the format of malls and the type of commodities that can be sold by the malls, which have to be always kept in mind.

Data Collection

All the variables other than government policy could be measured by administering a questionnaire (Refer to Appendix I). The questionnaire was developed keeping in mind the variables and our respondents (in our case, rural farmers). For each variable, sets of questions (on an average 4) were created that could measure it effectively. In total, we had 26. We found that Likert Scale rating would be best suited for measuring our variables through the questionnaire. And accordingly the questionnaire was prepared giving five options to the respondents viz.

- Strongly Disagree
- Disagree
- Neutral/ Can't Say
- Agree
- Strongly Agree

However, government policy will be analyzed with the help of secondary data.

The questionnaire measures the various variables as shown below:

A. Satisfaction level with the present outlets.

   Question no. A1 - A5 measure this variable.

B. Awareness about rural mall.

   Question no. B6 measures this variable.

C. Need for procurement centres

Question no. C7 - C 10 measure this variable.

D. Availability of credit facilities for purchases.

Question no. D11 - D15 measure this variable.

E. Accessibility of the mall

Question no. E18 - E22 measure this variable.

F. Spending pattern of rural households.

Question no. F23- F27 measures this variable.

G. Acceptance level of the mall among rural people

Question no. G 28 measures this variable

H. Government policy

We will use secondary data to measure this variable.

As the major clientele of the envisaged rural mall are the village farmers, so our respondents consisted of rural farmers of Puri district from different strata of society and income group. We surveyed 102 farmers of two villages, namely Kumudia and Nathapur, both situated near the Dhauli Stupa. While the average farmer in the village of Kumudia is pretty well off, Nathapur had a different story to narrate with most farmers just managing the bare necessities.

As most of the farmers didn't know English, we explained them in local language (Oriya) and helped them in filling up the questionnaire. At first they were a bit apprehensive, but when we explained them our purpose of study, they were very co-operative.

Data Analysis

We used the statistical package SPSS for analyzing the data we collected. We undertook different tests for data analysis. The data is shown in Appendix II.

Reliability Analysis: The reliability analysis of the measurement questions were done to find the reliability of questions that measure a particular variable. Reliability test basically tests whether the answers to the questions that measure the particular variable are consistent. If any question measuring a particular variable has contradicting answers, then the reliability for that particular variable is low.

We got responses for 26 questions which were utilized for measuring 7 variables. The reliability test for all the variables is attached in the appendix III.

Reliability test for all the variables except credit facility was successful. For credit facilities, the reliability test failed. Upon examining the data, it becomes clear that questionnaire being followed contains independent questions which measure the usage of various credit options available currently. Hence, we understood that only one question was sufficient for accurately measuring the credit facility available. We consider only one question (D15) in measuring this variable.

Factor Analysis: We planned to do factor analysis to find the variables that contribute the most towards the research question. Factor analysis provides information on which all variables are highly correlated. If a respondent answers positively for a variable, he will be positive to the correlated variable too.

The factor analysis results are shown below:

KMO and Bartlett's Test

Kaiser-Meyer-Olkin Measure of Sampling Adequacy.		.779
Bartlett's Test of Sphericity	Approx. Chi-Square	307.079
	df	21
	Sig.	.000

This table shows two tests which indicate the suitability of data for factor analysis.

The Kaiser-Meyer-Olkin Measure of Sampling Adequacy is a statistic that indicates the proportion of variance in variables, which is common variance, i.e. which might be caused by underlying factors. High values (close to 1.0) generally indicate that a factor analysis may be useful with your data. If the value is less than .50, the results of the factor analysis probably won't be very useful. Since in our case the value is 0.779, we can conclude that factor analysis maybe helpful to us.

Bartlett's test of sphericity indicates whether our correlation matrix is an identity matrix, which would indicate that our variables are unrelated. The significance level gives the result of the test. Very small values (less than .05) indicate that there are probably significant relationships among the variables. Hence in our case, there seems to be some significant relationship among variables.

Communalities

	Initial	Extraction
SATIS	1.000	.814
AWARE	1.000	.881
PROCURE	1.000	.564
CREDIT	1.000	.365
ACCESS	1.000	.637
SPEND	1.000	.453
ACCEPT	1.000	.702

Extraction Method: Principal Component Analysis.

Communalities indicate the amount of variance in each variable that is accounted for. For principal components analysis, initial communality is always equal to 1.0 (for correlation analyses) or the variance of the variable (for covariance analyses).

Extraction communalities are estimates of the variance in each variable accounted for by the factors (or components) in the factor solution. Small values indicate variables that do not fit well with the factor solution, and should possibly be dropped from the analysis. Low value for credit seems to suggest that we better drop this variable from further factor analysis. This also goes well logically, since credit facilities depend on easy availability of loans from individuals or financial institutions, and thus does not really go with other variables like awareness about rural mall or satisfaction level.

Hence, we redo the factor analysis dropping credit facility.

This time above analyzed values is as shown below:

KMO and Bartlett's Test

Kaiser-Meyer-Olkin Measure of Sampling Adequacy.		.781
Bartlett's Test of Sphericity	Approx. Chi-Square	270.786
	df	15
	Sig.	.000

Communalities

	Initial	Extraction
SATIS	1.000	.797
AWARE	1.000	.935
PROCURE	1.000	.576
ACCESS	1.000	.654
SPEND	1.000	.506
ACCEPT	1.000	.708

Extraction Method: Principal Component Analysis.

Component Matrix[a]

	Component	
	1	2
SATIS	.893	8.586E-03
AWARE	.154	.955
PROCURE	.696	-.302
ACCESS	.808	-2.46E-02
SPEND	.703	.109
ACCEPT	.842	-1.22E-03

Extraction Method: Principal Component Analysis.

a. 2 components extracted.

This table reports the factor loadings for each variable on the factors. Each number represents the correlation between the item and the factor. We see that Satisfaction, Procurement need, Accessibility, Spending, and Acceptance all have large loading (above 0.8) on component 1. Hence Component 1 can be referred as Retail Value. Awareness is a separate factor. This is understandable, since awareness is influenced by availability of media, educational facilities, etc., and is not affected by things that determine the value of the other factors like satisfaction, etc.

Thus, we see that three factors explain much of the variance in data – Credit Facilities, Awareness and Retail Value as is evident from the previous discussion.

Cluster Analysis: Cluster analysis was planned to find out the common taste or preference in the target population. For example, if the target population in two villages is very much common in their tastes and preferences then a single model of the mall may be successful. If we find a clustering of respondents from different villages then we may need to think of different strategy to cater to different set of target population.

We use Hierarchical Cluster Analysis. This procedure attempts to identify relatively homogeneous groups of cases (or variables) based on selected characteristics, using an algorithm that starts with each case (or variable) in a separate cluster and combines clusters until only one is left. Through this preference we basically wish to find out groups amongst the respondents according to the demographic characteristics. The Appendix V contains the output of the cluster analysis.

The coefficients column in agglomeration schedule indicates the distance between the two clusters (or cases) joined at each stage. The values here depend on the proximity measure and linkage method used in the analysis. For a good cluster solution, you will see a sudden jump in the distance coefficient (or a sudden drop in the similarity coefficient) as you read down the table. After the 95th stage there is sudden jump in distance from 6.327 to 10.740. Hence considering this table, the respondents can be broken into different clusters using 6 distance space. Though we did not find much commonality between the respondents in clusters, it still can be noticed that most of the respondents who favour rural mall actually come from income group above 100,000 per household per annum and age group above 35 years.

Secondary data analysis: The variable government policy is measured by secondary data analysis. The state government of Orissa has a very favourable retail policy and aims to maintain an efficient, competitive and innovative retail sector. It envisages retail development in locations where the proximity of business facilitates competitions, from which all consumers are able to benefit. The government also wants to ensure the availability of a wide range of shops, employment, services and other facilities by encouraging the retail sector.

Recently there was protest by locals against Reliance Fresh outlets. But the government gave full support to Reliance Fresh and provided adequate police protection to them to enable their normal functioning, though it was disrupted for few days.

So, we can conclude that government policy is very encouraging for rural malls. Subsidies can also be expected from the government for a rural mall.

CONCLUSION

The variables we chose are able to give an indication as to the factors that affect the feasibility of rural malls in the Puri district villages where population mainly thrives on agriculture.

As is clear from Factor Analysis, retail value that comprised of the variables satisfaction, need for Procurement, accessibility, spending and acceptance primarily determines the feasibility of rural malls. Other factors, namely, credit availability and awareness about rural malls also independently affects the setting up rural malls.

Though cluster analysis did not clearly bring out any particular cluster clearly, it shows that people aged more than 35 and whose household income is greater than Rs. 100, 000 are in favour of rural malls being set up in Puri district.

Most of the factors in our study point that rural mall will be feasible in Puri district. However our study did not comprise of a rural area with an existing rural mall. Hence, we are unable to ascertain whether rural mall is feasible in Puri. To draw a final conclusion on hypothesis we need to administer the questionnaire to those currently visiting and not visiting an existing rural mall in similar geographical locations (Probably ITC's E-choupal in Madhya Pradesh). Then, we can take the respondent purchasing from rural mall as dependent variable (0 for not visiting the rural mall and 1 for visiting the rural mall) and the other variables obtained from the respondent as independent variables. We can then do a linear regression analysis and get equation for feasibility. We can then use the data we collected to determine the feasibility. However we can provide the following recommendations for success of rural mall in Puri from the data we collected:

- Only 53% of respondents were aware of rural malls. Hence increasing awareness is important for success of rural mall.
- Rural malls should give access to credit facility as 58% were willing to purchase from rural malls giving credit facility.
- Rural mall should also act as procurement centres as 80% of respondent were willing to sell their produce to rural malls.
- About 90% of respondents like the concept of a rural mall - an indication that rural mall will most probably be successful in Puri district.
- People aged more than 35 with income level greater than 100,000 are in favour of rural mall. Hence they can be targeted initially. After establishing a presence, other segments can be targeted.

However, this paper gives a systematic procedure to study the feasibility of rural mall in rural India. This process can be easily replicated in other parts of India to study the feasibility.

LIMITATIONS AND FUTURE STUDY

There were few limitations in our research. We could only sample two villages. The villages were basically taken based on convenience and it was assumed that they would be representative of the entire Puri district. The response obtained was not with any specific brand/company in mind. The response for questions on variables like acceptability might have different responses based on the company that might set up the mall. For example, Tata and Reliance might get different responses for questions on the variable - acceptability. The feasibility is mainly tested based on whether people are willing to buy from mall. Company-specific factors like supply chain are not taken into consideration.

There is also scope for future study on this research. As indicated in conclusion, a rural area with rural mall can be studied. The same questionnaire can be administered to visitors to a mall and those not visiting the mall. Analysis of their answers would provide insight into the kind of people who would prefer rural mall. Also, it would give an insight into the reason for people not visiting a rural mall. A linear regression can also be performed on the factors to get an equation. This equation can be used in other similar areas to test the feasibility.

REFERENCES

Rural Retail – The Next Phase in Retailing; The Great Indian Retail Boom, March 2007. Economic Research and Policy Division http://www.smisme.com/images/marketplace 20070308ERPD%20Economic%20 Update%20March%202007%20Edition.pdf

B. Bowonder B, Gupta Vinay and Singh Amit, "*Developing A Rural Market e-Hub, The Case Study of e-Choupal experience of ITC*". http://planningcommission.nic.in/reports/sereport/ser/stdy_ict/4_e-choupal%20.pdf

Prerna Raturi And Gouri Shukla, "Ground Reality", *Business Standard* June 2005. http:// www.destinationmadhyapradesh.com/state-profile/Short-project-profiles/15-Rural_Shopping_Mall.pdf

R Panneerselvam, *Research Methodology*, Prentice Hall of India, New Delhi, 2004.

14

A Study on Health of Women in IT/ITES Sector

Ms. SHANTHI NACHIAPPAN*
DR.B.DHARMALINGAM**

"The secret of health for both mind and body is not to mourn the past, not to worry about the future, or not to anticipate troubles, but to live the present moment wisely and earnestly"

– The Buddha

Today, the term Information Technology has ballooned to encompass many aspects of computing and technology. IT professionals perform a variety of duties that range from installing applications to designing complex computer networks and information databases. As women in India enter the rapidly expanding Information Technology (IT) workforce, it can be predicted that their active participation in this sector will change their socio-economic status within the employing organization and the communities in which they reside.

It is often expected that women's participation in the professional realm will contribute to a breakdown of traditional gender roles. Women working in this sector may be earning attractive salaries, but suffer from physiological and psychological problems due to a sedentary lifestyle.

That women are physically weaker than men is a proven scientific fact and if women suffer from biological imbalance because of night shifts and extended lengthy work hours during nights in this sector, what will happen to their health in the long run? As of now, when they are young (average age in IT/ITES is 27 years), they do not face much of a problem, but when they become old their health will become a matter of concern. In the future, the expenditure towards healthcare will be huge. It is being said that "prevention is better than cure"; it is

* HOD, Department of Management Studies, VCMCS (Research Scholar, Alagappa University), Velammal College of Management & Computer Studies, Ambattur-Redhills Road, Chennai.

** Director-In-Charge, Centre for Rural Development, Alagappa University, Karaikudi.

high time to take care of the food and other healthy habits of our young IT professionals. What we could see among our IT youth now is premature greying, potbellies, graveyard (or night guard) shifts, lonely hearts, etc.

The slogan, "Healthy Women, Healthy World" embodies the fact that as custodians of family health, women play a unique role in maintaining the health and well-being of their communities. Illness or death of a woman has serious and far-reaching consequences for the health of her children, family and community.

Young women professionals of IT industry are overloaded with productive, reproductive and social roles. Young mothers having toddlers at home prefer to work in the night shifts as they can spent quality time with their kids in the day time and share the breadwinning load of their counterparts during nights. Because of this type of sacrifice, what we see now is that women suffer from having several problems like anaemia, hair loss, obesity, etc.

At this crucial juncture, in this research paper, we have made an attempt to find out the food habits and lifestyle of women who are employed in the sunrise IT/ITES sector of India.

INTRODUCTION

"The body is like a piano, and happiness is like music. It is needful to have the instrument in good order"

– Beecher

Women experience adverse reproductive health issues. Improving the health status of women remains an unmet challenge, with great disparities existing between low- and high-income countries. Young people's knowledge and awareness about sexual and reproductive health is increasing but safe practice is on the decrease. Gender power imbalances makes risky behaviour more acceptable - encourages secrecy, fear of disclosure, and inhibits negotiation among partners. (Associated risky behaviours - drinking, smoking and drugs).

WORKING CONDITIONS AND HEALTH AMONG IT PROFESSIONALS

Workers in information technology working with visual display units are reported to have various health and psychosocial disorders. In India, the occupational health personnel is slowly awakening to this group of modern professionals. These problems, if ignored, can prove debilitating and cause crippling injuries, forcing one to change one's profession.

Among computer operators, risk factors associated with work-related muscular-skeletal disorders, include the integration of biomechanical factors such as static muscular overload, repetitive motions, conditions related to the work station and work environment and issues related to the working organization, as well as those associated with the psychological aspects of work.

The study noted the continued stress and strain at work. The major reasons cited for quitting the job by employees, were inconvenience of shifts, increased stress, and lack of career prospects. The Burn Out Stress Syndrome (BOSS) is commonly observed among young people working in the IT sector. The symptoms of this syndrome include chronic fatigue, insomnia and complete alteration of the 24-hour biological rhythm of the body, leading to sickness and absenteeism.

The IT professionals are under tremendous stress at work. They don't follow any timing, face the pressure of deadlines, have irregular meals, work at night and have only time to sit in front of the computer for hours and hours without any physical exercise.

The Diagnostic and Statistical Of Mental Disorders (DSM-IV-TR) defines a psycho-social stressor as "any life event or life change that may be associated temporally (and perhaps causally) with the onset, occurrence, or exacerbation [worsening] of a mental disorder." A severe acute stressor may result in stress-response syndrome such as an acute stress disorder or a post-traumatic disorder.

Acute Stress Disorder

In acute stress, the mind and body respond with a fight or flight response. It begins with the activation of a section of the brain and release of steroid hormones, which are also known as glucocorticoids. The HPA system then releases a set of neurotransmitters known as catecholamines, which have three important effects:

- They activate the amygdala, an almond-shaped structure in the limbic system that triggers an emotional response of fear.
- They signal the hippocampus, another part of the limbic system, to store the emotional experience in long-term memory.
- They suppress activity in parts of the brain associated with short-term memory, concentration, and rational thinking. This suppression allows a human to react quickly to a stressful situation, but it also lowers ability to deal with complex social or intellectual tasks that may be part of the situation.

Post-traumatic Disorder

People with such a disorder may have intrusive remembrances, nightmares, or even flashbacks of the stress event. These can alternate with emotional numbing, interpersonal alienation, and extreme avoidance of traumatic reminders. A diagnosis of posttraumatic stress disorder (PTSD) is made if these symptoms persist longer than one month.

Symptoms

The symptoms include twitching, trembling, muscle tension, headache, sweating, dry mouth, difficulty in swallowing, dizziness, rapid or irregular heart rate, rapid breathing, diarrhea, fatigue, irritability, loss of temper, sleeping difficulties and nightmares, decreased concentration and sexual problems. Chronic over-activation of stress response may predispose an individual to greater risk for physical illness such as heart disease. Overly intense exposure to an acute stressor may result in a stress response syndrome with potentially disabling consequences.

T.T. Ashok, Chairman, Corporate Social Responsibility, Sub-Committee, CII - Southern Region, in his article "Vulnerability of Workforce in IT & ITES Sectors", has conducted a pilot study on the most critical and pressing health issue: HIV/AIDS. The study attributes that the health and lifestyle are interrelated and the following factors influence the health of women:

- Changing food habits ("from Pongal to Pizzas")
- Erratic sleeping pattern ("changes with every new shift")
- Lack of exercise ("no regular exercise regimen")
- Few recreation activities ("very little time or energy for anything else")
- Large disposable incomes at young age ("don't know what to do with it")
- Consumption-oriented lifestyles ("expensive consumer goods")

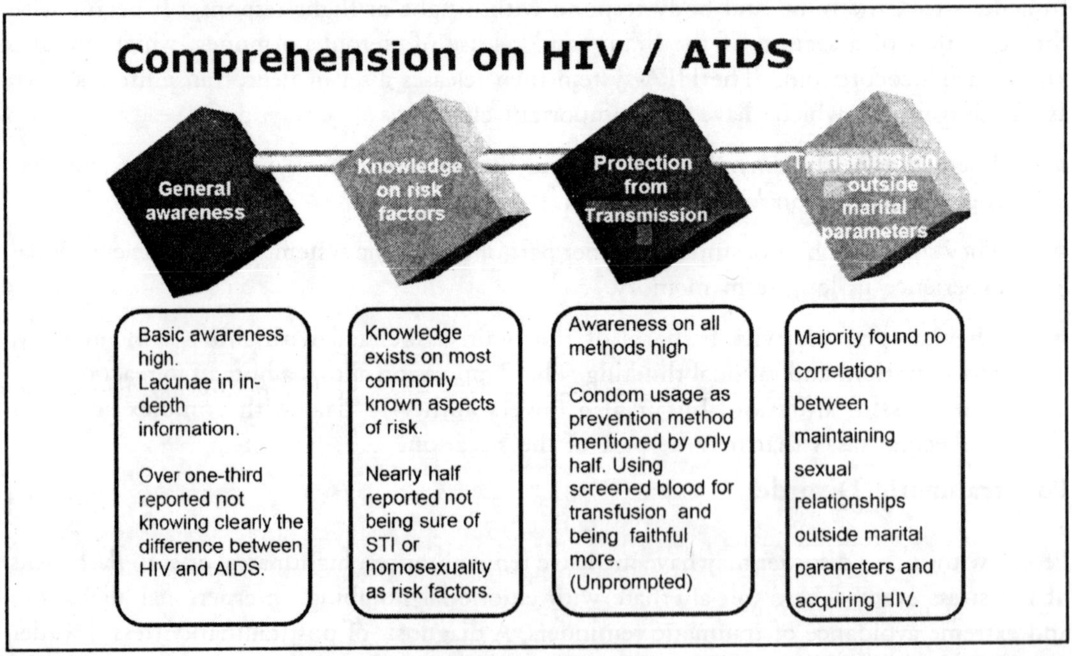

In an article published on December 1998 on "Women's health in India" by Victoria A. Velkoff and Arjun Adlakha, U.S. Department of Commerce, Economics and Statistics Administration, states that Indian women have high mortality rates, particularly during childhood and in their reproductive years. The research focuses on only five key issues: Reproductive health, Violence against women, Nutritional status, Unequal treatment of girls and boys, and HIV/AIDS. The article concludes that the health of Indian women is intrinsically linked to their status in society.

An research conducted by National Cancer Research Institute (NCRI), UK, on "LIFESTYLE CHANGES COULD PREVENT ONE IN TEN CASES OF BREAST CANCER BY 2024", states how a number of factors can influence a woman's risk of breast cancer. The research gives some predictions based on the following:

- That prolonged hormone replacement therapy (HRT) use will continue to fall at the same rate as currently (by almost 50%) over the next five years;
- That levels of obesity over the next 10 years will return to 1980 levels when 8% of women were obese compared with 23% today;
- That exercise levels will increase so that, within three years, all women will exercise for at least 30 minutes five days a week;
- That, within three years, all women will drink within the government recommendations of no more than two alcoholic units a day;
- That (as in Sweden) 72% of women in the UK breast feed for six months, currently achieved by 21%.

The research concludes that every woman will make choices about her health based on her individual circumstances. For instance, there are good medical reasons why some women take HRT where the benefits outweigh the disadvantages.

"Leading a healthy life with a good diet, plenty of exercise and drinking a limited amount of alcohol does not guarantee that a person won't get cancer but these healthy habits can help to cut the chances."

NEED FOR THE STUDY

Six software professionals under the age of 33 have died and 2 top executives from renowned software companies have become paralyzed because of stress-related heart ailments in the last six months in Chennai, says a study by Mitran Foundation, a Bangalore-based doctors' voluntary association.All the six who died, and the two who became invalid, had no family history of heart attacks or any pre-history of heart ailments or paralysis. They were all in their prime, between 27 and 33 years and handled challenging projects at work. They worked long and continuous hours. The end struck them very suddenly, and it looked as if their hearts refused to take any more stress," said Dr Dwarakanath, director of Mitran Foundation, who has studied stress components in 40 software companies in Chennai during the last six months.

Most married women prefer night shifts in ITES as they can take care of their children during the day/evening time and work during nights, which results in weight loss, psychological problems and others.

At this crucial juncture, in this research paper, we have made an attempt to find out the food habits and lifestyle of women who are employed in the sunrise IT/ITES sector of India.

RESEARCH METHODOLOGY

Type of research	:	Descriptive research was adopted
Sample size	:	75
Sampling technique	:	Convenient sampling method was used for sample selection.
Data Sources	:	Primary and secondary data were used for analysis, interpretation and report preparation.
Research Instrument	:	Structured questionnaire with open ended and close ended questions.
Sampling Unit	:	Women employed in IT and ITES sector in India.
Analysis	:	Both quantitative and qualitative data analysis was carried out.

Objectives of the Study

The main objectives of the study are

- To find the demographic profile (age, education, experience, etc.,) of women employees of IT & ITES
- To know about their awareness level about the health problems.
- To identify the health problems of women working in IT/ITES sector.
- To give suitable suggestions to corporate to frame their HR policies.

RESEARCH FINDINGS

- *Age:* Nearly three fourth of the respondents working in IT and ITES sector were in the age group of 20-25 years. The average age of the people working in this sector was around 27 years. This clearly indicates that the industry is very young with the intake of fresh blood into it.
- *Type of family:* Nearly three fourth [70%] of the respondents working in IT and ITES sector hailed from a nuclear family.
- *Marital Status:* Majority of the respondents [67%] working in this sector were unmarried and work for continuously 10-14 hours per day. Probably this could be the reason behind the industry's preference of very young unmarried women who did not have any family commitments. As unmarried women did not have the work-life balance challenge.
- *Shift:* More than half of the women [53%] were working in night shifts which show a drastic change in the respondent's perception of working in nights. This has also

lead to many health-related problems - most significantly stress problem, biological imbalance, etc.

Food Habits:

- Majority of the respondents [59%] working in this sector did not have breakfast on time and 49% didn't have lunch on time because of the night shift. Health specialists strongly argue that skipping breakfast was a most dangerous tendency. This would for sure lead to many health problems though not now, but definitely in the future. This is further proved statistically by the Anova analysis which revealed that the respondents of different age categories have average food habits.
- Nearly 36% of the respondents didn't have dinner on time because of the shift, which was frightening and shocking. It is further proved by chi-square results that more than one third of married and unmarried women skip dinner.
- More than one third [39%] of the respondents have fresh fruits once in two days and around two third [60%] have vegetables daily which is slightly encouraging.
- Consumption of junk food is yet another problem found among these young professionals. Anova 2 revealed that junk food is consumed equally by almost all with different educational qualification and different age categories have it equally, which was proved by the chi-square results.
- Almost three fourth [71%] of the respondents were having milk daily, which was found to be positive and 39% were not taking milk. Having milk though shows a good sign must be complimented with other good practices like exercise and other physical activity.

Exercising:

- 2/3rd of the respondents did not answer question regarding exercise, which means they were not doing it because of shifts and other reasons.

Health Problems:

- Nearly two third [69%] respondents replied that they were having acidity problems and nearly 87% have said they were not having insomnia.
- Half of the respondents [51%] said that they were having no stress against 49% replying that they were having stress, which was highly disturbing. Stress is high among night shift employees, which was proved by the Chi-square 2 results.
- More number [60%] of the respondents were suffering from hair fall which is alarming. This is proved statistically by the Chi-square results which revealed that hair fall was higher among the age category of 20 -25 years, which shows their stress level and lack of protein.
- Majority of the women (89%) respondents did not have obesity problem.

- More than half of the Indian IT professionals (51%) were found to be anemic, which is upsetting. This is similar to other Indian women, and education and economic empowerment haven't changed the position of Indian IT women in terms of health. This implies an evidence of the respondents prone to health problems in future.
- More than half of the respondents were in-energetic (56%) which is distressing. This is further proved statistically by the Chi-square results that both married and unmarried women were equally inenergic. Almost many were having back pain (59%), as it could be an occupational disease as the nature of work was sitting in front of the monitor for hours together.
- Around half (45%) of the respondents working in the sector were having eye problem which is worrying.
- It is heartening to note that majority (93%) of the respondents were not diabetic and were not having blood pressure. Probably as they were young, they were not having such health problems.

CONCLUSION

- ***Providing fresh fruit juice/milk in the morning in the work-place:*** It was observed that majority of the IT and ITES women employees were either skipping break-fast or dinner. They were having irregular food habits. So, organizations that employ huge number of women should take care of their health by providing them healthy fresh fruit juices/milk in the morning. This will help them to earn more in the long run as the health of their valuable employees is the real wealth for them.
- ***Strategies for occupational hazards:*** Women employees of IT /ITES were facing back pain problems, which could be avoided by proper exercising (compulsory exercises in the morning and in the evening). Eye strain could be overcome by proper relaxation. Once in two hours, regular two minutes breaks should be provided to all employees for this purpose.
- ***Empowering women in health:*** Real empowerment includes health empowerment of women. Women should be made aware of their health significance. Economic empowerment of women should not result in their health deterioration. They need not stay late nights or work beyond a limit to achieve their organizational goals, which will result in stress or strain and subsequently health problems. They should take care of their health by proper food habits (not by eating pizzas, burgers, biscuits , wafers or chat items or some other junk food which will fill in their stomach, but are not healthy).
- ***Health awareness from primary courses:*** As IT has become a sunrise industry and a comfortable choice of work for women, definitely more and more women would join the sector in the future. Hence health habits can be created right from the young age through the primary education system. Health consciousness and proper health habits have to be cultivated from the young age.

- *Common health hazards of IT employees:* A recent study conducted by Dr.Dwarakanath among IT employees revealed that BP, diabetes and mental pressure were common diseases. Suicides, divorce and heart ailments were highest among them.

  Cervical spondilitis and wrist problems due to uncomfortable handling of the computer mouse, eye problems and discomfort in bowel movements were also common. Fat salaries did not result in comfort. The results of this survey are almost similar to the above study. So stress management techniques like yoga, meditation, etc. to be taught to IT employees and they should be informed to practice it daily.

- *Regular Medical Check Ups in IT:* HR departments should make proper arrangement for regular medical check-ups at least twice in a year so that IT employees know their health status clearly. Prevention is always better than cure, as majority of the IT employees are young they think that they would not have such diseases but the problem is as they are workaholic they catch diseases at a very young age.

- *Night Shifts:* Women who were working in the night shift were reported to have insomnia and also stress problems. So awareness has to be created among women, as they were inenergic and anemic. So it is strongly recommended that such women to move from night shift to day shifts/work.

BIBLIOGRAPHY

Publications of:

1. National Cancer Research Institute, UK.
2. Confederation of Indian Industry.
3. U.S. Bureau of Statistics (Article issued on December 1998).

Websites

- www.marketresearch.com/product/display
- www.census.gov/ipc/prod/wid-9803.pdf

15 Sensory Branding for Sensible Differentiation in the Marketplace

S. VICTOR ANANDKUMAR*

Commodity status is the nightmare of every marketer. Once customers view a product or service as a commodity, the most important thing to them is price and that can trigger a race among the marketers to the bottom. To avoid this and to take the road to profitability and growth, most marketers differentiate their product or service offering apart from those of competitors in meaningful ways other than price. While several differentiators are available in the marketers' tool kit, an effective differentiator is branding. But with the proliferation of brands, the marketplace is increasingly competitive for the marketers and confusingly crowded for the customers. The consumer behaviour literature identifies exposure-attention-perception as the front end of information processing for consumer decision-making. This in turn affects what consumers comprehend, what attitudes they have, what they remember and finally, what decisions they make. In this context, sensory branding emerges as an approach that appeals to all five senses - touch, taste and smell, not just sight and hearing - in order to foster a lasting emotional connection between the brand and the consumer that optimizes purchasing and brand loyalty.

Sensory branding is likely to become an important aspect of the way brands will create true points of difference in an increasingly competitive market. The underlying logic is that appealing to all five is likely to heighten the brand awareness and strengthen the impression a brand leaves on its audience. A collection of case studies are assembled to probe into the principles and practices of sensory branding. An analysis of these case studies brings to surface many generalizations, which will be of value to marketers wanting to appeal to all the five senses. The product or service suitability to sensory branding is discussed and potential marketplace applications are presented. This paper uses case studies from global brands to illustrate the effectiveness of sensory branding.

Keywords: Branding, Differentiation, Sensory perception, Sensory branding, Case studies.

* Department of Management Studies, School of Management, Pondicherry University, Pondicherry.

INTRODUCTION

A commodity is a product or service for which there are no differentiating features (HBSP 2006): a plastic card, a postal mail, a retail store, a litre of milk. Once customers view a product or service as a commodity, the most important thing to them is price and that can trigger a race among the marketers to the bottom. To get orders, producers must meet the expected standards of quality and have the lowest price. Today, many products, unless differentiated, run the risk of turning into commodities. Even the personal computer (PC), a unique and highly differentiated product when it went mainstream in the 1980s, is now approaching commodity status. More than 90% of current PCs used the same operating systems and compatible microprocessors. The PC is fast on its way to joining the refrigerator and the television set as a commodity product.

Certain terms that are routinely used to distinguish between commodity and non-commodity products and services are summarized in the following table.

Table 1: Commodity vs. non-commodity: the differentiating terms

Commodity	Non-commodity
• Widely available	• Exclusive
• Cheap and getting cheaper	• Expensive
• Standard	• Unique
• Low status	• High status
• Undifferentiated	• Differentiated
• Goes by generic name	• Goes by brand name
• Meets needs	• Meets wants

[Source: Adopted from HBS, 2006]

Sellers want to avoid a commodity image, because doing so usually allows them to command a higher price. Ideally, they would like to differentiate themselves, set their offering apart and surround it with a positive aura. The road to profitability and growth for most enterprises is through differentiation - offering consumers something they value that competitors don't have. Approaches to differentiation are limited only by human creativity, but generally take one of the following forms:

- Appealing design and looks - for example, Apple's iMac
- Superior performance - for example, BMW automobiles
- Technical innovation - for example, Nokia mobile phones
- Services - for example, Cemex using just-in-time delivery of ready-mix concrete
- Reliability and durability - for example, Tupperware plastic kitchenware

- Channel of distribution - for example, Dell with its direct marketing model
- Convenience and ease of ordering - for example, Amazon.com
- Owner safety - for example, Volvo cars
- Image - for example, Harley-Davidson motorbikes

CONCEPT OF BRANDING

Branding is another approach to differentiation. Business historian Nancy F. Koehn defines brand as "a name, logo or symbol intended to distinguish a particular seller's offering from those of competitors (Koehn 2001)". It also embodies the abundant marketing messages connected with the offering and the complex set of customer expectations that arise from it. Branding refers to the communication effort that aims to differentiate a product or service from its rivals and to create a positive attitude towards it (HBS 2006). One could make a case that branding is the culmination of efforts to differentiate product or service. By building a familiar and favourable image for an offering, the marketer has a better than even chance of becoming the buyer's first choice among many competitors.

Whether they deserve it or not, brand-name products have an aura of quality or utility that rival products in the same category do not possess. That aura usually translates into premium prices over non-branded rivals. Brand power also leads to higher unit sales, because customers don't have to agonize over whether or not to buy them. Familiar brands reduce risks in a reliable, affordable and convenience way (Barwise and Meehan, 2004). A recognizable brand acts as an imprimatur of reliability, making the customer's choice easy.

Modern branding is only a 50+ year old discipline. The following table illustrates the evolution of branding since the 1950s and highlights the branding focus and critical success factor at different times. Branding guru Lindstrom (2005) identifies sensory experience as the critical success factor for today's branding. Arguments are presented to justify this position.

Table 2: Evolution of branding

Timeline	Focus and Critical Success Factor	Examples
1950s	Physical Product	
1960s	Emotional Attachment	Coke and Pepsi
1980s	Organization	Nike
Early 1990s	Brand	Harry Potter
Late 1990s	Consumer brand ownership	DeBeers
2000 and beyond	Sensory experience	

[Source: Adapted from Lindstrom, 2005]

As brands become commonplace and branding communication becomes ubiquitous, brand clutter and communication overload result. For example, with 35 varieties of bagels, 66 subbrands of GM cars and more than 13,000 mutual funds, American consumers are suffering a severe case of brand overload (Cristol and Sealey 2000). According to the Newspaper Advertising Bureau, in 1965 34% of consumers in the US could name the brand of a commercial aired during a show. Thirty years later, only 8% were capable of doing this. By the time the American consumers reach the ripe old age of 65, they have been exposed to two million television commercials. This means that they've spent an equivalent of eight hours each day, seven days a week, watching commercials without a break for close to six years (Lindstrom 2005). As a consequence of commonplace branding and pervasive branding communication, the brands face the following obstacles (Kahn 2007):

- *Overexposure:* this leads to brand dilution in terms of awareness, recognition and even confusion.
- *Product proliferation:* this leads to mindless brand extensions and thereby diminishing the brand value and positioning. Moreover, most offerings have similar quality and features. People have too many choices and too little time.
- *Higher new product failure rates:* this occurs as a result of too many brands chasing too few customers. There abound to be more losers than winners in the brand race.
- *Diminishing effectiveness of mass media advertising:* the methods by which consumers absorb information and entertainment and the ways they perceive, retain, and engage with brands and brand messages have changed irrevocably. As a result, mass media advertising effectiveness is on the decline.
- *Product commoditization:* As product lifecycles become increasingly shorter, many products quickly reach commodity status where price and not brand name becomes the single biggest buying driver.
- *Shift towards electronic interactions with brands:* this leads to customer-initiated interactions with the markets, thus reducing brand impact.

SENSORY BRANDING

When faced with the above mentioned obstacles, Lindstrom (2005) says: Marketers have to go back to the basics and identify what actually appeals to human beings on an ordinary, everyday basis. Almost our entire understanding of the world is experienced through our senses. Our senses are our link to memory and can tap right into emotion. A bright fresh spring day has a particular smell to it. Manufacturers try to bottle this feeling of life's renewal. Then the marketers use the emotional connection to spring to sell their dishwashing liquids, toilet cleaners, shampoos, soaps, window cleaners and so on. Branding is all about building emotional ties between consumer and product.

The senses offer more than just a means to satisfy basic needs. The senses offer one of the most compelling ways to create competitive advantage. They offer an opportunity to create a unique brand experience, support a distinctive brand identity, create a strong emotional bond, and ultimately create a compelling reason to buy the brand. The more senses you appeal to, the stronger the message. When applying this information to a branding context, the general rule of thumb is that the more senses a brand appeals to, the stronger the message will be perceived. Interestingly, stronger bonding directly translates to higher prices that consumers will be prepared to pay.

Sensory branding is defined as the purposeful design and deployment of the interaction between the senses in order to stimulate a consumer's relationship with a brand; and to foster a lasting emotional connection that optimizes purchasing and brand loyalty (Kahn 2007).

THEORETICAL BACKGROUND

Consumer decision-making involves information processing, which is a series of activities by which stimuli are perceived, transformed into information and stored (Hawkins et al 2004). Figure 1 illustrates a useful information processing model having four major stages, namely exposure, attention, interpretation and memory. The first three of these constitute perception. Exposure occurs when a stimulus comes within range of a person's sensory receptor nerves (in vision or hearing or smell or touch or taste). Attention occurs when the stimulus is taken notice of. Interpretation is the assignment of meaning to the received sensations.

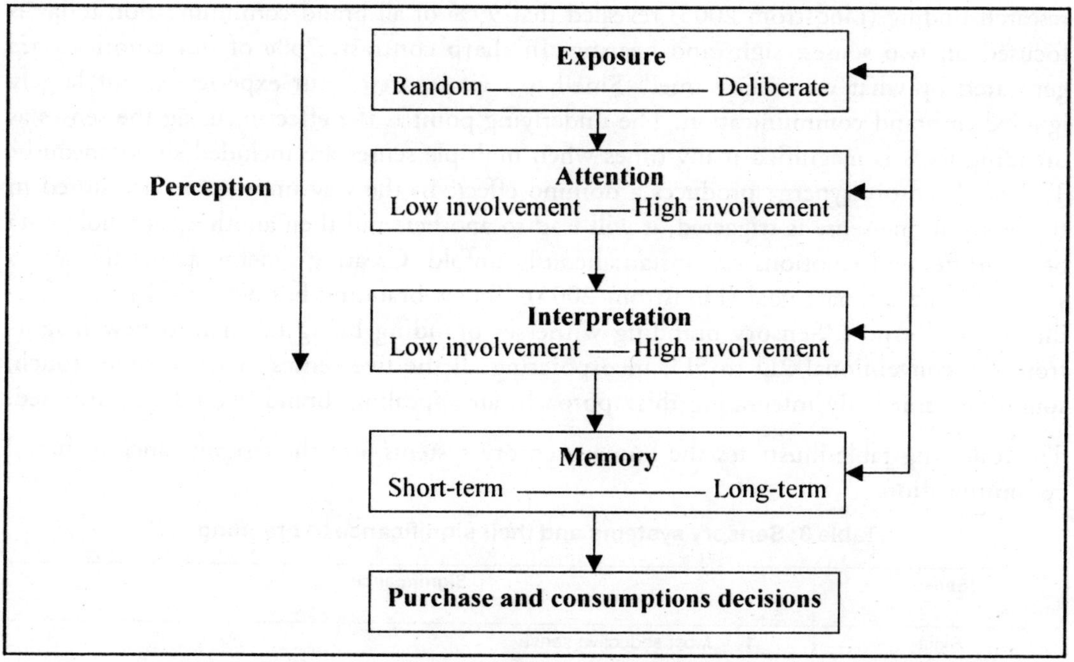

Figure 1: Information processing for consumer decision-making

The human body consists of five sensory systems that provide sensations when an external stimuli or sensory inputs are given. The following figure illustrates the role of the sensory systems in the perceptual process.

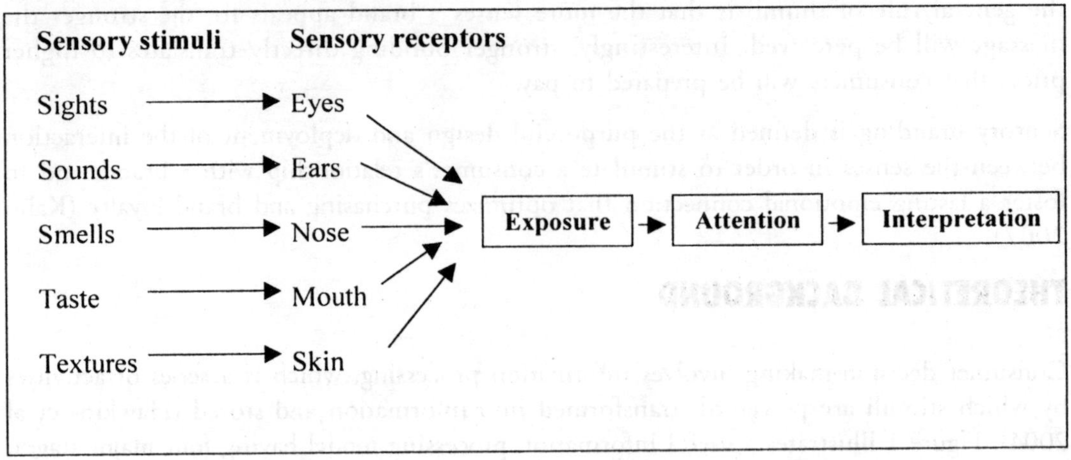

Figure 2: An overview of the perceptual process

The massive influx of visual stimulus that is encountered everyday in the marketplace has long dimmed the awareness of and need for integrated other senses. However, other sensory stimulus - sound, smell, touch, taste - still affect consumer mood and decision-making. A research finding (Lindstrom 2005) revealed that 99% of all brand communication today is focused on two senses: sight and hearing. In sharp contrast, 75% of our emotions are generated by what we in fact smell. Smell is a vital part of our experience, but largely ignored in brand communication. The underlying point is the effect of using the senses as branding tools is magnified many times when multiple senses are included simultaneously. This total sensory synergy produces a domino effect. In the way impressions are stored in the brain, if one sense is triggered, it will lead to another, and then another…a whole vista of memories and emotions can instantaneously unfold. Creating synergy across the senses should be the ultimate goal (Lindstrom 2005). Today, branding has developed into a five-dimensional aspect. Sensory branding witnesses branding being taken into new heights from the conventional 2D to 5D; incorporating all the five senses of taste, sight, touch, sound and smell. By integrating this approach, an appealing 'brand' would be harnessed.

The following table illustrates the human sensory systems and their significance in brand communication.

Table 3: Sensory systems and their significance to branding

Sense	Significance
Sight	1. Most seductive sense 2. Often overrules the other senses 3. Colour plays an important role
Sound	• Connected to mood • Only 4% of Fortune 500 brands use sound online

Contd...

	• Role of music is important
Smell	• Evokes memory, alters mood and influences choice • 10,000 times more sensitive than taste • 75% of human emotions are generated by scent
Taste	• Sweet, salty, sour or bitter • Hard to introduce but highly effective • Develops linkage in the memory
Touch	• Skin is the largest organ in the body • Alerts us to a sense of well being or pain • Texture of products and experiences

Park, Jaworski, and MacInnis (1986) identified three types of consumer need: functional, symbolic and experiential. The functional and symbolic needs are fulfilled by mass production and overwhelming commercial advertising. What is left, the experiential need, becomes the key to distinguishing brand offerings. Branding through experience - sensory branding, to be exact, has evolved from interior design and merchandise display into a more holistic approach, and has become a crucial facet of the marketing mix.

CASE STUDIES

This paper analyzes product categories that meet universal and non-gender-specific needs (e.g. FMCG products, plastic cards, entertainment, retail and public mail service) and the brands that have developed sensory branding strategies. International case studies have been included. Secondary data sources (such as sensory marketing books, websites, consumer behaviour texts and so on) have been relied upon, with the recency of the case studies as the inclusion criteria for analysis and discussion in the paper. Diverse product categories have been chosen to arrive at generalizable conclusions.

Case-1: FMCG

Avon, whose products are sold primarily door to door, now uses scent strips or scented pages for products from perfume to bubble bath in most of its product catalogues (Kang and Byron 2006). One of its recent catalogues features actress Jennifer Hudson on the cover, along with a sample of a new fragrance, Imari Seduction, encased beneath an adhesive strip. The extra cost is worth it, says Avon, which uses Arcade Marketing (one of the major players in creating ads that emit different smells to make scent strips in its catalogues). Avon says it can regularly see the high return on investment, according to Lily DeStefano, executive director of Avon's U.S. fragrances. The beauty company, based in New York, uses scented spots on its pages or fragrance strips for new and longstanding products because it translates to stronger sales for both and helps attract new customers. Still, the technique requires logistical planning to avoid one fragrance's aroma mixing with another. "It is a bit of a challenge because we don't want to compromise the quality of the scent," Ms. DeStefano says. "We just examine the brochure and place the scent pages strategically throughout so they don't clash." Beauty companies, not surprisingly, still dominate the market for scent ads. The beauty sector accounts for more than half of Arcade's business. Competition for shoppers' attention has become intense in the fragrance market amid record numbers of new product introductions over the past few years. The extra competition makes sampling a crucial tool in luring buyers, Arcade says.

Associative memories are those that are retrieved from the memory in response to an external stimulus processed by the human sensory system. Tapping into powerful associative memories are one of the paths into the heart of the consumer. California Milk Processor Board celebrated the hippy nostalgia of cookies in the oven (Weiss 2006). The project involved five downtown bus shelters that carried a stark black ad with the words "Got Milk?" on it. Hidden around the shelter were the carefully placed scent strips (that emit the aroma of freshly baked chocolate cookies) set for optimal downwind distribution. The subliminal scent was to entice those waiting for the bus to smell the cookies and think about having a cookie and a glass of milk. The campaign kicked off with distribution of cookies and milk around the bus shelters during the day. The hope: Once pedestrians pass the sweetly scented "Got Milk" bus shelters, they'll crave a tall glass of milk.

Case-2: Plastic cards

Forget about low interest rates, rewards points and free balance transfers. To attract new customers in a crowded market, credit-card issuers are pitching cards with sleek features, including a hefty one that its promoters say has "plunk factor" (Sidel 2006). Inspired by consumer interest in eye-catching products like retro toasters and fashionable can openers that have moved from the cupboard to the countertop, credit-card companies are creating unique cards aimed at winning the coveted "top of wallet" position - the card pulled out the most often. American Express Co. is testing a "Butterfly" card that folds in half and pops out of a silver case attached to a key ring. Other issuers and card-makers are experimenting with cards that feature various textures, light and sound, as well as high-tech security features. American Express believes card design is part of the innovation in credit-card market. Versatile Card Technology Inc. (VCT) is hustling to develop sample designs that it can pitch to banks, retailers and direct-mail companies. The company has manufactured dozens of unusual cards in the past several years. Some ideas, though, might have limited appeal. VCT makes a scratch-and-sniff model that smells like coffee, as well as about 90 other aromas. It even discussed with a retailer for a perfume-scented card.

Case-3: Entertainment

A scent-strip ad in the August 24, 2006 issue of Rolling Stone Magazine to promote the second season of Showtime's "Weeds" may smell like pot getting smoked, or marijuana in a bag or even hippies (Jossip.com 2006). To promote the second-season premiere of its pot-themed domestic drama, Showtime inserted perfume-style scent strips into a Rolling Stone issue. The fold-out strips emit an odour familiar to marijuana. The network is also passing out "Weeds"-themed brownies at major transportation hubs. A Munchie Mobile is distributing merchandise at Los Angeles and New York concerts and sporting events. Showtime Executive VP of Creative Marketing Len Fogge said the network went to several scent-manufacturing companies before finding the perfect herbal essence. "We experimented with several scents before we chose one - not that anyone here knows firsthand what it might smell like," he said. The concern here is that maybe some people may find this kind of thing edgy.

Case-4: Retail

Retailers know how you'll approach a store, where you'll hesitate, how to affect your mood, how to pique your desires, how to play to your aspirations. Everything in a store, from lighting to floor colour to music to how goods are displayed, is meant in some way to get you to not just shop, but spend. Today's retail is a highly orchestrated retail environment (Fetterman and O'Donnell 2006). At a Sony Style store, for instance, the subtle fragrance of vanilla and mandarin orange - designed exclusively for Sony - wafts down on shoppers, relaxing them and helping them believe that this is a very nice place to be. Everything in the store is designed to encourage touch, from the silk wallpaper to the smooth maple wood cabinets to the etched-glass countertops. Products are displayed like museum pieces and set up to touch and try.

Retailers such as Sony are developing "signature scents" that you smell only in their stores. Sony decided to create its own scent for its Sony Style stores as one way to make the consumer electronics it sells less intimidating, particularly to women. "From research, we found that scent is closest to the brain and will evoke the most emotion, even faster than the eye," says Dennis Syracuse, senior vice president of consumer retail sales. "Our scent helps us create an environment like no other." "Scent is so closely aligned with your emotions, it's so primitive," says David Van Epps, president of ScentAir, a US-based company that develops exclusive scents for businesses, including Sony. His firm's revenue, number of employees and output have tripled in the past two years, he says. Other retailers might not have signature scents, but they use fragrance. Bloomingdale's uses different essences in different departments: baby powder in the baby store; sun tan lotion in the bathing suit area; lilacs in lingerie; cinnamon and pine scent during the holiday season.

Music has been used by retailers for decades as a way to identify their stores and affect a shopper's mood, to make you feel happy, nostalgic or relaxed so you linger. But retailers are becoming more sophisticated in how they use music. J.C. Penney has installed a new system for its stores that allows certain music to be played at certain times of the day. It can "zone" music by demographics, playing more Latin music in stores where there's a higher Hispanic population - all controlled by headquarters in Plano, Texas.

Japan's choosy consumers are world leaders at sniffing out bargains, but in a bold advertising experiment in Tokyo, one restaurant will appeal to prospective diners' sense of smell in a more literal sense (McCurry 2007). Kirin City beer hall in the bowels of Tokyo railway station has been releasing computer-controlled aromas into the air in front of its entrance in the hope that it will draw extra diners. The hi-tech sales strategy - known as aroma digital signage - will run until the end of the year and the results will be used to gauge whether a whiff of refreshing orange or lemon at lunchtime, or the scent of wood in the evenings, really does put passersby in the mood for a meal or an after-work pint. The technology, in which the scents are released in bursts by a computer-controlled device hooked up to the internet, is being developed by NTT Communications. During an experiment with "calming" lavender and orange scents at a Tokyo shopping mall earlier this year, NTT saw sales rise by an average of 4.8%, according to Shunichi Hamada of the firm's net business division.

PUBLIC MAIL SERVICE

Britain's Royal Mail is seeking to bulk up its direct mail business by teaming with Brand Sense to promote the sensory potential of mail, suggesting marketers include scents and sounds with their appeals (Royal Mail Group 2007). Branded as 'Sensational Mail', it is a new direct marketing solution enabling advertisers to build sensory triggers into their direct mail. The logic is that a brand needs rational and emotional appeal to overcome customer inertia and differentiate itself against competitors. Therefore, get multi-sensory right and the prize is substantial.

Sensational Mail abilities include: adding a scent or your brand's signature fragrance to DM, using the latest micro-encapsulation technology; adding a fragrance to all types of paper and self-adhesive labels, fabric, plastic and metal so that when the consumer touches the micro-capsules, the fragrance is released; capture the flavour of food or drink on a wafer thin gel strip and attach it to your DM for people to taste; and put your sonic logo in a sound chip that can be sent to your customer. Royal Mail believes that such emotional connections provide higher margins, protection from price based competition, more effective communications, increased brand loyalty and greater advocacy.

Discussion and Implications for Marketers

Overlooking some of the senses in brand communication can jeopardize a brand. The goal therefore should be to include as many sensory touch points as possible. Many companies have to date been totally unaware of their major sensory touch-point advantages. The special tactile feeling of the product, the characteristic smell, the interesting taste - far too often companies neglect these senses. The case studies discussed in this paper have shown just how important the senses are in establishing an emotional connection.

Sensory branding offers certain clear benefits for marketers and their brands. They provide a greater impact for enhanced interruption and acquisition by longer attention, higher recall and by bringing the product experience into the communications. They also contribute to the bottom line by increasing the value of purchase. Sensory branding is useful to marketers to develop branding and touchpoint strategies and to strengthen capabilities in such areas as new product and retail space development. The concept of sensory branding is likely to become an important aspect of the way brands will create sensible points of difference in increasingly competitive markets. Sensory branding holds the key to establish points of differentiation in the global market. After years of bombarding consumers with ads aimed at their eyes and their ears, marketers are focusing more on the nose, the skin and the mouth - with ads that rely on smell, touch and taste - to get attention.

There is a perception that sensory branding is more applicable for the service industry where there is a combination of goods/ products and experience. But as illustrated by the case studies discussed in the paper, sensory branding is relevant for all products and services in the 'experience economy'. As goods and services become commoditized, the customer experiences that companies create will matter most (Pine and Gilmore 1998) and in order to create these experiences, sensory branding is essential.

CONCLUSION

We are all intimately familiar with our senses. They fully convey the picture of our daily life. In the unfortunate situation where one fails to function, the loss only underscores how much depend on it. However, for some mysterious reason, the advertising and communication agencies have always lived in a two-dimensional world. Messages almost exclusively appeal to sight and sound, neglecting the full five-dimensional picture. Nevertheless, as illustrated by the case studies analyzed in this paper, several marketers are taking sensory branding seriously to sensibly differentiate their offerings in the crowded marketplace.

Despite the recent rise in implementation of sensory stimulus, all this sensory progress is non-branded (Lindstrom 2005). The stimulus still tends to be added randomly, and revolves more around generating traffic than generating loyalty. Sensory appeal has not yet been defined as essential among even the world's famous companies, nor have they examined the major potential that sensory branding can unleash. The benefit of sensory branding is to achieve a better brand awareness through multi-sensual experience, consistency, and effective process that can penetrate consumers' memories. The aim is to generate not only new customers but returning customers. Because the returning customers are vital to brand equity; they are the evidence of a successful sensory branding programme.

REFERENCES

Barwise, Patrick and Sean Meehan. *Simply better.* Boston, MA: Harvard Business School Press, 2004.

Clegg, Alicia. "Senses Cue Brand Recognition", *Business Week*, 15 Mar. 2006. 26 Nov. 2007 <http://www.businessweek.com/print/innovate/content/mar2006/id20060315_501684.htm>.

Cristol, Stephen and Peter Sealey. *Simplicity marketing,* clutter, and confusion, New York: Free Press, 2000.

Fetterman, Mindy and Jayne O'Donnell, "*Just browsing at the mall?* That's what you think", USA Today, 9 Jan. 2006. 26 Nov. 2007 <http://www.usatoday.com/money/industries/retail/2006-09-01-retail-cover-usat_x.htm>.

Gobe, Marc, *Emotional Branding branding: The new paradigm for connecting brands to people.* New York: Allworth Press, 2001.

Harvard University, Harvard Business School Press (HBSP), Marketer's toolkit Chapter 6. *Branding: Differentiation that customers value,* Boston, MA, 2006.

Hawkins, Del., Roger Best and Kenneth Coney, *Consumer behaviour: Building marketing strategy,* New Delhi: Tata McGraw-Hill, 2004.

Jossip.com. 10 Aug. 2006. 10 Dec. 2007 <http://www.jossip.com/gossip/rolling-stone/>.

Kang, Stephanie, and Ellen Byron. "Scent noses its way into more ad efforts." *The Wall Street Journal,* 10 Aug. 2007. 26 Nov. 2007 < http://online.wsj.com/article/SB119180534945551750.html?mod=dist_smartbrief>.

Kahn, Randolph, "*5-D Sensory Branding.*" Kahn Consulting Inc. 2007. 25 Nov. 2007 <http://www.kahnconsulting.com/images/Kahn_5-D_branding.pdf>.

Koehn, Nancy, *Brand new.* Boston, MA: Harvard Business School Press, 2001.

Lindstrom, Martin. *Brand Sense: Build powerful brands through touch, taste, smell, sight, and sound*, New York: Free Press, 2005.

McCurry, Justin. "The sweet smell of success", *The Guardian Unlimited*, 8 Nov. 2007. 12 Dec. 2007 <http://www.guardian.co.uk/business/2007/nov/08/japan>.

Park, Whan.,Bernard Jaworski and Deborah MacInnis, "Strategic brand concept-image management", *Journal of Marketing*, 50 (1986): 135.

Pine, Joseph., and James Gilmore, "Welcome to the experience economy." *Harvard Business Review*, July-August (1998): 97-105.

Royal Mail Group. 2007. 2 Dec. 2007 <http://www.royalmail.com/portal/rm jump1? catId=65700705 &mediaId=65700710>.

Sidel, Robin. "Credit-card appeal: a new look, smell." *The Wall Street Journal*, 15 Nov. 2006

Solomon, Michael. *Consumer behaviour: Buying, having and being*. Singapore: Pearson Education, 2002.

Weiss, Tara. "Marketing Milk." *Forbes*, 1 Dec. 2006. 25 Nov. 2007 <http://www.forbes.com/leadership/2006/12/01/leadership-milk-advertising-lead-innovation-cx_tw_1201milk.html>.

16

Business Policy and Strategic Management at Bhagwanpura Mills - A Case Study

DR. SOLAI BASKARAN*
DR. REKHA ARUNKUMAR**

Bhagwanpura Sugar mills, situated at Dhuri, Punjab in the northern part of India, had been incurring heavy loses at the rate of around Rs.4 crores per annum and was on the verge of sick and being referred to BIFR for rehabilitation. The external factors were not favourable to this industry during this period. However, this mill also had many strengths and opportunities which could be exploited to turn it around into a successful enterprise. The new management group headed by the CEO and the VP had conceived a detailed turnaround plan for improving the overall effectiveness of organization.

This particular case focuses on how a sick sugar mill could be turned around by crafting and implementing cross functional strategies. This case can be quite useful to the faculty while teaching business strategy course, management change and organizational development interventions. The students, academicians and practitioners can learn a lot for undertaking management change and turnaround activities.

The management began undertaking a series of initiatives to diagnose the situation in detail with a view to define the problem in the right framework. A detailed examination had been done in terms of capacity utilization of the plant, cane availability, breakdown, fuel cost and other important cost, quality of sugar and the selling price of sugar. A detailed attitude survey of workers and officers was undertaken to ascertain their opinion and recommendations. Accordingly, they formed different committees like technical, commercial, financial, cane and general management and advised them to start analyzing issues, formulating strategies and ensuring the effective implementation for achieving the desired result.

This mill had come out of sickness by producing 3,500 bags of good quality sugar per day at a competitive cost. The management team was happy about the achievement in terms of

* Associate Professor, Alliance Business School, Bangalore.
** Assistant Professor, Alliance Business School, Bangalore.

production, productivity, effective governance, cordial and effective teamwork and financial viability.

...... Change is never-ending and needs to be attended and embraced as an opportunity........

Keywords: turnaround, strategies, management.

PRELIMINARIES

Indian sugar industries were going through turbulent conditions due to control of the industry by both the central and state government upon purchasing of sugarcane as raw material from farmers, fixation of sugar selling prices, releasing of sugar quota to be sold every month and fixation of salary and wages to the workers. Most of the small and medium size industries have already become sick and were on the verge of closure. Sugar mills with bigger capacities were trying to survive by increasing the economics of scale and diversification in to power production along with alcohol manufacturing.

Bhagwanpura Sugar Mills, in north India, had been incurring heavy loses at the rate of around Rs 4 crores per annum and at the verge of sick and being referred to the BIFR for rehabilitation. The external factors were not favourable to this industry during this period. However, this mill also had many strengths and opportunities that could be exploited to turn it around into a successful enterprise. The new management group headed by the CEO and the VP has conceived a detailed turnaround plan for improving the overall effectiveness of organisation.

BACKGROUND

Bhagwanpura Mills had the capacity to produce 2500 bags of sugar per day. It was a highly capital and labour intensive industry. It employed around 1,000 employees and nearly 100 officers including, engineers, chemists and managers. The raw material was sugarcane, produced by farmers from the field. The technology included the power turbine, mills, boilers, centrifugal machines, pumps and motors. The mill was initially set up in 100 acres of land and the real estate value of the land has gone up very significantly over a period of time due to urbanization around the mill. The industry was getting the raw material and cane from nearby villages comprising of thousands of farmers. The central as well as the state government fixed the purchasing price of cane on a year-to-year basis and the government always tried to fix an arbitrarily high price favourable to the farmers. The salary and wages of employees were also fixed by the wage board authorized by the central government. The selling of the final product, sugar, was also controlled by the government through a mechanism with a view to ensure cheaper price of sugar available to the consumer. Thus the industry was forced to buy the raw material at very high uncompetitive price fixed by the authorities and to sell the products in an unremunerative manner. In other words, the industry was totally controlled by the government to a very large extent, thereby leaving little scope for the management to control the business activities. This mill became financially sick and was on the verge of filing for rehabilitation from concerned authorities. The mill could not generate enough revenue to pay even the workers' salary in time and the management could not undertake proper repair and maintenance of the plant to attain the industry efficiency norms.

As most of the sugar mills had become sick, they could not pay the farmers the cane price in time and therefore the farmers stopped producing cane and diverted to other crops. As a consequence, the overall sugar production had come down very significantly. The government started importing sugar from sugar surplus countries to meet the domestic sugar consumption by spending a huge amount of foreign exchange. While the Indian sugar mills had been controlled by the government, on the other side they were made to face global competition to produce sugar at a competitive price against the imported sugar. The situation further worsened and the industry associations began getting panicky about development. With this background, the new management team had to work out turnaround strategies to revive this mill in order to build and sustain competitive advantage.

DIAGNOSIS OF THE MANAGEMENT COMMITTEE

The management started undertaking a series of initiatives to understand the situation in detail with a view to define the problem in the right framework. Accordingly, they formed different committees like technical, commercial, cane and general management and advised them to start analyzing the status and to formulate strategies for implementation. These committees undertook pilot studies and held discussions with all concerned in a micro level. The management committee conducted extensive discussions with the bankers, suppliers, union members, local government agencies and the industry associations to collect adequate information before finalizing the action programme. They had also examined all the reports and management information like daily crushing, cane availability, sugar sales report, sugar recovery analysis, inventory report, absenteeism report, plant breakdown details, fuel utilization report etc. A detailed examination had been done in terms of capacity utilization of the plant, cane availability, breakdown, fuel cost and other important cost, quality of sugar and the selling price of sugar. A detailed attitude survey of workers and officers were undertaken to get their opinion and recommendations.

INTERVENTION STRATEGIES FOR INITIATING MANAGEMENT CHANGE

Based on the above mentioned detailed exercise, the management had initiated the following major changes with a view to improve the production, productivity and profitability of the organisation.

Changes at the technology front

It was found that the production cost of sugar compared to the industry norm was high due to major breakdowns in the plant, obsolete machinery and the related high cost of power and fuel. Further, the plant capacity utilization on per day basis was not achieved and therefore the direct and the indirect cost were significantly higher than the competitors.

The quality of sugar in terms of grain size and colour was not up to the quality specification. Accordingly, the following actions were undertaken.

The necessary plant and machinery were repaired and replaced keeping in view the latest technology available and it was aimed that the production losses would be reduced significantly. The boilers were modified with the external consultants to reduce the power and fuel cost and thereby to improve the profitability. The entire manufacturing process was reengineered as per the state-of-the-art technology to have a smooth crushing without break down. The training department conducted extensive programmes to improve the technical and specialized knowledge requirement of operators, technicians, engineers and chemists. The manufacturing process had been changed to double curing in order to improve the quality of sizes, purity and colour.

Improving the quality and quantity of sugarcane availability

The major factor for the survival and the growth of this mill depends on the availability of adequate quantity and variety of sugarcane. If the quantity of cane during the season of six month did not meet the requirement of the factory, the mill could not achieve the full capacity utilization. Further, the different variety of cane like, early, middle and late maturing variety of cane should be made available to attain maximum recovery of sugar from the cane. If the mill had to crush the middle variety cane in the early period of sugar season, the sugar recovery would be definitely much lower and thereby the cost of production would be too high, leading to a loss for the mill. Thus, effective cane management practices with right varietal cane balance were taken up as one of the key activity to be implemented and monitored by the top management.

The cane department was reorganized and headed by a senior professional and assisted by a complete team of employees based on geography of cane area. The mission and objectives of this department were clearly communicated along with the performance requirement. A separate budget was given to promote cane development activities. This department began working on two major sub-divisions: one on the cane supply to the factory for crushing and the other for developing cane in the area. They were called cane marketing and cane development sections. The cane development section concentrated on cane seed farming, propagation of right cane seed for plantation. It supplied the fertilizers, chemicals and pesticides at an economical price to the canegrowers. They had also conducted a lot of training programmes for the canegrowers on the cane cultivation methods, crop protection, and disease control. All these activities resulted in growing the right variety and quantity of cane as per mill requirement. It further resulted in maximum of 300 tons per acre of output to farmers as against 200 tons per acre. The farmers got more money because of more yield and it was more remunerative for them compared to other crops. The other important agenda was to include different village representatives in the cane development committee for framing and implementing development plans. The mill undertook lots of community development activities in different villages and helped the farmers more than one ways. The factory ensured the timely payment of the right cane price to growers regularly.

Human resources development activities

During the study and discussion it was brought to the knowledge of management that the leadership styles of supervisors and managers were autocratic and no effort was initiated at any level to boost the individual development and entrepreneurial aspect of the employee. The employees were not clear about the corporate objective and their role in achieving the organizational goals. Most of the time, the employees were in a total state of confusion and found themselves in the state of insecurity.

The committee had initiated the following actions to improve the morale of employees to achieve the objectives as well as to provide maximum satisfaction to them.

- *Management Style:* The management style was changed from an autocratic/bureaucratic way to a more focused and participatory style. Functional autonomy was provided to the employees and they were asked to come out of their fear and get their doubts/queries cleared. The organizational structure was redesigned with proper flow of information. The employees were encouraged to come out with their suggestions for better working style in order to increase the production and performance.
- *Role Clarity:* Each employee designed his own work pattern and appraised himself regularly. The committee was entrusted to educate each employee about his role in the development of the organization and he was made responsible for his action. A sense of responsibility and sensitivity towards the organization was developed in him.
- *Communication Channels:* Effective two-way communication channels were developed so that there was no scope for grapevine to take place. It was ensured that the corporate objective, goals, policies were clear to all the employees without any ambiguity and they all understood and appreciated it.
- *Review Committee:* A review committee reviewed the changes that were taking place and its impact in relation to the corporate objective and passed down the information from top to bottom.

Change from groupism to team development

Team development work was undertaken by the change committee. Different teams were made comprising of technical staff, commercial staff, and departmental heads Chief Engineer, Chief Chemist, Shift Supervisors etc., using the following change procedure.

- *Unfreezing:* The first task was to make this team aware of the need for change by sharing the vision of the mill. A climate of openness and trust was developed so as to enable the group to accept and initiate the change.
- *Moving:* The results of the survey feedback were shown to the participants and they were asked to come out with their suggestions. The team was made to diagnose where the mill was and where it should be going in another few years.

- *Refreezing:* Once the diagnosis or the change areas were identified and evaluation done, the team was made to execute the plans into more effective performance.
- *Team Skill workshops:* Workshops were conducted for the team depending upon their area of work. The production team was made to understand the latest production techniques and other team-building exercises. The motto behind such training was to prepare them to accept and implement change.
- *Data Collection:* The primary and secondary data collected at various study levels were compiled and circulated among the team members; it showed their responses on organizational climate, supervisory behaviour and job content. This made them more understanding as a team to initiate the change.
- *Action Planning:* On the basis of above steps, the teams developed specific plans as discussed above for the changes to be carried out on the job.
- *Team Building:* All the team members met as a whole to identify the barriers to effectiveness and developed ways of eliminating the barriers and agreed upon plans to accomplish the desired changes. For instance, Purchase and Accounts were made to sit together and were asked to come out in the open with their receptive problems and they themselves were later asked the solution to it in a combined effort.
- *Intergroup building:* In the final phase, a two-day meeting was held between teams that were interdependent in accomplishing goals. Like stores and purchase were made to sit together and were asked to sort out the ways to meet the store requirement and at the same time not piling up inventory. The purpose behind this was to establish collaboration on shared goals and problems of total organization.

The top management, including the internal change agent i.e. Vice President of the company were all committed towards bringing the change and the internal agent felt that without the support and involvement of the top management i.e. the promoters of the organization it wouldn't have been possible to bring in the change. The review committee found that the change in the organization had taken place in terms of better productivity and performance; the mill was running in its full capacity and full captive utilization was concentrated on. Every employee felt responsible and was taking full initiative to give his maximum and was seeing that no resources were wasted; consumption of power and fuel has decreased with modification of machineries and by regular workshops of employees. Industrial relations were much better and weekly meetings of representatives of workers were held in which ideas, problems and future goals and strategies / course of actions were discussed in association with them so as to make them feel as part of a team besides initiating a better team development and communication channel. There was a better coordination in between the departments and it was ensured that the work did not suffer under any circumstances; all the employees felt responsible for their action. All these efforts resulted in increased production and profitability of the organization. The top management in order to motivate the employees and to keep this process of change as an ongoing process rewarded them with double increment in their salary and a good bonus. This announcement worked like magic and employees felt more committed towards the organization. On the raw material front, the mill started getting regular and adequate supply of good quality cane at its gate. The farmers felt satisfied and were happy with the mill management as they were getting all support of the mill whether it was for seeds, fertilizers, pesticides etc. All these efforts improved the image of the mill in the local area.

FINANCIAL DIMENSION OF THE MILL

The government enacted the Sick Industrial Companies Act, 1987. Under this act (SICA) it was mandatory on the part of the Directors of the Company to file a memorandum with the Board for Industrial and Financial Reconstruction in case the net worth of the company fell by 50% during the year compared to last audited accounts.

PRE-EXPANSION PLANT OPERATION RESULTS

	1983-84	1984-85	1985-86	1986-87
CANE CRUSED (LAC QTLs.)	9.40	6.90	7.80	13.20
RECOVERY (%)	8.66	9.75	9.17	9.32
PRODUCTION OF SUGAR (QTLs.)	86480	73970	76160	123041
NET OPERATIONAL PROFIT/(LOSS) (Rs.in Lacs)	(13.95)	(44.21)	(6.82)	(48.89)

NET WORTH FALL

(Rs. In Lacs)

	1983-84	1984-85	1985-86	1986-87	1987-88
SHARE CAPITAL	58.75	58.75	58.75	58.75	99.82
RESERVES &SURPLUS	4.61	4.61	8.58	8.38	8.38
ACCUMULATED PROFIT/(LOSS)	(50.06)	(94.28)	(101.10)	(149.99)	(411.11)
NET WORTH	13.30	(30.92)	(33.77)	(88.86)	(302.91)
WORKING CAPITAL	(69.22)	(173.39)	(221.88)	(260.51)	(486.76)

The sugar mills accounts showed the results as prescribed by the SICA. It filed the necessary papers with BIFR, and got registration as a sick company in need of rehabilitation. The BIFR, as per its procedure, appointed an operating agency. IRBI (Industrial Reconstruction Bank of India) was appointed the operating agency (OA). As per requirement OA prepared a rehabilitation scheme and envisaged an enhancement-cum-modernization in the capacity of the plant from 800 TCD to 2000 TCD. According to this scheme, the financial institutions, banks and Sugar Development Fund of the government of India shall have to advance loans to the factory as well as the banks shall have to provide need based working capital. The BIFR hearings were on towards approval of the scheme. Meanwhile, the government of India, Sugar Directorate brought out a Sugar Incentive Scheme, according to which the factories expanding to 2500 TCD under a reconstruction scheme shall be eligible for the incentive by the of 93% free sale sugar up to six years. The factory then made an application for grant of industrial license for the expansion to 2500 TCD. The license was granted vide LDI dated August 1990. In the meantime, BIFR, on application granted preparation of a fresh rehabilitation scheme for expansion to 2500 TCD. The operating agency prepared the fresh report which envisaged:

- Merger of the BSML with another existing operational and profitable company of the Promoters.
- Induction of fresh funds by the promoters.
- Tax benefits to be made available to the merged company in respect of unabsorbed depreciation and accumulated business loss of the BSML.

BIFR approved the scheme and accordingly expansion and modernisation loans were granted by:

IRBI	-	Rs.797.00 Lacs
IFCI	-	Rs.131.00 Lacs
SBOP	-	Rs.200.75 Lacs
BOB	-	Rs.133.75 Lacs
SDF	-	Rs.489.00 Lacs
Total		Rs.1451.50 Lacs

The factory started operating on the expanded capacity from 27th Jan. 1992 although the scheme envisaged that the expanded capacity operation to commence in the season 1990-91. Thus, there was a delay of almost one year and half in implementation. This delay was harmful as on one hand it increased the interest liability on the term borrowings, which were at very high rates of interest, and on the other it ate away one year from the incentive scheme. Merger having taken place with the Saraya Distillery, the factory dependent heavily on the distillery unit for its finance requirement both for working capital margin as well as to keep the debt service commitments.

The distillery being a highly profitable venture was being run highly professionally and generated goad profits. The term loans from banks & FIs thus, were fully paid, however, that from SDF was not, as the repayment schedule was like that.

Operation of season 2000-01

The crushing operation for the season 2000-01 started with a target of crushing above 25 lac qtls. and tried to achieve 30 lac qtls. depending on cane arrivals. Up to 100th day of crushing on 24th Feb. 2001 the factory did 24.30 lac qtls. crush. The average recovery was 9.15% as against the target of 9.25%. Therefore, if the factory could muster cane for another 15 days; consistent crushing as well as recovery was achieved. The plant efficiency was also better in so far as the total loss in 2.08 as against the government prescribed standard of 2.00. The total stoppages of mechanical/electrical nature had also been within control. The boiler operation had been satisfactory for a large part of the season and it consumed extra fuel of about Rs. 15 lacs. However, it had been consistently saving bagasse and about 5000 qtls. of bagasse had accumulated in the yard. The sugar quality was much better and white. This meant better price realization per qtl. of sugar in the current year. The bank and financial institutes' interest installments were being paid as per schedule. The mill could attract further loans and unsecured loans from others for meeting additional cash credit limit.

CHANGE IS NEVER ENDING AND NEEDS TO BE ATTENDED AND EMBRACED AS AN OPPORTUNITY

This mill had come out of sickness by producing 3,500 bags of good quality sugar per day at a competitive cost. The management team was happy about the achievement in terms of production, productivity and financial viability. They could clear the old dues of mills to all parties inclusive of workers, suppliers and the statutory payments. Alas, this was a temporary phenomenon and there was a major development in this industry. The government began decontrolling the industry, export of sugar started taking place, the quality aspect of sugar by global standard needed different process, technology.

All this called for a drastic change in the strategy formulation of sustaining the viability of sugar industries. For instance, the economies of scale could be up to 7,000 bags per day. Alternatively, keeping the same level of production of 3,500 bags, one could concentrate on producing healthy sugar like sulphurless sugar for export which could fetch premium price. It is possible to create a brand name of sugar and in small pockets. There are sugar industries who are even thinking of sugar as a byproduct rather than main product through the route of diversifying into alcohol and power production along with sugar production. The real estate value of 100 acres of land of this sugar mill also went up significantly whereas modern factories could be set up in only 50 acres. This would mean to a total relook at the strategy in terms of internal strength/resources of the company, external developments, core competency and a whole lot of other issues towards building and sustaining the competitive advantage of this industry. As a strategic planner, please help the industry to work out the strategic planning in this scenario.

ANNEXURE – 1

ORGANISATION STRUCTURE

BHAGWAN SUGAR MILLS LTD.,

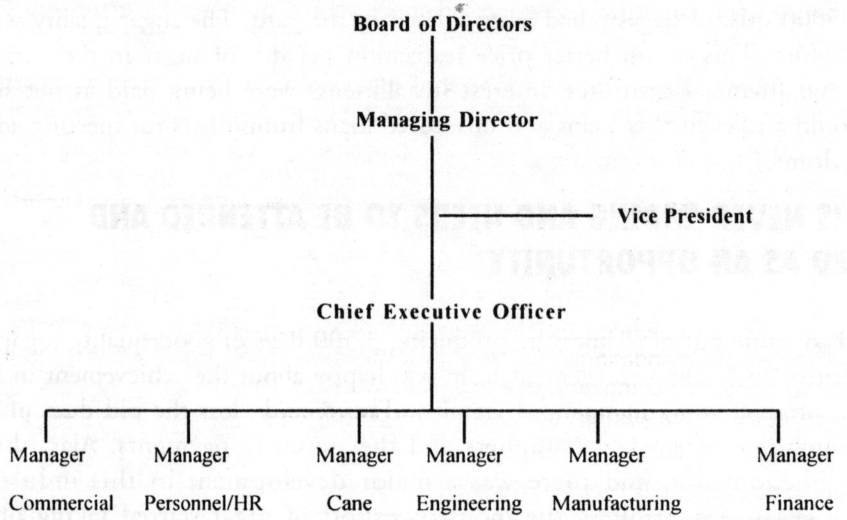

ANNEXURE - 2

SWOT ANALYSIS OF THIS MILL

A. STRENGTHS

1. The trend of improvement in cane availability and growers interest in cane cultivation in the mill area could go up to 20 to 25 lac qtls. as gate cane in 2001-02 season and 25 to 30 lac qtls. as gate cane in 2002 -03 season. This was the studied estimate of the management. Accordingly cane cost (transportation included) should go down as compared to current season.

   Thus, the dependency on out area cane shall greatly reduce. Cane management in the yard should therefore improve to a large extent. This factor could directly improve the sugar recovery.

2. High value of land as it was in the midst of the town.

3. Operational costs like labour and staff strength were lower, further scope to lower.

B. OPPORTUNITIES

1. The sugar policy formulated by the government was presently in line with the Mahajan Committee Recommendations. Accordingly, it was reasonably expected that the levy sugar requirement could be completely phased out in two years time. Not only that, the government could by 2005, if not earlier, completely decontrol sugar. The Mahajan Committee had recommended decontrol by 2002.

2. One could plan for a distillery plant with ETP at a capital cost of Rs. 5 crores. The profit from the activity could be provided for the borrowings cost and principal. After five years the profits could emerge, as the loans will liquidate.

C. WEAKNESSES

Commitments towards the loan liabilities. The loan liabilities are to —

SDF (Sugar Development Fund) — Rs. 8.00 crores

Agricultural Loan — Rs. 8.25 crores

Both are of course cheap loans, as the interest rates were low.
However, the repayment of these loans could keep the pressure on the cash flows of the factory for four to five years to come.

D. THREATS

1. In order to maintain the factory's efficiencies and also to keep pace with technology, gradual replacement and modernization-oriented capital expenditure shall have to be undertaken. These may, in the next three to five years, come to around Rs. 6 crores.

2. The huge contingent liabilities of the company towards 'Extra Levy Price Realization' and 'Purchase Tax Arrears' were becoming too large to be claimed by the government .

17 Entrepreneurship Development and Family Business-A Study in Export Oriented Match Units in Sivakasi

DR. M. JEYARATHNAM*
B.MAHESWARI**

INTRODUCTION

Development of any nation primarily depends upon its industrial development. Industrial growth builds prosperity and the image of any nation. The growth of industries in a country paves way for the effective utilization of resources like men, material and capital. However, the strenuous efforts of the entrepreneurs are the key drivers for the industrial development.

In India, there has been a phenomenal development of small scale units, contributing significantly to the overall development of the country. The number of registered units surged from 16,000 in 1950 to 6.5 lakh units in 2001, thus constituting over 92% of all manufacturing units in India. Its contribution to the national industrial output is 25%, value addition 20%, employment generation 40% and exports 29%.

The wide variety of advantages offered by small scale industrial sector has enabled men with qualities of initiative, vision and leadership to become successful entrepreneurs. It acts as a channel through which talented and motivated individuals can play a dynamic role. As such, the small scale sector is usually described as a seedbed or nursery for entrepreneurs. Entrepreneurship has been recognized as an essential ingredient of economic development of our country. Thus, greater emphasis has been laid on the development of entrepreneurship in small manufacturing units by the government.

To promote and encourage entrepreneurship in SSI sector, the central and state governments have been providing financial and non-financial incentives to the prospective entrepreneurs. These efforts have led to the growth of entrepreneurship.

* Professor, K.L.N. College of Engineering, Madurai.
** Lecturer, Ayya Nadar Janaki Ammal College, Sivakasi.

EVOLUTION OF HANDMADE MATCH INDUSTRY IN SIVAKASI

The seeds of industrial growth were sown back in 1922, when the late Shri. P. Ayya Nadar and his cousin Shri A. Shanmuga Nadar, went to Calcutta, after seeing an advertisement of "Cent percent profit in matches", to learn the art of match-manufacturing. They returned with enthusiasm to set up the first match unit in the small sector. After eight months stay in Calcutta they returned to Sivakasi, and Shri P. Ayya Nadar purchased an imported German machine, thus starting a semi-mechanized operation on match manufacturing. Some of the process of production of matches was carried out by machines and some by hand.

Those were the days of the freedom movement and the Swadeshi spirit was catching on. An eminent industrialist, Shri Ayya Nadar found that he could make better quality matches by hand. So he sold the imported machine. That was how the hand made cottage match industry originated in and around Sivakasi.

Established in 1923 as an insignificant cottage industry in Sivakasi town, the handmade sector had an annual turnover of about 60 crores of rupees, employing 3 lakhs of people directly. 75% of the total match production of India is carried out in Tamil Nadu.

Since 1961, the stick contents for a box have been standardized at 50 sticks per box. In 1967, the match factories were classified into mechanized sector and handmade sector. According to the excise department statistics, the excise duty levied during1994 is mechanized sector - Rs. 2.40 per unit and for hand made sector - Rs. 0.50 per units.

In the handmade sector, a tiny sector consisting of units producing less than 75 million sticks per annum was introduced, in order to help small entrepreneurs with meager resources to take up this labour intensive, rural industry.

The mushrooming growth of handmade match units in and around Sivakasi cannot be underestimated. Shri P. Ayya Nadar can be described as the Father of Match Industry of Sivakasi and he is called the chief architect of handmade match industries on India. He proved that production of goods through small scale units can be made viable and profitable and that a country like India with millions of unemployed can solve its problems only through rural and cottage industries, as envisaged by Gandhiji.

Objectives of the Study

1. To study the factors influencing the growth of entrepreneurs in export-oriented match units in Sivakasi.
2. To study the government assistance in export promotion.

DESIGN OF THE STUDY

Today, there are about 2,000 small scale units and 10,000 cottage units in Sivakasi. Together they account for about 80% of the country's total output. Match units in other parts of the country accounts for about 20%. The match entrepreneurs of Sivakasi, who have been flourishing since the pre-independence days, have chalked out appropriate growth strategies and entered the international market. The study covers the entrepreneurial development in ten export-oriented match units in Sivakasi.

As there are ten units exporting matches on regular basis in Sivakasi, the study has used the census method or complete enumeration method. The primary data were collected by the researcher from the entrepreneurs with the help of the schedule. The researcher also personally interviewed the entrepreneurs.

SCOPE OF THE STUDY

In Tamil Nadu, greater emphasis is being laid on the development of entrepreneurship in small manufacturing units. The success of small units largely depends on the technical expertise and the experience of the entrepreneurs. This growth of entrepreneurial class calls for a congenial environment. Sivakasi, popularly known as "Kutti Japan", by our late Prime Minister, Pandit Jawaharlal Nehru provides such environment to the local entrepreneurs to grow, expend and diversity. The establishment of match units in Sivakasi, during 1922, paved way for the development of fireworks, printing press and other allied industries. It is also interesting to note that, they no longer remained confined to matches, fireworks and printing, but were compelled to diversity into capital-intensive, mechanized activities like manufacturing of ink, manufacturing and processing of chemicals, engineering, electrical appliances, cements and cems, manufacturing of chloride and potassium nitrate etc., to meet the requirements of the match works and fireworks. This increasing trend of wide varieties of SSI units in Sivakasi motivated the development of new budding entrepreneurs into the business field. As there is more scope for the development of entrepreneurs in this town, the present study discusses the entrepreneurial development with respect to export of matches.

S.No	NAME OF THE EXPORT COMPANIES IN SIVAKASI
1.	Pioneer Group
2.	Sundaravel Match Industries Private Limited
3.	Thangavel Match Industries
4.	The Hind Matches Private Limited
5.	Supreme Match works
6.	The Arasan Group of Industries
7.	Premier Match Industries
8.	Janaki Match Company
9.	Standard Fire works Limited
10.	We Two Fireworks Factory

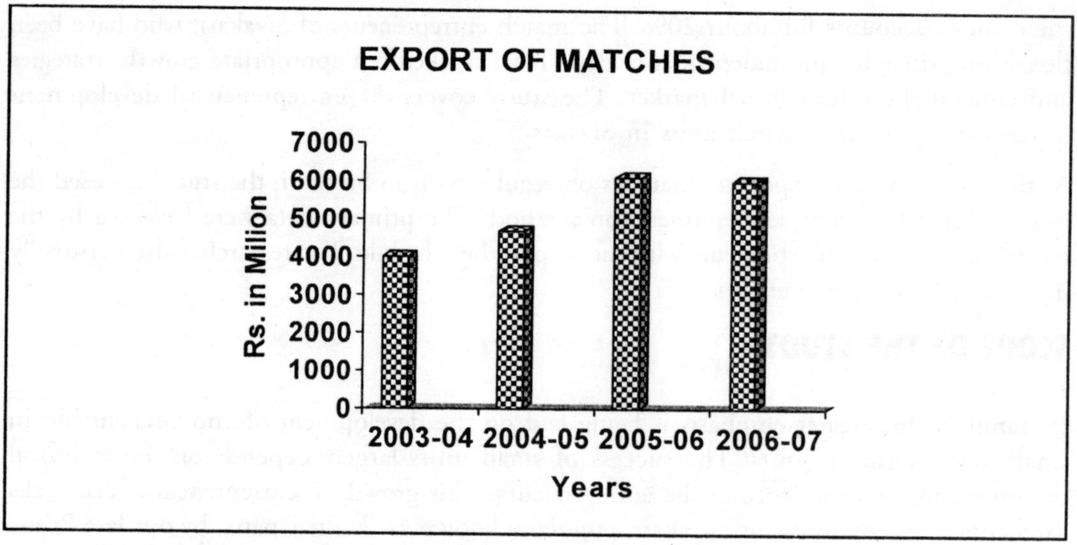

Factors Influencing the Entrepreneurial Development in Match Export Units

An attempt has been made to analyze the various factors influencing the entrepreneurial development in export match units in Sivakasi. Entrepreneurial development is a process and the entrepreneur as an individual plays a significant role in the process. The key factors that foster the entrepreneurial development in the match units at Sivakasi are as follows:

i. Abundant supply of cheap labour due to low level of agricultural operations.

ii. Low rainfall and dry weather for the major part of the year, suited to match production.

iii. Concession in excise duty in the small scale sector and curbs on the growth of the mechanized sector.

iv. Price competitiveness due to cheap labour, easy availability of raw materials and climatic conditions.

v. Immediate payment by the importers.

PERIOD OF MANUFACTURING AND EXPORTING MATCHES

Since 1934, increase of import duty and prohibition on import of matches by the Indian government has led to the growth of match units. As a result, the growth of semi-mechanized and cottage match units increased in number, which resulted in exports in the subsequent years. Table 1 shows the study units' experience in match manufacturing and exporting.

Table 1: Experience of study units in manufacturing and exporting

SL.NO.	TOTAL YEARS OF EXPERIENCE IN MATCH PRODUCTION	YEARS OF EXPERIENCE IN EXPORTS			TOTAL
		LESS THAN 5 YEARS	5 TO 6 YEARS	10 TO 15 YEARS	
1.	Less than 10 years	1	-	-	1

Contd...

2.	10 to 20 years	-	1	1	2
3.	20 to 30 year	1	1	-	2
4.	Above 30 years	2	1	2	5
	Total	4	3	3	10

SOURCE: Field data

It is apparent form the Table 1 that out of the ten sample entrepreneurs, one entrepreneur has less than ten years experience and is exporting for a period of less than 5 years. Two entrepreneurs have 10 to 20 years experience, and one entrepreneur exports for 10 to 15 years, and another one exports for 5 to 10 years. Two entrepreneurs have 20 to 30 years of experience in match production, out of whom one entrepreneur has less than 5 years of experience in exports and another has 5 - 15 years of experience in the exports. Five entrepreneurs have more than 30 years of experience in match production, out of them two entrepreneurs deal with exports for less than 5 years and one deal with exports for 5 to 10 years and the remaining two entrepreneurs deal with exports for 10 to 15 years.

It is evident from Table 1 that 50% of the respondents are highly experienced and knowledgeable in match exports than the other entrepreneurs.

FORMS OF ORGANISATION

An entrepreneur with a sound family background and seed capital, usually starts the unit as a family firm. However, the partnership firm of organization facilitates the pooling of resources and skill of different entrepreneurs who are relatives of the same family, known to each other. If the entrepreneur has adequate capital and skill, he starts the match unit as a sole proprietorship concern. So the form of organization has been considered as one of the conducive factors influencing the entrepreneurial development in match units. Table 2 shows the form of organization used in the study units.

Table 2: Forms of organisation of the study units

SL.NO.	TYPE OF ORGANISATION	TOTAL
1.	Sole Proprietorship	1
2.	Partnership	2
3.	Private Limited	7
4.	Public Limited	-
	Total	10

SOURCE: Field data

It is inferred from Table 2 that 1 match unit is owned and run by the sole traders, 2 match units have been started as a partnership form of organization. 7 private limited companies are working successfully. No public limited form of organization has been adopted. So it is evident that the private limited form of organization is familiar in the town.

EDUCATIONAL QUALIFICATION OF THE ENTREPRENEURS

Education is said to be an important factor, which influences the growth of entrepreneur. Educated entrepreneurs find it easy to create contact with officials and mostly they have the interest to attend meetings and programs meant for entrepreneurs. Many entrepreneurs with low level of education feel shy and hence are not able to create proper rapport with government officials. Educational qualifications enables the entrepreneur to contact government offices and banks, catering to their needs. They are able to avail themselves of the various incentives given to the match units. Education also improves the mental make-up of the entrepreneurs which will help them to acquire new skills and techniques of production. Hence the educational qualification has been identified as an important factor, which influences the growth of entrepreneurs. Table 3 shows the educational qualification of the entrepreneurs.

Table 3: Educational qualification of the entrepreneurs of the study units

SL.NO.	LEVEL OF EDUCATION	NUMBER OF RESPONDENTS	PERCENTAGE
1.	SSLC / Matric	1	10
2.	Under Graduate	7	70
3.	Post Graduate	1	10
4.	Professional Studies	1	10

SOURCE: Field data

It is inferred from Table 3 that 10% of the respondents have completed the SSLC course. 70% of the entrepreneurs have studied upto undergraduate level, whereas 10% of the remaining entrepreneurs completed post-graduate and professional courses. It is evident that the entrepreneurs of Sivakasi have a strong educational background to unleash the possibilities in the export trade.

MOTIVATIONS FOR STARTING THE MATCH UNIT

An efficient entrepreneur has a will to surmount the impossible. He utilizes the productive resources and opportunities before him, and starts the business with his own ideas in a meaningful way. If the entrepreneur has a business background, he finds it easy to start and manage the established units. The skills required to manage the units' passes on from the father to the son. Sometimes, the motivation from his friends and relatives prompt him to start a business. Hence these motivational forces have been taken as one of the factors influencing the entrepreneurial development in export match units. Table 4 shows the reasons stated by the respondents for starting match units.

Table 4: Motivational factors for starting the match unit

SL.NO.	PARTICULARS	NUMBER OF RESPONDENTS	PERCENTAGE
1.	Own Idea	2	12
2.	Idea from friends and relatives	3	18
3.	Hereditary business	5	29
4.	Spirit of adventure	7	41

SOURCE: Field data

It is identified from Table 4 that 12% of the respondents have started the match units based on their own idea and prospects in exports. 18% of the entrepreneurs have started the match units based on the idea from friends and relatives. 29% of the entrepreneurs have continued their father's and forefather's business and 41% of the match entrepreneurs had started the match units with a spirit of adventurism to succeed in the match business and have risen to be a "match exporter".

MEMBERSHIP IN TRADE ASSOCIATION

Each trade has its own trade association. The trade association looks after the welfare of the member business units. By becoming a member in the particular trade association, entrepreneurs have a chance to discuss the problems in marketing, finance and so on. The trade association also helps the entrepreneurs in solving their problems and this will speed up their growth. Hence the membership in trade association has been identified as one of the factors influencing the growth of entrepreneurship.

Table 5 shows the assistance received by the match entrepreneurs from the All India Chambers of Match Association.

Table 5: Assistance from the All India Chamber of Match Association

SL.NO.	PARTICULARS	NUMBER OF RESPONDENTS	PERCENTAGE
1.	Notification of the export Policy changes	9	53
2.	Addresses of the importers	8	47
3.	Information about the importers needs	-	-
4.	Marketing assistance	-	-

SOURCE: Field data

It is obvious from the Table 5 that, 53% of the sample entrepreneurs get assistance in the form of notification of the changes in the Export Policy, through the Association. 47% of the entrepreneurs get the addresses of the importers through the Match Association, which enables them to have a reliable contact with the importers of matches. The information relating to the importers' needs and wants are supplied by the Indian ambassadors in the importing country and not by the trade association. Marketing is undertaken by all the entrepreneurs themselves, matches, being a cheap consumer product.

AVAILABILITY OF INSTITUTIONAL FINANCE

Finance is the life blood of any business. With abundant supply of bank finance, the entrepreneurs dare to start a new unit or to run and expand the present match unit in an efficient manner. Finance is an essential input of the business and its availability enables the match units to grow further. Hence the availability of finance is taken as one of the factors influencing the development of entrepreneurs in the match export line. Table 6 explains the availing of institutional finance by the respondents.

Table 6: Source of finance

SL.NO.	PARTICULARS	PERCENTAGE
1.	SBI and its subsidiaries	46
2.	National banks	32
3.	Money lenders	10
4.	Financial institutions	8
5.	Friends and relatives	4
	Total	100

SOURCE: Field survey

It is inferred from Table 6 that the 46% of the total source of finance is availed form the SBI, its easy for the entrepreneurs to get loan based on some securities, 32% of the total source of finance is availed from nationalized banks, 10% from the money lenders, 8% from financial Institutions and 4% from friends and relatives.

GOVERNMENT ASSISTANCE FOR EXPORT PROMOTION

Any government that wants to motivate export should compensate its entrepreneurs in many ways, to make them internally competitive. Export policy as a conscious effort in influencing the volume and composition of export trade was clearly recognized from 1962. Export promotion was recognized as one of the important objective of the Five Year Plans. It has therefore been given an important place in the overall strategy for development. This is for higher profits and faster growth, for increased efficiency, a greater ability to withstand competition, a better image for domestic sales, as well as to bring in foreign exchange. Various supporting measures like the Export Entitlement Scheme, the Duty Drawbacks, and Cash Compensatory Support etc. were introduced. Broadly speaking, the export promotion efforts of a country may be considered in two parts. Firstly, export incentives are offered with a view to assist the exporters in overcoming his disadvantages as against the competitors in the world market. Secondly, export services enable the exporters to reduce the degree and dimension of the disadvantages.

A number of promotional measures have been instituted by the government and they are as follows.

(a) Cash assistance through banks

(b) Credit facilities at concessional rates.

(c) Import replenishment license for the raw materials used in export matches.

(d) Advance licensing for the import of 50% of the raw materials to be used in the production of export matches. So here customs duty is exempted.

(e) Export tax exemption to the 'H Form' holders, to the extent of 5% of the total finished product. The 'H Form' holders are also exempted from sales tax, for the packing cartons.

QUALITY OF EXPORT MATCHES

Quality is the only measure, through which an industry can effectively thrive in the market. The entrepreneurs of Sivakasi, through their in-house R & D efforts and by establishing quality control laboratory facilities, conduct the performance tests, for the match to be exported. With the locally available raw materials, the entrepreneurs of Sivakasi strive hard to produce good quality matches for export purpose. The quality of materials are superior than the domestically traded matches, in certain characteristics, which is shown in Table 7.

Table 7: Difference between export matches and domestically traded matches

S.No.	PARTICULARS	NUMBER OF RESPONDENTS	PERCENTAGE
1.	Damp proofness	6	60
2.	Strong splints	2	20
3.	Number of sticks	1	10
4.	Smooth flame	1	10
		10	**100**

SOURCE: Field data

Table 7 shows that the entrepreneurs have identified more than one reason. 60% of the entrepreneurs are differentiating exports, through damp proofness. This is because, as matches are exported to various countries through seaways, and as the moisture level also differs in different countries, it becomes imperative to improve the quality of glowing, on first striking. 20% of entrepreneurs differentiate their export matches through strong splints, to avoid breakage while striking. 10% of the entrepreneurs differentiate the number of sticks from 47 to 55, which are normally 50 in the domestic market. 10% of the respondents give importance to the smooth flame, which glows in pleasant colours.

MODE OF PACKING

Packing, important for effective sales promotion, is a silent and persuasive salesman. A good match box packaging depends upon the colour, quality of paper, design of packing, attractive labels and slips of finished goods. Thus, packing plays a vital role in maintaining the performance characteristic of matches and therefore improved new packaging techniques are developed by the sample entrepreneurs of Sivakasi.

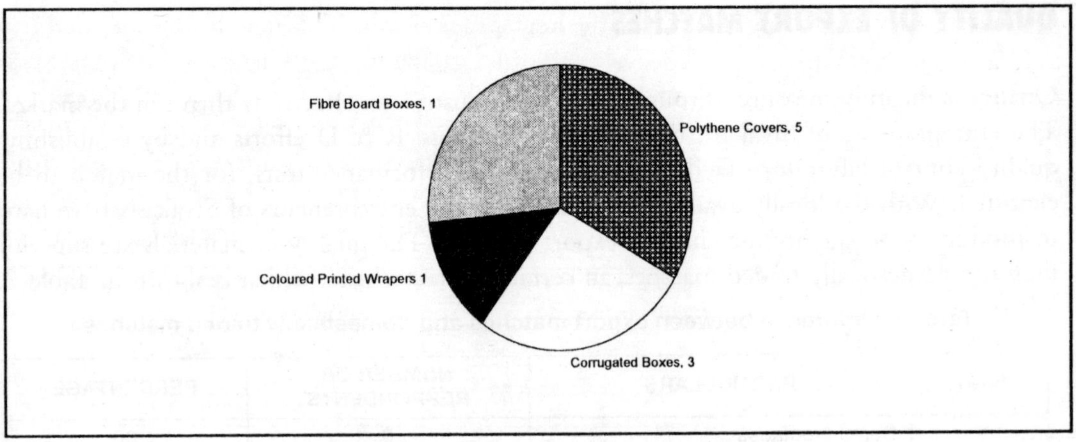

Figure 1: Materials used for packing

As the new matches of Sivakasi are mostly exported by the sea route, they are protected from constantly changing environmental conditions. Therefore, the materials used for packing are given more importance by the Sivakasi match entrepreneurs, which are shown in Table 8 below.

Table 8: Materials used for packaging

S.No.	PARTICULARS	NUMBER OF RESPONDENTS	PERCENTAGE
1.	Polythene covers	5	50
2.	Corrugated boxes	3	30
3.	Coloured printed wrapers	1	10
4.	Fibre board boxes	1	10
		10	100

SOURCE: Field data

Table 8 indicates that the sample entrepreneurs have adopted more than one technique for packing the matches meant for exports. 50% of the respondents have utilized polythene covers. 10% of the respondents have used fibre board boxes, 10% use coloured printed wrappers and 30% utilize corrugated boxes for exporting the matches.

PLACE

India is a developing country and exports matches to a number of developing and advanced countries in the world. In the wake of unprecedented increase in competition as well as protectionism in the world markets, it becomes imperative for the entrepreneurs of our country to get more and more energetically involved in the export business and make the dictum, "export and flourish", a really new proposition. The match entrepreneurs of Sivakasi, stand to gain more progressively and earn a good reputation for India internationally, in the match industry.

Table 9 shows the match exports to the leading international markets, by the sample entrepreneurs of Sivakasi.

Table 9: Area of marketing

S.No.	Countries	Number of respondents	%	Values In Crores Per Annum For 1995	%
1.	Africa	8	54	10 Crores	50
2.	Central Asian countries	2	13	6 Crores	30
3.	Russia	2	13	2 Crores	10
4.	Brazil	1	7	.50 Crores	2.5
5.	Singapore	2	13	1.50 Crores	7.5
		15	**100**	**20 Crores**	**100**

SOURCE: Field data

It is apparent from the Table 9 that the 50% of the entrepreneurs are exporting 54% for percent of the total value of exports to Africa alone, as there is more demand for matches there. This is due to the high cost of raw materials and the labour shortage in Africa. 30% of the entrepreneurs export their products to Central Asian countries, to the extent of 13% of the total export value.

CHANNELS OF DISTRIBUTION

In India, entrepreneurs market their product directly, i.e., through their own sales depot, set up through out the country, or through the distributors, covering almost all the territories. In the international trade, the entrepreneurs make their sale, either directly to the importers or through the middlemen located in the overseas market or through the agent. Table 10 shows the mode of exporting strategy adopted by the entrepreneurs to export their products.

Table 10: Mode of exporting of matches

S.No.	Particulars	Number of Respondents	%	Values in Crores for 1995	%
1.	Direct Export	1	10	2	10
2.	Through middle men in the overseas market	2	20	3	15
3.	Through agents	7	70	15	75
		10	**100**	**20**	**100**

SOURCE: Field data

It is clear from Table 10 that 10% of the entrepreneurs, who have considerable export business, resort to direct exporting, to the extent of 10% of the total value. They undertake this risk with heavy capital investment. 20% of the entrepreneurs market to the extent of 15% of the total value through the overseas middlemen, who carries out the marketing activities effectively in the export market. This helps the entrepreneurs to engage on production alone. 70% of the entrepreneurs market their matches through the agent in the domestic market, to the extent of 75% of the total value. Thus, they get themselves relieved from the various export formalities and concentrate on the production only.

MEANS OF TRANSPORTATION

It is said if the industries are flesh and bones of the country, then transport system will be the nervous system of the same. As the means of transportation are considered to be the cornerstone of the modern industry system, the entrepreneurs of Sivakasi, adopted various means to sell their products. The means of transport being followed for inland are by road and rail, and at times by air, in case of urgency. For exporting, the regular means of transportation is by sea and road, and air transport is also used.

Table 11: Means of transportation for export matches

S.No.	PARTICULARS	QUANTITY EXPORTED IN GROSS UNITS PER ANNUM (App).	NUMBER OF REPONDENTS	%
1.	Roadways	3,07,000 units	2	20
2.	Seaways	10,20,000 units	8	80
			10	**100**

SOURCE: Field data

It is inferred from Table 11 that 20% of the sample entrepreneurs adopt road transport, exporting worth 3, 07,000 gross units per annum to the neighboring countries, which are cheap and economical. 80% of the entrepreneurs export 10, 20,000 gross units per annum, through waterways to other countries, as they are also considered to be cheap. It is also inferred from the survey that all the respondents do not prefer to export through any other means of transport, which are considered to be costly.

PORT THROUGH WHICH MATCHES ARE EXPORTED

Selection of port through which the Sivakasi matches are exported, very much depends upon the attitude of the entrepreneurs. Table 12 shows the port selected by ten sample entrepreneurs to export their product in 2007.

Table 12: Port selected for export

S.No.	Particulars	Exported Value in Crores Per Annum	%	Respondents	%
1.	Tuticorin	15 crores	75	9	69
2.	Chennai	4.5 crores	22.5	1	8
3.	Bombay	.50 lakhs	22.5	3	23
		2	**100**	**13**	**100**

SOURCE: Field data

Table 12 indicates that the ten sample entrepreneurs have chosen more than one port to export their matches. 8% of them are exporting 22.5% of the total value through the Chennai port in a year. 23% of the entrepreneurs export to the extent of 25% of the total value, through the Bombay port, 75% of the total value through the Tuticorin port, in a year. So, depending upon the easy accessibility, good port services, local language etc, the Sivakasi entrepreneurs choose the port to export matches.

REASONS FOR SELECTING THE PARTICULAR PORT

The volume of export depends upon the various facilities available in the port. The ten respondents have given the reasons for selecting the ports, for exporting matches. The respondents were asked to rank them in the order of preference. Weighted Arithmetic Mean was used to rank the reasons. The reasons were given weightage for ranking purposes. Table 13 shows the opinion and reasons of the entrepreneurs for selecting the particular port.

Table 13: Reasons for selecting the port

S.No.	Particulars	Ranks	Points	Weighted Arithmetic Mean
1.	Easy to ship to various countries	I	5	4.8
2.	Near the place of production	II	4	4.2
3.	Cheap	III	3	2.4
4.	Good service	IV	2	2.1
5.	Local language	V	1	1.5

SOURCE: Field Survey

As per the survey, the reasons for selecting the particular port to export matches, are in the following order, viz, easy to ship to various countries (4.8), near to the place of production (4.2), cheap (2.4), good services (2.1), and local language (1.5). As per the entrepreneur's opinion, due to easy accessibility, Tuticorin port finds favour with them to ship their products to various countries.

SUMMARY

The process of emergence and development of entrepreneur cannot be explained by one single factor, but a host of factors.

The period of manufacturing and exporting of matches are evenly distributed. The entrepreneurs who have more than 30 years of experience in match production tend to take up export naturally.

Due to the inter-family relations, adequate finance, trust and managerial skills, the partnership form of organization is found to be very common in the Sivakasi match units.

90% of the educated entrepreneurs are able to influence a tremendous growth in match export, unleashing the impossibilities, which is due to the spirit of adventurism in them.

All the entrepreneurs avail different types of assistance from the All India Chambers of Match Association, as a result of their membership. 53% of the entrepreneurs have information relating to the Export Policy changes and 47% have the addresses of the importers.

Apart from their own investment in match units, the availability of finance from various sources such as SBI, nationalized banks, money lenders and financial institutions induces promotion of exports.

Regarding the availability of sources of finance, 46% of the total source of finance is availed by the match entrepreneurs from SBI and its subsidiaries alone.

The various assistances provided by the government, in the form of import replenishment license, duty drawbacks, tax exemptions and advance licensing system also influences the growth and development of the match entrepreneurs in the export business.

The quality of matches exported by all entrepreneurs is different when compared to that of the domestically traded matches. 60% of the entrepreneurs differentiate through damp proofness and 20% of them through strong splints, and 10% through the number of sticks.

Regarding the export market, 54% of them are exporting to Africa, 13% to Central Asian countries, Russia and Singapore each respectively and only 7% to Brazil.

70% of the entrepreneurs are exporting through agents, 20% through middlemen in the overseas market and 10% directly. It is also inferred that 80% of them are adopting sea transportation and 20% of them through roadways.

69% of the match entrepreneurs prefer to export through the Tuticorin port, 23% through the Bombay port and 3% through the Chennai port depending upon the easy accessibility, cheap tariff, local language etc. the entrepreneurs choose the port.

FINDINGS

As far as the total match production and the total match export is concerned, the compound growth rate of total match production of 18.68, which is grater than the compound growth rate of total match exports of 15.6. It is apparent that, there is wide variation between the two. This is due to the efforts of the match entrepreneurs in satisfying the demands of the domestic market first and then entering the international market. This is an indicator of the fact that in spite of increased demand in the domestic market itself, the match entrepreneurs concentrate and prosper in the international market.

80% of the sample entrepreneurs purchase the government fixed quota raw materials for producing the export matches, in the domestic market itself, due to its cost factor. Thus they relieve themselves from the irksome policies involved in importing the raw materials, which is done by 20% of the entrepreneurs.

An examination over the areas of marketing reveals that 54% of the sample match entrepreneurs are exporting to Africa to the extent of 10 crores rupees per annum, where there is more demand for Sivakasi matches.

Data regarding the means of transportation adopted by the match entrepreneurs reveals that 80% of them export through seaways, out of which 69% prefer the Tuticorin port, due to easy accessibility, cheap fare and good services.

70% of the sample match entrepreneurs export through the agents only, to the extent of 15 crores rupees per annum, thus avoiding the cumbersome export formalities and procedures, and concentrate only on the production of export matches.

Depending upon the availability of inputs, the price of the export matches is fixed. 82% of the sample entrepreneurs adopt cost plus profit pricing method, which is assessed to be practicable and profitable to them. The remaining 18% of the entrepreneurs fix the price either on the basis of the contract between themselves and the importers, or on the basis of the prevailing market conditions.

20% of the sample match entrepreneurs run their match units under the partnership form of organization, where there exists inter-family relations among the partners. This helps in pooling of sources and skills of one another in match export development.

Regarding educational qualifications, 70% of the entrepreneurs have undergone college studies till the undergraduate level, which enables them to tackle and handle all the procedures and formalities in export promotion.

50% of the sample entrepreneurs who have more than 30 years of experience in match production are highly experienced and knowledgeable in match exports, than the other entrepreneurs.

All the entrepreneurs avail of the various concessions and assistance of the government such as tax and duty exemption, advance licensing, and replenishment benefits.

PROBLEM AND SUGGESTIONS

Based on the findings, the following suggestions are made to overcome the problems and further streamline its development of exports.

The first problem relates to the purchasing and consumption of potassium chlorate and sulphur. The quantity of these two basic raw materials to be purchased and used at a time is fixed by the government. This restricts the entrepreneurs to meet an increased demand. The moment the entrepreneurs exhaust the annual quantity fixed for him, he has to go to the collector of the district and get his annual quantity raised. This results in waste of time and money to the entrepreneurs. Appropriate officials should be placed at the manufacturing centre, to have an easy approach to get the sanction.

Due to the absence of mechanization in match industries, filling up the boxes with exactly 50 sticks is impossible. The counting in the boxes varies from 47 to 55. But for export purposes, it is stressed legally by the export authorities. So, large scale production and mechanization of match industries will pave the way for the betterment of export matches.

Regarding the sources of finance available to the entrepreneurs, 46% of the total finance is procured from the commercial Banks, and the remaining from other sources. Due to the cumbersome procedures of filling up the numerous forms and formalities in banks, the match entrepreneurs are not availing of the finance from one source alone, viz. banks only. This aspect needs to be looked into by banks liberalizing its irksome procedures, which will help to increase our foreign exchanges.

The government should help the entrepreneurial development by training in management and marketing, assistance in product design and development, and in quality control. This can be easily achieved by getting the ISI mark.

REFERENCES

Laminayana. C. and Sakriya. D, *Yojana,* Vol. XVII, New Delhi, Publication House, March 15, 1994, P.24.

Krishna Prasad. M and Sharmala M.P, "Tomorrow's Techno shop", *Indian Express,* Sep. 29, 1987, P.9.

Government of Tamil Nadu Industries Department, *Guide to Entrepreneurs,* 1989, P. 38-45.

Swami M.M. and Reveendran M.M.S, *Mini Japan, Sivakasi,* 1985, P.20.

All India Chamber of Match Industries, Sivakasi, *Hand-made Safety Matches in India,* P. 2.

Indian Institute of Foreign Trade – *A Study of Safety Match Industries in India,* 1979, p.29.

All India Chambers of Match Industries, Sivakasi, *Sivakasi where Light and Sound are packaged"* Supra., p.2.

The Sparkling Affair in Sivakasi, Business Standard, Volume. 211, March 8, p.7.

All India Chambers of Match Industries, Sivakasi, *Handmade Safety Industry in India,* p.4.

Balagopal, T.A.S., *Export Management,* Bombay, Himalaya Publishing House, 1992, P. 26.

18

A Model to Resolve Supply Chain Constraints in Indian Ports

HARISH PK*

SUJAY KUMAR S*

Indian participation in international trade has been on the rise over the past decade. Movement by sea is the cheapest for international trade and it accounts to 95% of the volume and 77% of the value of the traded goods. Ports are the transit points for transfer of cargo from ship to shore and vice versa. Hence, a port is an essential infrastructure for trading. That the economy is growing is good news, but it is in the process, choking the gateways to trade. Despite the low tariffs and strategic location advantage (connecting the vibrant Asian markets and the prosperous European and American markets), Indian ports have failed badly. Five of the twelve major ports in India handle cargo, which is more than the installed capacity; another three are on the brink of being clogged. This means that more than half of the major ports are under capacity constraint. The constraint comes despite the ports adding 58 million ton (MT) capacity, as against the planned 34.14 MT addition during the year.

According to the figures from the Department of Shipping, the ports where cargo is spilling over include Haldia (near Kolkata), Jawahar Lal Nehru Port Trust (JNPT), Mumbai port, Murmagao and Visakhapatnam. On the other hand, ports like Chennai, Kandla and Kolkata Dock Complex have close to 2 MT of spare capacity.

The cause of the congestion could be related to growing trade, customs bottlenecks, infrastructure and most importantly SCMM - the Supply Chain Mismanagement-the figures given above indicate the later as the most probable single cause. The major Supply Chain related problems in Indian Ports are

1) Ships have to wait too long to get berthing space.
2) Handling is labour-intensive hence susceptible to low productivity.
3) Excessive demurrage caused due to non-movement and non-clearance of cargo.

* Students of Symbiosis Institute of Operations Management, Nashik.

4) Poor facilities including lack of mechanizing, difficult night travel, and storage facilities.

5) Poor connectivity to the storage locations in terms of roads and rails.

6) Time consuming administrative process including long customs clearance and unclear decision making process.

In comparison with other major international ports like Rotterdam, New York, Singapore etc, Indian Ports cut a sorry figure. Resolving the existing supply chain constraints is the only way to improve the Indian ports' functioning so that they can attain international standards. In this paper we aim at proposing a model involving Quantitative Techniques and Supply Chain Modelling to avoid the aforementioned shortcomings so that the port revenue could be tapped as well.

INTRODUCTION

The current international trade activities are a direct consequence of liberalization. Indian participation in international trade has been on the rise over the past decade. Movement by sea is the cheapest for international trade and it accounts for 95% of the volume and 77% of the value of the traded goods. Ports are the transit points for transfer of cargo from ship to shore and vice versa. Hence, a port is an essential infrastructure for trading. That the economy is growing is good news, but it is in the process, choking the gateways to trade. More than one reason have resulted in severe congestion in the ports of India resulting in major losses for shipping companies and the country, thereby making Indian ports less attractive. The cause of the congestion could be related to ineffective supply chain resulted by growing trade, customs bottlenecks and infrastructure shortcomings. The Planning Commission is very aggressive in expanding the capacity of ports but without strengthening the existing supply chain, capacity expansion could result in less return on huge investments. Inadequate supply chain management causes ineffective utilization of port capacity and navigational aids, bunching of vessels, limited cargo handling facilities, high down time of equipment, low labour productivity, shortage of storage space, in short contributing to the low efficiency of Indian ports.

Despite the low tariffs and strategic location advantage (connecting the vibrant Asian markets and the prosperous European and American markets), Indian ports have performed poorly. Five of the twelve major ports in India handle cargo, which is more than the installed capacity. Another three are on the brink of being clogged. Indian ports look completely out of sorts when compared to other international ports like Singapore, New York, Rotterdam, Shanghai, and Hong Kong. In fact the efficiency of a port is determined by the efficiency of its supply chain and that's where the Indian ports have failed badly.

Indian ports should improve their supply chain to be competitive on international arena much before even thinking of expansion. Inbound logistics which constitutes arrival of cargo to the port, material handling which constitutes loading/unloading of the cargo, and outbound logistics makes up the port supply chain and improvement can be made to each of these elements. A definite improvement in the supply chain can be achieved by resolving the issues in each of these elements. This paper aims at proposing a mathematical model to resolve the supply chain related inadequacies existing in Indian ports.

INDIAN PORTS-AN OVERVIEW

At present, India has twelve major ports which account for most of the trading activities. Apart from the twelve there are close to hundred and fifty minor ports along the coastline of about 5,500 km.

Location of the Major Ports

Table 1: Location of the Major Ports

S.No.	Name of the port	Coast associates	Latitude	Longitude	State
1.	Mumbai	Arabian Sea	18N	72E	Maharashtra
2.	Kolkata	Bay of Bengal	22N	88E	West Bengal
3.	Haldia	Bay of Bengal	22N	80E	West Bengal
4.	JNPT	Arabian Sea	18N	73E	Maharashtra
5.	Kandla	Arabian Sea	20N	70E	Gujarat
6.	Chennai	Bay of Bengal	13N	80E	Tamil Nadu
7.	Mangalore	Arabian Sea	12N	74E	Karnataka
8.	Mormugao	Arabian Sea	15N	73E	Goa
9.	Paradip	Bay of Bengal	20N	86E	Orissa
10.	Tuticorin	Bay of Bengal	8N	78E	Tamil Nadu
11.	Vishakhapatnam	Bay of Bengal	17N	83E	Andhara Pardesh
12.	Cochin	Arabian Sea	9N	76E	Kerala

Among the major ports, *Mumbai* handles over one-fifth of the bulk trade, which includes petroleum products and dry cargo. *JNPT* is equipped with modern facilities having mechanized container berths for handling dry bulk cargo. *Kandla* is a tidal port. A free trade zone has been set up here. It handles all type of traffic. *Mormugao* handles fifth position in terms of total quantum of traffic handled. Facilities for export of iron-ore were specially developed at *Mangalore*. *Cochin* is a natural harbour. *Tuticorin* handles coal traffic. *Chennai* is one of the oldest ports and it handles petroleum and crude oil trade. *Vishakhapatnam* is the deepest port in the country and it handles iron-ore. Recent addition of births has enabled it to handle petroleum and crude oil as well. *Paradip* handles iron-ore and some quantities of coal and dry cargo. *Kolkata* is a river line port handling diversified commodities. A fully mechanized *Haldia* port supplements its activities. *JNPT* and *Haldia* are the most modern of the ports.

SUPPLY CHAIN PROBLEMS EXISTING IN THE INDIAN PORTS

Vessels choose a port of their choice based on quick turn around time, productivity, quick discharge, besides destination of the cargo. In a port, a berth should wait for a vessel and not the other way around. The major supply chain related problems in Indian ports are:

(1) Ships have to wait too long to get berthing space.

(2) Handling is labour-intensive hence susceptible to low productivity.

(3) Excessive demurrage caused due to non-movement and non-clearance of cargo.

(4) Poor facilities including lack of mechanizing, difficult night travel, and storage facilities.

(5) Poor connectivity in terms of roads and rails.

(6) Time consuming administrative process including long customs clearance and unclear decision making process.

A study on the dwell time of cargo in Indian ports reveals that for containers the average at major container terminals is 1.88 days for imports and 3.78 days for exports. More importantly, the port authorities are responsible for only 3.5-5.5 hours for import containers and 3.3–5.3 hours for export boxes, while the rest of the wait is on account of other stakeholders such as shipping agents, Customs, clearing agents, transporters and others responsible for various pre- and post- shipment activities such as documentation, arranging for funds for port charges and organizing transport.

The average dwell time for dry bulk and break bulk cargoes is: Imports — dry bulk 38.23 days and break bulk 15.49 days; and exports — dry bulk 27.14 days and break bulk 17.2 days. The dwell time of liquid bulk is not important because of its fully mechanical handling. Dwell time is the duration for which an 'entity' stays in the port for service; in port parlance, the 'entities' are vessels and cargo (including containers). The vessel-related dwell time is the time between a vessel reporting at anchorage and its casting-off from the berth, which is also the turnaround time of the vessel. The cargo/container related dwell time is the time a consignment remains in a terminal's in-transit storage awaiting shipment (for exports) or evacuation by rail/road (for imports). Dwell time thus reflects the efficiency of the port. Higher the dwell time, lower is the efficiency.

According to the figures from the Department of Shipping, the ports where cargo is spilling over include Haldia (near Kolkata), Jawahar Lal Nehru Port Trust (JNPT), Mumbai port, Murmagao and Vishakhapatnam. On the other hand, ports like Chennai, Kandla and Kolkata Dock Complex have below 2 mt. of spare capacity. The constraint means ports may face a repeat of the congestion nightmare that JNPT port in Mumbai faced in 2003. This congestion comes despite the participation of private companies (Indian and foreign) in port operations.

Comparison with other Major International Ports

At Rotterdam, the dwell time for containers as well as break bulk cargoes, for both imports and exports, is higher than those in major ports in India and yet it is not a matter of concern because the port it is a component of the industrial complex similar to the Special Economic Zone in India. However, Singapore presents a different picture. At

Singapore, there is no dry bulk; only break bulk and containers and the dwell time of break bulk for both imports and exports is 0.85 day and for containers (both imports and exports) 0.6 days.

Foreign ports score on several factors, such as the high degree of mechanization in cargo handling as well as information exchange with the participation of highly-skilled workforce, availability of sufficient space for storage and allied activities and proper facilities for quick evacuation of cargoes. Vast differences have been observed in the availability of infrastructure, connectivity and electronic information exchange. Thus, the aggregation/evacuation of cargo in international ports is very quick due to several reasons such as seamless connectivity with various modes of transport, excellent rail/road/inland waterways network, higher carrying capacity of wagons and road carriers and conveyor system for handling bulk cargoes. India, despite having a vast coastline, large-sized ships could not call at its ports following draft restrictions. Usually, the majority of vessels plying between Europe and Far East go past India without touching any of the Indian ports. Privatization also has hit a major blockage in terms of high costs. Indian ports are so expensive that having a hub would be difficult. The cost at Indian ports was around 15% more compared to the Colombo and Salalah ports.

Table 2

Indian Ports	Port of Rotterdam
Cargo is predominantly by road and rail only.	Most of the bulk cargo and the containers movement through barges accounts for 50-60% transportation because of excellent inland water networking. Intermodal connectivity by rail / road is seamless.
The extent of mechanization is less in India's major ports.	The level of mechanization is very high with the latest technologies applied in all spheres.
Most of the manufacturing firms are located away from the ports.	Most of the manufacturing units are located within the port; thereby the evacuation is very fast.
We have dedicated terminals with less number of berths.	There is no concept of pre-berthing detention as the berths are waiting for ships and they have longer quay lengths.
EDI implementation is partial. Too many human interfaces and manual exchange of documents.	The total EDI networking is complete and total and hence, there is no physical movement of paper from any place. Human intervention is almost nil. All payments are also done electronically.
Work flow is manual and partly computerized and ERP is being envisaged for implementation.	The entire processing is computerized and Enterprise resource planning software is implemented years back.

Table 3

Indian Ports	PSA Singapore
The total number of terminals for handling containers at India's biggest Container Port–JNPT is three Terminals having linear quay length of 600 Mtr., adequate for nine vessels at a time.	PSA Singapore has four terminals having quay length of 11,754 mtrs. which can accommodate about 41 container vessels at a time.
There are draft limitations in the channel.	There are no draft limitations in the channel and the biggest ships in the world can visit Singapore Port at any point of time.
Handling of container cargo is only 4613 TEUs and JNPT, India's biggest container port handled 2667 TEUs in 2005-06.	The total volume of cargo handled at Singapore in the calendar year 2005 was 423.3 million tons of which, containers handled was 23.2 million TEUs. The volumes therefore are simply not comparable.
The equipments are handled by staff deployed at site. The average move per hour is about 20/25. Due to less deployment of cranes, the crane rate (total number of containers loaded/unloaded from a ship in one (hour) is about 60/70. This leads to late turnround of vessel.	The cranes are both operated by staff at site and also by automation through terminals control centre. The move per hour is about 25-30. They have the maximum reach across the biggest and widest generation vessels. Due to adequate deployment of cranes, the crane rate achieved is 100 per hour. This leads to quick turnround of vessel.

As compared to other international ports, it can be inferred that Indian ports cut a sorry figure in terms of efficiency, cargo handling, profitability and performance. This model helps in resolving the critical issues and also helps in arriving at realistic parameter values under the existing feasibility constraints.

PORT OPERATIONS TIME STUDY - IMPORT CYCLE - TOTAL TIME TAKEN: 3.5-5.5 HRS

Berthing of vessel

- Agencies Involved – Shipping Agent, Port, PHO, Police, Immigration Customs, Rummaging (for narcotics).
- Documents Required-ISPS declaration, copy of P&I cover, Application to DC, Details about crew, boarding set consisting ship and crew details, PHO form.
- Time Taken- **1 to 3 hrs.**

Discharging of import container

- Agencies Involved – Shipping Agent, Customs, Port, Port's Transporter.
- Documents required - Vessel, Yard Planning form, Tally Sheet.
- Time Taken - **20 min**

Movement to Out Gate

- Agencies Involved –Port, Shipping Agent, Port's Transporters.
- Documents Required- Advance list, Gate Pass,
- Time Taken- **30 min**

Request for berthing of vessel

- Agencies Involved – Shipping Agent, Port.
- Documents required- Berthing application, Payment.
- Receipt for berth hire and stevedoring, Certified hazardous cargo list.
- Time Taken- **30 min**

Submission of Advance list

- Agencies Involved – Shipping Agent, Port.
- Documents required- Hard copy of IGM, Port Payment Receipts.
- Time Taken - **30 min**

Vessel / Yard Planning

- Agencies Involved – Shipping Agent, Stevedores, port.
- Documents Required-Vessel Bayplan, Vessel, Yard planning form.
- Time Taken- **45 minutes**

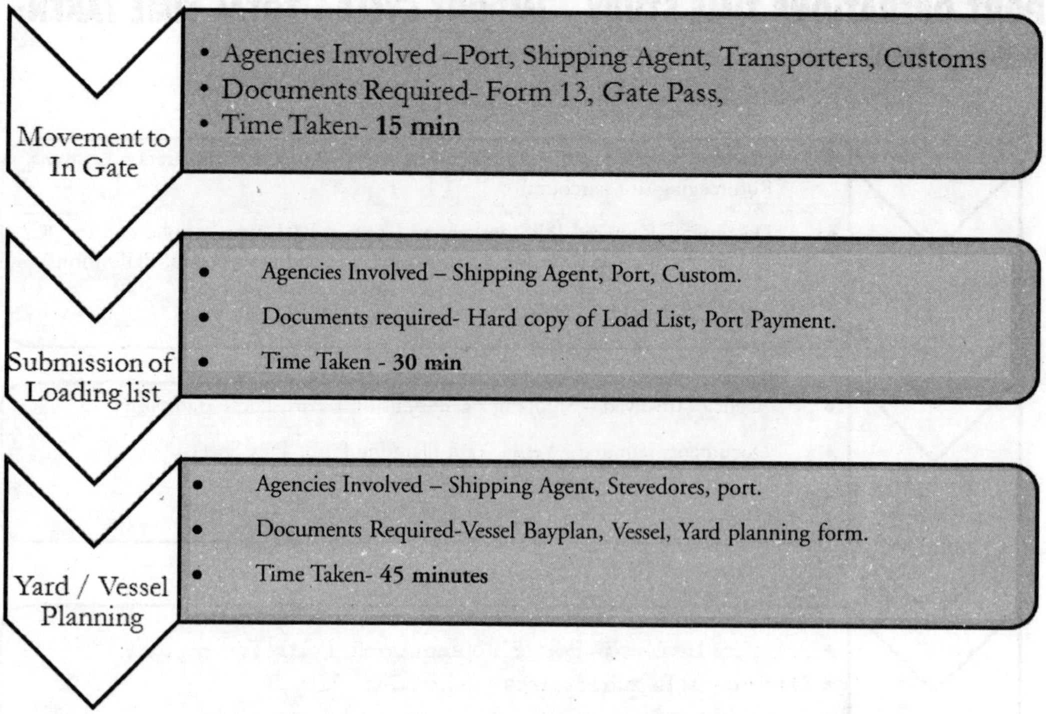

As it can be seen, both in the import and export cycles, the actual time spent on value adding work is only about 3-5 hrs, while the rest is spent on non-value adding activities. Therefore, it is of great importance that the other non-value adding parameters should be decreased.

FACTORS CONTRIBUTING TO PORT INEFFICIENCY

The port supply chain inefficiency is a result of a multitude of factors. The following are the major reasons:

- Inadequate port capacity.
- Inadequate navigational aids and facilities.
- Bunching of vessels.
- Poor road network within the port.
- Shortage of wagons and heavy duty trucks.
- Inadequate equipments.
- Low labour productivity.
- Low IT application.
- Systems and procedures.
- Excessive documentation.

SUPPLY CHAIN EFFICIENCY PARAMETERS

The supply chain of a port can be judged by measuring the following parameters

- Pre-Berthing Detention Time (PBD)
- Non-Working Time at Berth (NWT)
- Working Time (WT)
- Turn Round Time (TRT) and
- Output per Ship Berth day (OSB) of the vessels.

TRT = PBD + NWT + WT + Transit Time

Any reduction in TRT will improve the port efficiency and in turn increase the productivity and help in increasing the Supply Chain Surplus.

MODEL OBJECTIVES

The major reason behind developing this model is to improve the supply chain activities of a port. An attempt towards the same is made by developing linear goal programming problems (LGP).

The following are the objectives for developing this model

- To identify supply chain constraints that result in port parameter inefficiencies
- To achieve realistic parameter values under specified constraints using suitable quantitative tools to foster better supply chain efficiency
- To provide recommendations that help in achieving the values
- To quantify the resulting benefits in terms of increase in productivity.

Reduction in Pre-berth Detention and Non-working Time Values-A Goal Programming Approach

The PBD and NWT are two major constituents of TRT and a decrease in these values would contribute immensely towards increase in Port Productivity.

TRT is a function of Pre-Berth Detention Time (PBD), Non-Working Time (NWT) and Working Time (WT) and a negligible Transit Time. WT is a value addition activity, while PBD and NWT are non-value addition activities. Hence PBD and NWT should be minimized at any cost. Goal Programming Technique is adopted to minimize the above mentioned values.

Linear Goal Programming Problem to Minimize PBD and NWT

An LGP is developed to attain the following goals and QM Solver for Windows is used to solve the same.

P1: Minimize TRT and make it less than or equal to 60 hours instead of the existing 84 hours.

P2: Minimize PBD and make it less than or equal to 18 hours instead of the existing 27.15 hours.

P3: Minimize NWT and make it less than or equal to 10 hours instead of the existing 13 hours.

P4: The combined sum of non-value adding PBD and NWT should be exactly only two - fifth of TRT so that three-fifth of the TRT is spent on value adding WT:

Z = minimize (p1d1_ + p2d2_ + p3d3_ + p4d4)

Subject to the constraints

1.94 PBD + 1 NWT <= 60

PBD <= 18

NWT <= 10

PBD + NWT = 24

Solution obtained after simulations using QM Solver are as follows:

Table 4

```
Data and Summary ----------

Data

Minimize +1P1d+1 +1P2d+2 +1P2d+3 +1P3d+4 +1P3d-4
TRT: 1.94PBD +1NWT + d-1 -d+1 =60
PBD: 1PBD + d-2 -d+2 =18
NWT: 1NWT + d-3 -d+3 =10
PBD+NWT: 1PBD +1NWT + d-4 -d+4 =24

Summary of results

Decision variable analysis
PBD        18
NWT        6

Priority analysis   Nonachievement
Priority 1           0
Priority 2           0
Priority 3           0

Constraint Analysis RHS        d+          d-
TRT                  60        0           19.08
PBD                  18        0           0
NWT                  10        0           4
PBD+NWT              24        0           0
```

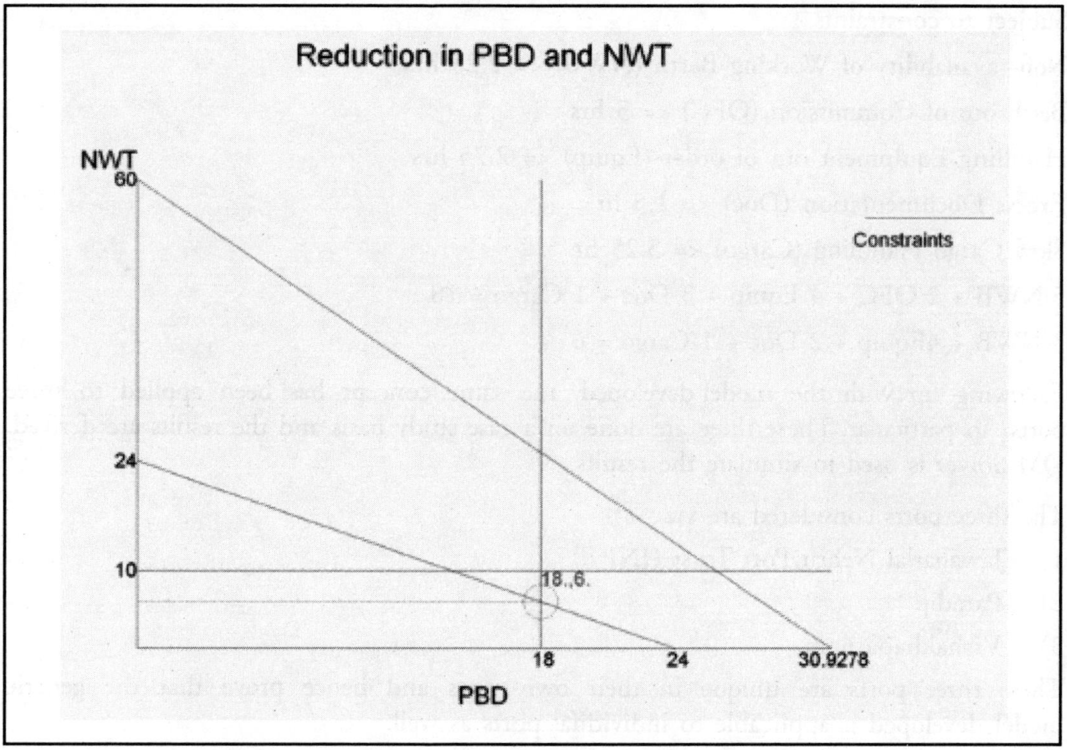

Figure 1

Further to the decrease in PBD and NWT, the value of the components constituting them should also be decreased.

A Linear Goal Program to Minimize the Major Components of PBD And NWT

The major components of high PBD and NWT are

1) Non-availability of working berth
2) Berth out of commission
3) Handling equipment out of order
4) Excess documentation
5) Slow cargo handling

The goals that need to be achieved are

P1-P5: To minimize all the components so that they meet benchmarked values

P2: To attain the pre-achieved values of PBD and NWT

Z= minimize (p1d1_ +p2 d2_ +p3 d3_ + p4d4_ + p5d5_) + p6 (d6_ + 6+ + d7_ + d7+))

Subject to constraints

Non- availability of Working Berth (NWB) <= 2.25 hrs

Berth out of Commission (OFC) <= 3 hrs

Handling Equipment out of order (Equip) <= 2.75 hrs

Excess Documentation (Doc) <= 1.5 hr

Slow Cargo Handling (Cargo) <= 3.25 hr

5 NWB + 2 OFC + 4 Equip + 3 Doc + 1 Cargo = 18

3 NWB + 4Equip + 2 Doc + 1 Cargo = 6

Following up with the model developed, the same concept has been applied to three ports in particular. These three are done on a case study basis and the results are derived. QM Solver is used to simulate the results.

The three ports considered are viz

1) Jawaharlal Nehru Port Trust (JNPT)
2) Paradip
3) Vishakhapatnam

These three ports are unique in their own ways and hence prove that the generic model developed is applicable to individual ports as well.

The models developed are presented and the results are derived as well.

Table 5

```
Data and Summary ----------

Data

Minimize +1P3d+3 +1P4d+4 +1P1d+5 +1P5d+6 +1P2d+7
PBD: 5NWB +2Out of Commission +4Equipment +3 Doc +1 Cargo + d-1 -d+1 =18
NWT: 4NWB +3Equipment +2 Doc +1 Cargo + d-2 -d+2 =6
Doc: 1 Doc + d-3 -d+3 =1.5
Cargo: 1 Cargo + d-4 -d+4 =3.25
NWB: 1NWB + d-5 -d+5 =2.25
Out of Commission: 1Out of Commission + d-6 -d+6 =3
Equipment: 1Equipment + d-7 -d+7 =2.75

Summary of results

Decision variable analysis
NWB          0
Out of Commission
             4.75
Equipment    1
 Doc         1.5
 Cargo       0

Priority analysis    Nonachievement
Priority 1            0
Priority 2            0
Priority 3            0
Priority 4            0
Priority 5           1.75

Constraint Analysis  RHS        d+        d-
PBD                  18         0         0
NWT                  6          0         0
Doc                  1.5        0         0
Cargo                3.25       0         3.25
NWB                  2.25       0         2.25
Out of Commission    3          1.75      0
Equipment            2.75       0         1.75
```

CASES - JNPT, PARADIP, AND VISHAK

JNPT

Data and Summary ----------

Data

```
Minimize +1P1d+1 +1P2d+2 +1P2d+3 +1P3d+4 +1P3d-
TRT: 10PBD +1NWT + d-1 -d+1 =24
PBD: 1PBD + d-2 -d+2 =8
NWT: 1NWT + d-3 -d+3 =0
PBD+NWT: 1PBD +1NWT + d-4 -d+4 =9.6
```

Summary of results

Decision variable analysis

PBD	2.4
NWT	0

Priority analysis	Nonachievement
Priority 1	0
Priority 2	0
Priority 3	7.2

Constraint Analysis	RHS	d+	d-
TRT	24	0	0
PBD	8	0	5.6
NWT	0	0	0
PBD+NWT	9.6	0	7.2

Table 6

Final Tableau ----------

	PBD	NWT	d- 1	d- 2	d- 3	d- 4	d+ 1	d+ 2
TRT	1	0	0.1	0	-0.1	0	-0.1	0
PBD	0	0	-0.1	1	0.1	0	0.1	-1
NWT	0	1	0	0	1	0	0	0
PBD+NWT	0	0	-0.1	0	-0.9	1	0.1	0
Priority 3	0	0	-0.1	0	-0.9	0	0.1	0
Priority 2	0	0	0	0	0	0	0	-1
Priority 1	0	0	0	0	0	0	-1	0

	d+ 3	d+ 4	RHS
TRT	0.1	0	2.4
PBD	-0.1	0	5.6
NWT	-1	0	0
PBD+NWT	0.9	-1	7.2
Priority 3	0.9	-2	7.2
Priority 2	-1	0	0
Priority 1	0	0	0

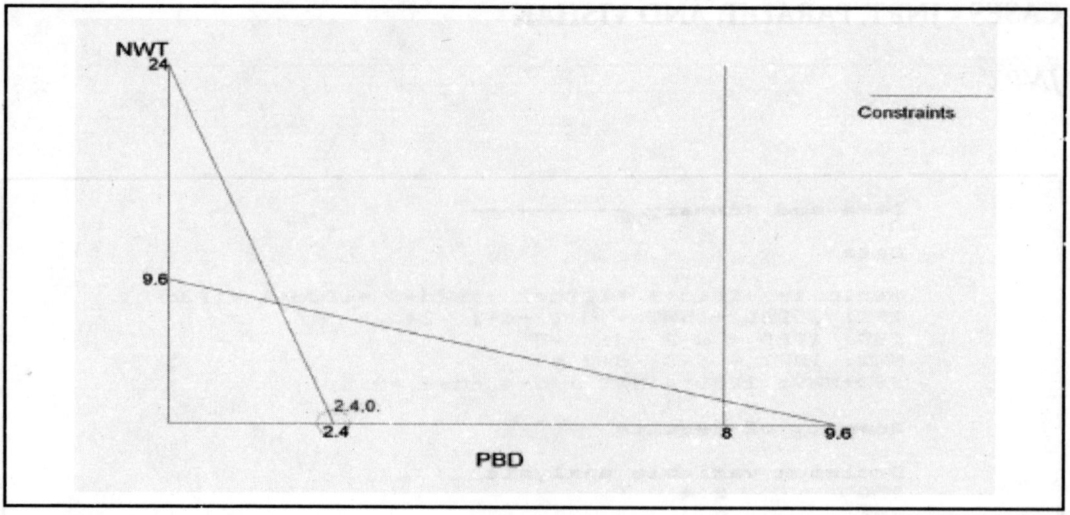

Figure 2

PARADIP

Table 7

Final Tableau ----------

	PBD	NWT	d- 1	d- 2	d- 3	d- 4	d+ 1	d+ 2
TRT	0	0	1	-0.8	0	-1	-1	0.8
PBD	1	0	0	1	0	0	0	-1
NWT	0	0	0	1	1	-1	0	-1
PBD+NWT	0	1	0	-1	0	1	0	1
Priority 3	0	0	0	6	0	-1	0	0
Priority 2	0	0	0	0	0	0	0	-1
Priority 1	0	0	0	0	0	0	-1	0

	d+ 3	d+ 4	RHS
TRT	0	1	18.6
PBD	0	0	15
NWT	-1	1	4.6
PBD+NWT	0	-1	5.4
Priority 3	0	-1	0
Priority 2	-1	0	0
Priority 1	0	0	0

Table 8

```
Data and Summary ----------

Data

Minimize +1P1d+1 +1P2d+2 +1P2d+3 +1P3d+4 +1P3d-4
TRT: 1.8PBD +1NWT + d-1 -d+1 =51
PBD: 1PBD + d-2 -d+2 =15
NWT: 1NWT + d-3 -d+3 =10
PBD+NWT: 1PBD +1NWT + d-4 -d+4 =20.4

Summary of results

Decision variable analysis
PBD          15
NWT          5.4

Priority analysis    Nonachievement
Priority 1             0
Priority 2             0
Priority 3             0

Constraint Analysis  RHS          d+          d-
TRT                    51          0           18.6
PBD                    15          0           0
NWT                    10          0           4.6
PBD+NWT                20.4        0           0
```

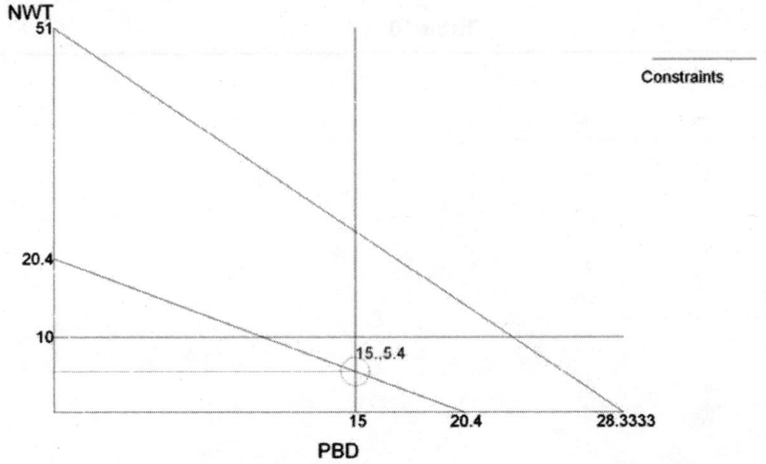

Figure 3

VISHAK

Table 9

Data and Summary ----------

Data

Minimize +1P1d+1 +1P2d+2 +1P2d+3 +1P3d+4 +1P3d-4
TRT: 2.25PBD +1NWT + d-1 -d+1 =72
PBD: 1PBD + d-2 -d+2 =22
NWT: 1NWT + d-3 -d+3 =8
PBD+NWT: 1PBD +1NWT + d-4 -d+4 =28.8

Summary of results

Decision variable analysis

PBD	22
NWT	6.8

Priority analysis	**Nonachievement**
Priority 1	0
Priority 2	0
Priority 3	0

Constraint Analysis	RHS	d+	d-
TRT	72	0	15.7
PBD	22	0	0
NWT	8	0	1.2
PBD+NWT	28.8	0	0

Table10

Final Tableau ----------

	PBD	NWT	d- 1	d- 2	d- 3	d- 4	d+ 1	d+ 2
TRT	0	0	1	-1.25	0	-1	-1	1.25
PBD	1	0	0	1	0	0	0	-1
NWT	0	0	0	1	1	-1	0	-1
PBD+NWT	0	1	0	-1	0	1	0	1
Priority 3	0	0	0	0	0	-1	0	0
Priority 2	0	0	0	0	0	0	0	-1
Priority 1	0	0	0	0	0	0	-1	0

	d+ 3	d+ 4	RHS
TRT	0	1	15.7
PBD	0	0	22
NWT	-1	1	1.2
PBD+NWT	0	-1	6.8
Priority 3	0	-1	0
Priority 2	-1	0	0
Priority 1	0	0	0

PROJECTED VALUES OF INCREASED PRODUCTIVITY

The decrease in TRT increases the productivity of the port and it is mandatory to quantify the results. Accordingly, the increase in OSB (Output per Ship Berthing Day) is calculated in proportion to the decrease in TRT and the corresponding decrease in its components, viz. PBD, NWT, and WT.

The calculated projected increase is tabulated and it can be concluded that without any heavy investment, close to 10% increase in productivity can be increased, which translates into huge monetary gains.

Table 11: Projected increase in Productivity

Port Name	TRT Current (A)	NWT Current (B)	PBD Current (C)	WT Current A-(B+C)	OSB Current (O)	TRT Projected (E)	NWT Projected (F)	PBD Projected (G)	WT Calculated E-(F+G)	OSB Calculated O* (A-(B+C))/(E-(F+G)
Over all	3.5	0.58	1.13	1.79	9267	2.5	0.25	0.75	1.5	11058.62
JNPT	1.96	0.08	0.92	0.96	15821	1	0	0.1	0.9	16172.58
Paradip	3.16	0.82	1.05	1.29	11316	2.125	0.225	0.625	1.275	11449.13
Vizag	3.8	0.54	1.04	2.22	10557	3	0.28	0.93	1.79	13093.03

RECOMMENDATIONS TO ACHIEVE THE ABOVE MENTIONED VALUES

To Achieve the Proposed PBD of 18 Hours

- Introduce 24 x 365 - round the clock port working.
- Deployment of VTMS in all ports
- Optimization of cargo handling systems and equipments
- Use IT as a strategic weapon in the port sector
- Introduce E-environment to eliminate physical interface
- Strengthen the IT backbone for port operations
- Implement Port Community System.

To Achieve the Proposed NWT of 6 Hours

- Synchronization of the landside operations with the seaside operations such as optimizing the rail operations, removal of road congestion within ports by efficient management of traffic flow etc.
- Maintenance management of the cargo handling equipments.
- Make it mandatory for ports to invest in 4-lane RCC roads laid using state-of-the-art technology within the port area.

- Port to implement immediately unidirectional traffic flow to eliminate cr isscrossing and traffic congestion.
- The approach roads to ports to be 6 lanes with no surface crossings.
- Improve the conditions of handling equipments.

CONCLUSION

The proposed model would immensely beneficial if implemented. The proposed model is also highly economical and it doesn't ask for any huge investments. The major beneficiaries include the following:

- Stakeholders
  1) Customs
  2) Terminal Operator
  3) Vessel Operating Agent
  4) Container Operating Agent
  5) Stevedore
  6) Importer / Exporter / Customs House Agents (Cha)
  7) Transport Operators
- Nation
- Ports & Terminals

Indian participation in world trade is expected to rise significantly and if it has to become a reality, then the efficiency of the gateways to trade should also be improved correspondingly. Our model attempts at doing the same.

REFERENCES

Andreas Klose, M.Grazia Speranza, Luk N.Van Wassenhove, *Quantitative Approaches to Distribution, Logistics, and Supply Chain*, Springer-Verlag Berlin Heilderberg, 2002.

Sunil Chopra, Peter Meindl, *Supply Chain Management Strategy, Planning, and Operation,* Prentice Hall of India, Third Edition 2007.

Barry Render, Ralph M. Stair Jr., Michael E. Hanna, *Quantitative Analysis for Management*, Prentice Hall of India, Ninth Edition 2007.

http://www.indiaseaports.com/isp/indexns.jsp

19

Learning Dynamics in Organizational Transformation: A Multi-dimensional Study of Strategic Change and Knowledge Innovation

ABDUL MAJID*

Organizational and individual learning are two different concepts in contemporary organizational context. Organizational learning is not a new concept, but it needs to be further elucidated at an understandable level for organizational practitioners at an actual work setting, specially in developing countries like Pakistan. This paper reviews the literature on organizational learning in transformational change, and the comparative learning processes in different geographical locations. We are dealing here with the so-called learning cycle in strategic change process with special reference to the textile sector in Pakistan.

Keywords: Learning cycle, Transformational change, Innovation, Geographical characteristics, Dynamics.

INTRODUCTION

Theories of organizational change are totally different from the theories of organizational learning. In the context of strategic change phenomenon, different authors have attempted to define the different perspectives of organizational change and the relationship between change and organizational characteristics, dimensions and variables. Some considered different theories as a basis of organizational change e.g. institutional theory [(Perrow1979)], Neo institutional [(DiMaggio,1983) 148]; some authors have worked on the need of organizational change [(Meyer,1982)515], some have worked on protocols and dynamics [(Hinning & Greenwood, 1988)], procedures of implementation [(Child & Smith,1987) 565,]; (Fomburn,1990) 298]; management [(Tushman, 1986), (Tichy,1983)]; sources and strategies [(Quinn,1980)]; failure [(Amburgey, Kalley, & Barnett,1993)51]; leadership

* Permanent faculty member of Hazara University, Mansehra, NWFP, Pakistan and PhD Research Scholar in University of Peshawar, Peshawar, Pakistan.

[(Tichy, 1984)240], conflicts and resistance [(Deutsch, 1971), (Argyris & Schon, 1978); (Kotter & Schlesinger,1979)106, (Folger & Skarlicki,1999) 35, (Hultman,1995)15 ; (Dent & Goldberg,1999) 25, (Piderit,2000) 783, (De jager,2001) 24, (Kegan & Lahey,2001) 86)]

To summarize the work of different authors is very difficult and beyond the scope of this research, but it is still necessary to identify some of the key areas of organizational change.

The key areas in the field of organizational change are pointed out by [(Pettigrew, Woodman; Cameron, 2001) 697], which are

1. The examination of multiple contexts and levels of analysis in studying organizational change.
2. Consideration of timeframe processes and protocols.
3. The link between change processes and organizational performance and outcomes.

This is simply the overview of the work under the heading of change. As far as learning is concerned, it remains vibrant in all types of strategic change process. We know that learning is a continuous process in the scenario of the modern organizational development, but its frequency is not the same in different levels and phases of change. In developmental or incremental change, the learning process is temporary and for a limited time period. While in a continuous change process, most of the organizational shifts are different from previous ones, and all new shifts generate new knowledge and learning portfolios.

This conference paper begins with the basic concepts of strategic change and organizational learning. The definition of those concepts provides us an analytical lens to deal with the complicated concept of knowledge innovation. After defining the basic concepts we will discuss the learning cycle in strategic change process, at different stages of transformational change by conducting the comparative analysis of the work force learning behavior in different work environments.

WHAT IS ORGANIZATIONAL CHANGE?

Environmental conditions and managerial decisions compel organizations to establish basic pattern of activity [(Boeker, 1989)490, (Selznick, 1948)25]. With the continuation of those activities, a shared understanding of that basic pattern is established [(Meyer & Rowan.1977)340]. That type of shared understanding also helps to develop organizational inertia [(Hannen & Freeman, 1984)150], and to break this inertia a new concept has emerged which is called organizational change, which is implemented in most of the organizational activities [(Romanelli & Tushman, 1994)1141].

According to Ven & Poole, change is a difference in the form, quality or state over time in an organization's alignment with its external environment. The same authors use the definition of Hofer & Schendel, [(1978)] to describe the organization's alignment with its external environment as "Fundamental pattern of present and planned resource deployments and the environmental interactions that indicates how the organization will achieve its objectives".

ORGANIZATIONAL TRANSFORMATION

The Greek word "metanoia" captures the meaning of transformation well. It literally means "beyond the mind." It is an idea of stretching or pushing beyond the boundaries with which we normally think and feel. It means a profound change in mind, a radical revision, a transformation of our whole mental process, a paradigm shift.

In the framework of organizational change, different organizational theorists have defined this concept in different ways. Senge [(1990)] called this generative learning, and Mohrman, Lawler, Ledford, & Cumming [(1989)] called this large-scale system change, [(Tushman,1985)171] reorientation, Tichy [(1983)] strategic change, Miller & Friesen [(1984)] quantum change, [(Argyris,1976) 363] double loop learning, and [(Golembiewski, Billingsley, Yeager,1974)135] called this a Gamma change.

Alfred Adler [(1998)] defines transformation in the following words "Transformation occurs when leaders create a vision for transformation and a system to continually question and challenge beliefs, assumptions, patterns, habits and paradigms with an aim of continually developing and applying management theory, through the lens of the system of profound knowledge. Transformation happens when people managing a system focus on creating a new future that has never existed before, and based on continual learning and a new mindset, take different actions than they would have taken in the past".

Difference between Transformational and other Types of Org-changes

There are more than one kinds of change and they need to be handled in particular way [(Wesis. J. W, 1994)]. There are three basic types of organizational change [(McEvoy, 2005)] which are incremental change [(Linda S. Ackerman, 1986)1], transitional change and transformational change [(John Kotter; 1995)]. Incremental or developmental change improves what the business is currently doing, rather than creating something new. Transitional change replaces what already exists with something completely new. The organization must dismantle and emotionally let go of the old way of operating while the new state is being put into place [(McEvoy, 2005)]. Transformational change introduced new and radically different forms of organization's mission, culture and leadership [(Ackerman, 1986)], which includes both radical and incremental changes [(Child & Smith,1987)570].

ORGANIZATIONAL LEARNING

There is no definition of organizational learning on which there is consensus amongst the Contributors of organizational theories. But there are some definitions that can translate the different characteristics of learning concept. For example, (cyert & March, (1963) says that organizations adopt different things with the passage of time, which is basically organizational learning. Duncan [(1979)133] defines learning as a knowledge about the transformation process with its environmental context. In contemporary organizational management, learning is considered as the acquisition and development of skills, knowledge, values, behaviours, memories, understanding, and wisdom of the workforce in the organization.

The purpose of this research paper is to analyze the learning process in transformational change. With that objective in mind, we have to understand that in transformational or strategic change process the learning process is different from the learning taking place in the rest of the change processes. As we already have discussed that transformational change is a continuous process, and with that process learning process, also present in a continuous shape, Danial R, Tobin [1996] called this a transformational learning, which is the identification, acquisition, and application of information that enables an organization and the people within that organization to reach their goals.

To undertake transformational learning, one must

1. Discover what he needs to know, that is, uncover their area of unconscious ignorance.
2. Locate the information they need.
3. Apply that information to their work.

Since organizational transformation generates a bundle of knowledge that is helpful in creating the learning organization [(Ehrenberg & Stupak 1994)75], which promotes communication and collaboration, that everyone is engaged in identifying and solving problems, enabling the organization to continuously experiment, improve and increase its capability [(Daft, 2000)]. With these complex activities, transformational learning is also there in strategic change process in one or other forms.

CHANGE CYCLE IN DIFFERENT GEOGRAPHIES

Learning is a developmental process with proper inception and demise. In organizational development, learning process goes side by side with strategic change process. We know that strategic change consists of different transitional phases, and in those transitional phases, learning process can start or stop at any point. Beginning of the transition is not an indicator of the start of the learning process or vice versa. In my opinion, there are no rigorous steps in learning cycle for contemporary workforce like any other cycle in business organizations.

Inception of Learning in Transformational Context

In transformational change, learning process do not start from zero, because, we are dealing with the era of learning organizations, with developed human resources, having up to date knowledge. In strategic change, the learning process starts at a point where they receive new knowledge to increase their capabilities, develop their skills, wisdom and understanding, and also the methodology to use that knowledge at actual work setting.

Dynamics of Transformational Learning

Learning process is not the same in all the regions of the world. In developed countries, the learning process is totally different than the learning process of the workforce in developing countries. This difference in learning behaviour is due to the difference in education, skills, opportunities; and motivational factors etc. This difference remains dynamic in different stages of whole transformation process.

At the start of first transition in transformational change, the learning behaviour of every individual is different from each other. In developing countries as mentioned in the Figure 01, the learning process starts from the lower level while on the other side, the learning process of the workforce in developed counties starts from the higher level due to the previous knowledge that they already have as mentioned in Figure 2.

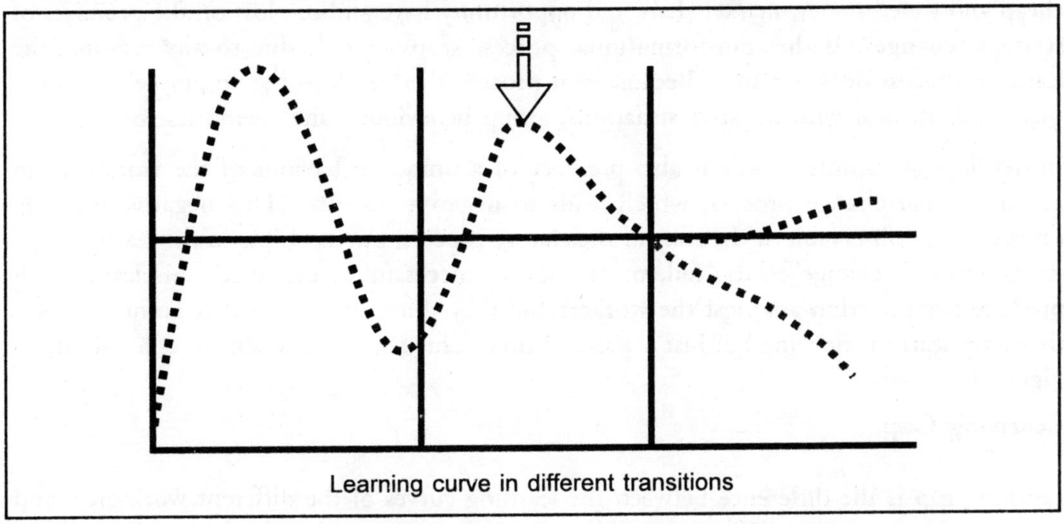

Figure 1: Learning curve in strategic change process in a developing country

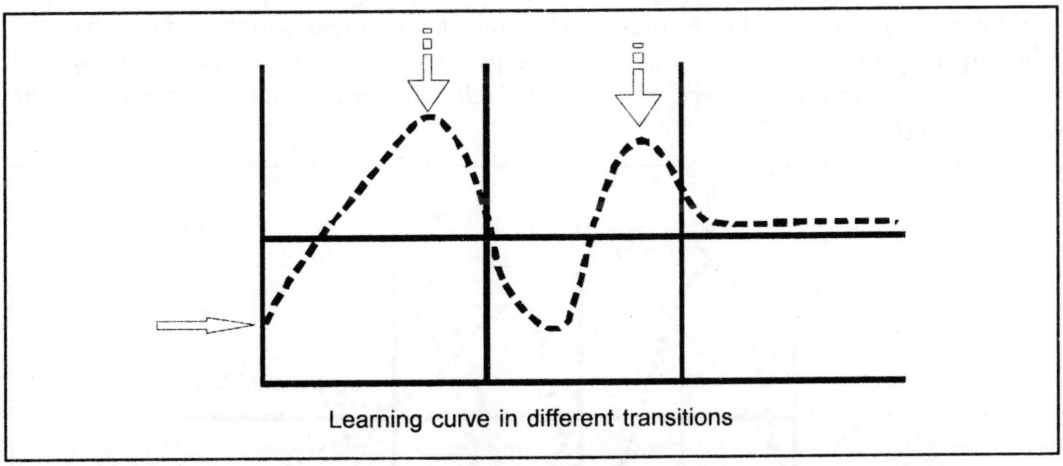

Figure 2: Learning curve in strategic change process in a developed country

Learning Acceleration

Learning acceleration is basically the speeding up of learning process in workforce during the transitional phases. At the beginning of the transitional phase, the learning process is relatively fast in both of the regions, in developed as well as developing countries. With the passage of time, the slope of the learning curve is downward which shows that the process of intellectual development is going to diminishing. In some cases, the downfall of the learning curves touches to zero, where there is no growth in mindset, behaviour, skills, and wisdom etc. The process of diminishing the learning curve can start at any point in strategic change process.

Transformation of the organization is a complex phenomenon and difficult to implement. According to J. Arthur, "Over half of all change efforts fail and the price of failure is not cheap and time, money, market share and opportunity have all been lost on the promises of strategic change". If the transformational process stops or fails due to any reasons, the learning process does not stop. Because that process also develops the employee's wisdom, their skills to deal with negative situations, group behaviours, and memories too.

In developing counties, there is also presence of a unique behaviour of the workforce in organizational change process, which leads to negative learning. This negative learning process is not observable at the start of the change process, but as visible in the textile sector in Pakistan. If change efforts fail, or are not so successful as expected, this failure will produce demotivation amongst the workers and they think that up to that point whatever they have learnt is nothing but just a waste of time. This behaviour is shown as a red line in Figure 1.

Learning Gap

Learning gap is the difference between the learning curves of the different workforce, and even in the curves of different workers in one stratum. In the beginning of the transformational phase, learning gap is in the favour of the organizations with less developed workforce. It means that the learning acceleration in that organization is more than the other organizations that have a relatively developed workforce. In the upcoming stages of the transitions, the learning acceleration of the different organizations approaches to the equivalent level.

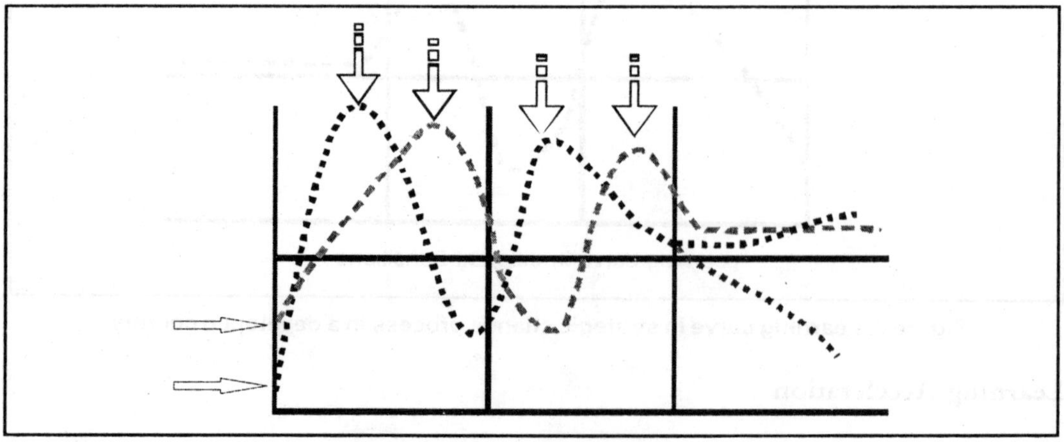

Figure 3: Comparative Analysis

Learning Maturity in Strategic Change

Learning maturity is a different point in different transitions in transformational change, where the learning process and behaviour is at its extreme level and after that point, learning process goes to diminishing. It is not necessary that the maturity of the transition phase for the organization is also a maturity stage for the learning process. This maturity point lies anywhere in the strategic change process. The behaviour of the learning curve is different from the behaviour of the transitional curve in strategic change process. At one transition the learning process will mature at the middle of the whole process while in the other cycle, the learning process may mature at the end of the transition. It totally depends upon the learning behaviour of the employees, which is beyond the scope of this paper.

ORGANIZATIONAL TRANSFORMATIONS THROUGH KNOWLEDGE INNOVATION

Learning generates the change or change process generates, the learning and knowledge this is a complex phenomenon. But most of the contributors to organizational theory considered transformational change as a kind of learning. For example, Senge, (1990) called this generative learning, [(Tushman,1985)] reorientation, [(Argyris,1978)] double loop learning, Russell Ackoff in his book *"Creating the Corporate Future"* [(1981)] says that: "Transformation is the creation and change of a whole new form, function or structure. To transform is to create something new that has never existed before and could not be predicted from the past. Transformation is a 'change' in mindset. It is based on learning a system of profound knowledge and taking actions based on leading with knowledge and courage"

All the viewpoints of different contributors demonstrate that transformational change and continuous learning go side by side, and both of them support each other. As mentioned earlier, transformational process starts with a strong base of knowledge. But to continue that process, innovative knowledge and contemporary learning is required in every new transition, because every new shift identifies new variables, generates new challenges and focuses on new priorities.

CONCLUSION

The study of learning dynamics in different geographies provides us a different lens to analyze the learning process. Most of the previous works on organizational learning deal only with the different dimensions of learning, and try to present different theories to conceptualize the learning process e.g. Estesw, (1950)94] deals with the basic definition of learning process, [(Postmanl, 1963)] verbal learning; [(Abelson,1977)] computer simulation as the process of learning; [(Greenoj,1980)713] individual learning; [(Argyris,1978)] basic characteristics, [(Shrivastava,1983)8] typologies of organizational learning systems, But the interesting thing in this study is that, this work has attempted to identify the learning potential and learning behaviours in the strategic change process, of the workforce of different geographic locations.

With the inception of the concept of globalization, the term, multi-national, does not remain as a new understanding; most of the organizations of European countries are now operating all over the world. In that scenario they have to understand the environment of every country and also try to transform it after a complete understanding of its characteristics. As far as learning is concerned, they have to develop the workforce over there by transfer of knowledge through training and development by any means, and at the time, they have to understand the protocols of learning in that specific environment, which is totally different from their own working conditions. Without understanding the environmental conditions, no one can achieve the specified targets, especially in the case of human development in learning organizations.

REFERENCES

Ackerman, L. "Development Transition or Transformation: The question of change in organizations." *OD Practitioner*, (1986): 1-8.

Ackoff, R. L. *Creating the Corporate Future.* New York: John Wiley & Sons.1981.

Adler, A. *Understanding Human Nature.* MN: Hazelden, Center Cit, 1998.

Amburgey, Kelly, & Barnett, W, P. "Resetting the Clock: The Dynamics of Organizational Change and Failure." *Administrative Science Quarterly* 38.1(1993):51-73. 17 Dec 2007 < http://links.jstor.org/sici?sici=0001-8392%28199303%2938%3A1%3C51%3ARTCTDO%3E2.0.CO%3B2-C>

Argyris, C. "Single- and double-loop models in research on decision making." *Administrative Science Quarterly* 24(1976): 363-375.

Argyris, & Schon, D. *Organizational Learning.* MA: Addison-Wesley, Reading.1978.

Boeker, W. "Strategic Change: The effects of founding and history." *Academy of Management Journal* 32(1989): 489-515.

Child, & Smith, C. "The context and process of organizational transformation Cadbury limited in its sector. *Journal of Management Studies* 24(1987): 565-593.

Cyert, & March. *A Behavioral Theory of the Firm.* Englewood Cliffs NJ: Prentice Hall, 1963.

Daft, R.L. Organization theory and design. Ed.7th. Mason: South-Western College Publishing, 2000.

De Jager, P. Resistance to change: a new view of an old problem. *The Futurist*, (2001): 24-27.

Dent, E. & Goldberg, S. "Challenging resistance to change." *Journal of Applied Behavioral Science* (1999): 25-41.

Deutsch, M. "Toward an understanding of conflict", *International Journal of Group Tensions*, 1(1971): 42-54.

DiMaggio & Powell. "The iron cage revisited: institutional isomorphism and collective rationality in organizational fields." *American Sociological Review* 48(1983): 147-60.

Duncan, R, & Weiss, A. "Organizational learning: Implications for organizational design." *Strategic Management Journal*, 3(1979) 133-146.

Ehrenberg, R, H. & Stupak, R, J. "Total Quality Management: Its relationship to administrative theory and organizational behavior in the public sector." *Public Administration Quarterly.* 18.1(1994): 75-98.

Estesw, K. "Toward a statistical theory of learning". *Psychological Review*, 57(1950): 94-107.

Folger, R. & Skarlicki, D. "Unfairness and resistance to change: hardship as mistreatment," *Journal of Organizational Change Management (1999)*, 35-50.

Fombburn, & Ginsberg, A. "Shifting gears: Enabling change in corporate aggressiveness." *Strategic Management Journal* 11(1990): 297-308.

Golembiewski, Billingsley, & Yeager, S. "Measuring change and persistence in human affairs: Types of changegenerated by OD design." *Journal of Applied Behavioral Sciences,* 12(1974), 133-57.

Greenoj, G. 'Psychology of learning." *American Psychologist,* 35.8 (1980): 713-26.

Greenwood, R. & Hinning, C,R,: Understanding Radical Organizational Change: Bringing together the Old and the New Institutionalism." *The Academy of Management Review,* 21.4(1996):1022-1054. 14 Dec, 2007.<http://links.jstor.org/sici?sici=0363-7425%28199610%2921%3A4%3C1022%3AUROCBT%3E2.0.CO%3B2-T>

Hannan, & Freeman, J. "Structural Inertia and Organizational Change." *American Sociological Review,* 49.2(1984): 149-164.

Hofer, C, Schendel, D. *Strategy Formulation: Analytical Concepts.* MN: West, St. Paul, 1978.

Hultman, K. "Scaling the wall of resistance." *Training & Development* (1995): 15-22.

Kegan, & Lahey, L. "The real reason people won't change."*Harvard Business Review* (2001):85-92.

Kotter, & Schlesinger, L.A. "Choosing strategies for change." *Harvard Business Review* (1979): 106-114.

Kotter, J. "Leading change: Why transformation efforts fail." *Harvard Business Review,* 73(1995):

L, Ackerman. "Development, Transition or Transformation: the Question of Change in Organizations." *OD Practitioner,* 1986: 1-8.

"Leading the process of change - Choose the Most Appropriate Change Strategy" *Mc Envoy Consulting,* 10, Dec, 2007. <http://www.mcevoyconsulting.co.uk/process/strategy.html>

Meyer, J., Rowan, B. "Institutionalized organizations: formal structure as myth and ceremony." *American journal of Sociology,* 83(1977): 340-363.

Meyer, A. "Adopting to environmental jolts." *Administrative Science Quarterly* 27(1982):515-37.

Miller, & Friesen, P. "Momentum and revolution in organizational adaptation." *Academy of Management Journal* 23(1980):591-614.

Miller, D., Friesen. *Organizations: A Quantum view.* New Jersey: Prentice Hall, Englewood Cliffs, 1984.

Mohrman, H., Lawler. Ledford, G., Mohrman, S., Cumming, T. *Large-scale organization change.* San Francisco: Jossey-Bass, 1989.

Morgan, G. *Images of organization,* Thousand Oaks, CA: Sage Publications, Inc.1997.

Nadler, & Tushman. *Managing strategic organizational change: frame bending and frame breaking.* New York: Delta consulting Group, 1986.

Perrow, C. *Complex Organizations: A critical essay.* New York: Random House, 1979.

Pettigrew, A. "Context and action in the Transformation of the firm." *Journal of Management Studies* 24(1987): 649-670.

Pettigrew; Woodman, & Cameron, S. "Studying Organizational Change and Development: Challenges for Future Research." *The Academy of Management Journal* 44.4(2001):697-713. 24 Dec 2007 http://links.jstor.org/sici?sici=0001-4273%28200108%2944%3A4%3C697%3ASOCADC%3E2.0.CO%3B2-4.

Piderit, S.K. "Rethinking resistance and recognizing ambivalence: a multidimensional view of attitudes toward an organizational change." *Academy of Management* (2000): 783-794.

Postmanl. *Verbal Behavior and Learning: Problems and Processes.* New York: McGraw-Hill.1963.

Quinn, J. *Strategies for change: logical incrementalism.* Homewood, IL: Irwin, 1980.

Romanelli & Tushman. "Organizational Transformation as Punctuated Equilibrium: An Empirical Test". *The Academy of Management Journal,* 37.5(1994): 1141-1166.

Senge, P. M. *The fifth discipline: The Art and practice of learning organization.* London,. Century Business, 1990.

Schankr, & Abelson. *Scripts, Plans, Goals and Understanding: An Inquiry into Human Knowledge Structures.* Hillsdale, N.J: Erlbaum, 1977.

Selznick, P. "Foundation of Theory of Organization." *American Sociological Review* 13.1(1948): 25-35.

Shrivastava, P. "A Typology of Organizational Learning systems." *Journal of Management Studies,* 10(1983): 8-28.

Tichy, N. *Managing strategic change: technical, political and cultural dynamics.* New York: John Wiley, 1983.

Tichy, N. & Ulrich, D. 1984. "Revitalizing organizations: The leadership role." *Managing organizational Transitions,* In J. R. Kimberly & J. B. Quinn (Eds.), Hornewood IL: Irwin: 240-264.

Tobin, D, R. Transformational Learning. New York: John Wiley & Sons Inc, 1996.

Tushman, M, L. & Romanelli, E. "Organizational evolution: a metamorphosis model of convergence and reorientation."*Res, Organizational Behavior* 7(1985): 171-222

Tushman, L. & Anderson, P. "Technological Discontinuities and Organizational Environments."

Administrative Science Quarterly, 31.3(1986): 439-465. 12 Dec, 2007 <http://links.jstor.org/sici?sici=0001-8392%28198609%2931%3A3%3C439%3ATDAOE%3E2.0.CO%3B2-L>

Van de Ven & Huber, G. "Longitudinal field research methods for studying processes of organizational change." *Organization Science* 1(1990): 213-219.

Wesis, J. W. *Business Ethics, A managerial stakeholder approach.* Belmont Calif: Wadsworth, 1994.

20

Fun and Laughter - An Indispensable Element for Work-place Happiness

K.SANGEETHA*

In the current, radically transforming business world and increased war for talent, attracting and retaining talented employees has become very crucial. There is an alarming rate of attrition due to dull and unpleasant work environment, boring and monotonous jobs etc. which affect the workforce performance and the company's productivity. Fun and laughter at workplace is one of the vital tools that can be used in an organization to motivate the employees to enjoy work. Many organizations have started realizing the need for creating a happier work environment infused with fun and laughter to retain the talented employees at any cost. Various studies have shown that workplaces which induce excellent performance are those filled with laughter and humour. Adding the element of fun and laughter to the workplace helps to bring about a significant positive change in the employee's attitude and behaviour; and on the company's bottom-line. It creates a competitive advantage to the company in the marketplace as it boosts employee morale and kindles their enthusiastic spirit to work sincerely and to give of their best potential in their work performance that has a significant impact upon the company's profits. A shared joke or introducing games that evoke fun and laughter in the workplace results in multiple benefits to both the employer and the employee - physically, emotionally and psychologically. A sense of humour allows the employees and the leaders to recognize and understand the incongruities of the workplace and life in general; and bring in a feeling of freshness and delight that promotes team spirit, creativity and esprit-de-corps. It inculcates the right attitude in them and helps them take pride in their job. A fun and humour-filled workplace motivates the employees to look at the brighter side of life, be creative, develop high morale and a balanced view of life and work. Fun may not be a recommendation for all companies but for certain organizations, it is a powerful tool that promotes morale and enthusiasm among the workers who take pride in working in the company. Getting proper ideas and 'how to go about' will make the programme implementation successful in making the workplace a happier one even during tough times. Laughter not only makes the external environment happy but also makes the workers work

* Faculty Associate and Consulting Editor, Icfai Business School Research Center, Chennai.

to their best potential with high quality that helps in the realization of the organizational goals. In a nutshell, a fun and laughter filled work environment will make the company a successful one and help them emerge as an 'employer of choice' or to be a great place to work for.

INTRODUCTION

The rapidly increasing fierce competition and increasing employee attrition levels across various industries globally have made business take care of their employees as never before. Fun and laughter in a workplace lends a competitive advantage to an organization through its human resources that boost employee's morale and enthusiasm and reduced work pressure. It instills a sense of joy among the employees that can go a long way in creating a bond between the employees and the employers. Companies that had appreciated and implemented fun at workplace had accomplished many wonders in terms of innovations, superior talent pool, good quality products, increased productivity and soaring revenues. In a nutshell, creating a fun and laughter filled work environment will pave way for the company's success in the marketplace and surely emerge as an 'employer of choice'.

FUN AND LAUGHTER AT WORKPLACE – MAKING COMPANIES EXCEL

Laughter really is the best medicine, and that goes for everything from the common cold to the bottom line

– An Old Adage

The relentlessly changing business scenario of ever-increasing talent war, and lesser retention levels, have made companies to comprehend the need for building a happier work atmosphere that is packed with fun and laughter. With rising attrition levels across diverse industries, it has become critical for the employers to hold the talented employees at any cost. Besides, there are being upsetting attrition levels due to boring and unpleasant job environment, dreary and monotonous jobs etc. which affect the workforce performance and the company's productivity. Hence it is a precondition of an employer to integrate the element of fun and laughter in the work place which helps in boosting employee morale and enkindles their enthusiastic spirit to work earnestly. It makes employees to be proud about their job and their employers; dwindle tardiness and stress at work, which perks up their work performance and productivity that makes company earn excellent profits and to earn a competitive advantage in comparison to their competitors in the marketplace. Winning companies such as Google and Genetech have emerged as market leaders as their employees enjoyed the work environment, took pride about their working and gave their best performance at work which made the company emerge as 'employer of choice.'/ 'great place to work for'.

Various studies have shown that fun-filled workplaces will result in excellent performance:

A study by the Business Council of Australia found that 'fun' was one of the key elements of extraordinary, productive workplaces which achieved outstanding performance are filled with laughter and humour[1]. Rogers (2002) found that based on 2,500 employees from different industries in Australia that "81% believe that they are more productive in a fun working environment; 93% informed that laughing during work helps in reducing job-related stress. And 55% were willing to take lesser pay to have more fun at work". From this survey Roger concludes that "people who have a fun spirit and can convey this in their workplace are to have low levels of job stress and burnout and high levels of job satisfaction and organizational commitment[2]. Fun at work reduces stress and improves productivity". When employees are working on a monotonous job, humour can increase length of time on job by reducing tension and boredom. And studies show humour does not detract from tasks requiring increased concentration" (Buxman, 2002,).[3]

A fun and laughter-filled workplace makes a significant positive change in the employee's attitude and behaviour and on the company's bottom –line. Introducing playful sport at work provides multiple benefits to both the employer and the employee – physically, emotionally and psychologically. It aids the employees look at the brighter side of life, be creative, have positive morale and to take a balanced view of the both - life and work. This enables the employee to resolve work conflicts; be a productive team member whose work contributes to the organizational productivity and profitability. As the saying goes, "Laughter is the shortest distance between two people" (Victor Borge) but that distance can be reduced when people laugh together.[4] The power of humour in business is very critical and this is more so in the areas of sales and marketing as it helps the customer to overcome the early hesitation and to develop a superior opinion towards the product/idea by holding the customer's attention and influencing their buying behaviour. Thus, the role of fun and humour has become an indispensable one in every day of business life. South West Airlines is a classic example of a company whose strategies to build fun at work had boosted employees' morale and had garnered laurels as a successful market leader in its business and as an 'Employer of Choice'.

FUN AND LAUGHTER AT WORKPLACE – THE BENEFITS

Laughter in the workplace has several proven benefits, for the mind, body and spirit and on social occasions.

Physiological Benefits

Humour and laughter causes a domino effect of delight and pleasure, and also many positive physical effects - strengthens one's immune system and recovers from illness, and also brings joy to lives. A study by Drs. Lee Berk and Stanley Tan of Loma Linda University

---

1 Hull, D. and V. Read, *Simply the Best Workplaces in Australia.* 2003, ACIRRT - University of Sydney + Business Council of Australia: Sydney. p. 41.

2 *Humour in the Workplace: Anecdotal Evidence Suggests Connection to Employee Performance by* Lauren Breeze, Adrienne Dawson, and Susanna Khazhinsky St. Edward's University.

3 *Humour in the Workplace: Anecdotal Evidence Suggests Connection to Employee Performance by* Lauren Breeze, Adrienne Dawson, and Susanna Khazhinsky St. Edward's University.

4 Make em' laugh, make em' laugh, make em' laugh! By Nina Spencer http://www.ninaspencer.com.

found that laughing decreases blood pressure, and stress hormones and improves muscle flexibility. Besides, the endorphins released during laughing enhance the general sense of well-being - a sense of happiness and optimism and reduced tension in a stressful situation.[5] Besides, these therapeutic benefits humour also provides various physiological benefits. They are:

- The endorphin produced makes one feel good.
- Improves muscle relaxation, boosts immunity and suppresses the stress hormone and fight/flight attitudes.
- Cures cancer and reduces body pain.
- Is an exceptional aerobic exercise and helps in losing weight.
- Improves breathing and blood circulation.
- Protects an individual from heart diseases by reducing high blood pressure.

Benefit to the Workers

A happy person is not a person in a certain set of situations, but rather a person with a certain set of attitudes.

Having fun and laughter at the workplace is of vital importance to an employee in all spheres of life and this is more crucial in relieving the employee's workplace stress and burnout. A stressed employee becomes sick, depressed, shows irritation and is unproductive. In such situations, laughter is the most economical and effective cure that reduces employee's stress and the attrition levels. A study by Duane Smelser highlighted that successful people are the ones who are cheerful, have fun and in good spirits. This optimistic feeling/attitude increases oxygen in the brain, endorphins and blood flow, which enables people to sense more obviously and creatively. [6]

- Laughter produces a sense of comfort and increases employee's alertness.
- Humour helps in balanced thinking.
- Brings in bright positive attitude and to evade negative emotions.
- Makes employees energetic and enthusiastic due to increased oxygen level in the blood.
- Builds self-confidence and courage to overcome any stressful situations.
- Boosts employee morale and a willingness to learn, share and contribute to the organizational success.
- A good sense of humour results in efficient communicators and makes them good team workers.
- Instills pride about their contribution, their job and on the management that would make the firm an 'Employer of Choice'.

---

5 *Laughter in the workplace can boost profits, reduce tension* by Laura Laaman,2005http://www.bizjournals.com/

6 *Laughter in the workplace can boost profits, reduce tension* by Laura Laaman,2005http://www.bizjournals.com/

- Helps in effective decision-making and in appreciating and implementing new initiatives both at workplace and in personal life.

Benefits to the Organizations

The smallest distance between two people is a smile. This distance can further be reduced when employees laugh together in workplace.[7]

Happy employees are the most productive workers who break workplace monotony and involve in creating a perfect place to work for as they pass on their exuberant mood to their colleagues and managers too. They serve as a source of motivation for everyone in the office. People who are witty are good communicators; take criticisms in a lighter vein; make effective presentations; and improve customer service and their retention levels. When leaders practice humour it helps in making their advices/ new ideas be acceptable to their employees in an amiable way that result in bonding relationships, especially when they laugh together. Such an environment makes employees confident team members who take a collective approach to resolve problems, have reduced work tension and takes pride about their employers. In brief, a leader who encourages humour and fun at workplace will have decreased absenteeism rate, win the war for talent, boost company's profits and emerge as employer of choice. Ex: Google, Southwest Airlines, IBM, Quad/Graphics, and Nucor Steel have less absenteeism rate compared to the industry standards.

FUN AND LAUGHTER AT WORKPLACE: HOW TO DIAGNOSE?

The benefits of incorporating fun and laughter in an organization and the benefits earned by implementing this programme can be measured by comparing the rate of absenteeism, tardiness, and employee turnover/ attrition with those of the rates before the programme implementation. The decrease in the rate of customer complaints is also taken into consideration. An employee satisfaction and motivation survey can also reveal crucial information for the employers to act upon – what the employees feel about their work, the company and its culture. To know whether the programme had to be implemented in an organization or not, Jody Urquhart provides a test for it to identify by scanning the workplace and taking note of the following questions:

1. Are your people seen laughing or smiling at work? Yes/ No
2. Do people stop and appreciate it when some funny or humorous incidents happen? Yes/ No
3. Does the company organize fun activities every month? Yes/ No
4. Are sufficient tools (fun giveaways, draws) available to request clients to take part in the fun work environment? Yes/ No
5. Is your manager generally positive and does he smile at work? Yes/ No

---

7 *Make em' laugh, make em' laugh, make em' laugh*! By Nina Spencer ***http://www.ninaspencer.com***

If 'no' is the answer for two or more of these questions, it highlights the fact that the staffs are suffering from "terminal seriousness," has a negative impact on the employee morale and productivity[8].

WORKPLACE FUN AND LAUGHTER: THE MYTH AND THE REALISM

Many organizations harbour a myth that having fun and laughter in work will have a negative impact upon the company's operation and on its market performance. They tend to believe that successful and effective organizations are those, whose work culture is defined by work seriousness, control and to be tough with employees. They believe that having humour at work causes diversion in work performance and on the employees' attitude and behaviour that negatively impacts upon the company's production and profit generation. They believe that playful behaviour and laughing at work are the signs of employees' immaturity, incompetence and ineptness. But, this is a myth, not the reality. A happier workplace has a profound positive effect on the company's operations and profitability. The concept of fun at workplace does not connote that workers are allowed to behave like jokers or clowns, but to have a refreshed mind that enables them to receive and perceive clearly the situations/ problems; to communicate efficiently and resolve things before they become complex. According to Dr. Trice's research, laughter will help one to get rid of negative feelings and allows one to get back to a task or go ahead with another assignment by being impassive to the past defeat.[9] A pleasant atmosphere helps them have a break from the serious work for a while to have a refreshed heart, mind and soul. Dr. David Abramis discovered that people who have fun at work are more creative and productive as also good decision-makers, and get along well with their co-workers. They have less absenteeism, late, and sick days than the people who do not have fun. Though some expenses are associated with "fun-at-work" activities and programmes, the benefits reaped are plentiful in terms of reduced cost of absenteeism, attrition, recruitment and poor productivity[10]. Google's and Genetech's fun-filled work environment had made its employees feel a sense of pride about their employers and made them emerge as an employer of choice/ great place to work for.

FUN AND LAUGHTER AT WORKPLACE: STRATEGIES TO BUILD IT

Humour loosens up the mental gears. It encourages out-of-the-ordinary ways of looking at things."[11]

Humour or fun at work is a great tool in increasing employees work performance and in building strong relationships but it should be remembered that no inappropriate joke or comments are made in any situation that would hurt anyone. It should not be distasteful nor divert the workers from their main work duties. One has to ensure that it synchronizes with the existing organizational culture, it is supported by the top management and is

[8] *Creating a Fun Workplace* by Jody Urquhart http://www.idoinspire.com/articles/article 010804182645.php.

[9] *Lighten Up: Humour In The Workplace* http://www.warrenshepell.com/NR/rdonlyres/DEE9FCA5-E7DF-48B3-B326-3711817D1CC0/0/humour.pdf

[10] *Humour and Fun in the Workplace* by Mary Rau-Foster, June/July 2000 , workplace issues.com

[11] Doskoch.P, *Happily Ever Laughter. Psychology Today* http://cms.psychologytoday.com/articles/index.php. Last accessed: 26/4/2005.

incorporated ingeniously in the routine work. It can be incorporated in many ways like including a joke-telling session during the break time, sending a card or a message for an employee's anniversary, or a CEO congratulating an employee's good work. But the key is to ensure that it always has a surprise element that makes people smile, enjoy and feel relieved from a tensed situation.

At workplace, humour can be encouraged during presentations, staff meetings, team work and negotiations which turn the work purpose more fruitful. Using funny toys such as Barbie dolls, Frisbees or clipping cartoons at the work desk, or having funny dressing competitions and get together will increase employee motivation, make them overcome stress and the employers have a good employee retention levels. Ex: Autodesk, a California-based software company, made its employees participate in its "bring-your-animal-to-work" programme. Such initiative to make the employees happy was received well though there were some conditions and expectations that accompanied the programme.[12]

Before saying a joke or making a humorous statement one had to ensure that it will:

- Make others feel happy.
- It is on situations and not on people.
- Not based on a person's looks, religion, or gender.
- Not complicating the existing problems or camouflaging workplace complaints.
- One should be more conscious of cultural differences.

A fun-filled workplace can be started in a small way at the workplace by creating a joke board in the staff room/ lunchroom where one can post good cartoons, jokes or crazy photos of themselves and their colleagues. Employee's suggestions to do ridiculous activities during the week could be displayed and implemented. Such employee participation creates a sense of oneness, promotes team work and resolves their differences or conflicts. It acts as an stress buster and boosted creativity. It reduces employees' stress, burnout, and tardiness and boosts their morale. Companies such as Google, IBM and South West Airlines believe strongly in the concept of fun at workplace and promote a fun-filled healthy environment that makes its workforce enjoy working for the company. It helps in perceiving and accepting changes, improves communication, creativity and confidence of the employees encouraging them to give their best performance. Offering stress busters such as yoga, meditation, family get together, Friday dressing, sports events, use of funny props at office helps the employee to be relaxed and to take note that the company take cares of their health too...

Many companies have different ways of creating and injecting fun and laughter and few of the suggested ways inferred from these companies are:

- Ensuring that the humorous and funny observations are scrutinized by the top management and accepted by them

[12] *Humour and Fun in the Workplace* by Mary Rau-Foster, June/July 2000 , workplace issues.com.

- Hiring competent employees who value fun and have a good sense of humour
- Establishing a Fun Committee
- Encouraging job spontaneity
- Developing the employees to have the habit of looking for humour in everyday workplace situations
- Encouraging the use of situational humour to lighten tense situations. Ex: In South West Airlines, an employee who initiates loads of fun in the workplace is rewarded with free flight air tickets
- Using humour as ice breaker before meetings or presentations
- Sharing a joke or a funny idea with colleagues – Ex: In Genetech, they have 'the Ho-Ho's programme' on every Friday afternoon where the employees take a break and talk about how the week went
- Telling stories and funny incidents in one's personal life to the fellow colleagues
- Creating a humour break room stored with cartoons, joke books, fun props, video and audio players so that employees can take short humour breaks
- Using fun props such as Hula Hoops, Yo-Yos, Tinkertoys, Frisbees, Silly Putty, Nerf Balls and Guns,
- Having funny dress-up days; wearing a silly hat/ guerilla caps. Ex: Genetech hosts annual conferences where the employees wear funny night caps and conduct games and parties for the employees
- Conducting funny game contests – paper plane contests, treasure hunt and cooking contests and the best childhood secret contests
- Having cartoon caption contests
- Clipping funny cartoons or a humorous advertisements from a newspaper or a magazine; crayons and drawings of the employees' children on the office bulletin board
- Sharing and pinning photos of colleagues or the family members etc.
- E-mailing good jokes to other colleagues or circulating a funny newsletter in the office
- Giving funny cards and gifts to the co-workers on special occasions such as on birthdays, wedding days, festive days or for thanksgiving
- Using humour to promote upcoming events/seasons
- Participating in a laughter club
- Operating a humour library at workplace
- Encouraging the workers to develop humorous skits and musical fun contests.

Ben-Jery Ice creams, a U.S. based ice cream manufacturer is a classic example of a company that has implemented many of the above suggestions. It established fun committees, humour bulletin board and break room, fun dress up day, cartoon caption contests, funny posters and pizza complaint party that made its employees enjoy their job. 'Managing Office Technology' magazine created a tension venting area in the office common place where stuffed pig toys called 'Babe' was used relieve the employees stress by kicking the doll. To quote further, Dick Kussman, VP, sales AT&T' encouraged his sales staff to have fun at work. He organized team chili cook-offs, employees' monthly unusual dress-up days and sharing of funny videos among the employees across the nation.

FUN AT WORKPLACE: THE ROLE OF LEADERSHIP

"It is inhumane if employees can't have natural fun at work. It is the role and responsibility of the leader to create workplace where people can enjoy themselves. I know that our company is doing well; when I walk, I can hear people laughing"

– Hal Rosenbluth, CEO of Rosenbluth International[13]

The role of leadership in creating a fulfilled environment is very crucial as it involves a change in the professional atmosphere and requires a lot of creative thinking on the part of the leaders. Hence their commitment to implement fun programmes successfully in an organization is a prerequisite. Getting proper ideas and 'how to go about' will make the programme implementation successful in making the workplace a happier one even during tough times. [14] The Hodge-Cronin & Associates survey had revealed that 98% of the 737 CEOs surveyed favoured candidates who had a good sense of humour and 84% of CEOs believed that employees having a good humorous sense would do best in their jobs compared to the people with less humour.

A leader who takes initiatives in making the workplace a fun-filled one is the one who knows how to identify, develop and retain employees who can execute work effectively even in a critical situation. A perfect leader is one who knows how to boost the team spirit, enthusiasm that leads to open communication, make his/her followers to enjoy the work place and make the corporate culture a lovable one to the employees even at odd times. The best example of a leader who encouraged the fun culture at workplace is Herb Kelleher, CEO of Southwest Airlines who hired employees with a good sense of humour and attitude. He did not care much about candidates' education and expertise because they could always be trained. Such an approach of the Southwest Airlines and its leaders had made the company a successful airline; and its employees loved working there. They worked harder to attain higher performance and quality in work to serve their customers and remain with the company. Employees who initiate fun in the workplace are rewarded with free flight air tickets. Due to its fun-filled work environment Southwest have received increased number of applicants to work for the company.

---

[13] *Changing Corporate Perceptions of the Value of Humour* by Paul McGhee, PhD, www.LaughterRemedy.com

[14] *Humour and Fun in the Workplace by* Mary Rau-Foster, June/July 2000 , http://www.workplaceissues.com/arhumour.htm

Even managers at IBM have ventured to make work fun. In 1996, an orchestra composed of skilful employees of the new IBM sales division was created to give a 15 min concert every morning at office. It generated a happier workplace filled with laughter that made its employees enthused to boost everyday sales and the units sales was increased by 30% in that year.[15] At Sun Microsystems Laboratories, Inc. the management encourages its engineers to come up with new ideas and be involved in funny pranks such as the April Fools' Day as they are influenced that it will boost morale and provokes teamwork.[16]

CONCLUSION

Fun and Laughter at Workplace – A Key to Organizational Success

A sense of humour and fun-filled work environment allows the employees and the leaders to recognize and understand workplace incongruities and of the personal life. The feeling of freshness and delight brought in by a happier humorous work atmosphere promotes team spirit, creativity, and esprit-de-corps and reduces employee attrition level. Such being the power of humour it has been taken to be one of the many motivating tools that can be practiced in an organization to make their workforce happy and enjoy work. Fun may not be a recommendation for all companies but for certain organizations, it is a powerful tool that promotes morale and enthusiasm among the workers who take pride in working in the company and stay for a longer period with the company. A sense of participation and ownership for the product or service rendered is felt by the workers who are in a happy work environment. A shared joke and laughter among the workers adds excitement and enchantment to work and gives pleasure to employees. It inculcates the right attitude in them and helps them take pride in their job. Laughter not only makes the external environment happy, but also makes the workers work to their best potential and with high quality. Such an environment brings the management and the employees together in the realization of the organizational goals and objectives in making the company a successful one in the marketplace. In a nutshell, building and sustaining a fun and laughter-filled organization is concerned with raising a strong business through its positive-minded people who always look forward to go to work every day; producing better products and services and to create an environment that attracts talented workforce and to emerge as 'employer of choice'.

[15] Lancaster, H. Your career may be a laugh track away from the fast track. *Wall Street Journal*, March 26, 1996, p. B1.

[16] Humour Improves Employee Morale by Paul McGhee, PhD, http://www.laughterremedy.com/articles/article_pages.html#anchor6

Case Study: Southwest Airlines Inc.

"We look for attitudes: people with a sense of humour who don't take themselves too seriously. We'll train people on whatever it is they need to do, but the one thing Southwest cannot change in people is inherent attitudes."

— Herb Kelleher, CEO Southwest Airlines[17]

Employees come first, customers come second' is the mantra of Southwest Airlines. It has a strong belief that its people who made it emerge as a business leader in the market place and were helpful for the Southwest's continuous success in the airlines industry. Southwest's employee-oriented corporate culture and its CEO Kelleher's charismatic leadership initiatives – giving freedom to employees and an inspiring fun-filled work to environment have boosted its employee morale. It strongly believes that such a work environment builds loyalty and nurturing employee morale can alone maintain sustainable profitability in the competitive world.

Herb Kelleher, who appears at public events dressed like Elvis and the Easter Bunny strongly believed on it workforce and on the concept of fun at workplace which had made it one of the most profitable airlines in the United States for more than 25 years running. The business mantra of the management is not based on 'being funny' but - it's about developing a humour sense, appreciating its value and applying its positive qualities to increase ones communication skills and to reinforce their persuasive abilities. The goal of is not to make people laugh but to incorporate the fun philosophy to create an environment where laughter and fun is appreciated and welcomed.

Besides the fun way at Southwest's recruitment process had gained more efficient employees to the company. Their unconventional and humorous job advertisements that emphasized its work culture attracted more people and motivated them to join southwest. Its job advertisements reads like this "Work in a place where Elvis has been spotted . . . The qualifications? It helps to be outgoing. Maybe even a bit off-center. And be prepared to stay awhile. After all, we have the lowest employee mover rate in the industry. If this sounds good to you, just phone our job line or send your resume. Attention: Elvis."[18] Its interview process is also conducted in an extraordinary way on the basis of selecting people who fits into the Southwest's corporate culture, had a good sense of humour and could make others happy. According to Southwest, "Fun is taken very seriously at Southwest Airlines, and the company's recruiting and hiring practices are built upon the idea that humour can help people thrive during change, remain creative under pressure, work more effectively, play more enthusiastically, and stay healthier and more positive in the process."[19] In 2006, Southwest received 284,827 resumes and hired only 3,363 new employees.[20] As

---

[17] *Ideas for Celebrating Humour in the Workplace* by Terrill Fischer, http://www.humouru.com/articles/art_workplacehumour.html

[18] Senthil Ganesan, "Southwest Airlines A Saga of Winning Attitude", *HRM Review*, ICFAI Press, January 2003.

[19] John Wagner, *"Humour Helps Profits Soar"*, http://www.wagnerseriouslyfunny.com/(bxfjke551lgj0b55l5andc45)/articles/Humour%20HELPS%20PROFITS%20SOAR.pdf

[20] "Southwest Airlines Fact Sheet", op.cit.

soon as the new employees entered the organization, they are accorded a celebration greeting and exposed to the history, mission, values and culture of the company.

Southwest developed a unique culture called 'Southwest Spirit' that aimed to keep its employees highly motivated. It has engaged in numerous organizational practices that focused on shared goals, profit sharing, shared knowledge and mutual respect among employees. It provided a variety of training programmes that aimed to inculcate leadership qualities among employees. Southwest has launched various motivational programmes such as - 'Mind the Gap', 'Walk-A-Mile' that aimed to foster team spirit and to learn more. It also launched an 'Employee Recognition Programme' and various get together programmes like 'Spirit Parties', 'Culture parties', and 'Weekly Deck Parties' etc. which encompasses activities like gong shows, talent shows, dance contests, limbo contests, karaoke, and famous person look-alike themes.[21] This fun way of Southwest had made its employees to be ambitious, creative, high morale and productivity. The company experienced less employee turnover coupled with incredible customer loyalty and growing profits.

Exhibit I

Southwest's Net Income (in millions)

Year	2002	2003	2004	2005	2006
Net Income	$188	$372	$215	$484	$499

Source: "Southwest Airlines Co. Annual Report 2006", http://www.southwest.com/investor_relations/swaar06.pdf, 2006

Such innovative HR practices and work environment had resulted in increased employee satisfaction and loyalty to the organization and enhanced employee morale and goodwill. Southwest was honored with several awards for best customer service with least complaints and *Fortune* has listed Southwest Airlines as number three among America's Top 10 Most Admired corporations in 2006.[22] For the fifth year in a row, *Business Ethics* magazine listed Southwest in its "100 Best Corporate Citizens" ranking.[23]

21 "Southwest Airlines Co.", http://www.greatplacetowork.com/education/innovate/honoree-2003-southwest.php.

22 "Southwest Airlines", http://www.uschamber.com/bclc/profiles/southwest.htm.

23 Ibid.

Exhibit II

Southwest's Airlines Recognitions

- In July 2007, Southwest Airlines was included in the Top 100 Most Innovative Technology Organizations by *InformationWeek* Magazine.
- For the 11th year in a row, *FORTUNE* magazine recognized Southwest Airlines in its annual survey of corporate reputations. Among all industries in 2006, *FORTUNE* has listed Southwest Airlines as number five among America's Top Ten most admired corporations.
- Southwest Airlines was named in the *Forbes* Platinum List in the category of Transportation in 2007.
- The American Brand Excellence Awards recognized leading national brands that best served the needs of small- and mid-sized businesses. Southwest Airlines was given the award in the Travel category in May of 2007.
- Southwest Airlines received the Dallas/Fort Worth Network of Hispanic Communicators Corporate Award at their Scholarship Awards Brunch in April of 2007.
- In April 2007, The Port of Portland presented Southwest Airlines with the Environmental Excellence Award in recognition of an exemplary effort in the category of Environmental Innovation.
- Keynote Systems ranked southwest.com number one in the Design and Organization category. The annual survey measures the online performance of 15 major airlines. In October 2006, southwest.com underwent a major design overhaul. The improved southwest.com design is founded on customer feedback and utilization.
- Southwest Airlines carried more domestic customers than any other U.S. airline in January 2007, according to the U.S. Department of Transportation's Bureau of Transportation Statistics.
- Southwest Airlines' Rapid Rewards programme was honored in *Inside Flyer* magazine's 2007 annual Freddie Awards for Best Award Redemption.
- For the eighth year in a row, *Business Ethics* magazine lists Southwest Airlines in its "100 Best Corporate Citizens," a list that ranks public companies based on their corporate service to various stakeholder groups.
- Southwest Airlines was named to *Business Week*'s first ever list of "Customer Service Champs." The *Business Week* list, which appeared in the March 5, 2007 issue, ranks the best providers of customer service, and digs into the techniques, strategies, and tools they use to deliver great service.
- Since 2000, *HISPANIC* magazine has listed Southwest Airlines as Corporate 100 for Leadership in providing opportunities for Hispanics and for supporting recruitment, scholarships, and minority vendor programmes.
- The Express Delivery & Logistics Association (XLA) honored Southwest Airlines as the "2007 Airline of the Year." This is the third consecutive year that Southwest Airlines Cargo has received this honor.
- *Business Week* along with The Boston Consulting Group named Southwest Airlines in their 2006 Top 25 ranking of "The World's Most Innovative Companies." Southwest was included in the list for being "a whiz at wielding operational improvements to outfly its competitors."
- Southwest Airlines was voted as Best Low-Cost Carrier by the readers of *Executive Travel Magazine* in the 2006 Executive Travel Leading Edge Awards.
- Travel and Leisure Magazine ranked Southwest Airlines 4th for Top Domestic Carriers in 2007.
- *Business Week* ranked Southwest Airlines as one of the top 50 Best Places to Launch a Career.

Source: "Southwest Airlines Fact Sheet",
www.southwest.com/about_swa/press/factsheet.html#Recognitions,August 6th 2007

21 The Lake Woebegone Syndrome - Its all Pervasiveness

DR. G. PRAGEETHA RAJU*

Lake Woebegone Syndrome is the human tendency to report pleasing beliefs about oneself and believe that one is above average. This syndrome is being nourished by Banks, VCs, Stock Market Analysts, Executives, Software Vendors, Entrepreneurs, Police Officers, Drivers, University Students, etc. Statistics say that it is preposterously implausible for a majority of people to be above average. Evidently, a great number of the self-proclaimed 'above average' individuals are in fact below average in those areas, and they are purely ignorant of their ineptitude. In a nutshell, some nominal skill and opinion is needed to be familiar with the fact that we possess very little talent or judgment and that we may end up average, below average, or hopeless.

This article examines various cases/situations of the Lake Woebegone Syndrome, its causes and discusses techniques to counteract this phenomenon.

INTRODUCTION

Hype is inbuilt in today's society. Mediocre or average is no better enough, be it in case of performance, competence and/or attitude. Everyone or nearly everyone believes to be above average and tend to get overconfident about them. This is understood to be the manifestation of the well known Lake Woebegone Syndrome. Just examine the following situations:

1. Entrepreneurs are too sanguine about their ventures. They are in fact, very positive about the functioning of their plan. It was found that financial modelling and scenario planning are the sole reasons behind this super optimism (*Cassar, Garry, 2007*). This over confidence in part appears to be driven by Lake Woebegone Syndrome.

* Faculty Member for HR at ICFAI Business School, Andhra Pradesh.

2. By visiting online business sites, it is often discovered that nearly all the stocks that are being written about are either "buy" or "strong buy" with rare "hold". Now the question is: where is "sell" and "strong sell"?

3. Take the case of excessive executive compensation, one fouling the reputation of numerous corporations. For example, Pfizer paid its CEO $ 45million during 2001 to 2005 and added $ 83 million as pension. Exxon-Mobil paid its CEO almost $ 400 million and Verizon, in 2005, paid its CEO a whopping $ 48 million. Every company's board supposes their CEO is above average thus becoming a prey to Lake Woebegone Syndrome.

4. CEOs who engage in M & A tend to be overconfident. Overconfident CEOs are inclined to chase risky deals, or pay too much because they overvalue the returns they can produce from an acquisition. Every CEO who walks into an acquisition assumes he is different, i.e., he will be able to pull it off; CEOs are badly affected with Lake Woebegone Syndrome.

5. 80% of the drivers think they are among the safest 30% of those driving. (*Svenson, Ole, 1981).*

6. Investors generally overestimate the precision of their knowledge about a security's value, and the probability that their assessment is more accurate than that of the others. The result is, more active trading but **not** better performance. They are affected by Lake Woebegone Syndrome. (*Barber, Brad & Odean, Terrance, 1999*).

All the above examples indicate the Lake Woebegone Syndrome, or Woebegone Effect, or Woebegonism – an idea where we all think we are above average at most things. More precisely, every human being tends to overvalue his/her achievements with regard to others. This is the buzzword in the rapidly developing world and it pertains to *hubris* (overconfidence) about ability. This syndrome is being nourished by banks, venture capitalists, and angel investors who need ostensible financial projections in order to analyze and appeal for capital. It is seeping into other occupations like stock market analysts, business executives, software vendors, entrepreneurs, CEOs, police officers, drivers, university students, and so on.

Research too reveals that majority of the people think that they possess characteristics that are better or more desirable than average. Social scientists have confirmed time and again that people generally overestimate their abilities and knowledge. (*Zuckerman, 2001)* Most people, in areas directly related to their specialization, believe themselves to have more knowledge and extrapolative skill than they actually have. Findings show surprisingly large incongruity between actual skill and self-assessed skill.

ORIGIN OF THE TERM

Lake Woebegone is a famous fictitious town in Minnesota and was popularized by Garrison Keillor, the famous radio personality of the US. The term has two possible meanings that are contradictory to each other. The word 'Woebegone' means "plagued with problem".

On examining the words, "Woe, be, gone", it clearly indicates a release of troubles. The Lake Woebegone is characterized by the famous saying, "*women are strong, men are handsome, and all children are above average,*". This is a delightful bit of imaginary tale that summarizes a significant message in impracticable expectations. This saying has been used to depict an authentic and all-encompassing human predisposition to overrate one's accomplishments and competencies with respect to others. For instance, many Infosec (Information Security) sellers are culpable of the "Woebegone Syndrome" as they pander to unworkable user requirements and make bizarre claims about their solutions.

ANALYSIS OF LAKE WOEBEGONE SYNDROME

Examine the third example (excessive executive compensation) at the beginning of the article. Most CEOs envelop themselves on their boards with obedient peers, willing to scratch backs for higher income. Compensation agencies employ consulting firms to read, learn, and benchmark existing pay levels. These firms recommend that all clients are certainly "above average," (the Lake Woebegone Syndrome) and suggest "above average" pay. In the interim, corporate status goes down even lower as stakeholders retort with skepticism and low confidence. Where are the Chief Risk Officers in this muddle? Most of them are so entangled with their econometric models that they overlook the shortcomings of disproportionate compensation. This practice of paying too much executive compensation, far beyond rational limits, grinds down the trust and confidence so vital to an effectual and resourceful market economy. It creates a public perception of unrestrained greediness.

Corporate executives suffer from the Lake Woebegone Syndrome. Corporate executives are impressed with their own abilities. Corporate decisions offer ample examples of heuristic-driven bias and frame dependence. *Hubris,* however, is the primary bias involved in corporate takeovers because it leads to the phenomenon of winner's curse, where the acquiring firm overpays for the target.

The contrary side of *woebegone effect* is **worse than average effect** which is the tendency to undervalue oneself in certain situations. The overconfidence effect is the penchant to be more confident in his/her own attributes, behaviours, and physical nature than he/she ought to be. On examining example 5 (drivers case), overconfidence is mostly seen after a chain of triumphs or in cases where success is rare and can result in extreme risk taking. Sometimes, investors have too little diversification because of this.

Now, deviating slightly, what causes inflationary acclamation so troublesome is that, by retreating genuine accomplishments, it can debilitate our capability to recognize quality and make distinctions. A latest study tells that a good number of not-so-competent people are not aware that they are incompetent (lacking ability). When questioned, most individuals depict themselves as **better-than-average** in areas such as leadership, interpersonal skills, writing skills, or just about any taste of savoir-faire where the individual has an interest. Statistics say that it is preposterously implausible for a majority of people to be above average. Evidently, a great number of the self-proclaimed 'above average' individuals are in fact below average in those areas, and they are purely ignorant of their ineptitude. Dr. David Dunning, a Professor of Psychology at Cornell, established that people who fare badly in diverse tasks are ignorant of their ineptitude because the skills required to assess how well they're doing are frequently the same as those needed to do the job primarily. Thus, people who persistently narrate one lame joke after another are unsuccessful to make audience laugh but they are not likely to make out that we're not laughing. Bertrand Russell writes that "*the difficulty with the world is that the stupid are dead sure and the intellectuals are full of doubt.*" This is correct whether one construes *stupid* as 'silly' (less smart) or as 'ignorance' (less informed). Intentionally or if not, Charles Darwin, pointed out that "*ignorance more often results in confidence than does knowledge.*" The Internet is an authentic source of such mislaid confidence. Online, individuals frequently talk with confident clout on a given topic, yet, their conclusions are faulty. It is likely that such individuals are completely ignorant of their ignorance.

When an individual fails to identify his/her own below-average performance, their self-assessment doesn't comprise that negative information resulting in an unnaturally overblown view of one's own skills, often tampered by ego. This is likely to cause the incompetent congratulating one another as they fall short in detecting each others insufficiencies.

CAUSES OF LAKE WOEBEGONE SYNDROME

From the above analysis, the causes can be identified as,

- *Availability Bias:* People have trouble imagining all the possible ways that events could open up. Therefore, we tend to take for granted that everything will go normally.
- *Confirmation Bias:* Mostly people begin with a best guess, their best guess 'anchors' their thinking, and prevents them envisaging conditions that might nullify it.
- *Groupthink:* When the majority in a group have a particular opinion, minority opinions may be suspended for fear of condemnation or appearing foolish.

Counteracting Lake Woebegone Syndrome

Anyway, this syndrome is not a psychological impairment. This is just a mistake, an error. It is explainable. It happens over and over again in history. This syndrome can be detrimental to organizational success because this makes individuals overvalue their coherent cognitive structures (frame of thought) and undervalue the relevance of the same possessed by others. To examine further, overconfidence can be of two types, namely, optimistic overconfidence where the probability that one's favoured outcome will take place and over estimation of knowledge is the second type which is commonly seen among Venture Capitalists who overestimate their own judgment when they do not have a personally favoured end result. Also, confidence is good for entrepreneurs, but blind hope can be a costly mistake. Though Lake Woebegone Syndrome doesn't lead to a wrong decision, the bias is likely to inhibit learning and becomes an impediment in improving the decision process. Reference point thinking leads people to give opportunity costs less weight than out-of-packet costs of the same magnitude.

In a nutshell, some nominal skill and opinion is needed to be familiar with the fact that we possess very little talent or judgment and that we may end up average, below average, or hopeless. Professionals need to calibrate their own knowledge and skills, to know when to be certain, and when to have doubts. Pointless doubts may debilitate the professional, and create a notion of ineptitude, but unwarranted contentment can be equally devastating in the long run. (*Russoe & Schoemaker, 1992*). Some ways to offset Lake Woebegone Syndrome would be:

1. Conduct a training programme in which case studies are administered to allow the trainees to see how frequently they get their answers accurate.
2. An exercise to show to a person that his/her knowledge is less than what he/she thinks may pin down overconfidence.
3. Encourage group decision making methods like Delphi or NGT.

If all of us begin to view ourselves as amazing, outstanding, and above average and ceaselessly adorn our fashionable caps to purchase strong stocks that always progress, the definition of superlatives will start vanishing and critical evaluation will slowly turn into empty congratulations.

BIBLIOGRAPHY

Barber M Brad M. & Odean, Terrance, *"Boys will be Boys: Gender, Overconfidence, and Common Stock Investment"*, American Public Media, University of California, February, 1999.

Cassar, Garry, *"Are individuals entering self-employment overly optimistic? An Empirical Test of Plans and Projections on Nascent Entrepreneur Expectations"* (Doctoral Dissertation), Wharton School, University of Pennsylvania, Jan, 2007.

Svenson, O, "Are we all less risky and more skillful than our fellow drivers"? *Acta Psychologica,* Vol. 47, 1981.

Zuckerman, E. W, & Jost, J. T, "What makes you think you're so popular? Self Evaluation Maintenance and the Subjective Side of the "Friendship Paradox" *Social Psychology Quarterly,* 64(3), 2001.

Russo, J.E. &. Schoemaker, P.J.H., "Managing Overconfidence" *Sloan Management Review* Winter 1992, 33 (2).

